GUINEAS AND GUNPOWDER

BRITISH FOREIGN AID IN THE WARS WITH FRANCE
1793-1815

William Pitt the Younger, by John Hoppner

GUINEAS AND GUNPOWDER

BRITISH FOREIGN AID

IN THE WARS WITH FRANCE

1793-1815

JOHN M. SHERWIG

HARVARD UNIVERSITY PRESS

Cambridge, Massachusetts

TO THE MEMORY OF MY MOTHER AND FATHER

PREFACE

During the century and a half since the Battle of Waterloo, a vast literature has appeared dealing with almost every aspect of the Wars of the French Revolution and Napoleon. This book is concerned with an important but strangely neglected feature of that struggle: Britain's financial aid to her continental allies between 1793 and 1815. Every serious account of the war makes peripheral reference to British subsidies, but the subject has never received the attention it merits. It is hoped that the work here offered will meet that need.

In examining Britain's use of subsidies as an instrument of war, answers will be sought to two major questions. Did subsidization involve any clear policy? If so, did that policy undergo any change between the outbreak of war and its conclusion twenty-two years later? This is primarily a study of diplomatic and military history. The economics of subsidization is an important subject in itself, but its history has yet to be written.

Much of the research for this work was done at the Public Record Office, and I gratefully acknowledge the kindness of the Keeper of Public Records for permission to make use of the British government archives for the period. Transcripts of Crown-copyright records in the Public Record Office appear by permission of the Controller of Her Majesty's Stationery Office. The time I spent at the Record Office was all the more profitable thanks to the invaluable assistance given me by H. N. Blakiston and E. K. Timings, Principal Assistant Keepers. They helped me find my way through the archival maze and brought much important material to my attention which I would otherwise have overlooked. Two other members of the Record Office staff, S. R. Bickell and E. E. Coleman, also made me their debtor. They cheerfully produced many hundreds of bundles and volumes of material for me. The many kindnesses of all the Record Office staff made my two sojourns in Chancery Lane a delight.

I am grateful to the Trustees of the British Museum for permission to make use of the collections of private papers deposited there. Acknowledgment is also due Howard H. Peckham, director of the William L. Clements Library, the University of Michigan, Ann Arbor, for the opportunity to examine the typescript copies of the unpublished correspondence of George III. The editor of the *Journal of Modern History,* published by the University of Chicago, has kindly permitted me to incorporate in this work parts of my article, "Lord Grenville's Plan for a Concert of Europe, 1797-1799," which appeared in vol. 34 (1962) of that periodical.

To the late Professor David Owen of Harvard University and to Professor William B. Willcox of the University of Michigan I owe a special debt. They initiated me into the mysteries of the historian's craft and their suggestions led me to take up the problem of British subsidies in earnest. The late Sir Charles K. Webster also took a kind interest in my endeavor and gave generously of his time in sharing with me his vast knowledge and understanding of the period.

In bringing to completion a work which has occupied so many years, I cannot hope to acknowledge all of the many debts I have incurred. The staff of my college library merit a special mention, however. I have often taxed their patience, but never their resources. I am also particularly obliged to the Widener Library at Harvard University for the opportunity to use their rich storehouse of material. My faculty colleagues have been unsparing in their encouragement and assistance. Professor George A. Schnell kindly prepared the maps and graphs. The manuscript was read in its entirety by Professor Lawrence W. Sullivan who offered many helpful suggestions. Mrs. Lester F. Tubby typed the final manuscript and her sharp eyes saved me from a number of pitfalls.

Finally, I acknowledge a particular debt to my wife, Mary Jane, whose courage and confidence at a critical moment helped me complete this study.

Waterloo Day, 1968   John M. Sherwig
State University of New York
New Paltz, New York

CONTENTS

ILLUSTRATIONS

Illustrations

MAPS

GUINEAS AND GUNPOWDER

The character of this country had suffered by its inflexible perseverance in the present war; even our allies had said, that the English covered Germany with blood and gold.
—Mr. Nicholls in a speech to the House of Commons, July 9, 1800

If you . . . could open the eyes of the continental nations to their true interests, if you could clearly shew them that not only their interests but their salvation depended upon their joining you in opposing an enemy whose object it was to destroy you both, then surely it was not only not unjust, but it was even meritorious, to secure their co-operation if possible.
—William Pitt, speaking to the House of Commons, June 21, 1805

INTRODUCTION

As February 1, 1793 drew to a close, the Reverend James Woodforde of the parish of Weston Longeville, Norfolk, set down in his diary the few events of that quiet day which seemed worth recording. He noted with regret the death of one of his parishoners, "beloved by all that knew him it is said as being a very good natured, inoffensive Man." The brief entry ended on a happier note since that evening the good parson had won sixpence from his niece at cribbage. Woodforde had no idea that on that same day the French National Convention had declared war on Great Britain.[1] At first neither the Norfolk parson nor his prime minister, William Pitt, suspected how much that war was to affect their lives and their country. Victory over France was won only after both had passed away, but parson and premier lived long enough to see the contest turn into a struggle for existence far more perilous than any their nation had ever known.

When the French Revolution broke out in 1789 there was no reason to believe that it would finally engulf all Europe. So far as Britain was concerned, every consideration of national self-interest warned her away from involvement in French affairs. Pitt's program of fiscal reform was just beginning to bear fruit, and nothing ought to be allowed to imperil the harvest. Furthermore, disagreements with Spain and Russia were threatening to develop into major diplomatic crises of far more immediate concern to Britain than France's struggle for constitutional government. By the spring of 1792, however, the Revolution had become a whirlpool which threatened to draw Europe into its vortex. In Britain the Revolution had inspired a political reform movement which aroused the worst fears of the conservatives. France's

---

1. *The Diary of a Country Parson: The Reverend James Woodforde,* ed. John Beresford (London, 1924-1931), IV, 5.

1

declaration of war against Austria in 1792 prompted Pitt's government to issue a declaration of neutrality in an effort to escape the coming violence.

Less than a year later, Britain and France were at war. The creation of the French Republic in September 1792 had little effect on Pitt's foreign policy, but the unexpected victories of the Revolutionary armies in the Low Countries presented him with a crisis. Before the close of that year, the French controlled a large part of the Austrian Netherlands and crowned their success by opening the Scheldt river to navigation. This not only violated a long-standing international agreement, it virtually guaranteed a French attack on Holland. Pitt hoped to meet the Republican threat by diplomacy, but each passing week proved this wishful thinking. Only the strongest countermeasures could check Republican aggression in Europe and French-inspired treason in Britain itself. War was now inevitable. The February 1 manifesto by the Revolutionary Convention in Paris settled the matter and thrust upon Pitt the unwanted mantle of a war leader.

The events leading to the war defined the goals which Britain must now seek on the battlefield; the balance of power had to be restored and the sanctity of international agreements upheld. Such was the prime minister's position in his first war speech to the House of Commons: "England will never consent that France shall arrogate the power of annulling at her pleasure, and under the pretence of a natural right of which she makes herself the only judge, the political system of Europe, established by solemn treaties, and guaranteed by the consent of all the powers."[2] Despite the eloquent urging of Edmund Burke and the Royalists, Pitt steadily refused to take up the cause of the *ancien régime*. For the remainder of his life, he insisted that Britain's paramount concern was the restoration of the balance of power as the best hope for an enduring peace. In 1805 Pitt embodied this viewpoint in a concrete plan for the reconstruction of Europe, a plan which profoundly influenced Lord Castlereagh's diplomacy during the final stages of the war.

What part was Britain to play in this contest with France which had now begun? Her troops were soon on their way to Flanders to

2. *The Parliamentary History of England, from the Earliest Period to the Year 1803 . . .* , ed. William Cobbett (London, 1806-1820), XXX, 283.

join with the German powers in driving back the enemy, but even when enlarged by recruitment and the employment of mercenaries they would play a subordinate role to the Prussians and the Austrians. The Royal Navy was sent out to destroy the enemy's fleets, seize her colonial possessions, and protect friendly shipping. An important war function was assigned to Britain's diplomatic service: the negotiation of treaties with the other powers at war with France, binding all of them together in an effective coalition. Once formed, this grand alliance would have to be enlarged to include Russia. Anxious as Pitt was to create such a league, he was not ready to pay for it by sharing his nation's wealth with the major allies. The war would probably be brief, surely not long enough to strain unduly the resources of the continental powers. For that matter, it could be argued that Britain and Holland, as powers attacked by France, were entitled to claim military assistance from Prussia by the terms of their defensive alliance of 1788.

Nearly all the assumptions which shaped Britain's war plans in 1793 soon proved false. The allied armies were powerless to stem the advancing French tide in the Low Countries, and soon even Holland was overrun. All Britain's diplomatic skill was insufficient to create the great war confederacy which Pitt desired. In the end he was finally forced to pay Prussia and Austria in order to keep alive Britain's war partnership with them. One by one, the easy assumptions of 1793 had to be abandoned and more realistic ones found to take their place.

By the time the war reached its climax in 1813-1814, Britain's role was dramatically different from what it had been twenty years before. Several of these changes deserve special comment. The Grand Alliance, which finally broke Napoleon's hold on Europe, was largely the creation of Pitt's pupil and successor, Lord Castlereagh, whose leadership contrasts sharply with the ineffectiveness of British diplomats during the initial stages of the war. Equally impressive was the important role played by the British army in overturning Napoleon. Wellington's force in the Peninsula was no auxiliary unit but the embodiment of Britain's resurgent military power. To say that it contributed to Napoleon's defeat is to do simple justice to the men who triumphed at Badajoz and Vittoria.

One of the most significant changes in Britain's war program was the evolution of her subsidy policy between 1793 and 1815. Pitt had no desire to subsidize his country's major allies in 1793, but by 1805, circumstances obliged him to pay them all as a matter of general policy. During the final year of the war, Britain spent £10,000,000 on her allies in a massive aid program which would have astounded Pitt. Nor was this all. In 1808 the British aid program took on a different character when arms and supplies, in addition to money, were sent to support the Spanish and Portuguese uprisings. Four years later, the other European powers rose against France and looked to Britain for weapons as well as subsidies. In response to this appeal, Britain sent them nearly one million muskets during the year 1813 alone. The changing character and expansion of Britain's foreign aid program materially added to her war debt. More than £1,500,000,000 had to be raised in loans and taxes between 1793 and 1816 to finance the struggle with France; only the nation's rapidly expanding economy made it possible for her to do this.[3]

The development of the British foreign aid program cannot be studied in isolation. That the early coalitions against France quickly weakened and fell apart was due in large measure to rivalries whose origins antedate the war. The methods of Britain's diplomatic service must at least be summarized since it was an important ingredient in the formation of nearly every coalition. Something ought also to be said of Britain's war economy, which made it possible for the government to help its allies with money and arms. Finally, Britain's ability to wage war on land and sea deserves comment, for by the time the war ended, the goverment had coordinated its military effort and its foreign aid program.

To some degree, the wars of the French Revolution represent simply an extension of the drives for territorial aggrandizement which characterized international politics in the eighteenth century. Austria and Prussia were at least as anxious to plunder France as they were to make the world safe for absolute monarchy. When the chance for easy victory faded, they were tempted to withdraw from that profitless struggle and look elsewhere for gain.

3. Leland H. Jenks, *The Migration of British Capital to 1875* (New York and London, 1927), p. 17.

The Austro-Prussian alliance against the Revolution was an uneasy marriage of powers who had been deadly rivals for nearly a century. In 1742 Frederick the Great wrenched Silesia from Austria's hold and thereafter blocked all her efforts to find compensation elsewhere. Thanks to Prussia's opposition, Vienna was never able to carry out her favorite plan of exchanging Belgium for Bavaria. Disappointed in the west, Austria joined forces with Russia in 1788 to make war on the Ottoman Empire—only to meet with failure again. From her contest with Revolutionary France, which began in 1792, Austria hoped to win the territorial prizes which had hitherto been beyond her grasp. As for Prussia, the First Polish Partition (1772) climaxed Frederick the Great's ambition, and he spent the remainder of his life protecting the loot. Under his successor, Prussia again grew land hungry and joined with Austria in waging war against France in an effort to satisfy her appetite. Of all the powers, Russia alone came closest to realizing her territorial ambitions in the decade before 1792. Catherine the Great's gains at the expense of Turkey inspired the envy of her neighbors. While Austria and Prussia undertook to pillage the French Republic, the Tsarina remained at peace in order to consolidate the position of strength she had won in eastern Europe.

Britain played little part in this continental scramble for land and influence. The American War had left her friendless and financially exhausted to such a degree that she was powerless to prevent France from meddling in the political affairs of Holland. By 1787, however, Pitt was able to take a stronger line when a crisis developed between the supporters of the Stadtholder and the French-directed "Patriot" party. Joint intervention by Prussia and Britain forced France to release Holland from her orbit. To cap this victory, Pitt threw up a barrier against future French aggression by uniting Britain, Prussia, and Holland in a defensive compact. The Triple Alliance of 1788, largely the work of the British diplomat, Lord Malmesbury, was a major diplomatic triumph for the prime minister, but events soon made clear how small a community of interest existed among the allies.

Britain hoped to use the Triple Alliance to restrain France; Prussia regarded it as a useful tool to further her own territorial ambitions. When Frederick William II demanded another slice of Poland to offset any gains Austria and Russia might obtain from their war with Turkey, he found Britain reluctant to support him. If Prussia must go empty-handed, then the eastern powers should be forced to end their war with Turkey on a status quo ante basis. Austria would probably agree; should Russia refuse, Frederick William hoped Pitt would join him in threatening her with war. The proposal seriously divided the British Cabinet, but it finally agreed to send such an ultimatum. A few days later, London learned that Austria might support the Tsarina in the event she found herself at war with the Triple Alliance. Parliamentary approval of the government's Russian policy, never enthusiastic, soon evaporated. Pitt had no choice but to suppress the ultimatum which he had already sent to St. Petersburg. The "Humiliation of Oczakoff" embarrassed Pitt at home and shattered his diplomatic union with Prussia. Incensed by what appeared to be British perfidy and cowardice, Frederick William refused to cooperate with her any longer and turned toward union with Austria against Revolutionary France in the hope of territorial gains along the Rhine.

These diplomatic struggles profoundly affected the fate of the coalitions. The German powers were soon disappointed in their contest with France, and Prussia began to cast covetous glances toward Poland. In 1792 Catherine the Great and Frederick William agreed on terms of a new Polish partition, but no provision was made for Austria to share the plunder. Early in the following year Prussian troops moved into Poland, thereby relieving pressure on the Revolutionary armies in the West. Since Austria was to have none of Poland, she demanded compensation elsewhere. Not only did Prussia refuse to placate her partner, but arrogantly declared that Austria was entitled to nothing. By the time Britain entered the war with France, the German allies were at each other's throats.

The military reverses of 1793 heightened Austro-Prussian bickering, and Pitt was forced to take up the delicate role of mediator. Prussia's heart was no longer in the war with France, while failure to obtain territory clouded Austria's outlook. The apparent ease with which Britain picked up French colonies did not pass unnoticed by her partners. When Prussia finally abandoned the war in 1795, the coalition began to crumble; two years later, Vienna made her peace with the French Revolution. Compelled to yield Belgium, which the Hofburg had long wanted to be rid of, Austria at least found some solace in the north Italian lands France allowed her to annex.

Jealousy among the allies hastened the death of the First Coalition and thereafter plagued Britain's efforts to create new and more effective leagues. Austro-Prussian rivalry was so virulent that the two powers did not again stand together against France until 1813. Russia's reluctance to become involved in the war against France proved especially difficult for Britain to overcome. Indeed, it was not until 1813 that the lengthening shadow of the French imperium forced the continental powers to see that their only hope was in union. Until then, British subsidies could do little more than briefly prolong the life of alliances doomed as much by internal discord as by the military prowess of the enemy.

Pitt enjoyed considerable freedom in directing the British war program, but there were certain political and constitutional restraints on his power. A broad area of agreement had always to be maintained between prime minister and foreign secretary, while major war plans regularly went before the Cabinet for discussion and approval. Significant policy decisions also required royal consent, and to secure it Pitt sometimes had to spend long hours in conference with George III.[4]

The excesses of the French Revolution made King George III a zealous supporter of any plan to break its hold on Europe. For that reason, Pitt's fondness for colonial expeditions was coldly regarded by his sovereign, who foresaw from the beginning that the contest would finally be decided on the battlefields of Europe. When the prime minister hinted at the desirability of peace discussions, George III reacted with characteristic Hanoverian stubbornness. So long as ministers shared the King's determination to crush France, however, he allowed them a free hand in the management of the war. Even so, George III insisted on being kept well informed concerning their plans.

As for the Cabinet, Pitt was careful to keep his colleagues in touch with the latest developments, and they often held their meetings at the Foreign Office in order to have easy access to

4. The King's role in the formulation of war plans has been examined in detail in Donald G. Barnes, *George III and William Pitt, 1783-1806* (Stanford Calif., 1939), pp. 269-301.

documents and dispatches. The Cabinet usually supported its leader, but his subsidy proposals sometimes aroused opposition. In cases of severe disagreement, Pitt usually yielded and either modified or withdrew his plan.

Provision for the payment of subsidies was the business of the House of Commons. There, ministers were obliged to defend their requests for appropriations. Even the opposition was willing to allow the government to hire German mercenaries, but any proposal to subsidize a major ally always found them ready to give battle. The whigs opposed subsidies because they opposed the war, but one of their leaders confessed during a debate on a proposed grant to Russia in 1799 that, in his opinion, "if more blood is to be shed, it should be any other than English blood."[5] During the closing years of the war, the number of allies receiving money grew so large that legislative action on each subsidy treaty proved cumbersome. To obviate this difficulty, the government often asked for a general "Vote of Credit" for foreign aid which would leave the allocation of the money to ministers themselves. So strong was the government's position throughout the war that the Commons approved every request made to it for subsidies.

Between 1793 and 1801 Pitt shared the direction of the war with Henry Dundas and Lord Grenville. Dundas was secretary of state for war, with major responsibility for military operations and colonial affairs. War diplomacy was of little interest or concern to him, but in this area Grenville's role was as important as that of the prime minister.

It has been said that an appreciation of the Grenvilles "is certainly an acquired taste," and even their defenders admit that they were a troublesome tribe.[6] William, the youngest son of George Grenville, author of the ill-fated American Stamp Act, entered Parliament in 1782 and attached himself to the fortunes of his cousin, William Pitt. Thereafter, he enjoyed a succession of offices and in 1790 was created Baron Grenville. A year later, he became foreign secretary and served his cousin until Pitt left office in 1801. Grenville's ties with the Pitt family were strengthened by his marriage to Anne Pitt, a distant relative of the prime minister.

5. *Parliamentary History*, XXXIV, 1045.
6. The expression appeared in a book review published in the *Times Literary Supplement*, December 31, 1954, p. 851.

The bride's father, Lord Camelford, described his new son-in-law as "one of the most sensible, most honourable, and best temper'd of human beings."[7] Unlike Camelford, whose own opinion may have changed in time, Grenville's associates found him stiff, dour, and unimaginative. They never had occasion, however, to question his honesty and diligence, and only rarely his good sense.

The organization of the Foreign Office, which Grenville headed, had attained considerable maturity by 1793, but its staff was very small. Provision was made for two undersecretaries whose appointment was pretty much within the gift of the foreign secretary they were to serve. The clerical business of the office was handled by a staff of clerks responsible for the preparation of fair copies, ciphering, and filing. The name of only one of these scriveners survives: a Mr. Rolleston, who engrossed every treaty negotiated by Great Britain between 1793 and 1815.[8] For carrying dispatches, the three secretaries of state had the service of a pool of about thirty couriers. Romantic as the life of a King's Messenger may have been, it was full of perils, and more than one set out on a mission from which he never returned.

Delay in communication was one of the most vexing problems for the Foreign Office. In peacetime, dispatches to British embassies in northern Europe were usually sent via The Hague, but the French conquest of Holland in 1795 forced the Foreign Office to use a north German port (usually Hamburg), and the resulting delays were serious. During the winter, London was often out of touch with its embassy in St. Petersburg for months at a time.

The quality of service performed by British envoys varied greatly, but it could seldom be described as excellent. Even though salaries for foreign service had been increased, diplomatic appointments usually went to men who regarded them as stepping stones to more attractive positions at home. Quite exceptional was the case of Sir William Hamilton, who represented Britain at Naples for thirty-six years. Naples was one of the most attractive posts, however, and its duties were not usually exacting. Far more typical was the career of Sir Morton Eden, an unexceptional time-server, whose service at numerous capitals was climaxed in

7. Lord Camelford to an unknown correspondent, July 21, 1792; from a manuscript letter in the author's possession.
8. John Tilley and Stephen Gaselee, *The Foreign Office* (London, 1933), p. 51.

1794 by his appointment as British minister at Vienna. The fact that Eden was related to Lord Auckland may explain why he ended his career with an Irish peerage and an annual pension of two thousand pounds. Berlin appears to have been the least attractive foreign embassy; nearly every minister sent there soon requested a transfer. By the standards of the time, Britain was well served by Charles Whitworth, her envoy to Russia between 1789 and 1800. On leaving the service in 1803, he was sent to Ireland as Lord Lieutenant in possession of the prize which all diplomats sought, an English peerage. Downing Street often entrusted negotiations with allied governments to special agents rather than to resident ministers. Training and experience seem not to have been regarded as essential in a special agent. Assignments of major importance twice went to the foreign secretary's brother, Thomas Grenville, who at best was an intelligent amateur.

Foreign representatives in London were generally no better than their British counterparts abroad. Throughout the period, Prussian interests were represented by Baron Jacobi Kloest, for whom Grenville had an ill-concealed dislike. The Austrian ambassador, Count Louis Starhemberg, was personally more acceptable but his abilities were slight. Between 1785 and 1806 Russia was served by Count Simon Vorontzoff, the only foreign diplomat of the period who merits special attention. Vorontzoff was so ardent an Anglophile that his government often had to remind him that his duty was to represent Russia's interests. Pitt's death was a severe personal loss to Vorontzoff, and shortly thereafter he retired into private life. Completely westernized, he remained in London until his death in 1832.

Only a few changes in detail are required to apply this description of the British diplomatic machine to the decade of war which remained after Pitt died in 1806. Following the incapacity of George III, the Prince Regent supported Perceval and Liverpool as earnestly as his father had their great predecessor. George Canning's leadership of the Foreign Office between 1807 and 1809 maintained the traditions which Grenville had established in that department. By 1812 the rapid spread of French power had reduced the number of British embassies in Europe to only six. Lord Wellesley's negligence and sloth during these years left the Foreign Office badly in need of reorganization when he resigned as foreign secretary in the spring of 1812.

Appointed to succeed Wellesley, Castlereagh held a position in the Cabinet such as no foreign secretary before him had enjoyed, not even Grenville. The Cabinet's confidence in Castlereagh was never more striking than when, at the end of 1813, it decided that he must go to the Continent for direct negotiation with the allied foreign ministers. The era of "personal diplomacy" which followed was unique, although as early as 1798 Grenville had glimpsed the possibility of a central council of foreign ministers. Direct negotiation with the allies, taking place almost on the battlefield itself, ended at once the problem of communication which had hampered British diplomacy in the past. It also allowed for an ease of interchange among the allied governments such as had never before been possible.

A forceful allied offensive undertaken even as late as the autumn of 1793 might have swept the Revolutionary armies from the field. In default of such a campaign, the scales of war turned slowly against France's enemies. Prussia's withdrawal from the war in 1795 left Austria alone to struggle with the Republican forces that came pouring across the Rhine into Germany. Twenty more years of desperate fighting would be needed to defeat France, and then it would require an allied military force much larger than any that would have been possible at the outset. In 1793 the combined armies of all France's opponents numbered about 350,000 men; during the climactic campaign of 1814, Russia and the German powers alone threw nearly twice that many troops against Napoleon. Without British aid in money and arms, this tremendous expansion of the allied war effort would scarcely have been possible.

The economic weakness of the continental powers in 1793 made their war with France less of an unequal struggle than it appeared. Prussia was on the verge of bankruptcy, while Austria had to borrow heavily abroad to meet her current expenses. Thanks to Catherine the Great's wars with Turkey, Russia's economic health was even worse than her neighbors'. The Tsarina staved off disaster only by massive loans from Dutch bankers and by flooding her country with paper money.

By the end of the first year of the war, the resources of the continental allies began to dry up and they turned to Britain for help. Thereafter, Britain had to bear not only her own war costs, but a part of her allies' burden as well. Assuming at first that the war would be brief, Pitt planned to meet his country's financial needs by heavy reliance on loans. A succession of military and economic crises in 1796-1797 made clear that a new system of war finance would have to be devised to support a long and expensive struggle. The Bank of England suspended payments in specie and a host of new taxes were introduced in order to minimize the Treasury's dependence on high interest-bearing loans. Even so, the government still had to borrow heavily, and by the end of the war the national debt was close to £700,000,000—considerably more than twice what it had been when Pitt came to power.[9]

Survival in the war with France depended on the strength of Britain's economy and her world trade. The rapid growth of industry during these years provided the nation with the means of victory. Expansion of the iron and steel industry freed her from dependence on imports. The value of cotton textiles sent abroad rose at a phenomenal rate; by 1815 it was fifteen times greater than at the beginning of the war. Curiously, Britain lagged badly in the production of arms, artillery, and gunpowder until the turn of the century, when steps were taken to insure an ample supply of equipment for her own army and those of her allies.

Britain's export trade paid for a large part of her war costs in Europe between 1793 and 1815. Three of these expenses were especially important: the cost of her military operations, subsidies to the allies, and the purchase of foreign grain to make good deficiencies in the home harvest. For reasons peculiar to the military service, the army always had to be provided with a large amount of hard money. Subsidies and grain purchases, however, could be paid for by drawing on whatever credits British trade had accumulated on the Continent.

Thanks to the rapid expansion of British trade with Germany between 1788 and 1801, the government could pay its bills on the Continent without resorting to heavy export of specie. The introduction of Napoleon's Continental System in 1806 disrupted the normal channels of British commerce, forcing her merchants to undertake major adjustments. Probably the most important of these was the entry of the British trader into the colonial markets

---

9. Elie Halévy, *A History of the English People in the Nineteenth Century,* trans. E. I. Watkin and D. A. Barker (New York, 1945), I, 370.

of South America. Another step taken to frustrate Napoleon's design was the establishment of entrepôts for British goods along the perimeter of Europe. Adjustments in trading practices such as these enabled Britain to prosper, and by the end of the war the value of her exports exceeded £51,000,000 a year.

Students of the Continental System disagree about the effectiveness of Napoleon's blockade in reducing the flow of British goods into Europe. One thing is certain, however; after 1808 Britain's war expenses on the Continent shot upward. The maintenance of Wellington's army in the Peninsula between 1808 and 1814 was a special strain since a large part of its bills had to be met by specie sent from Britain. To offset this drain, subsidies and food purchases could be financed by drawing on British trade credits on the Continent. The final years of the war were characterized in Britain by high taxes, shortage of hard money, and great difficulty with the balance of payments. Because subsidies to foreign powers were unpopular in England, the government's critics indicted the foreign aid program as the primary cause of these problems. Final judgment on this question must await answers to two questions. First, how did the cost of foreign aid compare with the money Britain spent to maintain her own army, navy, and ordnance services during the war years? Second, how important were subsidies in causing the balance of payment problem, as compared to the cost of British military operations abroad and the purchase of foreign grain?

At the conclusion of his skillful analysis of the British navy during this period, the French historian Elie Halévy shrewdly observed, "It was that they had the country behind them, and they knew it."[10] Presumably this did not apply to the army, which, at least until the Peninsular War, suffered from deplorable morale. Accepting this generalization, it seems possible to supplement it in certain particulars.

The navy was in good condition when war came in 1793, due largely to the careful attention Pitt had given it during the years of peace and retrenchment. Twenty-five ships of the line and twice as many frigates were already in commission in home waters, while several times that number of vessels, now in ordinary or under construction, would soon be ready for sea. New operational

10. *Ibid.*, I, 65.

techniques had recently been developed which were soon to be tried out in war. In 1790 the navy adopted an improved signaling system which allowed greater flexibility in fleet control than in the past. Naval officers were also coming to believe that in fleet action the chances of success would be greatest if, after breaking the enemy line, the work was finished off by bringing on a general melee. Lord Howe's victory on the Glorious First of June, 1794, proved the theory; Trafalgar was its classic exemplification.

After Trafalgar, France never again challenged Britain's control of the open seas. The possibility that the French might do so, however, combined with the duties of blockade, condemned the British navy to constant surveillance of Europe's coasts. Nelson embodied the fighting spirit of the pre-Trafalgar navy. Thereafter, the navy was symbolized by Lord Collingwood, who commanded the Mediterranean fleet on blockade until his death in 1810 ended five years of unexciting service on that station.

Why did the army operate so often in the shadow of defeat, at least during the first half of the war? Part of the answer is to be found in the government's persistent misuse of its land forces. Pitt dribbled away manpower in expeditions to Flanders, the West Indies, Toulon, Corsica, and in amphibious attacks on the coast of France. The prime minister had no monopoly on military mismanagement. Henry Dundas proved that political skill alone did not qualify a man to be a successful secretary of war. There is some justice in the verdict passed on the amiable Scot by the historian of the British army: "Yet so profoundly ignorant was Dundas of war that he was not even conscious of his ignorance."[11]

Confusion at the Horse Guards was only one of the army's troubles. The quality of the officers who led the raw recruit of 1793 inspired no confidence. Whatever the Duke of York's capacities might have been, his conduct of the Flanders campaign during the first years of the war proved that he lacked elements of greatness as a field commander. Incompetence was more conspicuous at the higher levels, but was not confined there. While serving in the West Indies, General Sir John Moore saw how disastrous poor leadership could be for troop morale. "Indeed, if the War continues," he wrote, "some strong measure must be

11. John W. Fortescue, *A History of the British Army* (London, 1899-1930), IV, 72.

adopted for the Army in general. For with blockheads at the heads of regiments and the bad condition of the officers, the Army has degenerated to such a degree that we shall lose, very soon, even our character for spirit."[12]

Before the century ended the army began to show improvement, although poor management, bad training, and incompetent officers never entirely disappeared. The Duke of York finally found his proper niche as commander-in-chief of the forces, an administrative post he first held between 1798 and 1809. At the Horse Guards, he undertook a long overdue reform of the operational functions of the army and its supply service. A new era of military development began at the tactical level with the formation of the experimental Rifle Corps. The Light Infantry, under Moore's enlightened leadership, ultimately redeemed the army's reputation by its successes on the battlefields of the Peninsula. The war years cost the lives of many good officers, but many poor ones were also driven from the service. By the time a new front opened in Portugal in 1808 there was a respectable supply of leaders who had learned their trade in the years of adversity. The names of Moore, Wellington, Picton, Hill, and Graham were to become monuments to the renaissance of Britain's military power.

In Wellington's hands, the army in the Peninsula became a deadly weapon, but it was not exclusively a British force. By 1814 nearly half the men in that army were Portuguese and Spanish levies. The nationalists fought side by side with their British allies, and received their arms, clothes, food, pay, and supplies under the British foreign aid program.

The British expedition to the island of Walcheren in 1809 exhibited nearly every fault which had marked the army's history since the beginning of the war, but the same year also witnessed a British victory over the French at Talavera in Spain. This victory taught the British and their Spanish allies that, having beaten the French once, they could do it again. The road from Talavera was neither straight nor easy, but Wellington's men were now ready to follow it until, five years later, they came to the crest of the Pyrenees from which they could look down and behold France.

12. Carola Oman, *Sir John Moore* (London, 1953), p. 153.

I

THE FORMATION OF THE FIRST COALITION

As a February afternoon yielded to dusk, the embarkation officers at Greenwich hurried aboard ship the last of the troops which had come down from London. Early that morning, February 25, 1793, two thousand Foot Guards marched out of the capital on their way to the embarkation point. The head of the column reached Greenwich in fairly good condition, but many in the rear drank too freely of the refreshment offered them by patriotic well-wishers along the way. Those who fell by the roadside finished their journey in carts stacked like cord wood. By nightfall all were at last on board the transports, and the first British expeditionary force of the war was ready to sail for Flanders.[1]

The hiring of German mercenaries was the cheapest and fastest means by which the government could enlarge its contribution to the allied cause. Within a month after the outbreak of war, Hanover agreed to send 10,000 infantrymen, together with units of artillery and cavalry, into Britain's pay and service.[2] A year later, the Electorate furnished an additional 5,299 men on the same terms, thus bringing to more than 16,000 the total of the King's German subjects in Britain's service.[3]

During the American War, the German states of Hesse-Cassel and Hesse-Darmstadt had rented men to fight in King George's army and they were ready to do so again. The negotiation with Hesse-Cassel was entrusted to the Earl of Elgin who, in April 1793,

1. Fortescue, *British Army*, IV, 65-66.
2. George Martens and Charles Martens, *Recueil des Principaux Traités d'Alliance . . . Conclus par les Puissances de l'Europe . . .* , 2d ed. (Göttingen, 1817-1835), V, 422-429.
3. Treaty with Hanover, January 7, 1794, *Journal of the House of Commons*, XLIX, 197-198.

concluded a treaty which added 8,000 men to the Duke of York's command in Flanders.[4] To mobilize this force, Britain undertook to pay levy money at the rate of £7 4s. for each foot soldier and £19 5s. for each cavalryman. The Hessians were to serve Britain for three years, during which time they would be paid and maintained by their employer. While the landgrave's troops were away Britain would give him £54,140 each year for his own use. On the expiration of the treaty, Britain would make a final payment to replace lost equipment and meet the expense of bringing the corps back to its original strength.[5] The Hessians were good soldiers, and in August 1793 another 4,000 men were hired on the same terms.[6] Like most German princelings, the landgrave refused to have his men serve in the West Indies, but he did offer to rent Britain a "Body of Foreigners" for this purpose. Since they were suspected to be French deserters living in Cassel, London declined the offer.[7]

Arranging subsidy agreements with the German states soon required the services of a special agent, and Pitt assigned this responsibility to Lord Yarmouth.[8] The ruler of Württemberg refused the terms Yarmouth offered him, but Baden was eager to strike a bargain. In return for the customary levy money and an annual subsidy of £5,013, Baden sent 754 men to serve under the British flag.[9] Yarmouth moved on to Hesse-Darmstadt and obtained 3,000 men on essentially the same terms as in the agreement concluded with Hesse-Cassel.[10] By August 1793 more than 17,000 hired German troops were under the Duke of York's command, which numbered only 6,500 British soldiers.[11] The German princes saw to it that their men were well clothed and generously supplied with equipment, but Yarmouth suspected that

4. Thomas Bruce, seventh Earl of Elgin (1766-1841) was to have a long career in the diplomatic service, but is today best remembered as the collector of the Elgin Marbles.

5. Treaty with Hesse-Cassel, April 10, 1793, Public Record Office, London, MSS., Foreign Office (hereafter cited as "FO"), 93/43(2).

6. Treaty with Hesse-Cassel, August 23, 1793, FO 93/43(3).

7. Yarmouth to Grenville, September 5, 1793, FO 29/2.

8. Francis Seymour Conway (1719-1794) was Sir Robert Walpole's nephew, and at one time, had served as British minister to France. He was made Earl of Yarmouth in 1793. His health soon collapsed under the strain of traveling in Germany.

9. Treaty with Baden, September 21, 1793, FO 93/12(1A).

10. Treaty with Hesse-Darmstadt, October 5, 1793, FO 93/44(1).

11. Fortescue, *British Army,* IV, 120n.

the Hessian landgraves secretly encouraged their subjects to desert so that they could again be offered to Britain for hire.[12]

Nearly all the mercenaries were sent to Flanders, but some were employed elsewhere. In September 1793, 4,000 Hessians were sent to help hold the French port of Toulon which had fallen to the allies. During their transfer from the Low Countries, some were temporarily put in barracks at Portsmouth and on the Isle of Wight. When this was announced to the House of Commons, Charles James Fox and Charles Grey (the future Earl Grey of the Reform Bill) protested that their presence violated the Bill of Rights and threatened English liberty. Despite the vigor of their attack, the whig leaders won little support for their motion.[13]

The opposition was ready to raise a storm over Hessians in Hampshire, but it did not oppose their employment as soldiers. No debate occurred on the appropriation of £455,851 in the 1793 Budget to pay for the Hanoverians, and in the following year the Commons voted £1,169,000 to meet the cost of all "Foreign Troops."[14] Thereafter, the expenses of the mercenaries usually appeared as a part of the "Army Extraordinaries" rather than being included as a separate budget item. So well established was the practice of hiring German troops that the whigs never seriously attacked it.

Mercenaries permitted a rapid buildup of the British army, but a prolonged war would force the government to rely increasingly on its own national manpower resources. Between 1793 and 1795 the British military establishment for home service increased from 17,344 to 119,380 men; by 1795 the ratio of British troops to mercenaries was about four to one. The invasion of Germany by the French forced many of the German princes to make peace, and by 1798 the total of all foreign troops in Britain's service fell to less than 5,000.[15]

Hiring mercenaries to swell her army was certainly important to Britain, but her major diplomatic goal was the creation of a grand alliance against France. Austria and Prussia were bound by their

12. Major William Gunn to Grenville, October 27, 1793, FO 29/3; Yarmouth to Grenville, December 6, 1793, FO 29/3.
13. *Parliamentary History,* XXX, 1363-1391.
14. *Ibid.,* XXX, 559-560, 1355.
15. Fortescue, *British Army,* IV, 938-939.

war pact of 1792, but Britain's only tie with the belligerents was her 1788 alliance with Holland and Prussia. What was needed was a coalition of all the powers in arms against France that would be founded on specific war goals acceptable to all the allies. If Russia could be persuaded to adhere, then the French Republic would surely go down to defeat before a united Europe.

British plans to create such a coalition were doomed from the start by the side effects of the Second Polish Partition. Prussia and Russia had made their arrangements for the partition only a few months before Britain entered the war. Austria's consent to these arrangements had apparently been won in exchange for a Prussian promise no longer to oppose Hapsburg efforts to exchange Belgium for Bavaria. In January 1793 Prussian troops invaded Poland to divide the loot between Frederick William and the Tsarina. When the robber-rulers' gains far exceeded what Austria had been led to expect, the Hofburg grew suspicious. All doubt disappeared after the partition was complete, when Prussia declared that she would oppose any sort of territorial compensation for Austria.[16]

The Polish crisis may have saved the life of the French Republic. Had Prussia thrown all her military might against the enemy in the West, instead of becoming involved in Poland, the campaign in the Low Countries would probably have ended in an allied victory. Thanks also to the Polish problem, Austro-Prussian relations were now worse than ever. How much interest was Russia likely to show in the war against France now that she was heavily involved in Polish politics? In February 1793 Catherine instructed her envoy in London to propose an alliance and, as proof of her zeal for the good cause, she also offered fourteen Russian warships for service with the Royal Navy against France.[17] The Tsarina's motives were probably less obvious than they appeared. An outward display of friendship for Britain at this time might neutralize Pitt's well-known opposition to the Polish Partition. Charles Whitworth, the British minister at St. Petersburg, sensed

16. Heinrich von Sybel, *History of the French Revolution,* trans. from the 3d ed. by W. C. Perry (London, 1867-1869), II, 355 and *passim*; A. W. Ward and G. P. Gooch, eds., *The Cambridge History of British Foreign Policy, 1783-1919* (Cambridge, 1922), I, 236-239.

17. Copy of instructions to Count Vorontzoff signed by Catherine, February 7, 1793, FO 65/24; Whitworth to Grenville, February 7, 1793, FO 65/24.

the direction in which Russian policy was moving and warned that Catherine's only real interest was in Poland.[18]

Lord Grenville's negotiation with the Russian minister, Count Vorontzoff, got off to an excellent start when the latter announced that the Tsarina had also empowered him to sign a new commercial treaty. Renewal of the Anglo-Russian trade pact of 1766 was greatly to Britain's interest. When the foreign secretary turned the discussion to the matter of joint military action against France, he found Vorontzoff hesitant and evasive. Catherine was anxious to conclude a defense agreement with Britain, but Vorontzoff confessed that his instructions left it unclear whether she was ready to send troops against France at this time. This was exactly the point closest to Grenville's heart. Under pressure, the Russian envoy admitted that he could not go that far. As a stopgap measure, however, he offered to conclude a general alliance with Britain at once, leaving the negotiation of a specific agreement to Whitworth and Catherine's ministers at St. Petersburg.[19] There was little the foreign secretary could do but agree, and on March 25, he signed two conventions with Vorontzoff. One renewed the commercial treaty of 1766; the other was a loose pact pledging both powers to carry on the war with France "as far as the circumstances in which they may find themselves shall permit."[20] This loose language left Catherine free to do as much or as little as she might wish. The next day instructions were sent by Grenville to Whitworth directing him to arrange a firm military treaty with Russia. Catherine's offer of warships would have to be politely declined. What Britain needed was the service of 12,000 Russian troops in the Low Countries. "His Majesty's principal object," Grenville explained, "is to obtain the co-operation of a body of troops which may act in conjunction with His against the common Enemy. You will urge this point to the utmost, and make use of every argument."[21]

The Second Polish Partition had been carried out by the time

18. Whitworth to Grenville, February 12, 1793, FO 65/24.
19. Duke of Richmond to Grenville, March 15, 1793, Historical Manuscripts Commission, *Report on the Manuscripts of J. B. Fortescue, Esq., Preserved at Dropmore* (London, 1892-1927), II, 384-385; Minute of a conference with Count Vorontzoff, March 15, 1793, FO 97/342.
20. Treaties with Russia, March 25, 1793, FO 97/342.
21. Grenville to Whitworth, March 26, 1793, FO 65/24.

these instructions reached St. Petersburg. Since Britain was now a suitor for Catherine's favor, Whitworth could hardly protest Russia's part in that affair. The diplomatic advantage was now all with Catherine, who could maintain Britain's goodwill indefinitely by holding out the hope of her eventual cooperation in the war against France. At Whitworth's first meeting with Vice-Chancellor Ostermann, he was amazed to learn that Catherine expected a British subsidy of between £500,000 and £600,000 in return for sending 10,000 troops to the West. Not only was the demand unexpected, it was exorbitant. Whitworth rejected it at once and confessed his amazement at such a request from a ruler "who has not only constantly taken the lead in exciting others, to put themselves above personal considerations... but who had also begun by indemnifying Herself so amply." Ostermann had nothing to say beyond the obvious fact that affairs in the West were of more immediate concern to Britain than to Russia. Since there was no basis for any negotiation, the matter was referred back to London.[22]

Grenville was in no mood for diplomatic niceties when he resumed his meetings with Vorontzoff in mid-June. The Russian demand for money was outrageous! More than half-persuaded to this opinion himself, Vorontzoff used his discretionary authority to reduce the price from £600,000 to £300,000. The foreign secretary was unimpressed and demanded to know why Britain should pay the Tsarina even £300,000 when for a fraction of that sum she could hire 50,000 German mercenaries? At this point Vorontzoff poured oil on the troubled waters by predicting that Catherine would finally settle for a smaller subsidy. Rather than abandon the negotiation, he urged Grenville to give the matter his cool consideration before making any decision. Privately, the Russian envoy found the whole business distasteful and predicted that Britain would never yield. Writing to his brother Alexander, he sadly observed, "The whole thing was quite impossible. I foresaw it, I wrote about it, and the minister's reply confirmed it."[23]

22. Whitworth to Grenville, April 29, 1793, FO 65/24; Fedor F. Martens, *Recueil des Traités et Conventions Conclus par la Russie avec les Puissances Etrangères* (St. Petersburg, 1874-1909), IX, 363-364 (hereafter cited as F. Martens, *Recueil des Traités*).
23. F. Martens, *Recueil des Traités,* IX, 364; Simon Vorontzoff to Alexander Vorontzoff, June 14, 1793, in *Arkhiv Kniazia Vorontsova,* ed. P. I. Bartenev (Moscow, 1870-1895), IX, 303-304.

Vorontzoff was right. Almost at once, Grenville informed Whitworth of his decision: the Tsarina must be told "that unless the idea of a subsidy is abandoned, all possibility of a future concert is at an end."[24] This ultimatum put an end to all discussion of an Anglo-Russian alliance, and Whitworth was now convinced more than ever that the Tsarina would remain aloof from the war. "All which we have seen happen," he wrote Grenville, "seems to justify the Opinion I entertained from the Beginning, that it would be the Policy of this Court to engage as many as it could in the Broil, and to keep as clear as possible of it, itself."[25] Ostensibly, Catherine's refusal to take arms was the result of Britain's unwillingness to finance her. In fact, it is hard to believe that she had ever meant to become involved.

The Polish Partition was also responsible in large measure for Grenville's failure to form a diplomatic union with Austria and Prussia. Originally he hoped to create a single alliance binding all three powers to remain at war until France had restored her conquests.[26] This emphasis on a status quo ante settlement partly grew out of Britain's desire to keep Austria in the Low Countries as a barrier against France. The possibility that Austria might someday succeed in exchanging Belgium for Bavaria had always made the Foreign Office uneasy.[27] In the spring of 1793 Vienna searched feverishly for some territorial compensation to match Prussia's recent gains in Poland. She might force a defeated France to yield Alsace to her or agree to a generous enlargement of Belgium's frontier. Both possibilities were attractive, and in April 1793 the new head of the Austrian foreign department, Baron Johann Thugut, told the British ambassador that he was seriously considering giving up the Belgium-Bavaria exchange plan.[28] London responded eagerly to this announcement by proposing that any territorial settlement with France must provide for an important cession of land to Belgium. By such an enlargement of Belgium, it might be possible for Britain to wean Vienna away from any thought of exchanging it for Bavaria.

---

24. Grenville to Whitworth, June 14, 1793, FO 65/24.
25. Whitworth to Grenville, June 28, 1793, FO 65/24.
26. Grenville to Sir James Murray, February 6, 1793, FO 29/1.
27. Austria's victory at Neerwinden (March 18, 1793) encouraged hopes that the French would finally be driven from Belgium. In such a case, the Belgium-Bavaria exchange plan might be revived.
28. However, he added that he was unwilling to "bind himself down never to resume it," Morton Eden to Grenville, April 15, 1793, FO 7/33.

British plans overlooked the fact that Prussia was determined to see that Austria got nothing at all. The quarrel between the German allies in the spring of 1793 waxed so violent that Grenville abandoned all thought of arranging a single alliance with them. All he could hope for was to negotiate separate treaties. The negotiation with Prussia was assigned to Lord Yarmouth, who reached Frederick William's camp at Mainz in June to find his hosts elated by the prospect of early success in their siege of that city. Frederick William received the British diplomat cordially and their discussion of terms ended in prompt agreement. When his ministers protested that the country could not afford another campaign, the King brushed aside their objections and on July 14 the treaty was signed. It consisted of five brief articles binding both powers to continue the war until France had returned all her conquests.[29] The alliance with Austria was negotiated by Grenville himself, in conjunction with Count Louis Starhemberg, the Hapsburg envoy in London. On August 30 the two men affixed their names to an agreement much like the one Yarmouth had signed at Mainz one month before.[30]

What Grenville's diplomacy achieved hardly bore any relation to his original plan for a grand alliance of all the powers. That plan had been wrecked by Catherine's dissimulation and by Austro-Prussian jealousy. Instead of a firmly knit coalition, there was only a confused combination of interlocking agreements. Possibly even this precarious confederacy might succeed in spite of its poor foundations. During July 1793 the French suffered a serious reversal in Belgium and the Prussians at last captured Mainz. With the approach of autumn, France's borders were more exposed to her enemies than at any time during the past year.

Britain gave highest priority to the negotiation of treaties with Russia, Prussia, and Austria, but she did not neglect bringing the smaller states into the coalition. During the first year of the war she undertook engagements with Spain, Portugal, Naples, and

29. Treaty with Prussia, July 14, 1793, FO 93/78(4C).
30. Treaty with Austria, August 30, 1793, FO 93/11(1A).

Sardinia. Of these, only that with Sardinia called for the payment of British subsidies.[31]

The Anglo-Sardinian alliance, signed on April 25, 1793, almost exactly recreated the union which had existed between the two powers nearly a century before. During the War of the Spanish Succession, Britain paid Sardinia to help maintain an army of 45,000 men against Louis XIV. When France invaded Nice and Savoy in 1792, the government at Turin turned to Britain for help. By the terms of their alliance, Britain promised to provide an annual subsidy of £200,000, to be paid quarterly, in return for which Sardinia was to maintain 50,000 soldiers in the field against the French Republic. The first quarterly payment of the Sardinian subsidy, amounting to £50,000, was remitted to her envoy in London the following June. Payments made during the remainder of the year brought the total to £150,000, while in the following year, she received £200,000.[32] In this way, Britain helped finance the counteroffensive which Sardinia launched in the summer of 1793. Successful at first, the Sardinians were finally forced back and escaped destruction only because the French suspended the campaign. London grew uneasy at reports that her ally's army was far below the 50,000 quota specified in their treaty, and Grenville threatened to suspend subsidy payments until the Sardinian force was increased to that figure.[33]

31. Britain's alliance with Spain of May 25, 1793, FO 93/99(5A), provided for joint cooperation in the war and the exclusion of French commerce from the ports of both nations. Spain still smarted from her defeat at Britain's hands in the Nootka Sound affair three years before. Grenville was not pleased with the treaty of alliance and feared that it "cannot be considered as a very solid foundation of friendship" (Grenville to Lord St. Helens, June 21, 1793, *Manuscripts of J. B. Fortescue,* II, 398). The treaty with Portugal of September 26, 1793, FO 93/77(1A), simply renewed the old Anglo-Portuguese alliance and bound Portugal to break off trade relations with France. The Treaty with Naples, signed by Sir William Hamilton on July 12, 1793, FO 93/96(1A), obliged Naples to maintain at least 6,000 troops at her own expense. Should it be necessary for those troops to serve outside Naples, they would be provided with transportation by the British navy. These treaties have been examined both in their protocol form and as they were finally ratified. None of them made any provision for the payment of British subsidies.

32. Treaty with Sardinia, April 25, 1793, FO 93/87(1A). Payments of the Sardinian subsidy are recorded in the King's Warrant Books, part of the Treasury Papers (hereafter cited as "Ty.") in the Public Record Office, London, 52/80,351; Ty. 52/81, 13; Ty. 52/82, 31, 103-104; Ty. 52/83, 91.

33. Grenville to John Trevor, October 8, 1793, FO 67/13.

The Sardinian treaty provided the only opportunity for the House of Commons to debate the question of foreign aid during the first year of the war. Although the treaty was presented to the Commons in June 1793, it was not until the following January that Pitt requested the necessary appropriation of funds. Fox opposed the agreement, not because it involved a subsidy, but because he "had never conceived that it could be wise to enter into any treaty by which we were to receive nothing and to give everything." So far as subsidies were concerned, the whig leader admitted that he had nothing against them in principle. "He knew, that in every war to be carried on by a confederacy, we must pay the weaker powers whom we engaged in that confederacy."[34]

Pitt took no part in the debate, but his views were doubtless those of the young member who replied to Fox. In this, his maiden speech, George Canning upbraided the whigs for their limited vision and declared that the treaty, as well as the war itself, could be justified on the same grounds: the salvation of England, as well as the European equilibrium, would be decided by the outcome of the present contest.[35] The course of the debate clearly showed that the Sardinian treaty was in no danger and the government's request for money was finally adopted without division.

Examination of Britain's treaties with her war partners now makes it possible to define the role of subsidies in the formation of the First Coalition. British money was spent generously to hire German mercenaries, but this was a time-honored device to expand the British army as rapidly as possible. On the other hand, no financial aid was offered to the allies other than to Sardinia. Britain's refusal to act as paymaster to the coalition is clearly revealed in her summary rejection of Russia's demand for money, even though that decision gave Catherine the Great an excuse to remain at peace. Pitt and Grenville must surely have seen this as a pretext; Russia had nothing to gain from a war with France. British diplomacy encountered difficulties with Prussia and

34. *Parliamentary History,* XXX, 1310-1313.
35. *Ibid.,* XXX, 1317-1329; Dorothy Marshall, *The Rise of George Canning* (London, 1938), pp. 53-54.

Austria, but not over the question of subsidies.[36] The treaties with the German allies, concluded during the summer of 1793, made no provision for any British financial assistance. Except for the pledge of aid given Sardinia, Britain was not ready to underwrite the war expenses of any of the major powers who were now her allies.

Britain's refusal to subsidize the major allies reflected her leaders' confidence that the war would not last long. In the late summer of 1793 the fortunes of war turned in favor of the coalition, and the road to Paris at last lay open to their armies. However, a new outbreak of Austro-Prussian jealousy blighted this last chance for easy victory over France. It began at the Prussian headquarters in August when the Marquis Lucchesini, Frederick William's trusted advisor, provoked a violent quarrel with the Hapsburg envoy, Count Lehrbach. In recent months, the Polish Diet had attempted to recover some part of Prussia's share in the recent partition, and Lucchesini now charged Lehrbach's government with secretly encouraging the Poles. In vain, Lord Yarmouth intervened to bring the rival ministers back to what seemed to him the immediate question: agreement on the campaign against France.

Thoroughly alarmed at the turn affairs had taken in Poland, Frederick William decided to intervene. Henceforth, he would give highest priority to the protection of his Polish interests, rather than to the war with France. Orders were issued transferring a large part of his army to Poland. Troops now being mobilized at home would be sent to join units already in the East rather than toward the Rhine. To dramatize this change of policy, the King left for Posen to take personal command of his forces.[37]

A few days after these decisions had been announced, Lucchesini explained to Lord Yarmouth why the King had been forced to make them. Frederick William's heart was still in the war with France and he was anxious to remain a principal, but the

---

36. Two months after the Prussian treaty was signed, Lord Yarmouth admitted that during its negotiation the Prussian ministers broadly hinted that British funds would be welcome. Yarmouth ignored the hint, however, and the matter was not pressed; Yarmouth to Grenville, September 29, 1793, FO 29/2.

37. Sybel, *French Revolution,* III, 135-148.

recent Polish troubles, combined with the oppressive expense of maintaining armies on two fronts, were sapping his resources. For Prussia to continue to play a major role in the war against the Republic, two new articles must be added to her recent alliance with Britain: first, Britain must formally guarantee Prussia's Polish lands against attack by another power; and, second, she must give Prussia a subsidy and urge the other allies to follow her example. Yarmouth refused to discuss these demands, although he promised to send them on to London at once.[38]

Prussia's appeal for money was not unexpected in Downing Street; for the past few months, the British chargé d'affaires at Berlin had warned that something of the sort was in the wind. Frederick William's advisors were pressing him to end the war with France as the only means of averting bankruptcy. Equally disturbing was their insistence that the contest with France served no important Prussian interest.[39] Grenville had little sympathy for Prussia and her problems. Early in October Frederick William's demands reached him and his response was immediate: the Polish guarantee was inadmissable and he urged Pitt to reject the demand for subsidies.

Pitt's reaction to the Prussian note was more considered and thoughtful than his foreign minister's. He entirely agreed that Britain could do nothing to help defend her ally's Polish lands. An outright rejection of Prussia's request for money, as Grenville recommended, would only antagonize the volatile Frederick William and play into the hands of the peace faction at Berlin. Would it not be wiser to accept at face value the King's protest of good faith and then consider what could be done to help him? This approach would cost nothing and it might put him in a mood to be reasonable. After all, there was one side of the problem which no one had yet considered: the mutual defense obligations undertaken by Prussia, Britain, and Holland in the Triple Alliance of 1788. So far nothing had been said about that treaty even though it clearly had application to the present war. As the parties attacked by France, Britain and Holland had a right to ask Prussia to provide 32,000 troops (20,000 for Britain and 12,000 for

38. The Prussian memorandum is to be found in FO 29/2. See also J. B. Burges' letter to Grenville of September 30, 1793, *Manuscripts of J. B. Fortescue*, II, 430-431.
39. George Rose to Grenville, July 20,27, September 17, 1793, FO 64/28.

Holland). In return, they were treaty-bound to supply these troops with "bread and forage." Much the same arrangement was included in the Austro-Prussian alliance of 1792, which entitled Austria to call on her ally for 20,000 troops in the event of attack. By the terms of these two conventions, Prussia was obliged to furnish her three allies with a total of 52,000 men whose "bread and forage" expenses would be a charge on Britain, Holland, and Austria. Pitt estimated that on this basis the three powers would owe Prussia somewhat more than £1,000,000 a year.

Careful consideration of the question led the prime minister to propose that Prussia be invited to meet her obligations to the allies under these treaties. Should Frederick William then be able to supply additional troops for the war against France, the allies ought to underwrite their total expense. In such a case, the subsidized corps must be completely at their disposal. In effect, Pitt recommended that once Prussia had met her debts to the allies, they ought to hire a second Prussian army on nearly the same basis as Britain employed Hessian mercenaries. He urged Grenville to consider whether it might not be wise to offer such a counterproposal: "I think this mode will be less likely to produce a coldness between us and the Court of Berlin; and if he [Frederick William] agrees to the idea, it would be more advantageous than any co-operation he has yet afforded in the war. The expense will be comparatively speaking no object, if it produces a real and efficient force at our disposal, in a quarter where it is essential to act with vigour, as part of the general plan for the next campaign."[40]

Grenville admitted that Britain was clearly obliged to provide "bread and forage" for any Prussian troops she might claim under the terms of the 1788 alliance, but the idea of subsidizing additional Prussians was repugnant to him. Unable to agree, Pitt and Grenville decided to submit the question to the Cabinet at its meeting on October 9. The Cabinet listened to the arguments advanced on both sides and, in the end, supported Grenville's position. Pitt accepted his defeat, but urged that the foreign secretary's reply to Prussia be temperate. There was no point in giving unnecessary offence. As finally drafted, the British note sent to Berlin rejected the requested Polish guarantee and called

40. Pitt to Grenville, October 2, 1793, *Manuscripts of J. B. Fortescue,* II, 433.

on Prussia to meet her obligations under the Triple Alliance. At the same time, Britain acknowledged her obligation to pay the "bread and forage" expenses of the force to be furnished.[41]

So far, Prussia's request for subsidies had been expressed only in general terms, but early in November Frederick William's envoy in London announced that the King would require £3,500,000 from his allies to finance another campaign. Britain was expected to furnish half this sum, while Austria and the Empire would be asked to supply the balance.[42] Grenville responded to Baron Jacobi's announcement by informing him of the decision which the Cabinet had already reached on this question: to invite Prussia to fulfill her obligations under the 1788 treaty. On hearing this, Jacobi turned petulant and declared that his government no longer considered that treaty operative. The foreign secretary took up the point in a flash since it was basic to the entire British position. Would Jacobi be willing to put that statement in writing? The Prussian backed off at once. Grenville put an end to the meeting with the forceful declaration that Prussia's obligations to Britain were clear-cut and that George III "never would submit to purchase succours which He had a right to from the treaty of Alliance."[43]

Frederick William returned from Poland to his capital early in November 1793, to discover how profitless his appeal to the allies had been. Austria's refusal to help came as no surprise, but there was something about the cool British demand for implementation of the 1788 alliance which infuriated the King. After all he had done for the cause, it was the worst sort of cheese-paring for her to demand fresh exertions under a treaty whose meaning had been rendered obsolete by events since 1788. The King's vexation was eagerly cultivated by those of his ministers who were anxious for him to end the war. Prussia was nearly bankrupt and the nation cried for peace. All this was reported by the British chargé d'affaires who warned Grenville that not one voice was heard at Berlin in favor of continuing the war against France.[44]

41. Pitt to Grenville, October 10, 1793, *ibid.,* II, 441-443. The official British reply to Prussia, dated November 13, 1793, is to be found in FO 97/324.

42. Frederick William to Jacobi, October 26, 1793, FO 97/324.

43. Minute respecting Lord Grenville's conversation with Jacobi, November 7-8, 1793, FO 64/28.

44. Rose to Grenville, November 3, 1793, FO 64/28.

Prussia's reply to the British demand took the form of a letter from the King to Jacobi which the latter was expected to lay before Pitt and Grenville. London's ungenerous attitude did him less than justice, Frederick William wrote, since it entirely overlooked his exertions in the good cause for nearly a year before Britain entered the war. The allies could not honestly deny that he had already done more then enough to meet his obligations to them. Therefore, he must reject Britain's demand. Unless Austria and Britain provided the money he required, he would be forced to limit severely his part in the spring campaign.[45]

The rapid collapse of the allies' position in Flanders during the closing months of the year underscored the threat contained in the King's letter. In September 1793 the Revolutionary armies regained the offensive and forced the Duke of York to abandon his siege of Dunkirk. A month later, the Austrians also suffered a severe setback. The Prussians had taken Mainz during the summer and moved on to attack Landau, but before the year ended, they, too, were forced to fall back. With the arrival of the New Year, France held a position from which her rejuvenated armies would be able to launch an offensive against the allies.

Frederick William's ultimatum presented the British Cabinet with what was essentially a military problem: was there any chance of victory over France without the support of Prussia as a major ally? Austria could not enlarge her forces to make up for the withdrawal of the Prussians, and Russia was as far as ever from taking any part in the war. There was no choice but to work out some sort of agreement with Berlin. In mid-November, the prime minister brought forward the plan the Cabinet had rejected one month before. Prussia must be persuaded to honor her treaty obligations to the allies who, in turn, would pay her at least £1,000,000 in "bread and forage" money. Once that had been done, Pitt recommended that Prussia be asked to bring forward another army to be entirely paid for and used by her partners. Circumstances left the Cabinet no choice but to endorse this proposal and authorize a special mission to Berlin.

There were clear advantages in carrying on the negotiation at the Prussian capital, rather than in London. The Prussian envoy, Jacobi, was a time-server who could not speak with any real

45. Frederick William to Jacobi, November 10, 1793, FO 97/324.

authority; furthermore, Grenville found it hard to bear with him. Much to be preferred was a special British agent working with Prussian ministers at Berlin. Lord Yarmouth was certainly not the man for this mission, even though he was now in Germany. His steadily worsening health was seriously eroding what little talent he possessed. All agreed that the special assignment at Berlin must be entrusted to Lord Malmesbury. Still less than fifty years old, Malmesbury had spent nearly half his life in his country's service at Madrid, Berlin, St. Petersburg, and The Hague. The Triple Alliance had been his masterpiece, and since Britain's approach to Prussia involved that treaty, Malmesbury's qualifications for this service were indisputable. By now, the ways of diplomacy were second nature to this dean of the British diplomatic service. In semiretirement since 1788, Malmesbury was anxious to resume his career, and when Pitt offered him the Prussian post, he gladly accepted.

Grenville carefully prepared instructions to guide the new envoy. Malmesbury's immediate goal was to bring Prussia to recognize that not only was the 1788 treaty still binding, but that it specifically applied to the present war. "If the King of Prussia," Grenville explained, "admitting the force of all His Treaties, and actually furnishing the contingents respectively due to the Empire, to the Emperor, to His Majesty [George III] and to Holland, is yet willing to concert measures for a further co-operation in the War against France, there could be no objection to discuss with Him the means of facilitating such further exertions by the supply of whatever pecuniary assistance might be necessary." There must be no misunderstanding on one point: any additional force subsidized by the allies must "act under their direction and control." London would make no specific offer until after receiving Malmesbury's report on conditions at Berlin.[46] Privately, Grenville urged his envoy to carry on discussions so far as possible with the Prussian king himself, "from whose sense of his engagements more may, perhaps, be expected than from the principles or policy of those by whom he is advised." Obviously, Prussia's complaints of poverty must be carefully investigated. Finally, since the British

46. Instructions for Malmesbury, November, 1793, FO 64/31.

plan to aid Prussia looked to a joint effort by all the major allies, Malmesbury ought to discuss the question with Dutch leaders at The Hague on his way to Berlin. He would certainly invite the support of the Austrian minister to Prussia, even though "the utmost jealousy prevails between the two Courts of Vienna and Berlin."[47]

Prussia's conduct had been a puzzle to British leaders for nearly a year. The wretched business of Poland had combined with Austro-Prussian antagonism to dash to pieces Grenville's plan for a grand alliance of all the powers. Still, even that did not explain Frederick William's odd conduct toward Britain. Perhaps Malmesbury could find some solution which would enable the coalition to make war successfully against France in the spring of 1794. When Malmesbury came to the Foreign Office to take his leave, Grenville tried not to appear pessimistic. Only in a private letter to his brother did the foreign secretary admit his fears: "Lord Malmesbury is going to Berlin, to bring our good ally to a point—ay or no. I think it will end in no."[48]

47. Grenville to Malmesbury, November 20, 1793, *Diaries and Correspondence of James Harris, First Earl of Malmesbury* . . . , ed. by his grandson, the third Earl, 2d ed. (London, 1845), III, 1-5 (hereafter cited as *Malmesbury*).

48. Grenville to the Marquis of Buckingham, November 21, 1793, *Memoirs of the Court and Cabinets of George the Third,* ed. the Duke of Buckingham and Chandos (London, 1853-1855), II, 247.

II

THE PRUSSIAN SUBSIDY

Lord Malmesbury reached Berlin in time to have his first audience with Frederick William on Christmas Eve. Darkness had come, wrapping the northern capital in the cold winds of a winter night when the envoy was ushered into the presence of the Prussian monarch. Frederick William had not seen his English friend since their meeting five years before at The Hague when they had concluded the Triple Alliance, and he now greeted him with sincere warmth. Malmesbury was shocked to see what a toll these years had taken of the King's health even though he was still not fifty. It was more than the fact that he had lost a few teeth. Unmistakable signs of both physical and moral decay were stamped on this man who, indeed, had only three more years to live.[1]

Unlike his predecessor, the great Frederick, this Prussian monarch was totally lacking in self-discipline. Warm and impulsive by nature, he had never learned to master his passions and, on coming to the throne in 1786, he gave up the unequal contest altogether. Even worse than his personal immorality was the coarseness which characterized it. In preparing for a journey he carefully selected several female traveling companions as another man might choose books from his library to ease the tedium of travel. The King flew from one diversion to another, stunning his court more by his lack of discrimination than by his fickleness.[2]

1. *Malmesbury*, III, 27.
2. *The Journal of Elizabeth, Lady Holland, 1791-1801,* ed. Earl of Ilchester (London, 1908), I, 168-169; Malmesbury to Grenville, January 9, 1794, *Manuscripts of J. B. Fortescue*, II, 492-494.

He would dabble with Rosicrucianism for a while and then, losing interest, feed his hunger for music by creating one of the finest court orchestras in Europe. Sustained effort and enduring interest were foreign to him. In the person of the king of Prussia was the heart and mind of a spoiled and very bored child. Malmesbury might well have wondered whether this ruler was really master of his own state.

Although their first meeting was brief, Malmesbury went to the heart of his business at once by asking the King whether he still considered the Triple Alliance binding. Frederick William seemed astonished at the question. Without a moment's hesitation he replied that, so far as he was concerned, the treaty was as effective now as on the day it had been signed. Let there be no doubt about that. The hard fact was, however, that without money from the allies, Prussia could no longer make war on France. Very solemnly the King assured Malmesbury that *"on the faith of an honest man . . .* I have not in my treasure enough to pay the expenses of a third campaign." So completely was he dedicated to the good cause that not even Austria's treacherous conduct toward him had weakened his zeal.[3]

In the days that followed this interview, Malmesbury carefully studied conditions at Berlin. He made a special point of discussing the war with the three Prussian foreign ministers and found none of them an enthusiastic supporter of the coalition. From what Malmesbury could discover, Prussia's financial condition was every bit as bad as Frederick William claimed. Of £13,000,000 left by Frederick the Great, less than £3,000,000 remained, and the annual revenue regularly fell short of expenses. The British envoy's conversations with officers of the Prussian army revealed that they were more interested in discussing the errors of the last campaign than in planning for the next. Some insisted that at least three months would be required to put the army in shape to move against the French. What had happened to the military traditions of Frederick the Great?[4]

News of allied defeats along the Rhine and the French recapture of Toulon alarmed Malmesbury and he at once began negotiations

3. Malmesbury to Grenville, December 26, 1793, *Malmesbury,* III, 28-31.
4. Malmesbury to Grenville, December 26, 1793, FO 64/31; and *Malmesbury,* III, 34-38.

with the King. Frederick William assured him that with financial support from his allies he could put 100,000 effective troops in the field by the spring. He eagerly suggested ways by which the allies could raise the money he needed. Funds could surely be obtained by means of an international loan with the French nation offered as collateral. Another possibility suggested to the King by the Dutch was that the allied powers issue a paper currency to be redeemed after the war ended. Malmesbury wisely refrained from asking for further details, nor did Frederick William supply them. Instead, with his imagination now fired by warlike visions, the King vowed, "That at the head of this army he would begin the campaign, by acting in such a manner as he trusted would leave no doubt of his sentiments on the present war, or of his invariable wish to fulfil his engagement to the utmost of his power."[5]

On January 9, 1794 the British agent sent Pitt a detailed report of his findings. It was impossible to exaggerate the wretched state of affairs he had found at Berlin. Frederick William's intentions were good enough, but they surely could not be relied on. "The irresolution and weakness of his character," Malmesbury observed, "is indeed such that I cannot venture to pronounce that, if he is allowed to cool, this disposition will last." Malmesbury went to the heart of the matter by asking, *"Can we do without the King of Prussia or can we not.* If we can, he is not worth the giving a guinea for; if we cannot, I am afraid we cannot give too many." Certain of the answer to this question, Malmesbury made his own recommendation: "We must only look to the making the best and quickest bargain possible, to the purchasing him as reasonably, and to the binding him as fast and as securely as we can." Even if this was done, Pitt must remember that "The greatest difficulty is to secure the hearty co-operation of His Prussian Majesty till the end of the war, and on this point I am quite at a loss what is to be done."[6]

Parliament reconvened early in 1794, and the King's Speech made clear the government's decision to carry on the war with

5. Malmesbury to Grenville, January 5, 1794, *Malmesbury,* III, 38-41. See also Grenville to Lord Auckland, January 16, 1794, *The Journal and Correspondence of William, Lord Auckland* (London, 1861-1862), III, 168-170 (hereafter cited as *Auckland*). The proposal that the allies issue a paper currency to pay their war costs was finally adopted during the last phase of the Napoleonic war.

6. Malmesbury to Pitt, January 9, 1794, *Manuscripts of J. B. Fortescue,* II, 494-495.

renewed determination. Fox's motion for peace provoked a spirited response from the prime minister who declared that his policy was "to resist, where resistance alone can be effectual, till such time, as by the blessing of Providence upon our endeavours, we shall have secured the independence of this country, and the general interests of Europe."[7] This was also the spirit of the Cabinet, which authorized the subsidy proposal Grenville sent to Malmesbury on January 28. Strategy for the 1794 campaign called for the Austrian and British forces to resume the offensive in Flanders, while at least 100,000 Prussians provided support along the Rhine. Holland had decided not to claim the 12,000 Prussians due her under the Triple Alliance and Grenville therefore fixed at 40,000 the force Frederick William was treaty-bound to furnish Britain and Austria. If he could enlarge this force to 100,000 men, then the allies might be willing to pay him a £2,000,000 subsidy. The foreign secretary recommended that the allies undertake this financial obligation jointly since "The whole burthen of the above mentioned Sum is far beyond what it is possible to propose that His Majesty should take upon himself."[8] Britain was willing to pay two fifths of the total (£800,000) but Austria, Holland, and Prussia would each have to contribute one fifth.

Strange as it might seem to require Prussia to pay £400,000 toward her own subsidy, Pitt and Grenville were both firm on this point. From the outset the prime minister feared that subsidizing Prussia might have the effect of making her appear to be merely a troop-renting agency.[9] Less sensitive to Prussia's feelings, Grenville argued that for Prussia to share the financial burden would give her "a direct and immediate interest in the success of the War." Frederick William might be more energetic if he thought that a defeated France could be made to reimburse him.[10] Writing confidentially to Malmesbury, Grenville complained that "German Princes think England a pretty good milch cow."[11]

7. *Parliamentary History*, XXX, 1045-1047, 1286.

8. In Grenville's first draft, he described the £2,000,000 subsidy as "beyond what it is possible." In the final draft, he altered this to read "far beyond what it is possible."

9. Pitt to Grenville, October 2, 1793, *Manuscripts of J. B. Fortescue*, II, 434-435.

10. Pitt's biographer aptly describes this device as "suggestive of that of the rustic who tempts his beast of burden onwards by dangling a choice vegetable before his nose" (John Holland Rose, *William Pitt and the Great War* [London, 1911], p. 202).

11. Grenville to Malmesbury, January 28, 1794, FO 64/31; Grenville to Malmesbury, January 17, 1794, *Manuscripts of J. B. Fortescue*, II, 497.

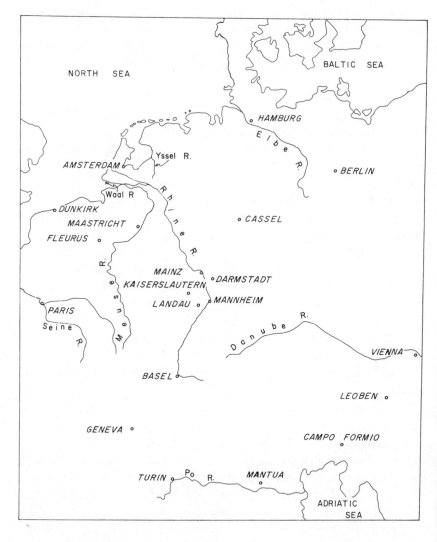

1. Campaign Area of the First Coalition

The British proposal was based on foolish hopes, and it was also contrived and complicated. Prussia refused to contribute to her own subsidy unless the total was increased to provide her with the means to do so.[12] The Dutch were willing to bear that part of the burden Britain had assigned to them, but in February Grenville learned that Austria would pay nothing.[13]

By this time, the Prussian government had produced a subsidy plan which Malmesbury sent to London in February. Not only did the Prussians want vastly more money than they had previously asked for, but they demanded that the monthly payments be made retroactive to the first of the year.[14] So extreme were these demands that Grenville was sure they had been "brought forward for the purpose of being negatived," and his notes on the proposal are generously sprinkled with such phrases as "highly objectionable," "wholly inadmissible," and finally "utterly inadmissible."[15]

Within a few weeks the spring campaign against France was due to begin, and the Cabinet had no choice but to produce a counterproposal. In the middle of March Grenville forwarded this new plan to Malmesbury and described it as "Final." If Prussia would maintain 62,000 troops against the enemy (including the 32,000 men Holland and Britain were entitled to by the 1788 alliance), Britain would pay her a subsidy of £1,000,000 a year. Malmesbury was empowered to offer two additional concessions if they were needed: first, to accept the demand for monthly payments retroactive to the first of the year; and second, to offer still an additional sum to meet the "bread and forage" costs of the 20,000 troops Prussia was bound to furnish Britain by the terms of the Triple Alliance. This second concession would add about £400,000 a year, bringing the total subsidy close to £1,500,000.[16]

The coming of spring found Frederick William ready to compromise his differences with Britain, and even before Grenville's final offer reached Berlin, Malmesbury was presented with a new Prussian plan more reasonable than the last. Sixty-two

12. Malmesbury to Grenville, February 16, 1794, *Malmesbury*, III, 51-66.
13. Thugut was horrified by the prospect of 100,000 subsidized Prussians operating in an area from which they might launch an attack on the Hapsburg possessions; Grenville to Malmesbury, February 3, 1794, FO 64/31.
14. The Prussian proposal is found in FO 64/32.
15. Grenville to Malmesbury, March 7, 1794, *Manuscripts of J. B. Fortescue,* II, 516; Grenville's notes on the Prussian proposal, FO 64/31.
16. Grenville to Malmesbury, March 7, 1794, FO 64/32.

thousand troops would be mobilized for service in the Low Countries, for which the Maritime Powers (as Britain and Holland were referred to) must pay £800,000 a year, together with an extra sum to meet the expenses of this force.[17] The Prussian offer was no bargain, but Grenville wearily instructed Malmesbury to continue negotiations and resolve the differences between the two governments.[18] Meanwhile, Malmesbury had proposed to Count Kurt von Haugwitz, his Prussian counterpart, that their future discussions be continued at The Hague. Ostensibly this would permit the Dutch to take part in the final settlement of terms. In fact, Malmesbury feared that the growing antiwar sentiment at Berlin would prove fatal to his mission if he remained there much longer.[19]

Hard bargaining marked the closing phases of the negotiation at The Hague, but by April 1, 1794 terms had been agreed to which, in general, fell within the limits Grenville had prescribed. Gone entirely was the clumsy distinction Pitt had made between the troops Prussia was treaty-bound to supply and an additional contingent. Now it was simply agreed that Prussia would place 62,400 men at the disposal of the Maritime Powers who would pay her a monthly subsidy of £50,000 to be counted from April 1. An additional sum would be due for the upkeep of this force, bringing the total monthly payment to £150,000. To gain this much, Malmesbury had been forced to go beyond Grenville's offer in certain respects. In order to escape Haugwitz' demand that monthly subsidies be made retroactive to January 1794, Malmesbury had to agree to the payment of "preparation money." After much haggling, the British envoy offered £400,000 for this purpose and it was accepted.[20] Prussia balked at the demand that the Maritime Powers have absolute control of the subsidized force, as if it were a corps of Hessian mercenaries. The text of the treaty, which was signed on April 19, left this important question in some confusion. Provision was made for the creation of a military commission, representing Britain and Holland, to arrange with the Prussian commander for the employment of the subsidized army

17. Malmesbury to Grenville, March 13, 1794, FO 64/32.

18. Grenville to Malmesbury, March 28, 1794, FO 64/33.

19. Moving to The Hague would also bring Malmesbury into closer communication with London. See Malmesbury to Grenville, March 13, 1794, *Malmesbury*, III, 75-80.

20. Malmesbury to Grenville, April 19, 1794, *Manuscripts of J. B. Fortescue*, II, 552.

"where it will be judged most agreeable to the Maritime Powers."[21]

While at The Hague, Malmesbury also reached an understanding with the Dutch regarding their responsibility for subsidy payments. The Stadtholder's government consented to pay £100,000 of the "preparation money" due Prussia as well as £400,000 of the annual subsidy of £1,350,000. Privately, the Dutch ministers confessed that this obligation would be difficult for them to meet. To save the Dutch embarrassment, Malmesbury promised that his government would sponsor a £400,000 loan for the Stadtholder from the Bank of England. This courteous gesture greatly annoyed Pitt when he later learned of it.[22]

On hearing that the Prussian subsidy treaty had finally been signed, Pitt declared that he was "sincerely glad." George III's reactions are in some respects more interesting and penetrating. On the whole, the King was pleased with the result, but added that "perhaps a little more firmness in Ld. Malmesbury's manner of treating might have in some particulars rendered the terms more Advantageous; but as the main object is so essential, I think it best not to look out for any objections."[23] The King's advice was sound, for the treaty could hardly be considered as a diplomatic victory for Pitt. In fact, the agreement did violence to each of the four major points on which the prime minister had insisted at the outset of the negotiation.

First, the treaty ignored entirely the distinction Pitt had made between the troops due Britain under the 1788 alliance and the additional corps she was willing to subsidize. Instead, the Maritime Powers acknowledged that the subsidy treaty of 1794 in fact freed Prussia from her obligations to them under the Triple Alliance. Second, nothing at all remained of Pitt's original insistence that any subsidy for Prussia must be financed collectively by the allies. The entire expense was now to be borne by Britain and Holland with every likelihood that the Dutch would pass on their share to Britain.

21. Treaty with Prussia, April 19, 1794, FO 94/183(3),(4).

22. Treaty with Holland, April 19, 1794, FO 93/46 (1D); and Pitt to Grenville, April 24, 1794, *Manuscripts of J. B. Fortescue,* II, 552.

23. Pitt to Grenville, April 24, 1794, *Manuscripts of J. B. Fortescue,* II, 552; George III to Pitt, April 28, 1794, in the papers of William Pitt included in the Chatham Papers on deposit at the Public Record Office, London, 30/8, vol. 103.

Lord Grenville, by John Hoppner

Lord Malmesbury, by Sir Joshua Reynolds

Sir Charles Whitworth, by Sir Thomas Lawrence

George Canning, by Sir Thomas Lawrence

Third, throughout the negotiation Pitt had been forced to offer Prussia more and more money. In January an annual subsidy of £800,000 was considered to be the limit, but the April treaty saddled Britain with a bill which would amount to about £1,500,000 by the time the year ended. Finally, Britain had all along insisted that the subsidized Prussians must be under the control of the allies who provided the money. Whether or not the military commission, created by the treaty, would actually exercise this sort of control remained to be seen.

Important as these considerations are, they must not obscure the main point: Britain could find no other way to carry on the war without Prussia's cooperation as a principal partner. Military necessity was the determining consideration before which lesser interests had to yield. This was the point the prime minister stressed when, on April 30, he presented the Prussian treaty to the House of Commons. He frankly confessed "that it would be much more satisfactory to me to be able to state that the king of Prussia still continued to take part in the war as a principal, acting on his own bottom, and from his own resources." That was no longer possible. "How much soever we may regret, or disapprove the secession of the king of Prussia from the common cause," he continued, "there can be no doubt that if his efforts can at all be effectual to the purposes of the war, it is still desirable to secure the use of them." The House should note that it would cost Britain much more to add 62,400 men to her own army than it would to obtain the service of as many Prussians by a subsidy. Pitt readily conceded that Britain could not hope to control the subsidized Prussians as if they were German mercenaries. It was, perhaps, as well that he neglected to mention it was exactly that sort of control he had originally hoped to obtain.[24]

Although Fox had no hope of defeating the treaty, he was anxious to make as good a fight as possible. With the skill of an experienced debater, he fastened tenaciously to the weakest part of the government's case. If military necessity compels us to submit to Prussia's demands, then "Spain, Austria, and all the other powers, might come to the same resolution." Could the prime minister "give the people of this country any ground to

24. *Parliamentary History*, XXXI, 437-442.

hope that the same difficulty would not be felt by the other powers as had been expressed by Prussia?" Certainly not! "What, then, was to be expected to be the result of all this?" Fox asked. "Why, that the whole expence would eventually fall on Great Britain."[25] Had members known how accurate this prediction was to prove, perhaps more than thirty-three of them would have voted in favor of Fox's motion to deny the subsidy. Instead, the treaty was upheld by more than a hundred votes, and Pitt might have congratulated himself on carrying off the business with so little trouble.

Grenville's defense of the agreement, made the same day in the Lords, dealt at length with the principles which justified the payment of subsidies. War with France had always obliged Britain "to seek for aid on the continent; for though our superiority over France, in point of national vigour, of naval power, of commerce and of wealth was manifest, yet in point of population, and of the means of raising armies, Britain must yield to her rival; and thus it had always been our system to seek on the continent for additional land force." The employment of mercenaries and subsidy agreements with the allies had "at all times, been our policy, not merely from necessity, as we could not raise great land armies ourselves, but also from economy, as it was certainly cheaper and more politic to pay foreign troops, than to take our own youth from the plough, and the loom, and thereby not merely put a stop to all domestic industry, but also drain the island of its population, and diminish our natural strength." This had certainly been the case with the 1758 Prussian subsidy treaty which Grenville pointed to as a precedent.[26]

Even though Britain's population was more than double that of Prussia, she had chosen to pay Frederick William to maintain 62,400 men under arms against the French Republic.[27] Not only would it have cost her more than the subsidy to enlarge her own army by that number, but such a diversion of manpower would

25. *Ibid.*, XXXI, 442-451.
26. *Ibid.*, XXXI, 452-455.
27. It has been estimated that at the close of the eighteenth century the combined population of England, Wales, Scotland, and Ireland was about 15,600,000 while the population of Brandenburg–Prussia was only around 6,200,000; see Herbert Moller, ed., *Population Movements in Modern European History* (New York and London, 1964), p. 5.

impair Britain's ability to create wealth. In the face of such a double loss, the Prussian subsidy treaty might seem a bargain. The point probably struck most peers as self-evident, for when the House of Lords finally voted, only six members expressed themselves as "Not-content" with the subsidy to Prussia.

The subsidy treaty with Britain renewed Frederick William's commitment to the war in the West, and for that reason, some of the King's advisors bitterly opposed it. Prussia's real interest, they insisted, was territorial expansion in the East, not war with the French Republic. Shortly before the signing of the treaty, events took a turn in Poland which added weight to their argument. Ever since the partition of the previous year, Poland had been restive, and in March 1794 a revolt flared up which quickly turned into a war of liberation against Prussia and Russia. Within a month, Polish patriots drove their oppressors from Warsaw and reasserted the independence of their nation. Had the conclusion of the subsidy agreement with Britain been delayed much longer, Frederick William's ministers might have persuaded him to end the negotiation. As it was, the Berlin peace party now set about to convince the King that, regardless of his new obligation to Britain, his chief responsibility was to suppress the Polish rebels and then preside over a final partition of that country. Torn between the arguments of his ministers and his own sense of obligation to the allies, Frederick William compromised: the forces subsidized by Britain and Holland would remain on the Rhine, but the rest of his army would move into Poland. This decision reflected the dualism of Prussia's policy which soon reduced her subsidy treaty with Britain to scrap paper.[28]

Pitt unwittingly played into the hands of the Prussian peace faction by his careless tardiness in remitting the subsidy payments. At the signing of the treaty, Malmesbury promised Haugwitz that the preparation money and the April subsidy would be sent from England at once.[29] On his return to London a few weeks later he discovered that Pitt and Grenville were so absorbed in rooting out

28. A. W. Ward, G. W. Prothero, and Stanley Leathes, eds., *The Cambridge Modern History* (Cambridge, 1934), VIII, 542-544.

29. In March Malmesbury was told that Prussia's military chest would be exhausted within another month; Malmesbury to Grenville, March 8, 1794, FO 64/32.

sedition at home that they had altogether neglected their responsibility to Prussia. The diplomat was horrified and begged ministers to attend to the Prussian business at once.[30]

It was not until May 20, one month after the treaty had been signed, that Pitt directed the Bank of England to supply £600,000 in specie to pay Prussia the preparation money and the subsidies for April and May.[31] Arrangements were also made with the London bank of Harman, Hoare, and Harman to handle the remittances in return for a commission of 1/3 *d.* percent.[32] By the terms of the treaty, Britain was to appoint a member of the special military commission which would direct the operations of the subsidized force. For this post the prime minister selected Lord Cornwallis who had just returned from service in India. All Britain's obligations under the treaty had been met by the end of May when Malmesbury left England to resume his diplomatic duties at the Prussian headquarters.

At Maastricht the British envoy encountered Count Haugwitz, from whom he learned that Frederick William was still in Poland but was expected to return to the Rhine within a few weeks. Malmesbury indicated that the Cabinet wished the subsidized Prussians to take a new position between the Meuse and the sea in order to cooperate with the allies in the defense of Holland. Although Haugwitz approved this plan, he noted that the Prussians could not be moved until after the receipt of the subsidy money. So far no payment of any kind had been made. Malmesbury ruefully admitted that Prussia was entirely within her rights. This was exactly the danger about which he had warned Pitt; not a Prussian soldier would stir until at least the first subsidy remittance was at Berlin.[33]

On June 7, H.M.S. *Active* worked her way up the Thames and dropped anchor near the Tower of London in order to take aboard a quantity of kegs packed with Spanish silver dollars. She was soon joined by H.M.S. *Syren* under orders to take delivery of 231 kegs of silver. The crew of the *Active* was more fortunate, for, in addition to the specie, they loaded thirty puncheons of beer. Both

30. *Malmesbury*, III, 93.

31. Pitt to the Governor of the Bank of England, May 20, 1794, and Pitt to Jacobi, May 28, 1794, Chatham Papers, vol. 195.

32. Treasury Minute, May 31, 1794, Ty. 29/66, 466-467.

33. Malmesbury to Grenville, June 2, 1794, FO 64/33.

vessels sailed with the tide on June 9, outward bound for Hamburg, carrying between them £600,000 in silver. Ten days later, both ships were in the Elbe and the silver was conveyed by a guard of marines to the Hamburg bank of Parish and Company, correspondents of Harman and Hoare.[34] The Hamburg bankers made arrangements for the specie to be sent to the Prussian treasury at Berlin.

Meanwhile, Malmesbury and Haugwitz remained at Maastricht awaiting the arrival of Lord Cornwallis. The British general joined them early in June, bringing with him Brook Watson, commissary general to the Duke of York's army.[35] Watson offered to help the Prussian army get moving at once by lending them sixty days' rations from his own stores. Haugwitz curtly rejected this offer, pointing out that it was a shortage of money, not rations, which kept the army immobilized.[36] So forcefully was the point made that Cornwallis began to doubt whether Prussia had any intention of joining in the defense of Holland.[37]

A few days after this unhappy meeting, Malmesbury and Cornwallis set out for the Prussian headquarters at Mainz to confer with the commander of the subsidized army, Marshal Möllendorf. They were accompanied by Baron Kinckel, who had been appointed as Holland's representative on the military commission. Arriving at Mainz, the envoys discovered that instead of the 62,400 troops called for by the treaty, the Prussian army numbered only about 40,000 men in deplorable condition.[38] Möllendorf provided a chilly reception for his visitors, making clear that he really wished they had not come. Overlooking this discourtesy, Malmesbury turned at once to business and informed Möllendorf that the military commission wished him to move his troops toward Flanders. The aging marshal bristled. No one but

---

34. Master's Log for H.M.S. *Syren,* 1794, Admiralty Papers deposited in the Public Record Office, London (hereafter cited as "Adm."), 52/3427; Master's Log for H.M.S. *Active,* 1794, Adm. 52/3520.

35. Brook Watson (1735-1807) had gone to sea as a boy and lost a leg to a shark while swimming in Havana harbor. The incident inspired a painting by John Singleton Copley. Watson served as commissary to the British army in Canada during the Seven Years War, after which he went into business in London. A member of Parliament and a director of the Bank of England, he was later elected Lord Mayor of London.

36. Malmesbury to Grenville, June 11, 1794, FO 64/34.

37. Cornwallis to the Duke of York, June 18, 1794, *Correspondence of Charles, First Marquis Cornwallis,* ed. Charles Ross (London, 1859), II, 248.

38. Fortescue, *British Army,* IV, 292.

the King could give such an order and he had not done so. The army would remain at Mainz. Malmesbury's patience had been worn away by the disappointments of the last few weeks, and he now lashed out at Möllendorf's refusal to abide by the clear meaning of the treaty. The military commission was present and demanded the right to decide where the Prussians were to fight. Möllendorf was not open to argument on this point. Until orders came from the King, the army would stay where it was.[39]

Malmesbury was now at his wits' end. The Prussians refused to move even though the subsidy had been paid. With Frederick William still in Poland, weeks of correspondence would be needed to clear up this tangle. To make matters worse, Cornwallis had begun to get on Malmesbury's nerves; the phlegmatic general had not uttered a word to support his colleague during all the discussions with Haugwitz and Möllendorf. In fact, Cornwallis was thoroughly weary of the whole business and when he announced his decision to return to England, Malmesbury offered no objection. By now, the Prussians were nagging the British minister about the subsidy payments for June and July. The first remittance of £600,000 brought the payments due only to the end of the month of May. Again the familiar refrain was heard: nothing could be done until the account was paid up to date. Malmesbury relayed their complaints to Grenville, adding with obvious weariness, "I am persuaded the same game will be play'd over again at the beginning of each month."[40]

The June subsidy was a month late in being sent from England. Early in July the Bank of England supplied £120,000 in Spanish dollars to be shipped aboard H.M.S. *Mermaid*. To complete the payment, Harman and Hoare purchased £30,000 in specie at Amsterdam for delivery at Hamburg. The treasure carried by *Mermaid* was delivered to Parish and Company in mid-July and was to have a significant part to play in the worsening of Anglo-Prussian relations.[41]

Malmesbury's reports from Mainz created a dismay in Downing Street which quickly turned to fury. While the Prussians did guard

---

39. Malmesbury to Grenville, June 21, 1794, FO 64/34.
40. Malmesbury to Grenville, July 12, 1794, FO 97/324.
41. Thomas Cotton to Grenville, June 27, 1794, FO 64/29; Master's Log for H.M.S. *Mermaid*, 1794, Adm. 52/3215.

duty on the Rhine, the Austrian army had been badly beaten at Fleurus on June 25. Unless the Prussians quickly moved to support the allies, all of Belgium would fall to the enemy. Grenville ordered Malmesbury to insist on the right of the Maritime Powers to use the troops they were paying: "This is a point in every light so important, and which was so clearly understood during the whole negotiation, and so plainly expressed in the Treaty itself, that it can never be given up."[42] Pitt was even more upset and bewailed the fact that "we are condemned to a *wretched defensive*" if Möllendorf did not soon move. At first, the prime minister was tempted to declare that Prussia's inaction had nullified the treaty, but he soon recognized that such an act would be foolish.[43] Certainly, there was much talk in government circles about stopping subsidy payments until the Prussians moved. At a Cabinet meeting in mid-July someone (it may have been Grenville) proposed such a step. Pitt and the Duke of Portland, however, argued that at this stage such a decision would probably do more harm than good.[44] In the end, this view prevailed, and on July 19 Grenville dispatched an appeal to Möllendorf to send at least 20,000 men to help the allies stem the onrushing French tide which threatened to engulf Holland.[45]

During this same month, a comedy of errors which nearly ended the Anglo-Prussian alliance was played out at Berlin involving the subsidy money brought by H.M.S. *Mermaid*. Early in July, Haugwitz informed George Rose, the British chargé d'affaires at Berlin, that a rumour was going around to the effect that London had stopped subsidy payments. If this were so, Haugwitz declared that all Prussian troops would be withdrawn from the western front.[46] Rose knew nothing of the matter. He had resigned his post and was only awaiting the arrival of his successor, Arthur Paget. A few days after Paget reached Berlin, Haugwitz had a stormy interview with him in which he announced that Parish and Company had refused to turn over the June subsidy money to the Prussian treasury. Paget protested that there had been a misunder-

42. Grenville to Malmesbury, July, 1794, FO 64/34.
43. "We ought to insist on an immediate order for the Prussians to march, or consider the treaty as broken" Pitt to Grenville, June 29, 1794, *Manuscripts of J. B. Fortescue*, II, 592-593.
44. Portland to Malmesbury, July 23, 1794, *Malmesbury*, III, 120.
45. Grenville to Malmesbury, July 19, 1794, FO 64/34.
46. Rose to Grenville, July 5, 1794, FO 64/29.

standing which he would correct. Despite Paget's eagerness to set things right, he could not appease Haugwitz, who forced him to accept a very stiff ministerial note of protest.[47]

Hurried enquiries revealed that Parish and Company had indeed refused to pay the June subsidy brought by *Mermaid.* As justification, the Hamburg bankers produced a letter from Harman and Hoare forbidding them to make any further payments without specific instructions from London.[48] What had happened now seems fairly clear. With rumours circulating in London that the subsidy was to be suspended, Harman and Hoare had ordered their Hamburg correspondents to delay payment until they could discover the truth. The matter was soon cleared up and the Prussians received their money. Haugwitz' conduct had perhaps been the most significant feature of the entire incident: the only major Prussian minister to support the subsidy treaty, he now appeared to have joined its opponents.[49]

Before July ended the French had driven the allies from Belgium. The Duke of York fell back into Holland, while the Austrians withdrew eastward toward the Rhine. With the allied armies now separated, the French turned against Möllendorf's Prussians and forced them to abandon Kaiserslautern. Under this pressure, the Prussian marshal bestirred himself and offered to unite with the Austrians in the defense of the Rhine. The British Cabinet endorsed Möllendorf's plan and agreed to continue the subsidy. This was just as well. Late in July Malmesbury learned of Frederick William's decision regarding the direction of the subsidized Prussians; it was left to Möllendorf to decide where they were to fight.[50]

The proposed union of the Prussian and Austrian armies never took place. With the French daily growing stronger in his front,

47. Paget to Grenville, July 26, 1794, FO 64/30.

48. Harman and Hoare's instructions to Parish and Co., dated July 11, 1794, read "be pleased to observe, that no part of the Silver is to be sent away until you shall have our instructions for it"; Paget to Grenville, July 26, 1794, FO 64/30.

49. If Pitt felt that Harman and Hoare were guilty of misconduct, he did nothing more than insist that for the future they act only on the government's instructions. For the details, see Grenville to Paget, August 16, 1794, FO 64/30; Harman and Hoare to Pitt, August 15, 1794, FO 64/30; and Harman and Hoare to Pitt, September 17, 1794, Chatham Papers, vol. 142.

50. Malmesbury to Grenville, July 29, 1794, *Malmesbury,* III, 118-119; Grenville to Malmesbury, August 16, 1794, and Malmesbury to Grenville, July 29, 1794, FO 64/34.

Möllendorf decided against moving north to join with the Imperial army. The Austrians were therefore obliged to continue their withdrawal, and early in October Möllendorf himself sought refuge by crossing to the right bank of the Rhine. Meanwhile, the French stabilized their position by uniting their scattered armies into a single arc, stretching from Mannheim roughly north and west through the south of Holland. Malmesbury remained with the Prussians, but his role was now that of an observer rather than an envoy. Each day made him more disgusted with the Prussians and their duplicity, and he compared them to the Algerian pirates "whom it is no disgrace to pay, or any impeachment of good sense to be cheated by." He longed only for release and confided to Grenville, "I lament every hour that I remain near them."[51]

When Pitt learned of Möllendorf's refusal to unite with the Austrians, fear overcame the little of his patience which remained. Since May more than £1,000,000 had been paid to the Prussians with absolutely no return. As early as August, Grenville was ready to wash his hands of the whole business and he told Malmesbury, "We have given the thing the best chance of success . . . It has not succeeded, and I am convinced that no further endeavours will obtain more from the Prussians than we have had for the last twelve or fourteen months, until events put us in a situation to speak in a higher tone."[52] Now the prime minister agreed. At the end of September, he informed Jacobi that the subsidy would be suspended until Möllendorf joined forces with the Duke of York in Holland.[53]

The blow which Britain had threatened all summer now fell on the Prussians, but circumstances made it anticlimactic. Berlin responded by declaring that the British decision put an end to their alliance.[54] Certainly, the Prussian peace faction was anxious to end the connection with London. Since spring nothing had quite gone as they wished. Operations against the Polish rebels had completely bogged down, and only the intervention of Russian troops ended the uprising. Catherine thereby won the right to dictate the terms of the final partition. Frederick William feared

51. Malmesbury to Portland, August 7, 1794, *Malmesbury*, III, 121-122; Malmesbury to Grenville, September 26, 1794, *Manuscripts of J. B. Fortescue*, II, 636.
52. Grenville to Malmesbury, August 16, 1794, *Manuscripts of J. B. Fortescue*, II, 621.
53. Grenville to Malmesbury, September 30, 1794, FO 64/35.
54. *Malmesbury*, III, 143.

that the Tsarina would favor Austria and grant him only a small share of Poland. This is what happened. For a time, the King was tempted to improve his position in the East by renewing his entente with Britain.[55] Pitt was always prepared to resume the subsidy if Prussian troops were sent to help defend Holland. During the autumn, Count Haugwitz tempted Arthur Paget by declaring that Prussia only waited for the payment of one more month's subsidy before sending her army to Holland. In the end, even Haugwitz wearied of the game and told Paget, "Pay the subsidies and then we will talk."[56]

Grenville would have none of it. He was barely civil to the Prussian minister, Jacobi, when the latter called on him in late October to express Frederick William's displeasure. So far as Grenville was concerned, the union with Prussia was broken, and on the following day, he sent Malmesbury permission to abandon the post which had become intolerable.[57]

The £1,200,000 paid to Prussia since June accomplished none of the things Pitt expected.[58] It is difficult to see how it could have been otherwise. When the treaty had been signed, British leaders hoped that the addition of 62,400 Prussians to the allied force in the Low Countries would bring victory. The Prussian argument that such a concentration would expose Germany to attack is probably valid from a military viewpoint. Even so, why did

55. The several communications made by Hardenberg to Malmesbury during the late summer of 1794 seem to bear this out; see *Malmesbury*, III, 131-133.

56. Paget to Malmesbury, October 20, 1794, *The Paget Papers; Diplomatic and Other Correspondence of the Right Hon. Sir Arthur Paget, G. C. B., 1794-1807*, ed. Sir Augustus Paget (London, 1896), I, 70-71.

57. Grenville's minute on a conference with Jacobi, October 23, 1794, FO 97/324; and Grenville to Malmesbury, October 24, 1794, *Manuscripts of J. B. Fortescue*, II, 642.

58. The King's Warrant Book (Ty. 52/81, 283) records warrants issued between June 4 and October 4, 1794, for a total of £1,306,495 for the Prussian subsidy. Of this sum, £720,000 was paid the Bank of England in June for the silver used in the first two remittances. The balance was paid to Harman and Hoare. In December 1794 that firm presented their final statement showing a credit of £80,000 to the British government, after deducting bankers' commissions and incidental expenses (Army Ledgers, Papers of the Pay Master General's Office, deposited in the Public Record Office, London [hereafter cited as "PMG"], 2/45, 330).

The fact that a warrant for the Prussian subsidy was signed on October 4 suggests that the payments to Prussia were resumed. However, the October warrant was to cover payments made to Harman and Hoare *prior* to the suspension in September (Pitt to George III, October 4, 1794, *The Later Correspondence of George III*, ed. Arthur Aspinall [London, 1963], II, 249).

Möllendorf remain totally inactive until the end of the summer when the French forced him to defend himself?

The answer to this question lies in the ambivalence which characterized Prussian policy throughout the entire year. Frederick William was torn between his interests in Poland and his obligation to the allies. His emotional attachment to the coalition's cause is beyond dispute. The hard fact was that the war with France offered Prussia very little opportunity to satisfy her craving for territorial gain. The Polish rebellion, coming almost at the same time as the subsidy treaty with Britain, placed him in a dilemma. If he devoted himself to the war in the West, Russia would doubtless settle the Polish crisis to Prussia's disadvantage. To renege on his treaty with the Maritime Powers would bring on him the charge of betrayal and, at the same time, deprive him of any share in the prizes which France might be obliged to yield to the allies. Because Prussia kept a foot in both camps she failed to meet her goals either in the East or the West. The performance of the Prussian army during the summer of 1794 nearly destroyed its reputation as one of Europe's finest military weapons. Möllendorf's inept operation along the Rhine was matched by the failure of Prussia's expedition against the Polish rebels. Victories could not be won by appeals to the memory of Frederick the Great.

Pitt contributed to the failure of the Prussian treaty by failing to pay the installments of the subsidy when they were due. From the very beginning, this provided Frederick William's ministers with the opportunity to charge Britain with bad faith. The ground was thus prepared for the bickering over pay and performance in which the allies engaged until the treaty was mercifully suppressed in October. One point is beyond all dispute: until Britain and the powers she assisted were of one mind regarding the purpose of the war, subsidies would make no contribution to victory, although they might postpone defeat.

53

III

A NEW ORIENTATION FOR THE COALITION

Prussia's withdrawal from the war disturbed Grenville far less than might be imagined. In one of his final dispatches to Malmesbury, the foreign secretary explained his lack of concern: "I am far from thinking it a disadvantage that the resolution of withdrawing the army has been so decisively and abruptly taken at Berlin. The season is, I trust, too far advanced to allow of any considerable impression being made on the German frontier in the course of this year; and we have the whole winter before us to take our measures for the next campaign, knowing what we have to trust to."[1] British and Dutch troops began to dig in behind the Waal river in a desperate last-ditch effort to hold that line against the French. By now, Pitt's confidence in the Duke of York had vanished and he pressed the Duke of Brunswick to accept the command. Brunswick declined the offer, but he did agree in November, to rent 2,289 of his soldiers to Britain for service in Holland. For this he would receive the customary levy money and an annual subsidy of £15,565.[2]

The formation of the coalition in 1793 created a partnership in arms among Britain, Prussia, and Holland—the powers who five years before had formed the Triple Alliance. By the opening of 1795 Prussia had abandoned the coalition and French armies threatened to overrun Holland. For the future, Britain would have to carry on the war in closer cooperation with Austria, her only remaining major ally. Information had reached Grenville indicating that the Tsarina might soon be ready to take an active part in the

1. Grenville to Malmesbury, October 24, 1794, *Manuscripts of J. B. Fortescue,* II, 642.
2. Treaty with Brunswick, November 8, 1794, FO 93/20(1).

contest with France. With the old Triple Alliance of 1788 in shambles, the foreign secretary proposed to provide the coalition with a new focus in the form of a British alliance with Austria and Russia. To accomplish this, Britain would certainly have to agree to supply her partners with money.

Austria's finances began to collapse in the autumn of 1793; at the same time Prussia made her first bid for British subsidies. Since the Prussian appeal initially had been rebuffed by London, Thugut seems to have concluded that an Austrian call for help would meet the same fate. Therefore, the Hofburg decided to borrow the money it required. With the Dutch money market almost destroyed by the war, application would have to be made to the bankers of England. Early in 1794 the Austrian minister in London, Count Starhemberg, was instructed to negotiate a private loan of £1,000,000, a sum soon raised to £3,000,000.[3]

Acting on these instructions, Starhemberg opened the matter with one of the City's leading banks: Boyd, Benfield and Company. Walter Boyd, senior partner in the firm, was highly regarded in financial circles, although some thought him more reckless than was desirable in a banker.[4] Boyd readily agreed to manage the Austrian business and he offered suggestions as to how £3,000,000 could be raised. As finally settled, there would be a £2,500,000 issue of Austrian 3 percent bonds. Bonds with a face value of £100 would be sold for £60 in cash, thus bringing Austria a total return of £1,500,000. The remaining half of the loan would take the form of twenty-five-year annuities yielding a 10 percent return.[5] Before going further, Boyd took the precaution of discussing the question with the prime minister. So far the government had remained out of the matter, although a foreign loan of this size was obviously a matter of concern to the Treasury. Certain City financiers had already urged Pitt to forbid the transaction. On May 6, 1794 the prime minister replied to Boyd's enquiry and indicated that he would not oppose the

3. Starhemberg to Thugut, April 1, 1794, in Alfred von Vivenot, *Quellen zur Geschichte der Deutschen Kaiserpolitik Oesterreichs während der Französischen Revolutionskriege, 1790-1801* (Vienna, 1873-1890), IV, 175; Karl F. Helleiner, *The Imperial Loans: A Study in Financial and Diplomatic History* (Oxford, 1965), pp. 2-16.

4. Walter Boyd (1754[?]-1837) began his banking career in Paris, but returned to England on the outbreak of the Revolution. Between 1796 and 1802, he was a member of Parliament and a regular supporter of Pitt's government.

5. *Parliamentary History*, XXXI, 1561-1564; Helleiner, *Imperial Loans*, pp. 8-9.

Austrian loan. So far as Pitt knew, there was nothing in British law to prevent a foreign government "in Amity with this country" from undertaking such a transaction.[6]

When the books on the Austrian loan were finally opened, the response was sluggish. Loans to foreign governments were always risky, and the security offered (the Emperor's hereditary revenues in Belgium) seemed inadequate, especially in view of Austria's setbacks in Flanders. Following the defeat of the Imperial army at Fleurus in June 1794, the loan came to a halt. The few who had agreed to buy now reneged, while some bondholders offered their securities to speculators at a 4 percent loss.[7] By July only £300,000 had been realized from a transaction intended to bring in £3,000,000.[8] At this point, Boyd proposed a remedy to rescue the loan and restore it to robust health; let the British government guarantee both the interest and the principal of its ally's loan and then potential investors would snap it up. Starhemberg doubted whether Pitt would agree to such a plan and nothing was done for the moment.[9]

During the summer of 1794 the collapse of the allied defense of the Low Countries brought Downing Street close to panic. With all hope of victory gone for the present year, plans had to be prepared for operations in 1795. Pitt had no genius for strategy and his proposals for future operations were unrealistic in the extreme. If Prussia increased Möllendorf's army to the 62,400 figure provided in her subsidy treaty with Britain *and* sent them into the Low Countries, Pitt intended to hire 30,000 more Prussians on the same terms. Austria was to be asked to enlarge her army in the Low Countries to 100,000 men and to find a new commander to replace Coburg. Pitt knew that Vienna was already suffering financial misery and conceded that he would have "to ascertain whether any pecuniary arrangements are necessary and practicable to enable Austria to prosecute the war vigorously for at least two campaigns after the present."[10]

6. Starhemberg to Thugut, May 6, 1794, Vivenot, *Quellen,* IV, 211; Pitt to Boyd, May 17, 1794, Chatham Papers, vol. 195.

7. Starhemberg to Thugut, June 27, 1794, Vivenot, *Quellen,* IV, 306.

8. Notes (in Pitt's handwriting) on a conversation with Desandrouin, July 25, 1794, Chatham Papers, vol. 195.

9. Starhemberg to Thugut, July 11, 1794, Vivenot, *Quellen,* IV, 332.

10. Minute of Mr. Pitt on Military Operations, July 15, 1794, *Manuscripts of J. B. Fortescue,* II, 599-600.

Britain could immediately aid Austria by guaranteeing the loan now languishing in Walter Boyd's care. Such a step was premature, however. No major commitment could be undertaken without the Cabinet's knowing more about Austria's resources, her willingness to name a new commander, and her real intentions toward Belgium. To obtain this information Pitt decided to send Earl Spencer on a special mission to Vienna for discussions with Thugut. Scion of one of the great whig houses, Spencer had no diplomatic experience at all. He was one of the most intelligent and effective defenders of the government in the Lords, however, and Pitt had great confidence in him. At the last moment, Spencer asked that the foreign secretary's older brother, Thomas Grenville, be named with him in a joint commission. The elder Grenville was agreeable and George III appointed both men as his envoys to the Hapsburg court.[11]

Pitt carefully explained to Spencer and Grenville the part he wished Austria to play during the next campaign. To help her undertake this assignment, Britain might agree to lend its "superior credit" to back the Hapsburg loan in London, but so far as a subsidy was concerned, "no encouragement can . . . be given to the Austrian Ministers which should lead them to form such an expectation." The envoys were to say nothing to Thugut about money and wait for a specific offer to be sent from London.[12]

The amateur diplomats arrived at Vienna in early August and at once conferred with Thugut, whom they found to occupy a commanding position in the Emperor's councils. Territorial gain was Thugut's lodestar and he was determined to see that Austria shared generously in the final Polish partition which was in the offing. As a step in that direction, he eagerly sought for a diplomatic entente with that giver-of-all-good-gifts in eastern Europe, Catherine of Russia. The formation of the Austro-Russian alliance was achieved early in 1795 and brought his plans closer to realization. Spencer and Grenville had the misfortune to be sent to Vienna at the very time Thugut was trying to disentangle his country from involvement in the Low Countries. The Hofburg was now far more interested in the possibility of expansion in Poland,

11. Grenville to George III, July 18, 1794, *Later Correspondence,* II, 225; George III to Grenville, July 19, 1794, *Manuscripts of J. B. Fortescue,* II, 601.

12. Grenville to Spencer, July 19, 1794, FO 7/38.

Turkey, and Italy than it was in recovering Belgium. If Britain expected Austria to spend her blood and treasure in rescuing the Low Countries, she must be prepared to pay well for it. This was the message which Thugut's agent, Count Mercy d'Argenteau, now en route to London, had been ordered to deliver to the British ministers.

Spencer and Grenville quickly discovered that only British money would induce Thugut to keep Austria's armies in the Low Countries. The expansion of that force, proposed by Pitt, was virtually impossible since Vienna "had neither money nor credit & could not without a subsidy hope to carry on any vigorous war." When the British envoys announced that they had no subsidy offer to propose, Thugut's disappointment was unmistakable. Until Britain had such a proposal to make, the Austrian foreign minister saw no point in carrying on any discussions with Pitt's agents. Thomas Grenville understood this immediately and warned his brother, "till they can hear the money jingle in Count Mercy's courier's portmanteau we shall not yet advance."[13]

The two Englishmen should have found Vienna in late summer a pleasant place to pass the time, but their letters home revealed that they were miserable. Held at arm's length by Thugut, Spencer and Grenville conscientiously gathered information and dutifully sent it on to London. No one in Vienna had any enthusiasm for the war and, so far as Belgium was concerned, its fate seemed to be a matter of indifference. It would be pointless to transfer the Prussian subsidy to Austria as the Hofburg desired, for as Thomas Grenville plainly warned, Britain "cannot buy what they have not to sell."[14] Within a month after their arrival, both agents were thoroughly weary of Vienna and Spencer requested permission to return to England.

Throughout August Thugut waited impatiently to learn what promises Count Mercy had been able to wring from Pitt, but fate intervened and that message never came. Mercy reached London about the same time that Spencer and Grenville sent home their

13. Spencer and T. Grenville to Lord Grenville, August 12, 1794, FO 7/38; T. Grenville to Lord Grenville, August 15, 1794, *Manuscripts of J. B. Fortescue,* II, 618.
14. T. Grenville to Lord Fitzwilliam, August 30, 1794, *Memoirs of the Court,* II, 281. See also T. Grenville to the Duke of Portland, August 24, 1794, *ibid.,* II, 259-267; Spencer and T. Grenville to Lord Grenville, August 12, 1794, *Cornwallis Correspondence,* II, 255-256.

first reports from Vienna, but he was too ill to attend to business. His condition turned critical and he finally died. On August 26 Count Starhemberg, the resident Hapsburg minister, presented Pitt with the three demands Mercy had been instructed to make: immediate financial help for the Austrian army in Flanders, a British guarantee for the Hapsburg loan, and a promise of a subsidy during 1795. Without this minimum aid, Starhemberg warned that Austria would have to give up the war in the Low Countries.[15]

Pitt's response to this ultimatum was powerfully influenced by recent events on the battlefields of Flanders. Once again the Imperial army had been driven back and was now desperately trying to stabilize its position along the Meuse. If this effort failed, the effect would be catastrophic. The prime minister was prepared to guarantee Austria's loan, but this would require legislation and Parliament had recessed for the summer. To provide immediate assistance, Pitt ordered the Duke of York to turn over as much as £150,000 in bills of exchange to the Austrians on condition that they hold their Meuse position. This would be considered as an advance which Austria could later repay from the proceeds of her loan in London.[16]

With Austria's immediate needs provided for, the Cabinet considered a long-range program of aid for her ally. Grenville had such a plan and he now offered it. To begin with, supreme command over all British, Dutch, and Austrian troops in the Low Countries must be vested in Lord Cornwallis. This was a *"sine quâ non,"* in return for which Britain would guarantee Austria's £3,000,000 loan as soon as Parliament assembled. As a further help, the subsidy now being paid to Prussia would be transferred to Austria. Two conditions were attached to this, however: that the Hofburg increase its army in Flanders to 160,000 men, and that the Empire undertake to pay Prussia during the coming year a subsidy of the same size she was now receiving from Britain. Ungenerous as the proposal was, Grenville had great difficulty in getting the Cabinet to approve it. Recent experience with Prussia had soured ministers on foreign aid. In the end, the plan was

15. Lord Grenville to Spencer and T. Grenville, August 26, 1794, FO 7/38; Starhemberg to Thugut, August 26, 1794, Vivenot, *Quellen,* IV, 403-407.
16. Lord Grenville to Spencer and T. Grenville, August 26, 1794, FO 7/38.

adopted, but with the clear understanding that Austria must accept Cornwallis as generalissimo of her forces.[17]

Britain's offer of help, which Thugut had long awaited, was so niggardly that he treated it with open contempt and poured out his wrath on Spencer and Grenville. It was outrageous to ask that the Imperial forces accept a British commander; to do so would oblige the Emperor "to disgrace himself by proclaiming to all Europe that he had not a General fit to command them."[18] Furthermore, Pitt must be totally out of touch with reality if he expected Austria to accept a subsidy and then pressure the Imperial Diet to pay Prussia. If the Diet had such resources, Austria would have appealed there for help rather than to Britain. Further discussion was clearly pointless and the two British agents prepared to leave for home.[19]

Pinchpenny though the British offer was, the Cabinet pared it down almost immediately. The collapse of the Austrian defense along the Meuse so frightened the Cabinet that it was at first inclined to cancel the proposal. With great difficulty, Grenville was able to salvage one of its parts: Britain would still agree to guarantee the Austrian loan if Vienna enlarged its army in the Low Countries to at least 80,000. Nothing was now said about the transfer of the Prussian subsidy or of Lord Cornwallis as supreme commander. The Duke of York had so far remitted only £50,000 to his Austrian allies and London now ordered him to pay no more. When Starhemberg pressed for an explanation, Grenville tartly told him that the Austrian army was not being paid to retreat.[20]

On the eve of their departure from Vienna, Spencer and Grenville were given a counterproposal by Thugut which he declared was his final offer. Let the British government guarantee

17. That the Cabinet seriously meant this is clear from Lord Grenville's letter to Spencer and T. Grenville of August 29, 1794, FO 7/38. See also Starhemberg to Thugut, August 26, 1794, Vivenot, *Quellen,* IV, 408-409.

18. On September 9, 1794, George III warned Pitt that Austria would never accept such a demand. See Lord Stanhope, *Life of the Right Honourable William Pitt* (London, 1861-1862), II, appendix, p. xxi.

19. Spencer and T. Grenville to Lord Grenville, September 15, 1794, FO 7/38.

20. Grenville's responsibility for saving this much of the original proposal is clear from a letter written by Lord Auckland to Lord Henry Spencer, September 18, 1794, in *Auckland,* III, 241. See also Starhemberg to Thugut, September 26, 1794, Vivenot, *Quellen,* IV, 454.

an Austrian loan of £6,000,000 (double that now pending) and he would provide an army of 100,000 for cooperation with her during the coming year. Without at least this much help, the envoys reported to London, "the Government here [Vienna] very explicitly state their utter inability to act in the war with any degree of vigour."[21]

Britain and Austria were now so close to agreement on terms that the remaining differences could certainly be compromised. Pitt's reluctance to abandon his connection with Prussia prevented this, however. While Grenville was ready to let the Prussians depart in peace and repair the damage by forming a strong union with Austria, the prime minister hesitated to take that decisive step. He postponed any decision on Thugut's latest offer, although he authorized the Duke of York to resume monthly cash advances to the Imperial army.[22] For months the prime minister's policy drifted. Unwilling to accept the fact that Prussia was now irretrievably lost to the coalition, he hesitated to effect the rapprochement with Austria which Grenville regarded as essential.

By the close of 1794 it was clear that Britain must come to some understanding with Austria if she meant to continue the war. Nothing short of a miracle could prevent the enemy from completing the conquest of Holland, and even George III recommended that his army be brought home. The campaign to save the Low Countries was over; henceforth, the war would be fought in Germany. Since nothing could be expected from Prussia, Britain must strengthen her union with Austria.[23] This had been Grenville's policy ever since the collapse of Britain's partnership with Prussia, and in December 1794 he proposed to the Cabinet a fundamental shift in military strategy involving close Anglo-Austrian cooperation. In line with the King's recommendation, British national troops would be recalled from Holland while the mercenaries would be sent to serve with the Imperial army. Austria must expand her force to 200,000 men and launch a major offensive against France's eastern frontier. Meanwhile, Britain

21. Spencer and T. Grenville to Lord Grenville, September 22, 1794, FO 7/38.
22. By May 1795 the Duke of York had advanced a total of £550,000 to the Austrians, which they finally repaid out of their loan; Grenville to Starhemberg, October 3, 1794, FO 7/37; Clerfait to Starhemberg, October 30, 1794, FO 7/37; Grenville to Eden, August 25, 1795, FO 7/42.
23. George III to Grenville, December 7, 1794, *Manuscripts of J. B. Fortescue*, II, 650.

would invade the Republic along her Atlantic coast, thus forcing her to fight a war on two fronts. To finance the Austrian campaign, Grenville recommended that Britain sponsor her loan for £6,000,000. Pitt acquiesced in this scheme, and on December 18 it was sent to Sir Morton Eden, recently appointed as British minister at Vienna.[24] Shortly afterwards, Grenville learned that Thugut had also realized the vital necessity of closer agreement between London and Vienna; he was now ready to offer 160,000 Imperial troops for service along the Rhine in return for a British guarantee of a £4,000,000 loan.[25] The difference between the British and Austrian plans was so slight that Grenville instructed Eden to conclude a treaty on the basis of either plan.[26]

Agreement between Britain and Austria could not come too soon. France's military victories of 1794 had gained greater stability and security for the Republic than it had known since its birth; her armies now numbered more than three quarters of a million men who had planted the tricolor far beyond their country's natural frontiers. In January 1795, during the worst winter within memory, Jourdan and Pichegru swarmed over Holland, forcing the Duke of York's army to withdraw into Germany. At the same time, London had positive information that Prussia had begun peace negotiations with France.

Since time was of the essence, Pitt agreed to ask Parliament at once to guarantee the Austrian loan without waiting to learn whether it would finally be for £4,000,000 or £6,000,000. On February 5 the prime minister explained to the Commons the stage which the Austrian negotiation had reached and requested support for the government's policy. While there was no question of the Emperor's good faith or sincerity, he admitted that some day Britain might have to pay the annual charges on the loan. This must not be a deterrent. The risk had to be taken unless the war with France was to be abandoned.[27]

Fox at once took issue with the prime minister and urged members to recall the history of the Prussian subsidy. Less than a year before, when the issue was before them, he had warned that

24. Grenville to Eden, December 18, 1794, FO 7/39.
25. Eden to Grenville, December 18, 1794, FO 7/39. Thugut actually offered 200,000 men but 40,000 of these would be for service in Italy.
26. Grenville to Eden, January 13, 1795, FO 7/40.
27. *Parliamentary History*, XXXI, 1294-1300.

other nations would surely follow Prussia's example. Then the prime minister had said as much about the good faith of the King of Prussia as he had just said about the Emperor. Lending money to the Emperor would only enable him to plunder Poland. If help must be given, let it be in some other shape. Subsidies were infinitely preferable to a loan guarantee because they "were paid by monthly instalments, and if the services stipulated for were not performed, we could stop farther payments, as in the case of the king of Prussia. But could we do so here? By no means; for if the Emperor should fail at any time to fulfill his engagement, we should still be obliged to pay the whole amount of the loan." The first lord of the Treasury counted upon France's resources to fail, "but it was the great business of that House to take care that the resources of England should not fail in contending with France."[28] When the House at last divided on the question, 173 members supported the government while only 57 joined with Fox.

The way was now open for the completion of Grenville's plan for a firm union with Vienna. More than ever he believed that such a war league could be expanded to include Russia, a development which would easily cancel out Prussia's loss to the coalition. Pitt had so far followed Grenville's lead in working for a new orientation for the coalition, but his support had never been enthusiastic. In February 1795 the prime minister convinced himself, on very slender evidence, that Prussia might yet resume her place in the coalition against France. He fanned this feeble ember with such complete concentration that once again the Austrian negotiation was allowed to dangle. With all his work now imperiled by Pitt's devotion to Prussia, Grenville threatened to resign from the government. A crisis in the Cabinet, as well as in the coalition, greeted the arrival of spring, 1795.

The same night that Pitt and Fox clashed in debate over the Austrian loan guarantee an obscure Prussian diplomat was dying in Basel. Count von der Goltz came to the Swiss city in December to discuss peace terms with a French emissary. The Prussian was already ailing on arrival, and overindulgence in good food and drink sealed his fate.[29] From the start of the negotiation it was

28. *Ibid.*, XXXI, 1300-1307.
29. The performance of an autopsy was needed to quiet Prussian fears that von der Goltz had been poisoned by Austrian agents. See Sydney S. Biro, *The German Policy of Revolutionary France* (Cambridge, Mass., 1957), I, 326-327.

clear that France would make Frederick William pay a high price for peace, and the King was sorely tempted to re-enter the war. Lord Malmesbury was still on the Continent, and this information was passed on to him, along with the report that even Marshal Möllendorf was hot to do battle again. Malmesbury forwarded this report to London, but he doubted whether it was worth much. The Prussian king might be ready to draw the sword again, but the peace policies of his ministers would finally prevail.[30]

That Baron Hardenberg was selected to replace von der Goltz at Basel perhaps was significant; during the past year he had been one of the few Prussian ministers to favor the alliance with Britain. En route to Basel, Hardenberg informed Malmesbury that he would delay the peace negotiation in order to allow Britain to make a new approach to Berlin. Renewal of the subsidy was recommended as an important step in bringing Prussia back into the coalition. Malmesbury's response to this overture was encouraging, but privately he doubted whether anything would come of it.[31] Evidence of a stiffening Prussian policy also reached London from another source. As early as January 1795, the newly appointed British minister at Berlin, Lord Henry Spencer, reported that Frederick William was ready to end the peace talks with France. Even Haugwitz was anxious "to prove his Prussian Majesty's readiness to forget all past misunderstandings, & to support the common cause."[32] If London wished to take advantage of this turn in the tide, Spencer urged that instructions be sent him without delay.

Pitt was overjoyed when he learned that Prussia might rejoin the coalition against France. The intervention of 60,000 fresh troops could prove to be the miracle needed to save Holland. To accomplish this he proposed to resurrect the 1794 subsidy treaty: £1,600,000 a year in return for a Prussian army to operate in Holland. This would be supplemented by a series of bonuses to spur Frederick William on to greater exertions. An additional £400,000 would be paid as soon as the Prussians crossed the river

---

30. Malmesbury to Grenville, February 3, 1795, and Malmesbury to General Harcourt, February 8, 1795, *Malmesbury,* III, 232-235.

31. Malmesbury to Harcourt, March 16, 1794, *ibid.,* III, 244-245.

32. Lord Henry Spencer to Grenville, January 20, and February 10, 1795, FO 64/37. Lord Henry Spencer (1770-1795) was a son of the Duke of Marlborough. Named British minister to Holland at twenty, he later served at Stockholm and finally at Berlin. His death in July 1795 prematurely ended a successful career in the diplomatic service.

Yssel, with £400,000 more due when the French were driven south of the Waal. Finally, a grateful Britain would turn over £1,200,000 upon the restoration of the Stadtholder's authority in Holland. Assuming that all this could be accomplished during 1795, and Pitt clearly believed it could, Frederick William would earn subsidies of more than £3,500,000.[33]

A comparison of Pitt's latest Prussian bid with the several offers made to Austria during the past year reveals his striking partiality for Prussia. Vienna had never been offered a subsidy, except on terms which were self-defeating. The most generous proposal ever sent the Hofburg, the one currently being considered, amounted only to a British guarantee for a £6,000,000 loan. Even this was conditional to Austria's maintaining an army more than three times larger than that for which Pitt intended to lavish gifts of money on Berlin. There was considerable justice in Thugut's complaints of Pitt's favoritism for Prussia.

This partiality for Prussia, so characteristic of Pitt, can be explained in several ways. As the lost sheep is always dearest to the shepherd, so the prime minister was ready to pay almost anything to halt Frederick William's drift toward peace. A vital strategic issue was involved as well. Unless Prussia returned to the coalition, Holland's doom was sealed. Only Prussia could be counted on to support Britain's plan to drive the enemy from the Low Countries. Proximity and dynastic connection with the House of Orange gave her an interest in the fate of the Dutch which Austria could never have. A coalition geared to Austria virtually committed Britain to fighting the war against France in Germany and northern Italy, areas which were of secondary interest to Pitt. In the latest news from Berlin, the prime minister found reason to hope that Prussia might yet be saved for the cause, Holland (now at the last gasp) preserved, and the old diplomatic union of Prussia and the Maritime Powers restored. A British entente with Austria, perhaps necessary as a last resort, would accomplish none of these goals.

Grenville regarded the proposed overture to Prussia as a dangerous threat to his own plan to reorient the coalition. In an

---

33. Pitt probably devised this plan during the last half of February. Its terms are clear from a reading of Grenville's analysis of it in a paper entitled Minute of Lord Grenville on the Project of a New Convention between Great Britain and Prussia, n.d., *Manuscripts of J. B. Fortescue*, III, 26-30.

impressive paper, prepared late in February or early March, he marshalled every possible argument to demonstrate that Pitt was being lured by a Prussian will-o'-the-wisp. Surely, the prime minister had not forgotten Frederick William's treacherous desertion less than six months before? He would use any offer Pitt might make him to win better terms of peace from France. Parliament had so far steadily supported the government's war program, but if Prussia once again accepted Britain's bounty only to turn about and repeat her desertion of the previous year, "the discredit it would throw upon Government must be such as to weaken if not destroy any hope of obtaining the support of Parliament for another campaign, supposing it should be found necessary to continue the war."

The gravest objection to the prime minister's plan was that it would end all chance of union with Austria and Russia. Agreement with Vienna was assured while recent dispatches from St. Petersburg encouraged the hope that Catherine would soon join forces with Austria and Britain.[34] Pitt must choose between union with Prussia and the two Imperial governments. Granted that he did not regard the Prussian plan as a substitute for alliance with the eastern powers, Grenville insisted that the schemes were mutually exclusive. "The danger that by negotiating at all with Prussia under the present circumstances," Grenville warned, "we alienate the Austrian and Russian Governments, with whom it should be our policy to endeavour to form the closest union; which can never happen while they are persuaded that we are ready at any moment to resume our former connections and intimacy with Berlin." Unless Pitt abandoned his plan, Grenville would resign.[35]

In the face of the foreign secretary's ultimatum, Pitt hesitated to make a decision. To make matters worse, the King joined with Grenville in disapproving the Prussian proposal and felt sure that Parliament would refuse to support it.[36] The prime minister was now at dead center. Unwilling to abandon the scheme, but opposed both by the King and Grenville, he could not make up his

34. In February Whitworth concluded a new alliance with Russia to take the place of the vague 1793 treaty.
35. Minute of Lord Grenville on the Project of a New Convention, and Pitt to Grenville, March 2, 1795, *Manuscripts of J. B. Fortescue,* III, 26-30.
36. George III to Pitt, March 3, 1795, *Later Correspondence,* II, 309-310

mind. A series of small incidents finally broke the deadlock early in April. Lord Henry Spencer's urgent appeals for positive instructions increased rapidly. Meanwhile, London learned that Thugut, with the worst possible timing, had begun to haggle over the financial terms of the Austrian loan. Finally, Malmesbury returned to England now completely convinced that Prussia was indeed ready to go to war. George III reluctantly agreed to withdraw his opposition to the Prussian plan, whereupon Pitt felt free to bring the matter before the Cabinet. On April 8 the proposal was approved and Grenville immediately announced that he would resign from the ministry.[37] To avoid embarrassment to the prime minister, he agreed to postpone a public announcement until the Parliamentary session ended. Meanwhile, the handling of the Foreign Office correspondence with Prussia was assigned to Dundas.[38]

Two days after the Cabinet gave the Prussian plan its approval, instructions were on their way to Lord Henry Spencer. Details of the proposal were also explained to Harry Calvert, aide-de-camp to the Duke of York, who was ordered to Berlin to support Spencer.[39] It was already too late. On April 5 Prussia and France signed a treaty of peace at Basel. Reporting this to London, Spencer ruefully observed, "Had I received them [details of the British offer] a few days sooner, I may venture to assert that England would have had at her disposal the best appointed Army in Europe."[40]

When Grenville learned of the Peace of Basel, he withdrew his resignation and threw himself into the work of bringing the Austrian negotiation to a quick conclusion. Naturally, he was vexed at Thugut's last-minute attempts to bargain for lower interest rates on the Austrian loan. The time had come to pull the Hofburg up short, and Eden was ordered to be stiff with the Austrian foreign minister: "You will apprize him, without

37. George III to Pitt, March 29, 1795, and Cabinet Minute, April 8, 1795, *Later Correspondence,* II, 323-324, 330-331.

38. Ephraim D. Adams, *The Influence of Grenville on Pitt's Foreign Policy, 1787-1798* (Washington, 1904), pp. 29-36.

39. The British offer was essentially the one Pitt first proposed. See Dundas to Spencer, April 10, 1795, FO 97/324; Dundas to Calvert, April 10, 1795, papers of the War Office, deposited in the Public Record Office, London (hereafter cited as "WO"), 1/408.

40. Spencer to Grenville, April 21, 1795, FO 64/37.

reservation that, unless, on the Receipt of this Messenger, You are enabled to return the Treaty signed, concluded, *and ratified* ... the whole Business [must] be considered as having fallen to the Ground." In a private letter to Eden, the foreign secretary was even more forceful: "For God's sake, enforce these Points, with all the Earnestness which I am sure you will feel, upon them. The People with whom You have to deal require a little spurring."[41]

Matters now moved swiftly, and a month later, London learned that Sir Morton Eden had concluded the business. On May 4 he signed a treaty with Thugut binding Britain to guarantee an Austrian loan of £4,600,000 on condition that the Emperor maintain 170,000 troops in Germany.[42] The loan was to be raised in London on the terms originally proposed and it would be secured by all the hereditary revenues of the Emperor. Austria also agreed to repay the advances made by the Duke of York during the past winter, although it was uncertain what the exact amount was. The £600,000 added to the loan of £4,000,000 was surely enough to provide for reimbursement. Britain was also to have the right, on which Grenville had all along insisted, to appoint inspectors to determine whether the Imperial Army in Germany actually reached the figure specified in the treaty.[43]

The signing of the Loan Convention cleared the way for the negotiation of a new mutual defense pact between Britain and Austria. In April Grenville had sent Eden a project of such a pact, which he hoped would ultimately be enlarged to include Russia. Austria and Britain mutually guaranteed their possessions against attack by a third party during the present war and thereafter. In the event of attack, the aggrieved power could expect her ally to provide her with a supporting army of 26,000 troops, or its equivalent in money. At first Thugut was inclined to boggle at the terms proposed, but on May 20 he accepted the British plan and signed a new alliance with Eden. Following the ceremony, the

41. Grenville to Eden, April 8, 14, 1795, FO 7/40; and Grenville to Eden, April 17, 1795, FO 7/41.

42. Austria actually was to furnish 200,000 men, of whom 30,000 were to be employed in the Italian campaign.

43. Eden to Grenville, May 4, 1795, FO 7/41; Loan Convention with Austria, May 4, 1795, FO 93/11 (1B). Strictly speaking, the treaty obliged Britain to guarantee the original loan of £3,000,000 and a new one for £1,600,000. The terms of both loans were the same. It seems less confusing to express them as a single loan. See Helleiner, *Imperial Loans*, pp. 48-50.

British minister handed Thugut £400,000 in bills of exchange as an advance on the Austrian loan. Boyd, Benfield and Company would repay this amount to the Treasury from the yield of the loan.[44]

Only a few details concerning the loan remained to be settled. On June 15 the House of Commons enacted the legislation providing for the loan guarantee. Should Austria default on her payments, Britain was now legally obliged to meet those payments, which amounted to £345,000 a year. As Walter Boyd had all along predicted, the success of the loan was now assured. The Hofburg kept its word and returned to the Treasury the £550,000 which the Duke of York had advanced to the Imperial Army during 1794–1795. In 1797 Vienna reneged on its obligation and never again resumed payments on the loan. Thus, as Fox prophesied, the entire charge fell on the Treasury, which carried the burden until 1823 when a final settlement of the matter was made with Vienna.[45]

The high hopes of a two-front assault on France which the loan was intended to finance proved a disappointment. Late in the summer of 1795 the French crossed the Rhine and drove the Imperial armies back in disorder. The seaborne invasion of France, undertaken by British and émigré troops in June, ended in disaster and despair at Quiberon. Grenville refused to allow these setbacks to deflect him from his course, however. His attention was now riveted on St. Petersburg, where his envoy worked tirelessly to bring Catherine into a military partnership with Britain and Austria.

Grenville's hope of bringing Russia into the coalition was as unrealistic as Pitt's feverish pursuit of Prussia. Catherine could win neither profit nor honor by sending troops to fight the French in western Europe, as Britain wished. She therefore created diplomatic obstacles in the path of her British suitors, being careful not

44. Grenville to Eden, April 24, 1795, FO 7/41; Treaty with Austria, May 20, 1795, FO 93/11(2); Memorandum of Walter Boyd, April 10, 1795, FO 7/40.

45. *Parliamentary History*, XXXII, 45-46; There was also an extra yearly charge of £4,312 for the management of the loan; see William Newmarch, "On the Loans Raised by Mr. Pitt during the First French War, 1793-1801 . . . ," *Quarterly Journal of the Statistical Society*, 18 (1855), 246. The King's Warrant Book (Ty. 52/82, 396) shows that Boyd, Benfield and Co. repaid the £550,000 on October 23, 1795.

to discourage them to the point of abandoning the chase. The first of these was the demand she made in 1793 for British subsidies. Within a year she constructed another: Britain must undertake to defend her against a Turkish attack and guarantee her possessions in Poland. These terms were hard, but Grenville was ready to accept them if Russia joined the coalition. The outbreak of the Polish rebellion in the spring of 1794 enabled Catherine to withdraw her offer; she could not go to war with France until Poland had been reduced to order.[46]

Failure to budge the Tsarina was not the fault of Charles Whitworth, who zealously urged his country's cause at the Court of St. Petersburg. In 1793 George III decided to reward his envoy's loyalty by granting him the Order of the Bath and he invited the Tsarina to perform the investiture. At the end of the ceremony, Catherine suggested to Sir Charles that his sovereign reciprocate the courtesy by allowing her to obtain an astronomical telescope from William Herschel. For years she had wanted such an instrument, but British law prohibited the export of scientific apparatus without special permission. She had made this request of Whitworth's predecessor, but nothing had come of it.[47] The newly made knight quickly took the hint. Earlier, he had sent home a request from a member of Catherine's family for a collection of seeds and plants "which have lately been discovered in the South Seas." Now he urged Grenville to give the Tsarina's personal request the attention it obviously deserved.

At once, the Foreign Office directed the great astonomer to produce a ten-foot telescope for Catherine as a gift from George III.[48] Meanwhile, the nation's foremost botanist, Sir Joseph Banks, was making a selection of tropical plants from the conservatory at Kew. In the spring of 1795 the telescope and plants were shipped aboard H.M.S. *Venus,* along with a company of gardeners. The precious cargo reached St. Petersburg that summer and the plants were set out in a conservatory especially built to protect them

46. Grenville to Whitworth, January 17, 1794, FO 65/26; Whitworth to Grenville, February 7, 1794, FO 65/26.
47. D. B. Horn, *The British Diplomatic Service, 1689-1789* (Oxford, 1961), p. 192.
48. Herschel's bill for the telescope and its packing came to £214.

against the frosts of the northern capital.[49] George III's act of generosity was symbolic, for at this same time his ministers were undertaking another campaign to win Catherine as an ally.

All the signs surrounding the arrival of the year 1795 seemed to favor Grenville's plan for a military partnership with Austria and Russia. His negotiation with Austria was moving toward a successful conclusion, and in January he learned that Russia and Austria had signed a treaty of alliance (January 3, 1795). Perhaps it was as well that the foreign secretary did not know that the basis of this entente was joint action against Turkey, rather than against France. Early in February he instructed Whitworth to renew efforts to obtain an alliance with Russia. The Tsarina's troops were badly needed to support the campaign against France in the West and Britain could now use the warships she had offered for service in 1793.[50] Meanwhile, at St. Petersburg, Catherine had decided to open very slightly the door she had so far kept shut against earlier British appeals. In February her ministers offered Whitworth a specific alliance to take the place of the loose convention Britain and Russia had concluded in 1793.

By the terms of the treaty Whitworth signed on February 18, Britain and Russia assumed joint defense obligations against an attack by a third nation for a period of eight years. In the event of attack, Britain could count on 12,000 Russian troops, while the Tsarina was entitled to claim twelve British warships to defend her. No part of the treaty applied to the current war against France except a separate article which bound Russia to send twelve ships of the line and six frigates to act with the British Navy in the Atlantic.[51]

---

49. Details of this pleasant episode will be found in numerous letters contained in FO 65/29, 30, 31, and FO 97/342. Unfortunately, Catherine's gratitude was slender. In 1794, she presented Britain with a bill for £9565. Her brother, the ruler of Anhalt-Zerbst had recently died and, as his heir, Catherine claimed that Britain still owed him this amount for the service of mercenaries rented from Anhalt-Zerbst during the American Revolution. The claim does not appear to have been honored. See Vorontzoff to Grenville, September 22, 1794, FO 65/28.

50. Grenville to Whitworth, February 6, 1795, FO 65/29.

51. Either party could claim an annual subsidy of 500,000 rubles in place of the military aid specified. The protocol form of the treaty, together with the separate articles, will be found in FO 65/30.

The alliance fell far short of Britain's desires, but as Whitworth pointed out, Catherine's involvement in the naval war with France might "lead Her further than She perhaps is at first aware of, so that we may find Her a powerful and persevering Ally."[52] Grenville learned of the treaty at the same time his negotiation of the Austrian loan convention was reaching a climax. He therefore welcomed the Russian pact as an important step toward the creation of a new Triple Alliance.[53] Whitworth must persuade Catherine to send troops to the West during the coming summer and, to help with the expense, Grenville authorized him to offer the Tsarina a subsidy: £500,000 a year, plus all expenses, for the cooperation of 55,000 Russians. If this was not enough, Whitworth could double the offer.[54] Even though Catherine had the promise of a subsidy, she refused to consider Grenville's plea for armed intervention. For the moment, she would do nothing more than meet the naval commitment she had undertaken in the February alliance. The Russian flotilla was to sail from Kronstadt in June under orders to join Admiral Duncan's fleet in the North Sea. Whitworth warned London not to expect too much of the squadron, which he described as "complete in every point, as it can be considering the state of the Navy of this Country, which is, at best, but in its infancy." The performance of the Russian ships more than justified this caveat.[55]

The Anglo-Russian alliance, on the basis of which Grenville built such extravagant hopes, was more a reflection of changes in the diplomatic balance of eastern Europe than any wish on Catherine's part to aid the coalition. The Tsarina's Polish policy had always been geared to close cooperation with Prussia. With Poland soon to be partitioned for the last time, it was to Russia's advantage to free herself from Prussia and seek an entente with Austria, looking to a partition of the Ottoman empire. This shift in the Tsarina's policy was at the heart of her alliance with Austria of January

52. Whitworth to Grenville, February 19, 1795, FO 65/29.
53. Simon Vorontzoff to Alexander Vorontzoff, March 24, 1795, *Vorontsova*, IX, 335.
54. Grenville to Whitworth, no. 4, March 9, 1795, FO 65/29.
55. Whitworth to Grenville, June 14, 1795, FO 65/30. For the performance of the Russian squadron, see the account contained in Edward P. Brenton, *The Naval History of Great Britain* . . . (London, 1837), I, 271. A recent study of the question is Eunice H. Turner, "The Russian Squadron with Admiral Duncan's North Sea Fleet, 1795-1800," *Mariner's Mirror*, 49 (1963), 212-222.

1795. In that agreement the two powers decided that Prussia was to have a much smaller share in the final Polish partition than she was expecting. Such a maneuver exposed Catherine to the threat of Prussian retaliation; her rapprochement with Britain throughout 1795 may have sprung from her search for security. Certainly, this was the motive behind the curious proposal she sent to London in June 1795. Would Britain provide Russia with subsidies in the event she became involved in a war with Prussia? After all, since the Peace of Basel, Prussia might as well be regarded as a French ally. This logic left Grenville cold, and in his reply he reasserted what had all along been his position: subsidies would be given Russia whenever she took arms against France, but not otherwise. As a major step in that direction, the foreign secretary proposed that Britain, Russia, and Austria merge their separate alliances of 1795 in a single system.[56] Grenville's suggestion was received in silence by Catherine's ministers and remained unanswered for the rest of the summer.

Early in August Prussia learned of the terms on which Russia and Austria had agreed to partition Poland. Frederick William blustered, but finally accepted the decision when a few face-saving modifications were made for his benefit. Significantly, it was during this critical period that Catherine finally acted on Grenville's proposal that the alliances negotiated by Britain, Russia, and Austria during 1795 be codified into a single Triple Alliance. On September 28, Russia issued a formal declaration to this effect, a declaration which Whitworth followed up with a request that Catherine send her troops to the support of her allies.[57] The Tsarina's only reply to this entreaty was that "as soon as the dispute with the Court of Berlin should be adjusted . . . it was Her intention to take such steps as should upon mature deliberation be judged most conducive to the great object in view."[58] Whitworth had heard this sort of language for the past two years and he doubtless recognized how empty and meaningless it was.

The new Triple Alliance was a hollow victory for Grenville's diplomacy, for it was merely the form and not the substance of

---

56. Grenville to Whitworth, June 23, 1795, FO 65/30; Starhemberg to Thugut, June 12, 1795 and July 10, 1795, Vivenot, *Quellen*, V, 237-239, 287-288.
57. F. Martens, *Recueil des Traités*, IX, 385-387.
58. Whitworth to Grenville, September 29, 1795, FO 65/31.

what he had sought for nearly a year. Only Austria had supported the idea of a three-power alliance as the nucleus of a rejuvenated coalition against France. Despite Catherine's treaties with Britain and Austria, she was nearly as free from involvement in the war as ever. On the other hand, she now had promises of military support from her two allies in the event of an attack on her possessions by Prussia or Turkey. Viewed from St. Petersburg, the war with Revolutionary France was a thing apart, and not even the offer of British subsidies could tempt the Tsarina to share the burden of that remote contest.[59]

By 1795 Britain was playing a major part in the management of the coalition she had joined two years before almost as a junior partner. Concern for the safety of Holland led Pitt, in 1795, to undertake a singlehanded effort to bring Prussia back into the war and save the Low Countries from the French. Only after Prussia made peace with the enemy, did the prime minister support Grenville's plan for a firm union with Austria and Russia.

If Britain wished to lead the coalition, she would have to buy that right either by greater participation in the continental campaigns or by providing her allies with the means to make war. The supply of German mercenaries was by now nearly exhausted, and she could play a major part in the European war only by reducing her overseas operations or by mobilizing a larger part of her own manpower. Neither of these steps was consistent with her interests. Therefore, Britain had no choice but to make her wealth available to those of her continental allies who were able to maintain large armies in the field.

If Pitt was prepared to spend British money, he wanted to use it where it would do the most good. So much importance was attached to bringing Prussia back into the war that the prime minister offered £3,500,000 in subsidies to Frederick William. Vienna's growing interest in eastern Europe and Italy was at cross-purposes with Britain's concern over the fate of the Low Countries. When an Anglo-Austrian agreement at last became essential, Pitt helped the Hofburg by means of a loan rather than a

59. In October 1795 Grenville was ready to give Catherine subsidies in the event of a Prussian attack on Russia. By now Frederick William had accepted the terms of the final Polish Partition, and the eastern diplomatic crisis was over. Consequently, Catherine was not interested in this latest British offer. See Grenville to Whitworth, October, 1795, FO 65/32.

subsidy. For the time being, this cost Britain nothing. The importance of coming to terms with Russia finally led him to offer Catherine the subsidies she had all along declared to be indispensable, but British and Russian goals were still too far apart for the offer to make any difference.

By the close of 1795, the First Coalition had indeed been reoriented, but not in such a way as either Pitt or Grenville preferred. Its focus now, and for the remainder of its existence, was in the union of Britain and Austria. Unless Prussia or Russia took up arms, Britain could remain at war with France in Europe only so long as Austria was willing to keep her armies in the field. Henceforth, Vienna would be able to demand additional British funds as the price of keeping the coalition alive.

IV

THE COLLAPSE OF THE FIRST COALITION

The First Coalition had suffered so many grievous wounds during 1795 that it was hard to see how it could survive much longer. Prussia had made peace with France in the spring, and a few months later Spain followed her example. Downing Street feared that France would soon absorb the Spanish fleet into her own navy, as she had that of the defeated Dutch.[1] For the time being, however, Spain chose to remain at peace, and more than a year passed before she became France's ally and England's enemy.

Grenville's attempts to offset the loss of Prussia by rebuilding the coalition on the basis of a firm union among Britain, Austria, and Russia had ended in complete failure. The coalition's misfortunes in diplomacy were matched by its military reverses. Britain's invasion of Brittany in June availed nothing and its failure dangerously crippled the counterrevolutionary movement in the Vendée. Later that year, the Imperial forces regained the initiative in Germany and drove the enemy back across the Rhine, a gain which the Hapsburg commander tossed away by offering an armistice to his defeated opponent. In the mountains of Savoy, Austrian and Sardinian troops fought bravely, but in vain, to deny the French possession of those strategic passes which controlled the north Italian plan.[2]

1. Grenville greatly feared such an increase in French naval power. On September 19, 1795 he informed Whitworth that, in the event of a Spanish attack on Britain, the Cabinet wished Catherine to fulfill her treaty obligations to Britain by sending her warships rather than troops, (FO 65/31).

2. Grenville had long been annoyed by Sardinia's refusal to keep her army up to the 50,000 figure specified in their 1793 treaty. In the autumn of 1795, he withheld the quarterly subsidy in an effort to prod her into enlarging her forces. However, the close of the year found no more than 15,000 Sardinians under arms; Eden to Lord Auckland, December 7, 1795, *Auckland*, III, 324.

The rebirth of France's national vigor during this same period contrasted dramatically with the ineffectiveness of the coalition. At the beginning of the war, Pitt was sure that the chaos generated by the Revolution would finally destroy the Republic and its military ambitions. By 1795 all chance of such a development had vanished. The overthrow of Robespierre in the previous year was followed by a determined search for national stability which culminated in the creation of the Directory in November 1795. Not only was the Republic now safe, but its military power had grown more dangerous than ever to its foes abroad. Three years of war had forged the armies of the Republic into a case-hardened weapon capable of dealing the coalition a fatal blow. Bonaparte's invasion of Italy in the spring of 1796 marked the beginning of a new phase in the war; the Republic was now on the offensive.

Britain's army in Europe had grown rapidly since 1793, when it numbered only about 17,000 men. By 1795 her home establishment included nearly 120,000 troops together with 35,820 mercenaries. Elsewhere in the world more than 50,000 other British soldiers fought to take the colonies of France and her new ally, Holland. The collapse of the Netherlands campaign in March 1795 led the Cabinet to call home what remained of the Duke of York's army and to direct the mercenary forces to join with the Austrians in the defense of Germany. One month later, British plans for the employment of her mercenaries were wrecked by the Peace of Basel, which provided for the creation of a German neutral zone with the Main river as its southern boundary. Prussia was obliged to guarantee the neutrality of this area. Since Hanover lay within the zone, Britain had either to demobilize her Hanoverian units or risk a Prussian invasion of the Electorate. Reluctantly, George III decided to send the Hanoverians home, although some were kept there under arms to defend the state. With the departure of the Hanoverians, Britain lost the services of nearly half the mercenary corps which had fought her battles since 1793.[3]

In 1795 France forced the landgrave of Hesse-Cassel to make peace, and as a part of the treaty he agreed to recall the 12,000

3. The final British payment for the Hanoverians was made on July 10, 1795, when £79,866 was remitted for their pay; King's Warrant Book, Ty. 52/82, 213. Additional payments were made in 1796 and 1803, but these were to cover invalids' pensions and claims arising out of the 1793-1795 period of service; *ibid.,* Ty. 52/83, 50; Ty. 52/88, 24, 91.

troops he had rented to Britain.[4] By the time the campaign opened in the spring of 1796, less than 5,000 men out of the original mercenary corps were in British pay. These were troops from Brunswick and Hesse-Darmstadt, of which only the latter remained in Britain's service a year later.[5] This withering away of Britain's military strength on the Continent left nearly the entire burden of the war to Austria—a condition which Vienna would use to justify her claim for more extensive financial aid.

Six months after the signing of the Austrian Loan Convention in 1795, Thugut informed Sir Morton Eden that the Hofburg must have a second loan of £3,000,000 to finance the war effort during the coming year. Considering how much the coalition now depended on the Imperial forces, Downing Street could not ignore this request. The war had put a great strain on Britain's economy, however, and a £3,000,000 loan to Austria at this time was more than it could bear. Three years of heavy remittances abroad for war expenses had eaten into British trade credits in Europe, a condition which resulted in a serious deficit in her balance of payments. As a sign of what was to come, the Bank of England's specie reserve dropped sharply during the last half of 1795. By the end of the year, conditions had become critical and Grenville recommended that Austria raise her new loan on the Continent rather than in London.[6]

Given all these circumstances, it is not surprising that Pitt began to consider the possibility of a peace negotiation with France. A hint of this had appeared in the King's Speech at the opening of Parliament in October 1795, and a month later the government sent a special agent to Vienna for a discussion of the matter with

4. Grenville to Colonel Charles Craufurd, September 18, 1795, FO 29/6; Biro, *German Policy,* I, 381-385. The last payment to Hesse-Cassel was in August 1795, when £68,850 was sent to settle the landgrave's claim for the service of his troops during the American Revolution; see King's Warrant Book, Ty. 52/82, 272.

5. The final payment to Baden was in June 1795; King's Warrant Book, Ty. 52/82, 175. Payments to Brunswick were continued until December 1796; *ibid.,* Ty. 52/83, 324. An additional payment of £15,565 was made in 1797 to settle claims; *ibid.,* Ty. 52/83, 103.

Fortescue's table (*British Army,* IV, 938) shows 12,000 "Foreign Troops" in British service in 1797. These consisted largely of émigré troops who had thrown in their lot with Britain. In 1797, Britain sent some regiments of French émigrés (about 4,000 men) to help with the defense of Portugal.

6. Eden to Grenville, October 10, 1795, FO 7/43; and Grenville to Eden, nos. 72 & 73, December 22, 1795, FO 7/43.

Thugut.[7] Meanwhile, Grenville considered what measures ought to be taken if peace proved unattainable. The only direction in which he could turn was toward Prussia, and in November he asked the new British minister, Lord Elgin, for a report on conditions at Berlin. Elgin's reply, which reached London in January 1796, was most discouraging. Prussian policy had undergone no change since the Peace of Basel and she would certainly not go to war again unless she was sure it would be profitable. "If it is wished to secure to the coalition the assistance of Prussia," Elgin wrote, "it will be found requisite to afford some pecuniary aid, or hold out some positive indemnification, without which any favourable dispositions which exist here can certainly not obtain a decided superiority."[8] Elgin's language was complex, but his meaning was unmistakable: Prussia could be bought only at a very high price.

In February 1796 the Cabinet met to decide whether to initiate peace talks with France. During the course of the discussion, Grenville offered a rough plan for reviving the coalition should the negotiation prove abortive. To bring Prussia back into the war, he suggested that she be given Belgium and the Westphalian provinces. As compensation for the loss of Belgium, Austria would be allowed to annex Bavaria.[9] The plan included no specific subsidy offer, but Prussia might rely upon reimbursement for her actual expenses by the British or Dutch governments at the end of the war.[10] This was surely a desperate measure for the foreign secretary to propose and there is some question how serious he was about it. The Cabinet agreed to consider the question again if peace could not be concluded. For the moment, highest priority would go to opening a discussion with the Directory.

It soon became clear that France would not agree to any peace terms that Britain could afford to accept, and Grenville should now have brought forward his Prussian plan once more. He did not

7. Unfortunately, Thugut took an instant dislike to the British envoy; Eden to Auckland, November 8, 1795, *Auckland*, III, 320-323.

8. Elgin to Grenville, December 26, 1795, *Manuscripts of J. B. Fortescue*, III, 163.

9. When Thugut first learned of the plan, he raised an interesting point. Austria had always been ready to give Belgium to the Elector of Bavaria in *exchange* for Bavaria. Grenville's plan made no provision for him. Thugut asked Eden whether Britain intended to dispose of the Elector by strangling him, or sending him to Botany Bay; Eden to Auckland, December 9, 1796, *Auckland*, III, 368.

10. Grenville to Elgin, February 9, 1796, FO 64/39; George III to Grenville, February 9, 1796, *Manuscripts of J. B. Fortescue*, III, 173.

do so. Elgin's latest dispatches were most discouraging. Haugwitz had frankly declared that Prussia's only policy was "*to mediate amicably;* and that, *in no event would Prussia make hostile demonstrations at this conjuncture, still less actually take up arms, in the cause of Holland.*"[11] Grenville's scheme had also encountered resistance at home. George III regarded it with the greatest distaste; dividing up innocent states to satisfy Prussia's land hunger struck him as "immoral and unjustifiable."[12] Less concerned with the morality of the matter, Grenville saw its real weakness: it was simply not attractive enough to tempt Prussia.

A more important matter demanded London's immediate attention in the opening months of 1796. The Foreign Office had received one dispatch after another from Vienna demanding that arrangements be made for floating Austria's new £3,000,000 loan.[13] Despite the urgency of these appeals, Pitt hesitated. During the past year, the Bank of England's specie supply had fallen by more than half and the directors begged him not to guarantee a new Hapsburg loan.[14] Rumours were also circulating that the Emperor would soon undertake separate peace negotiations with France.[15] It would be disastrous for the government to sponsor a new Austrian loan only to have her ally turn about and leave the coalition.

The opening of the spring campaign made it impossible for Pitt to delay a decision any longer. By the end of April 1796 the prime minister devised a workable scheme to pay Austria on the installment plan. Small monthly advances would be made to Austria which she was to repay from the proceeds of a loan to be arranged in the future. Britain's specie shortage, he hoped, would end by the close of 1796, at which time the loan could be negotiated.[16] Until then, monthly advances would meet Austria's immediate needs and strain Britain's balance of payments less than

11. Elgin to Grenville, February 23, March 10, 1796, FO 64/39.
12. George III to Grenville, February 9, 1796, *Manuscripts of J. B. Fortescue*, III, 173.
13. Eden to Grenville, January 22, February 19, 1796, and April 27, 1796, FO 7/44 and 45.
14. Starhemberg to Grenville, April 12, 1796, *Manuscripts of J. B. Fortescue*, III, 192; John Clapham, *The Bank of England: A History* (New York, 1945), I, 297; *Parliamentary History*, XXXIII, 322-333.
15. Grenville to Eden, May 24, 1796, *Manuscripts of J. B. Fortescue*, III, 206-207.
16. Grenville to Eden, May 20, 1796, FO 7/45.

a £3,000,000 loan. Since London's financial leaders bitterly opposed any loan to Austria, Pitt decided not to give his decision publicity. He therefore chose not to consult Parliament on the matter, even though it was in session. On April 29 Grenville instructed Colonel Charles Craufurd, on service with the Imperial forces in Germany, to give the Austrian commander £100,000 in Treasury Bills. A month later, Craufurd was ordered to pay an additional £150,000.[17]

Britain's specie supply shrank so rapidly that Pitt abandoned all plans of negotiating an Austrian loan in 1796. The monthly advances were continued at the rate of £150,000 a month, and by the close of the year the Treasury had remitted £950,000 to Vienna's account with Boyd, Benfield and Company. All this was forwarded to Vienna in bills of exchange, except for £172,500 which the bank used to pay the interest on the first loan, which fell due in November.[18]

The war continued to go against the allies, especially in Italy where Bonaparte now led France's armies. Sardinia was defeated and removed from the contest, and soon all Italy south of the Po lay open to the enemy. One by one the Italian ports were closed to the British navy, and in October 1796 Spain's declaration of war forced the fleet to abandon the Mediterranean. Grenville believed that Prussia's intervention was so desperately needed that he was ready to pay any price Berlin might set. In this spirit, he revived his Prussian plan of the previous February. Pitt was lukewarm to this counsel of despair. "I can conceive no objection," he wrote to Grenville on June 23, "in the mind of any of our colleagues to see whether the arrangement to which you have pointed can be made acceptable ... But though I think it should be tried, I do not flatter myself with much chance of success."[19] The foreign secretary was just as pessimistic, but he

---

17. Grenville to Craufurd, April 29, 1796 and May 20, 1796, FO 29/9 and 10. Charles Gregan Craufurd (1761-1821) had a distinguished military career before being attached to the Austrian army in 1795. However, his professional life was ended by an accident which befell him while on service there.

18. Grenville to Eden, June 10, 17, 1796, FO 7/45; Statement of Remittances and Payments by Boyd, Benfield and Co. for the Account of the Imperial Government, 1796, Chatham Papers, vol. 115.

19. Pitt to Grenville, June 23, 1796, *Manuscripts of J. B. Fortescue,* III, 214.

believed that the overture would have to be made. A personal appeal by both ministers was needed to overcome the King's opposition to the plan.[20]

The Berlin mission, undertaken by George Hammond in the summer of 1796, was a lamentable failure. Haugwitz received the British agent very coolly on his arrival early in August, and a month of fruitless parleys convinced Hammond that he would not succeed. Throughout the discussions, Haugwitz carefully concealed the fact that Prussia had just concluded a secret neutrality agreement with the Directory.[21] With the failure of the appeal to Prussia, Pitt once again proposed to negotiate peace with the enemy, and early in September the Cabinet invited Denmark to arrange the necessary preliminaries. Ordinarily the last to yield, even Grenville admitted that there was no other choice.

A few days after this decision was taken, dispatches reached the Foreign Office from Whitworth announcing that Russia was ready to send 60,000 troops to Austria's assistance. London had waited three years for such a change in Catherine's policy. Now it was too late. At least five months would be needed before any army sent by Catherine could reach the western front. Furthermore, the price which the Tsarina attached to even this modest help was enormous; a preparation subsidy of £300,000 was required at once, together with a promise of an additional £120,000 each month. Britain was also expected to pay the "bread and forage" expenses of the army and undertake to make a final payment of £300,000 at the close of the war as "return money." Should the war last for another year, Britain would have to pay the Tsarina more than £3,000,000.[22] The more Grenville considered the Russian offer, the less he was impressed with it. Britain's best hope was in negotiation with the Directory.[23]

Paris was now the center of all attention, even though the inauspicious way the peace talks began foreshadowed their failure.

20. Grenville to George III, July 31, 1796, and George III to Grenville, July 31, 1796, *ibid.,* III, 228-230.

21. George Hammond to Grenville, August 17, 22, and September 6, 1796, FO 64/41.

22. Whitworth to Grenville, August 23, 1796, FO 65/34; Ostermann to S. Vorontzoff, August 10 [o.s.], 1796, FO 65/34. On September 13, Whitworth informed Grenville that 6,000 cossacks were to be included in the Russian force. They were being trained so "as to render them more dangerous to the Enemy, and less to the Country through which they pass" (FO 65/34).

23. F. Martens, *Recueil des Traités,* IX, 412.

By October Grenville was sure that the negotiations would soon collapse and he sent off a counterproposal to St. Petersburg, which he hoped the Tsarina would accept in place of her original offer. Britain would pay the £300,000 preparation subsidy she required, but she could promise no more than £100,000 a month by way of a subsidy. If Whitworth found that it was absolutely necessary to raise this bid, he could offer up to £1,000,000 in "return money" payable at the end of the war.[24] The foreign secretary still hoped that Prussia might be persuaded to come back into the ranks of the coalition. Unaware of the recent Franco-Prussian neutrality agreement, he proposed to revive his plan to offer Belgium and the Westphalian provinces to Frederick William—the plan Hammond had carried to Berlin during the past summer. Before going further, however, Grenville decided to sound out Austria's feelings on the matter.[25]

Catherine's sudden death in November brought the foreign secretary's schemes tumbling down like a house of cards. Her successor, Paul I, was unwilling to embark on any major diplomatic undertaking, and a few weeks after his accession, Whitworth learned that Russia would remain at peace.[26] At Paris, news of Catherine's death encouraged the Directory to end its peace talks with Britain.[27] There was a good deal of justice in Pitt's bitter observation on Catherine's passing: "It is difficult to say whether one ought to regret the most that she had not died sooner or lived longer."[28] As the year waned, British leaders faced the cheerless prospect of continuing the war with only Austria's support.

In this dark mood Pitt presented his budget for the new year to the House of Commons on December 7, 1796. Military and naval appropriations were to be higher than ever before; each of the services would cost more than £10,000,000. He also announced that, since the dissolution of Parliament in the spring, the government had advanced about £1,200,000 to Austria. Nothing

24. Grenville to Whitworth, October 7, 1796, FO 65/34.
25. This caution was justified. On learning of the plan, Thugut declared that Austria would resist the proposed territorial redistribution by force if necessary; Eden to Grenville, November 26, 1796. FO 7/47.
26. Whitworth to Grenville, November 26, 1796, FO 65/35.
27. Malmesbury to Grenville, December 20, 1796, *Malmesbury*, III, 351.
28. Pitt to Dundas, December, 1796, Stanhope, *Pitt*, II, 405.

was said to reveal that the advances had actually begun prior to Parliament's dissolution. He justified the advances on two grounds. First, the Emperor's needs were so pressing that they required extraordinary measures. "I am persuaded," the prime minister declared, "no man will be of opinion that we ought to have withheld from a brave and faithful ally, the assistance necessary to preserve his independence." Second, advances were preferable to a new Austrian loan which might have upset the state of Britain's money market at the time. It was hoped that the House would empower the government to continue these advances and consent to the inclusion of £3,000,000 in the new budget for future aid to the allies.[29]

The next night, Fox unleashed a fierce attack on the King's ministers. If the House was not in session when the government began to advance money to Austria, why had ministers kept silent after the new session began in October? Nearly two months had passed without a single word being spoken on this question. "If parliament had not been sitting," Fox asked, "and ministers had thought it prudent to grant pecuniary assistance to the Emperor, I say it ought to have been assembled for the purpose of deliberating upon it; but when parliament was sitting, in God's name, why was not application made to the House?" To the whig leader the answer was clear and beyond dispute: ministers desired to establish the precedent that public money was at their absolute disposal.[30]

Never before had the whigs a more opportune moment to attack Pitt's war program. The decline of the nation's supply of specie was causing panic in financial circles. It was also becoming nearly impossible to believe that the allies could win the war in Europe. Even now a French armada was believed to be at sea, under orders to invade the British Isles. On December 13 Fox rose in the House to move a vote of censure against the government. Once again he scourged Pitt for the Austrian advances and ended by moving that ministers "have acted contrary to their duty, and to the trust reposed in them, and have violated the constitutional privileges of this House." Immediately, one of the City of London members announced that his constituents had instructed him to support the

29. *Parliamentary History*, XXXII, 1256-1264.
30. *Ibid.*, XXXII, 1273-1277.

motion as an expression of their discontent with the mischief the government's policies had done British trade.[31]

It was now Pitt's turn to speak, and he defended his conduct in one of the finest speeches of his career. Was the real complaint that he had given away the nation's money without the consent of its representatives? This was demonstrably false. The money had not been given away. This was no subsidy, but an advance on a future Austrian loan from which the Treasury would be repaid. There had been good reason for making the advances, rather than undertaking a loan. "I felt," Pitt said, "that in consequence of the extraordinary extent of the drain of money, some time would be necessary before the influx of trade would be such as to render a measure of that kind practicable in its execution or safe in its impression." This had not been his opinion alone. He had conferred with City financiers and bankers ("monied men," as he termed them) and "submitted whether a public loan would be prudent in such circumstances, but they were unanimous in preference of the adopted mode." Ministers were not seeking to establish a dangerous precedent. Military necessity had dictated the step they took. What had been the result? Thanks to the advances, the Imperial armies still held the foe in check in Italy, while in Germany they had recovered the ground lost during the summer. "I appeal to the justice of the House," the prime minister concluded, "I rely on their candour; but to gentlemen who can suppose ministers capable of those motives which have been imputed to them on this occasion, it must be evident that I can desire to make no such appeal."[32] The government's conduct was finally upheld by a vote of 285 to 81, but on this question the opposition mustered considerable more support than was usually the case.

Although the whigs failed in their attack on the government's policy of advancing money to Austria, they were able to return to the charge two months later. The financial crisis which had been threatening for a year finally broke in February 1797. When the government ordered a suspension of cash payments, the antiwar party immediately indicted subsidies in general and the Austrian

31. *Ibid.*, XXXII, 1297-1310.
32. *Ibid.*, XXXII, 1310-1332.

advances in particular as the cause of the specie shortage. At best the charge was a half-truth.

On the outbreak of war in 1793, the Bank of England's bullion reserve was adequate, and during the year, it increased to nearly £7,000,000. From that point, however, a steady decline set in which caused increasing anxiety. The bullion drain slowed down during 1796, but business and government leaders waited in vain for the tide to turn.[33] For this reason, the Cabinet refused to sponsor a new £3,000,000 loan for Austria and chose, instead, to aid her with small monthly advances. Pitt's announcement to Parliament in December 1796 that such advances had been made and would continue, alarmed British bankers already concerned about the shortage of hard money. Even more disturbing was the threat of invasion which resulted in heavy demands on the Bank's specie early in 1797. Fear turned to panic when reports reached the City that the enemy had landed in Wales. The government moved at once, and on February 26 an Order in Council was issued suspending specie payments.

The House of Commons learned of the Order the next day, whereupon Sheridan at once charged that the crisis was due to the heavy export of specie to the allies. He therefore moved that until the matter had been thoroughly investigated the government be prohibited from sending bullion abroad for foreign aid. Defeat of the motion did not discourage the whigs, who continued to blame subsidies, loans, and the Austrian advances for the present troubles. Their clamor reached such a pitch that Pitt finally agreed to the creation of a committee to investigate the Bank's condition.[34]

Probably the amount of bullion in Britain at the time of the crisis was much greater than the Bank's dwindling stock suggested. Before the end of the year, even the Bank's treasure had risen to its normal level. No doubt, the Bank of England had been the victim of abrupt and excessive demands upon it by provincial

33. According to Clapham (*Bank of England*, I, 297), between 1793 and 1797 the specie reserve of the Bank of England was as follows:

1793	Feb.	£ 4,011,000		Aug.	£ 5,136,000
	Aug.	5,322,000	1796	Feb.	2,540,000
1794	Feb.	6,987,000		Aug.	2,123,000
	Aug.	6,770,000	1797	Feb.	1,086,000
1795	Feb.	6,128,000		Aug.	4,090,000

34. *Parliamentary History*, XXXII, 1518-1562.

banks acting in a panic mood.[35] The causes of the panic went deeper than this, however. Since the beginning of the war, Britain's trade with the Continent had suffered a balance of payments problem.[36] To make matters worse, a considerable amount of gold was being smuggled from Britain to France in order to take advantage of the higher prices which prevailed there by 1796. The French monetary system was undergoing a reorganization which, in effect, restored the gold standard and established premium prices for bullion. How important this illegal export of hard money was in bringing on the 1797 crisis is a matter of dispute, however.[37]

Beyond dispute is the fact that, during the four years of war leading to the Bank Crisis of 1797, Britain's involvement in the coalition forced her to make heavy remittances to the Continent, which worsened the balance of payments problem. Even her healthy trade with the Continent was unable to make up for these outlays, of which subsidies was only one. More than £8,000,000 in specie or bills of exchange had to be sent to the Continent between 1793 and 1797 to pay and maintain the British army.[38] The purchase abroad of supplies and equipment for the use of the Royal Navy during the same period involved an additional expense of about £4,700,000.[39] Taken together, the needs of the two services alone obliged the government to remit at least £13,000,000, either in specie or bills, during the period 1793-1797.

The total of all subsidies, the Austrian loan of 1795, and the advances made to the Imperial government in 1796 is just over £10,000,000—that is, about three quarters of the total foreign remittances for Britain's army and navy. The *relative* importance

35. George Rose, *A Brief Examination into the Increase of the Revenue, Commerce, and Navigation of Great Britain during the Administration of the Rt. Hon. William Pitt* (London, 1806), p. 79.

36. Trade figures for these years are available, but their interpretation is subject to considerable disagreement. See Norman J. Silberling, "Financial and Monetary Policy of Great Britain during the Napoleonic Wars," *Quarterly Journal of Economics,* 38 (1923-1924), 229. A more extensive and technical analysis of the question is A. H. Imlah, "Real Values in British Foreign Trade, 1798-1853," *Journal of Economic History,* 8 (1948), 133-152.

37. Ralph G. Hawtrey, *Currency and Credit,* 4th ed. (London, 1950), pp. 274-277.

38. Silberling, "Financial and Monetary Policy," p. 227.

39. Thomas Tooke, *A History of Prices and of the State of Circulation from 1793 to 1837 . . .* (London, 1838-1857), I, 208.

of British aid to foreign powers in exhausting the nation's trade credits in Europe is even less than this figure suggests. During the year preceding the Bank Crisis, Britain spent more than £4,000,000 overseas for the purchase of grain.[40] This was the only occasion prior to 1797 when an inadequate home harvest compelled her to import such a large quantity of food. Although not a war expense, the grain purchase of 1796 clearly contributed to the balance of payments problem.

It was natural for Pitt's opponents to seize on subsidies as the chief cause for the nation's troubles in 1797. The debate on the Austrian advances had occurred only two months before the Bank Crisis. Payments to foreign powers were unpopular in England, and the whigs doubtless saw the political advantage to be gained by raising the issue. Even at the time, some thoughtful observers objected to singling out foreign aid as the chief cause of the Panic. Sir Francis Baring, a member of Parliament and a leading financier, correctly observed: "It must be indifferent to the country, if bullion is exported, to what service it shall be applied; but it is of infinite importance whether the magnitude of the sum shall exceed, or fall short, of the balance of trade. Whether money so exported shall be applied for the payment of British troops in Germany, for the foreign expenditure of fleets in the Mediterranean or Lisbon, or whether it shall be for an Imperial loan . . . is exactly the same to the country."[41]

The House of Commons Committee on the Bank Crisis naturally paid much attention to the recent export of specie. So far as aid to the allies was concerned, it discovered that most of it had been remitted in the form of bills of exchange rather than bullion. Silver had been used sparingly; gold hardly at all. Of the £1,200,000 sent Prussia in 1794, only £720,000 had been in silver. The £4,600,000 Austrian loan of 1795 had entailed the remittance of about £1,193,000 in hard money, the balance being paid in commercial paper. To be sure, a distinction between subsidies paid in specie and those remitted in bills of exchange was of limited value. The effect on the balance of payments was the same in both

40. Silberling, "Financial and Monetary Policy," p. 227.
41. Francis Baring, *Observations on the Establishment of the Bank of England and on the Paper Circulation of the Country* . . . ,2d ed. (London, 1797), pp. 50-51.

cases.[42] Even more satisfying to the government than the Committee's Report was the rapid recovery of the Bank's specie reserve. By the end of 1797 it had risen to the level which it occupied on the outbreak of war. Notwithstanding, the government refused to rescind its suspension order, and Britain remained off the gold standard during the rest of the war.

The Bank Crisis had very little effect on the government's subsidy program. Pitt continued advancing money to Austria, the only ally with whom he could share the nation's bounty. Even these advances stopped in the spring of 1797, when Vienna made peace with France. Subsidies would not again be an important British war expense until the formation of the Second Coalition two years later. By that time the Bank of England reported a bullion reserve of more than £10,000,000. This remarkable recovery can be explained in various ways. However, it should be observed that during the two years between the Bank Crisis and the formation of the Second Coalition, British foreign remittances for subsidies and military operations fell to the lowest level since the outbreak of the war.[43]

Four years of war had destroyed all of the First Coalition except Britain's union with Austria, and even that was beginning to disintegrate.[44] Thugut bitterly resented Pitt's Prussian bias and believed that Austria's military efforts, if not her accomplishments, deserved more generous recognition. In 1796 the Imperial armies received the full shock of the French attack in Germany and Italy. Each month, Britain advanced money to her ally, but scarcity of specie and foreign credit sometimes forced the Treasury to send less than the £150,000 Vienna expected. Thugut protested loudly on such occasions and threatened a proportional reduction in the Hapsburg war effort.[45] The stage was thus set for the bickering between London and Vienna which marked the

---

42. See particularly the appendices of the Third Report from the Committee of Secrecy on the Outstanding Demands on the Bank . . . , presented to the House of Commons on April 21, 1797, *Reports from Committees of the House of Commons* (London, 1803), XI. Appendix No. 3 is most important; *ibid.*, XI, 168.

43. Arthur Gayer, W. W. Rostow, and A. J. Schwartz, *The Growth and Fluctuation of the British Economy, 1790-1850* (Oxford, 1953), I, 52; Silberling, "Financial and Monetary Policy," p. 227.

44. *Camb. Hist. Brit. For. Pol.*,I, 269-272.

45. Eden to Grenville, October 23, 1796, FO 7/47.

coalition's final days. By the time their alliance collapsed in 1797, the two powers parted in the worst possible humor.

With the approach of autumn, 1796, Thugut made an estimate of the financial help he would need from Britain to carry on the war during the coming year. Since a large part of any new loan would go to repay the money she had advanced, Thugut recommended that the loan be set at £5,000,000. In forwarding this request to the Hapsburg minister in London, he loftily reminded him that "the wealth of England does not lack resources when it is a question of the most essential interests of her prosperity."[46]

If Grenville once thought German princes grasping, he now knew they were petty bandits when compared with the empires of eastern Europe. The Tsarina expected £3,000,000 for the service of 60,000 Russians, and now Vienna was demanding a £5,000,000 loan. Even if these requests were reduced to reasonable proportions, Britain would still have a crushing load to bear. Starhemberg's endless pleas that the monthly Austrian advances be raised from £150,000 to £200,000 wore away the foreign secretary's small stock of patience. In November 1796 he sent that envoy an ill-tempered note stating: "I would have wished that you had been spared the very useless task of once again requesting an increase of assistance already in excess of what had been thought possible."[47] The government soon decided to be more generous, and in January Grenville announced that the advances would be increased to £200,000.[48] Scarcely had this decision been made when the Bank Crisis occurred, making it impossible for London to carry out its pledge.[49]

Troubles overwhelmed Pitt in the opening months of 1797. Barely had the Bank Crisis been weathered when mutiny broke out in the British fleet at Spithead and the Nore. On the Continent, the French broke through the Austrian defense of Mantua, and in February they occupied that important stronghold. By spring the enemy held positions in Italy and along the

46. Thugut to Starhemberg, September 10, 1796, *Manuscripts of J. B. Fortescue* III, 249.

47. Grenville to Starhemberg, November 13, 1796, *ibid.*, III, 267.

48. An additional £100,000 was to be added to each of the payments for January and February; Grenville to Eden, January 3, 1797, FO 7/48

49. Grenville to Eden, May 2, 1797, FO 7/49.

Rhine, from which they would launch a fatal assault at Austria's heart.

London expected any day to learn that her ally had concluded an armistice as a preliminary to peace negotiations, in which event Pitt was anxious to join Austria in arranging a general peace. George Hammond was sent to Vienna in April to confer with Thugut regarding the terms which the allies should demand. In order to guarantee that they would negotiate from the strongest possible position, Pitt was ready to pour forth Britain's wealth in Austria's support. Time was fast running out. On April 7 the Austrian commander concluded an armistice with Bonaparte. The prime minister moved quickly and on April 29 he asked the Commons to guarantee a new Austrian loan.[50]

During the debate on the government's proposal, Pitt announced that a total of £1,620,000 had been advanced to Austria.* The government wished to continue these monthly remittances until £3,500,000 in all had been paid, the whole to be returned to the Treasury from the proceeds of an Austrian loan of that same amount. Fox attacked the plan along predictable lines: since Austria had already made an armistice, was it wise to endorse the government's scheme when at any moment we might learn that the Emperor had concluded peace? Pitt responded to this by

50. *Parliamentary History*, XXXIII, 463-464.

* Despite the government's official statement that the Austrian advances of 1796-1797 totaled £1,620,000, there is reason to believe that they were actually somewhat larger than that. The question turns on whether the official figure includes the £250,000 advanced, on Grenville's order, by Colonel Craufurd during the spring of 1796.

The evidence is contradictory. A statement of all advances, prepared by Grenville for Sir Morton Eden's information (enclosed in Grenville to Eden, May 2, 1797, FO 7/49), shows that £920,000 was advanced in 1796 and £700,000 in 1797. The sum, £1,620,000, is the amount which the government claimed Austria received. A statement prepared by Boyd, Benfield and Co., entitled "Statement of the remittances and Payments by Boyd, Benfield & Co. for the Account of the Imperial Government, 1796" (Chatham Papers, 115) bears out the claim that the 1796 advances amounted to £920,000. At the bottom of that statement, however, there is a notation in a different hand indicating that this did not include the £250,000 in advances made by Colonel Craufurd in the spring. Pitt's announcement to the Commons in December 1796, referred to £1,200,000 having been already advanced to Austria. This figure approximately represents Boyd, Benfield's remittances, together with those of Craufurd.

Probably the total amount advanced to Austria was £1,870,000. Given the confusion of the time, Pitt may have made an honest error in citing the smaller figure. However, it is just as likely that he deliberately chose to suppress all reference to Craufurd's advances. These two payments, totaling £250,000, had been authorized by London *before* the end of the Parliamentary session. For that reason, the government may have chosen to conceal them.

making clear that the government's overwhelming concern was to end the war on the best terms attainable for both Austria and Britain. "Will any one deny," he asked, "that a vote of the parliament of England, passed with unanimity and decision, granting ample pecuniary succours to our ally, may materially affect the terms on which peace may be concluded? Does it not immediately affect the question of the Emperor making a separate peace? And if he is unfortunately driven to that extremity, will it not enable him to conclude a peace on better terms for himself, and consequently on better terms for this country? For it ought to be recollected, that whatever additional concessions he extorts from the enemy for himself, it is so much gained to us, since they will help strike a balance of power more favourable to Great Britain."[51]

Even though the House adopted the motion, Pitt lost his gamble against time; on April 18 Austria signed a preliminary peace treaty with France at Leoben. On learning this, the prime minister announced that he would advance no more money to the Emperor. Instead, the government made arrangements to sponsor a new Austrian loan for £1,620,000, the proceeds of which would reimburse the Treasury for the 1796-1797 advances. Grenville encountered no difficulty in negotiating a treaty with Starhemberg along these lines, since it had been clearly understood from the outset that the advances would be repaid by an Imperial loan. Although not specifically empowered to conclude such an agreement, Starhemberg willingly signed the treaty on May 16. Austria was now bound to borrow £1,620,000 in London, on the same terms as the 1795 loan, and give the money to the British Treasury. In return, Britain would stand security for the Emperor's annual payments of £112,000 to meet the interest and amortization charges.[52]

Pitt was greatly upset by Austria's negotiation of a separate peace in violation of her treaty obligations to Britain. He was still more troubled by the Hofburg's mysterious conduct in the weeks which followed. Thugut absolutely refused to disclose the terms of

51. *Parliamentary History*, XXXIII, 471.
52. Starhemberg to Grenville, May 6, 1797, *Manuscripts of J. B. Fortescue*, III, 321; Grenville to Starhemberg, May 14, 1797, FO 7/49; Starhemberg to Grenville, May 14, 1797, FO 7/49 (however, see Helleiner, *Imperial Loans*, pp. 98-99); Treaty with Austria, May 16, 1797, FO 93/11(3).

the Leoben agreement either to Sir Morton Eden or Pitt's special envoy, George Hammond. This naturally aroused Pitt's fears that the Hapsburg foreign minister was engaged in some profitable double-dealing with the Directory. Worse yet was the news Eden sent to London early in June: Vienna refused to ratify Starhemberg's treaty of May and announced that she would make no more payments on the 1795 loan![53]

Austria's decision to renege on her debts probably came as no surprise to the prime minister, but he was deeply shocked to learn that the new loan convention was not to be ratified.[54] He had so often declared that the 1796-1797 advances were to be repaid, that it was the worst sort of humiliation for that proud man now to admit that he had been duped. Grenville shared this view completely and warned Starhemberg that his government was making a tragic mistake. "We will lose some money," he declared, "for having believed in the good faith and probity of the Austrian government. The Court of Vienna will forever lose its credit, its honour, and the chance of finding here any financial aid which it might require in the future. All things considered, I really believe that if we are the dupes, it is the *Duper* who will be the loser."[55]

Eden was ordered to insist upon immediate ratification of the treaty as the necessary first step in the re-establishment of good relations between London and Vienna.[56] At first the tone of Grenville's dispatches was moderate, but as the time approached for the reassembling of Parliament it grew more angry. In September he instructed Eden to inform Thugut that by his persistent refusal to ratify the convention "he is deciding at once and for ever the possibility not only of any future assistance of a pecuniary nature from Great Britain to Austria, but of any intercourse of Councils or confidential Concert between them, at a Moment when perhaps upon some such Intercourse and Concert being established depends the common safety of the Two Monarchies, and the fate of the rest of Europe."[57] Language of this sort had little effect on Thugut, whose policies were better

53. Eden to Grenville, June 1, 1797, FO 7/49.
54. See Pitt's statement on this matter to the Commons, *Parliamentary History*, XXXIII, 429.
55. Grenville to Starhemberg, July 4, 1797, *Manuscripts of J. B. Fortescue*, III, 332.
56. Grenville to Eden, July 7, 1797, FO 7/50.
57. Grenville to Eden, September 26, 1797, FO 7/50.

served by his final peace treaty with France, signed at Campo Formio in October 1797.

Austria's withdrawal from the war left Pitt no choice but to undertake a new peace negotiation with France in the summer of 1797. The failure of the discussions which ensued at Lille cast a still darker shadow over Britain. Her relations with Vienna were now hopelessly deadlocked by the unratified loan convention. Appeals to Russia for the assistance provided in their mutual defense pact of 1795 fell on deaf ears.[58] Prussia's policy sank into the deepest lethargy as her court waited for Frederick William to die. Of all the members of the First Coalition only one remained at Britain's side: her oldest ally, Portugal. Except for Admiral Duncan's victory over the Dutch fleet at Camperdown in October, the autumn of 1797 was a period of unrelieved gloom for Pitt.

Since it was Britain's destiny to continue the war with France, her leaders had to determine how to fight it with the greatest chance of success. Certain considerations must have been very clear to Pitt and Grenville at this time. To begin with, obviously Britain could not singlehandedly undertake a continental campaign against the Directory. She had virtually ceased to participate in the European war since the loss of Holland in 1795.[59] By the time Austria left the coalition, Britain's only continental army was a small force of uncertain value which had been sent to defend Portugal. Paradoxically, the British military establishment in 1797 was nearly four times as large as it had been in the first year of the war.[60] A large part of this force was tied down at home, however, by the threat of rebellion in Ireland, and many units were involved in colonial campaigns. Spain's declaration of war in 1796 had enlarged the theater of operations in the West Indies, while campaigns in India made new demands on the nation's manpower.[61]

The failure of Britain's efforts to negotiate peace underscored the fact that only defeat on Europe's battlefields would put the

---

58. F. Martens, *Recueil des Traités*, IX, 412. In December 1797, Paul I formally announced that he was unable to meet his obligations to Britain under the 1795 defense agreement; Whitworth to Grenville, December 8, 1797, FO 65/38.

59. Except for the mercenaries who were left to cooperate with the Austrians.

60. Fortescue, *British Army*, IV, 938-940.

61. Heavy demands for troops obliged Britain to reduce its military commitment in Portugal in 1798. See Fortescue, *British Army*, IV, 605.

Directory in a mood to listen to reasonable terms. Since Britain could not accomplish this by herself, she had to win the support of the continental powers in a new league. There was no other way. The counterrevolutionary movement within France was undependable. Unless Pitt was ready to surrender, he must take the initiative in arousing the European powers to act with Britain once again.

Past experience proved that the members of any new coalition would expect British subsidies. Pitt's early hope that subsidies would be needed only as an emergency measure broke down well before the First Coalition collapsed. At one time or another, Prussia, Austria, and Russia had all insisted on receiving British financial support. In any new alliance, Britain might be forced to accept subsidization of her partners as a regular war expense, to be borne in addition to her own heavy outlays for military and naval purposes.

This consideration provided still another argument in favor of restructuring the British system of war finance which had prevailed since 1793. So far, the war had been fought largely on borrowed money. To escape the ruinous interest charges which resulted, the Treasury would have to transfer a larger part of the war burden directly onto the shoulders of the British taxpayer. During the final years of the century, Pitt introduced an imposing collection of new taxes for this purpose. Results began to appear almost at once; between 1797 and 1799 the revenue rose from £23,000,000 to more than £35,000,000.[62] The new tax program would make it easier for the government to provide its future allies with the subsidies they would surely expect.

No matter how well financed, a new coalition would fail unless built upon a realistic and mutually acceptable set of goals. First, the European powers would have to be awakened to the dangers which hovered over them. At the moment, Prussia was blind to the massive power of the Directory which hung over her, while Austria's delight in the acquisition of Venetia (Treaty of Campo Formio) helped her forget her losses in the Low Countries. How could the eccentric Tsar be made to see that French hegemony in the West imperiled his own domain? British diplomacy must rouse

62. Gayer, Rostow, and Schwartz, *British Economy,* I, 44.

these powers from their sleep and guide them toward agreement on war aims. No one was more aware of this than Grenville. He had seen Austro-Prussian rivalry tear the league apart in 1794. During the final phase of the coalition, Austria's ambivalence concerning her real interests had weakened her partnership with Britain. A new league would have to be created by British diplomacy and financed by British subsidies. In the long run, however, it might be easier to satisfy the allies' demand for money than to bring them into agreement on their war goals.

V

ORIGINS OF THE SECOND COALITION

Lord Grenville was not surprised when the peace negotiations at Lille fell apart in September 1797.[1] More than ever he was convinced that only a union of all the great powers could restore the European balance. They must confront the Directory with a proposal for a comprehensive territorial settlement backed by the threat of war. Late in 1797 Grenville undertook to form such a concert, and his plan, as finally matured, anticipated the system Castlereagh was to create at the close of the Napoleonic Wars.[2] If possible, such a concert should be established before the Directory stabilized its recent territorial gains. In this way, France would be obliged to accept its terms. If war was to be the destiny of the league, however, Britain must be ready to lead it and subsidize its members as generously as her resources permitted.

The broad outline of such a scheme was probably already in Grenville's mind when he received a most interesting dispatch sent by Lord Elgin from Berlin on October 8. Frederick William II was dying and Elgin felt sure that the Prince Royal, who would ascend the throne within a matter of weeks, was ready to take a determined stand against France.[3] Even assuming that Elgin's estimate of the prince's character was too optimistic, Grenville

1. Grenville had no confidence in the Lille negotiation and tried to dissuade Pitt from undertaking it. See *Malmesbury*, III, 366; Rose, *Pitt and the Great War*, pp. 322-326.

2. Once France had been forced to accept a territorial settlement, Grenville proposed that the four Great Powers remain united in order to guarantee it. Should the concert be forced to go to war, he recommended the creation of a central council of ministers representing the allied powers. For an examination of the proposal, see John M. Sherwig, "Lord Grenville's Plan for a Concert of Europe, 1797-1799," *Journal of Modern History*, 34 (1962), 284-293.

3. Elgin to Grenville, October 8, 1797, FO 64/45.

knew that Prussian policy was as shifty as running water. Haugwitz and his fellow-ministers would cheerfully abandon their entente with France if it could be done with much profit and little risk.[4] Britain could not ignore even the slight possibility that a young and patriotic king might make his influence felt at Berlin.

The foreign secretary decided to sound out the Prince Royal, although the obvious delicacy of the situation obliged him to use a secret agent. The assignment fell to an unlikely member of George III's household, an emigrant Swiss scholar named Jean de Luc.[5] Grenville's instructions to his emissary were general, but they made clear that Britain desired a union with Prussia as the nucleus of a concert to include all the major powers. Special emphasis was placed on the liberation of Holland as mutually advantageous to Britain and Prussia. The Prince Royal must be made to see how little real security his country derived from its 1796 neutrality pact with France. De Luc's instructions made no mention of any war alliance, but referred instead to a "union of all the great powers" as the only means of re-establishing the European equilibrium. Specifically, Prussia was invited to join with Britain in creating a counterweight to French power. Should war come, Prussia could count on British subsidies, but only for "services *rendered* and not *to be rendered*."[6]

De Luc's mission was a disappointment from the start. On November 16, Frederick William III succeeded to the Prussian throne, but foreign affairs interested him so little that he asked Count Haugwitz to respond to the British overture. That minister regarded the proposal rather like an offer of help from a dying man. In his reply, which reached London in January 1798, he

4. Grenville had every right to this opinion. During the last days of the First Coalition, Haugwitz had discussed with Elgin the possibility that Prussia might renew her connection with England. Elgin believed that Berlin would demand both subsidies and the promise of territorial rewards. See Elgin's dispatches to Grenville of February and March, 1797, FO 64/43.

5. Jean de Luc (1727-1817) was a native of Geneva who came to England in 1773. He held the position of reader to Queen Charlotte. Presumably, he was chosen for the Berlin mission because, as a traveling man of science, he would attract little attention. Much of his correspondence with Grenville, written in French and in a very small hand, has been published in vol. IV of *Manuscripts of J. B. Fortescue.* The foreign secretary found him an exhausting correspondent and even George III described De Luc's letters as "very judicious, though most *tedious*" (George III to Pitt, January 11, 1798, Chatham Papers, vol. 104).

6. Grenville to De Luc, November 10, 1797, and De Luc to Grenville, December 25, 1797, *Manuscripts of J. B. Fortescue,* IV, 8-10, 47.

reaffirmed his belief that "the system adopted by Prussia since the peace of Basel is the only one agreeable to her true interests." Only overt French aggression against the north German neutral zone would justify Prussia in going to war and then only for defensive purposes. In such an event, Britain would be expected to provide subsidies, which Haugwitz called the "nerve of war." For the foreseeable future, cooperation between the two governments either for diplomatic or military purposes was out of the question.[7]

Grenville did not grieve over the failure of his bid to the new Prussian ruler. France was now making her intentions so clear that even Europe's most obtuse statesmen would soon be able to read in them his country's doom. In December a congress assembled at Rastadt to settle terms of peace between France and the Empire. Negotiations had hardly begun when the Directory's envoys demanded the cession of the entire left bank of the Rhine. Meanwhile, French intrigue in Switzerland gave advance notice that the Directory intended military intervention there.

Haugwitz' memorandum brought from the foreign secretary a stern warning against the dangers of complacency. If the Directory had not yet threatened north Germany, it was only because it wanted to lull Berlin into a false sense of security. The day would soon come when French armies would smash through the line of demarcation. When that happened, Britain would provide Prussia with subsidies to help her against the common enemy. With this pledge went the grim reminder that the security of north Germany was only one part of a far larger issue. No nation would be safe until French imperialism had been halted and that could be accomplished only by a union of all the powers. "In its present crisis," Grenville explained to Haugwitz, "Europe can be saved only by a reunion of the Great Powers, which would have for its purpose the re-establishment of the general peace, and thereupon the maintenance of the common tranquillity, and the guarantee of possessions by the respective governments. As long as war exists in part, the interests will be divided; as long as a general concert does not exist for the maintenance of peace, nothing can halt the designs of a government which dominates by disunion."

7. Memorandum of Count Haugwitz for Lord Grenville, n.d., enclosed in De Luc to Grenville, December 21, 1797, *ibid.,* IV, 41-43.

If Haugwitz wanted to promote his country's welfare, he should join with Britain in working for that union. "England and Prussia," Grenville declared, "concerting together, and establishing (if it is still possible) a real and sincere understanding with the two other Major Courts [Russia and Austria], would put all four of them in a position to present in an imposing manner to France the bases of the future tranquillity of Europe, founded on whatever arrangements may issue from their discussions."[8] In a private letter to Elgin, Grenville conceded that each passing day made it less likely that the league could have its way with France without war. The Cabinet had already earmarked £1,000,000 for a Prussian war subsidy.[9]

The foreign secretary attached the greatest importance to winning Russian support for his concert plan. Aside from the fact that no union would be complete without the Tsar, his adherence might be a powerful inducement for Prussia to join.[10] Hopefully, the Tsar would also be able to impose some degree of cooperation on Prussia and Austria, thereby sparing the concert that bitter rivalry which had weakened the First Coalition. So far Russia had remained aloof, but French aggression in Germany might prod her into action. Under the Treaty of Teschen (1779), Russia was one of the guarantors of the Empire's boundaries, which the Directory insisted on revising at Rastadt. A brief summary of the concert plan was sent to Whitworth in December 1797, along with instructions to do everything possible to attract the Tsar's interest and support.[11]

Britain's eager courting of the northern powers contrasted sharply with her marked coolness toward Austria, a contrast heightened by the fact that, so far, only Vienna had shown any interest in union with Britain. Although Thugut still refused to reveal the terms of the Campo Formio treaty, he was willing to talk with Eden about a new Anglo-Austrian alliance. As early as November 1797, Eden reported that the Hofburg "might find it expedient to have again recourse to Arms." In fact, Thugut had

8. Grenville to Haugwitz, n.d., enclosed in Grenville to De Luc, January 14, 1798, *ibid.*, IV, 58-60.
9. Grenville to Elgin, January 14, 1798, FO 64/47.
10. So the Duke of Brunswick wrote George III on November 27, 1797. See *Manuscripts of J. B. Fortescue*, IV, 25-26.
11. Grenville to Whitworth, December, 1797, FO 65/38.

gone so far as to direct his envoy in London to hint that a promise of British subsidies would be a powerful inducement for Austria to go to war.[12]

Distrust of Austria colored the Cabinet's outlook throughout this important period. Thugut's refusal to ratify the 1797 loan agreement destroyed what little faith Pitt and Grenville had in Hapsburg sincerity. Nor were they inclined to accept the justification Thugut offered: Austria's penury and the fear that ratification would prejudice the outcome of the Rastadt Congress. The foreign secretary considered this transparent dishonesty, and early in 1798 he threatened to sever diplomatic relations with Vienna unless the treaty was ratified.[13] More was involved than the disputed loan agreement, however. The liberation of the Low Countries was a major goal of Britain's war policy; so long as Austria was indifferent to that goal, Downing Street must give highest priority to winning Prussian support. Furthermore, if a concert could be formed which included Prussia and Russia, then Austria could not possibly remain aloof. In such a case, Grenville believed, the Hofburg must either petition for admission, or "leap into the arms of the Jacobin government of France."[14]

Events soon bore out this prediction. Early in 1798 an Austrian agent was sent to England in a futile effort to borrow money to pay the interest due on the 1795 Imperial loan. Grenville stonily refused to consider this as evidence of good faith, and described the mission as "perfectly insignificant, and calculated only to gain time."[15] A few months later, the unfavorable nature of the Rastadt negotiations prompted Thugut to attempt an accommodation with Britain. On April 1 Starhemberg informed Grenville that his government was ready to support a union of the great powers. With this went an Austrian request for the return of the British navy to the Mediterranean and a guarantee of subsidies in the event of war.[16]

---

12. Eden to Grenville, November 1, 1797, FO 7/50; Thugut to Starhemberg, November 2, 1797, in Hermann Hüffer, *Quellen zur Geschichte der Kriege von 1799 und 1800* (Leipzig, 1900-1907), III, 478-480.
13. Grenville to Eden, January 16, 1798, FO 7/51.
14. Grenville's Memoir for the Duke of Brunswick, November 10, 1797, *Manuscripts of J. B. Fortescue*, IV, 9.
15. Grenville to Eden, March 13, 1798, FO 7/51.
16. Grenville to Pitt, April 1, 1798, *Manuscripts of J. B. Fortescue*, IV, 150-151.

The Cabinet took two weeks to consider Austria's appeal. Pitt was full of misgivings, and the Admiralty frankly doubted whether it would be safe to send the navy back to the Mediterranean.[17] So far as Grenville was concerned there could never be any agreement with Vienna as long as the 1797 loan treaty remained unratified. The British reply given to Starhemberg fell far short of Vienna's expectations. An Anglo-Austrian union must be preceded by ratification of the 1797 pact, "an indispensable preliminary to all discussions on this point." Thugut's pleas for money could not even be considered. Only one of Austria's requests was granted: the fleet would return to the Mediterranean provided Naples opened her ports for its service.[18]

A few days after this British response had been delivered to Starhemberg, Grenville confided to Eden that there was more to the Cabinet's decision than had been disclosed. To be sure, Britain could have no confidence in Austria until the 1797 convention had been ratified, but once that had been done she would welcome alliance with her and promise a £1,000,000 subsidy in the event of war. Past experience ruled out a third loan. "If the present discussions should terminate in the establishment of the concert proposed," Grenville explained, "the King will send a Commissary to the Austrian army who shall have instructions that whenever that Army shall be actually put in motion, and hostilities be commenced with France, he is to supply the Commander of it with monthly bills on the Treasury in the proportion of one million Sterling for the twelve month—such payments . . . to continue for so long only as hostilities shall be carried on between Austria and France."[19]

Grenville never doubted for a moment that Austria would finally join the allies. On April 13 an attack by a Viennese mob on the French ambassador brought the Hofburg close to war—a war she could not fight without allies. Before the month ended, Starhemberg informed Grenville that he had been instructed to declare "officially and solemnly" that the 1797 treaty would soon be ratified. The foreign secretary insisted on performance rather than this promise, which he regarded "as very little if at all more

17. Pitt to Grenville, April 1, 1798, *ibid.,* IV, 152; Lord Spencer to Grenville, April 6, 1798, Rose, *Pitt and the Great War,* pp. 366-367.

18. Grenville to Starhemberg, April 18, 1798, *Manuscripts of J. B. Fortescue,* IV, 171-172.

19. Grenville to Eden, April 20, 1798, FO 7/51.

satisfactory than those which have been received before."[20] Meanwhile, Starhemberg tried to borrow money in the City to meet the charges on the 1795 loan only to discover that he could not raise a shilling without a British guarantee.[21]

France's conduct during 1798 provided the strongest argument in favor of European union. At Rastadt, the Empire finally accepted the Rhine river as her boundary. The long-expected French intervention in Switzerland occurred, resulting in the annexation of Geneva and the formation of the Helvetic Republic. Meanwhile, the Directory's armies poured southward into Italy and took Rome. This rapid spread of French power made a deep impression on the Tsar, whose attitude toward the Directory had undergone a steady change since the beginning of 1798. Whitworth skilfully employed every argument to engage Paul's interest in the concert, and early in May he was able to report some success to London. The Tsar was ready to support the concert's aims even though it might involve him in war. It must be understood, however, that Russia's participation in any war with the Directory would depend upon a generous grant of British subsidies. As proof of his dedication, the Tsar was sending a personal emissary to Berlin to persuade Frederick William III to declare for the good cause.[22] With the Tsar's mind at last made up and Austria soliciting for membership in the evolving concert, Grenville turned his full attention to winning Prussia's support. Elgin was sent the necessary powers to conclude a treaty which would bring Prussia in as a member of the four-power alliance.[23]

Britain's plans seemed headed for fulfillment in the spring of 1798, but it was the only bright spot on the horizon. The steady rumblings of discontent that had been heard for years in Ireland suddenly erupted into revolt in May. At almost the same time London learned that a major French armada was loose in the Mediterranean.[24] Clearly, any four-power concert to be formed

---

20. Starhemberg to Grenville, April 26, 1798, *Manuscripts of J. B. Fortescue,* IV, 178; Grenville to Eden, April 27, 1798, FO 7/51.

21. Even Boyd, Benfield and Co. would do nothing for Austria. See Starhemberg to Grenville, May, 1798, *Manuscripts of J. B. Fortescue,* IV, 203-204.

22. Whitworth to Grenville, May 4, 1798, FO 65/39; Elgin to Grenville, April 6, 1798, FO 64/48.

23. Grenville to Elgin, April 20, 1798, FO 64/49.

24. Grenville correctly guessed that the French fleet was bound for Egypt. See Grenville to Buckingham, June 13, 1798, *Memoirs of the Court,* II, 401.

must be a war coalition. With the Directory in control of Switzerland and fast extending its power in Italy, Vienna could not postpone a commitment much longer. All that now remained was for Frederick William to come forward manfully and close the circle around the common enemy.

As the clouds of war gathered in the summer of 1798, Berlin became the nerve center of European diplomacy. Emissaries of Britain, Russia, and Austria joined forces to persuade Prussia to declare for the emerging concert. In this they competed with French agents pressing for closer ties between Berlin and Paris. Count Haugwitz was placed in a position where one false step might prove disastrous. With a delicate sensitivity to the high stakes involved, he tried to avoid offending either camp. It was to his advantage to play for time until it became clear what course would be most profitable for him to take. There was always the danger, however, that by delaying too long, Prussian support would lose its value both to the Directory and the concert powers.[25] Throughout the summer Haugwitz deftly parried unwanted offers of alliance thrust at him from both sides. When the allied representatives finally admitted defeat, they at least found consolation in the fact that the French envoy, Abbé Sieyès, had been just as unsuccessful in moving Prussia from the dead center of neutralism.[26]

Quite different from Prussia's indecision was the Tsar's conduct on learning of the Directory's aggression in the Mediterranean. For the first time since 1793 French imperialism directly threatened a vital Russian interest. The seizure of Malta and Bonaparte's invasion of Egypt removed Paul's last doubts regarding union with Austria and Britain.[27] He ordered the mobilization of his army and instructed Vorontzoff to resume discussion of the subsidy proposal Catherine had made to Britain in 1796.[28] The French

25. For a discussion of Haugwitz' policies see Guy Stanton Ford, *Hanover and Prussia, 1795-1803: A Study in Neutrality* . . . (New York, 1903), p. 56 and *passim*.

26. Elgin's correspondence during this period makes clear that the question of subsidies played no part in his discussions with Haugwitz.

27. As late as June the Tsar was carrying on secret conversations with France looking to a settlement of their differences. See Andrei A. Lobanov-Rostovsky, *Russia and Europe, 1789-1825* (Durham, N.C., 1947), p. 18.

28. Whitworth to Grenville, July 24, 1798, FO 65/40.

threat to Naples seriously alarmed Thugut, and Eden reported that the Austrian leader had pledged his unqualified support to defend her.[29] Prussia's continued evasiveness was a disappointment, but Grenville was encouraged by the reports reaching him from St. Petersburg and Vienna. In a rare mood of good humor, he wrote his brother, "my Emperors are going to war like good boys, but they have been a long while bringing themselves to it."[30]

The conclusion of an Anglo-Russian subsidy pact was unlikely to be difficult since Vorontzoff found the Cabinet ready to go "as far to meet this overture as our pecuniary resources will allow." Pitt renewed his offer of 1796: in return for 60,000 Russians, Britain would pay a preparation subsidy of £300,000, monthly payments of £100,000, and a final postwar bonus amounting to £50,000 for each month the treaty was in effect. Vorontzoff was delighted with the proposal, and in August Grenville empowered Whitworth to sign a treaty with the Tsar on these terms.[31]

The foreign secretary took advantage of his conversations with Vorontzoff to touch on other problems related to the concert. Without the adherence of at least one of the major German states, an Anglo-Russian alliance would be of limited value. Since Prussia was likely to remain neutral, Grenville proposed that Britain's subsidy agreement with the Tsar become operative only after Austria broke with France and entered into alliance with London. In short, the foreign secretary wanted Paul to bring Austria into the concert and to persuade her to ratify the disputed loan treaty of 1797.

Even if Austria satisfied Britain on both points, Grenville could offer her neither subsidies nor a new loan. Four months before, the Cabinet had been ready to give Vienna £1,000,000, but changing circumstances now made that impossible. The return of the British fleet to the Mediterranean, an indirect but important benefit to Austria and her Neapolitan ally, would cost the government at least £1,500,000 a year. About as much would be required to pay the subsidies the Tsar needed. Smaller sums were allocated to aid Portugal and Switzerland. Finally, if Prussia

---

29. Eden to Grenville, August 18, 1798, FO 7/52; Eden to Auckland, June 19, 1798, *Auckland,* IV, 23.

30. Grenville to Buckingham [August], 1798. *Memoirs of the Court,* II, 407.

31. Pitt to Grenville, August 16, 1798, *Manuscripts of J. B. Fortescue,* IV, 283; Grenville to Whitworth, August 29, 1798, FO 65/40.

decided to enter the war, she too would expect financial aid. It was completely beyond Britain's resources to undertake all this and, at the same time, help finance Austria's war program. In asking the Tsar to win Austria's support for the concert, Britain regretted she could not facilitate his task by guaranteeing any direct financial aid to the Hofburg.[32]

What accounts for this steady hardening of Britain's heart toward Austria? Financial considerations were unquestionably involved, as Grenville claimed. The nation's economic health was infinitely better than it had been in 1797, but Pitt hoped to limit the total of all foreign aid to £2,000,000 a year.[33] To satisfy both Russia *and* Austria would cost him about £2,500,000, in which case there would be nothing left for Prussia. Certainly, Frederick William could not be turned away because of a lack of funds. More was involved in the British attitude toward Austria than economic necessity, however. Thugut's conduct during recent months aroused deep suspicion regarding his real intentions toward France.[34] Grenville counted on the Tsar to bring Austria into the coalition and ratify the 1797 treaty, all of which he hoped could be done without costing Britain anything.[35]

If London could appeal to the Tsar to intervene in her quarrel with Vienna, Vienna could do so as well. Following the signing of a new Austro-Russian alliance at St. Petersburg in July 1798, the Hapsburg envoy, Count Louis Cobenzl, urged Paul to support

32. Note by Lord Grenville on the heads of a conference with Count Vorontzoff, August, 1798, *Manuscripts of J. B. Fortescue,* IV, 297-298. Grenville informed Eden of this decision on September 4, 1798 (FO 7/53), and observed, "the King's Servants have felt that this Mode of assisting Austria by procuring for Her the Cooperation of a large military aid from Russia would probably be more effectual in its result, and is after what has passed infinitely less objectionable in other respects than any Plans of direct subsidy to that Power [Austria]."

33. Pitt to Grenville, October 6, 1798, *Manuscripts of J. B. Fortescue,* IV, 337-338.

34. *Cambridge Modern History,* VIII, 642 and *passim.*

35. There is good reason to believe that if Grenville could have won Prussian support, he would have abandoned Austria altogether. Near the close of August, he summarized his recent talks with Vorontzoff in a dispatch to Whitworth. Britain still wished to see the formation of a four-power concert, but Austria might refuse to join. "If for this reason," Grenville continued, "or from any other circumstance the establishment of such a concert as is now proposed should become impracticable, there is another idea which might be suggested to the Court of Petersburgh, and which indeed if it could be rendered palatable there, would in any case be very much preferred by His Majesty to the establishment of any concert for a cooperation in the military plans of Austria." What Grenville had in mind was a Russo-British invasion of Holland which might shake Prussia from her languor and bring her into alliance with the two governments. See Grenville to Whitworth, no. 20, August [29?], 1798, FO 65/40.

Vienna in this contest of wills. Whitworth immediately sensed the direction in which events were moving and challenged Cobenzl to prove the Hofburg's good faith by ratifying the disputed loan convention. The Austrian envoy refused. Instead, he declared that his government would do so only *after* receiving positive assurances of British financial aid.[36]

The fate of the concert now rested in the hands of Paul, acting as arbiter between London and Vienna. By the end of September he had decided in favor of Vienna, and Whitworth was told that the conclusion of the Russian subsidy treaty would be delayed "until the so much wished for Concert between His Majesty [George III] and the Court of Vienna shall be re-established."[37] In short, London must make her peace with Vienna as the price of a Russian alliance.

Nelson's Victory of the Nile was still being celebrated in Downing Street when Whitworth's latest dispatches arrived with news of Britain's diplomatic defeat. Grenville regarded this as further proof of Hapsburg treachery, and when Vorontzoff and Starhemberg called on him, he received them with austere dignity. He asked the Austrian minister one question: was he empowered to ratify the treaty the 1797 treaty? When Starhemberg admitted that he had no such instructions, the foreign secretary ended the meeting by reaffirming his original position that ratification was a preliminary to all further discussion.[38] What was now to be done? Grenville's recommendation to Pitt was straightforward and simple: "It sounds whimsical, but I am inclined to think that in this state of things, urgent as the moment is, the best resolution we can take is to do nothing; to declare that we consider the negotiation at Vienna as at an end; and to say, but without the least tincture of ill-humour, that we must now wait for proposals from our allies, those which we had made having failed."[39] The prime minister was nearly as unyielding as his cousin. Nothing could be

36. Whitworth to Grenville, September 5, 1798, FO 65/40. See also Eden to Grenville, September 1, 1798, FO 7/53.

37. Russian ministers explained this decision to Whitworth by pointing out that "such an Employment in favour of Russia, of the Resources destined by His Majesty for carrying on the War, may put it out of His Majesty's power to assist the Court of Vienna, as much as may be necessary, when that Court shall have satisfied His Majesty on the subject of the present Misunderstanding" (Whitworth to Grenville, September 25, 1798, FO 65/40); see also Whitworth to Grenville, October 4, 1798, FO 65/41.

38. Grenville to Whitworth, October 23, 1798, FO 65/41.

39. Grenville to Pitt, October 28, 1798, *Manuscripts of J. B. Fortescue*, IV, 354.

done for the Austrians, he agreed, "till they have, *at least, ratified* expressly the convention [of 1797]; I think, not till they have begun to *execute* it." Once that point had been gained, it might be possible to give Vienna something. Pitt confessed, however, that "I am not . . . very sanguine in my hopes of any thing, but our continuing to fight well our own battle, and Europe must probably be left for some time longer to its fate."[40]

The Cabinet decided to stand its ground on the question of Hapsburg ratification.[41] Austria's unwillingness to honor her debts was evidence of bad faith, especially since she was not required immediately to repay the £1,620,000.[42] Since Britain had failed to create a concert of the powers, there was nothing left but to invite the Tsar to try. On November 16 Grenville informed Whitworth of this decision: "His Majesty would therefore recommend that the Russian Ministers at Berlin and Vienna should be instructed to propose the immediate conclusion of a treaty between the four great Powers: the basis of which should be the employment of their united efforts to reduce France within her ancient limits . . . and to which every other Power should afterwards be invited to accede."[43] Let the Tsar see what he could accomplish!

Although the initiative had been handed to St. Petersburg, it was not in Grenville's nature to sit idly by and await the result. This was especially the case now that the weathervane of Prussian policy was beginning to veer toward the allies. The first hint of this change came in September.[44] A month later, Haugwitz confided to the Russian minister, Count Panin, that Prussia might soon intervene to liberate Holland. He was anxious to learn "the price which England attaches to the operation, and what she would give to help with its means." Panin at once communicated this to London.[45] Encouraging though such news was, Grenville admitted to Vorontzoff that the kaleidoscopic character of

40. Pitt to Grenville, October 6, 1798 and October 29, 1798, *ibid.*, IV, 337-338, 354-355.

41. Only the chancellor, Lord Loughborough, seems to have been willing to yield to Austria; Loughborough to Pitt, October 5, 1798, *ibid.*, IV, 335-336.

42. Grenville to George III, October 10, 1798, the transcript copies of the unpublished correspondence of George III, deposited in the William L. Clements Library, Ann Arbor, Michigan, VIII, 3954-3956 (hereafter cited as "Unpublished George III Letters").

43. Grenville to Whitworth, November 16, 1798, FO 65/41.

44. B. Garlike to Grenville, September 23, 1798, FO 64/51.

45. Panin to S. Vorontzoff, October 18, 1798, *Manuscripts of J. B. Fortescue,* IV, 346-348.

concert diplomacy made him dizzy: "Prussia will act only with our help; and *after* seeing Austria go ahead of her. The same applies to Russia, while Austria delays action until assured of our pecuniary assistance, Russia's cooperation, as well as Prussia's neutrality. We do not have resources enough to put in motion the armies of three Great continental Powers."[46] Notwithstanding, Britain had a responsibility to promote the concert, and the Cabinet decided to send a special agent to Berlin to help win Prussia to the cause.

The Berlin mission was given to the foreign secretary's oldest brother, Thomas Grenville, who had gone to Vienna with Lord Spencer in 1794. His immediate task was to support the efforts of the Russian minister at Berlin to bring the German powers into some degree of harmony. If that could be accomplished, Britain desired the formation of "a general and extensive concert, in which the objects to be pursued shall be previously explained and agreed upon, and in which the means to be employed shall also be regulated by positive stipulation."[47]

Pitt's subsidy policy had changed greatly in recent weeks, and this change was reflected in Thomas Grenville's instructions. Should a four-power alliance be formed, Britain would provide Prussia and Austria with an annual grant of £1,000,000 each. Of course, the Austrian subsidy was conditional upon the ratification of the 1797 treaty. The aid offered the German allies was in excess of the money already pledged to the Tsar. Pitt had finally been compelled to abandon his original limit of £2,000,000 for all foreign aid.[48] Lord Grenville explained this by observing that it was subsidies "to which the Continental Powers look with the greatest anxiety, and which may unquestionably be of the greatest importance to the success of the intended operations." If subsidies could make the coalition, it was folly for Britain to withhold them. The raising of the subsidy limit to more than £3,500,000 probably influenced Pitt's decision to propose a new tax on

46. Grenville to Vorontzoff, November 2, 1798, *ibid.*, IV, 358.
47. Grenville listed the terms of a proposed territorial settlement, which closely resemble those finally achieved at the Congress of Vienna. See John Holland Rose "Pitt's Plan for the Settlement of Europe," which appears in his *Napoleonic Studies,* 2d ed. (London, 1906), pp. 41-84.
48. Dundas strongly opposed this decision and recommended that the total of all foreign aid be kept below £1,200,000 a year. See his letter to Pitt of December 1798, *Manuscripts of J. B. Fortescue,* IV, 433-435.

incomes (December 3, 1798). But if Britain had to be generous, she would not be prodigal. Subsidies to Austria and Prussia would be paid monthly by British commissaries "who will continue the payment so long only as the troops continue to act on the footing, & for the objects, which may be pointed out by the treaty."[49] The experience of the 1794 Prussian subsidy treaty was not to be repeated.

Thomas Grenville's mission began under the worst possible auspices. Violent storms and fog delayed his sailing from Yarmouth for weeks and it was not until the end of January 1799 that H.M.S. *Proserpine,* the frigate assigned him, was able to get to sea. Bad luck shadowed the voyage. *Proserpine* was destroyed by a storm in the Elbe estuary, although no lives were lost. It was not until mid-February that the British envoy reached Berlin. Nearly all his personal belongings and papers had been lost in the wreck.[50]

The cheerless arrival of the New Year, 1799, found Lord Grenville ill-prepared to receive the bad news which Whitworth had sent from St. Petersburg. From dispatches received in Downing Street early in January, the foreign secretary learned that his envoy had signed a treaty with Cobenzl binding Britain to sponsor a new Austrian loan of £3,600,000. Uncertain whether he was still in his right mind, Grenville took a few moments to comprehend what he had just read. At last, the meaning was inescapable: Whitworth had been tricked into an unauthorized act by the wily Austrian minister. The foreign secreatry's fury was not lessened at all by learning that Whitworth had also signed a subsidy pact with Russia.

Whitworth's position at St. Petersburg had grown increasingly difficult after Cobenzl won the Tsar's sympathy and support for the Hofburg. In December Cobenzl presented him with a compromise plan which had already been approved by Paul: in return for a British guarantee of a £3,600,000 loan, Vienna would ratify the 1797 convention and repay that loan from the proceeds of the forthcoming one.[51] The British envoy resisted vigorously for

49. Lord Grenville to T. Grenville, December 1798, FO 64/52.
50. For an account of Thomas Grenville's voyage, see J. D. Spinney, "Some Vicissitudes of a 'V.I.P.,' "*Blackwood's Magazine,* 265 (1949), 301-312. See also William James, *The Naval History of Great Britain* . . . (London, 1822-1824), II, 373-377.
51. Whitworth to Grenville, December 4, 1798, FO 65/41.

more than a week, but on December 13 he at last gave way and signed, *sub spe rati*, the treaty offered by Cobenzl.[52] Whitworth knew very well that Grenville's orders postivitely prohibited such an act. However, the latest dispatches from London were weeks old and perhaps no longer reflected the foreign minister's thinking. He therefore decided to gamble. If his treaty was acceptable, the Cabinet could ratify it; if not, they were free to reject it. In justifying his decision to Grenville, he described the intense pressure put upon him by the Tsar. "God knows," he wrote, "what may be the real intentions of the Court of Vienna, but it certainly is felt here, that unless some solid assurance of support is held out, such is its want of confidence . . . it will in despair listen to the tempting offers now proposed by the Directory."[53]

With Austria at last satisfied, the Tsar was ready to conclude a subsidy agreement with Whitworth. On December 29 Russia promised to send 45,000 troops to cooperate with Prussia when that power declared war on France. These troops would be in addition to the army Paul had already sent off to help Austria. By the terms of the treaty, Britain agreed to provide subsidies in line with Pitt's offer of the previous August. The preparation payment was fixed at £225,000, in addition to which monthly subsidies of £75,000 would be paid as soon as the corps left Russia. A final sum, amounting to £37,500 for each month the treaty was in effect, would be given by Britain at the close of the war.[54]

Downing Street's reaction to Whitworth's two treaties was mixed. That with Austria, providing for a new loan, would not be ratified. Whitworth's act was disavowed and Grenville seriously considered recalling him in disgrace. Thanks to Vorontzoff's kindly intervention, however, the foreign secretary curbed his anger and sent instead a most severe reprimand to his agent.[55] The Russian subsidy treaty was certainly acceptable even though its implementation was conditional on Prussian cooperation.[56] As yet

52. The treaty is to be found in FO 65/41.
53. Whitworth to Grenville, December 13, 1798, FO 65/41.
54. Treaty with Russia, December 29, 1798, FO 94/206.
55. Vorontzoff to Grenville, January 22, 1799, *Manuscripts of J. B. Fortescue*, IV, 447-449; Minute of the Cabinet, January 10, 1799, Unpublished George III Letters, IX, 10-12. Grenville's dispatch to Whitworth of January 25, 1799 (FO 65/42), is probably one of the most stinging rebukes ever sent a British envoy from the Foreign Office.
56. Paul made clear in his letter to Vorontzoff of December 30, 1798 that this condition was to be taken seriously; *Manuscripts of J. B. Fortescue*, IV, 428.

there was no indication that Berlin was ready to act, and Grenville decided not to ratify the Russian convention for the time being.

By now Austria's duplicity had bred a hatred in the foreign secretary for which there was at least some justification. Despite the Hofburg's alliance with Naples, it refused to lift a finger to save that Italian state from the French assault which was launched in December 1798. Furthermore, it was hard to have faith in a government which, within the space of one week, could welcome the arrival of Russian troops in Vienna and engage in secret conversations with the Directory.[57] The unratified loan treaty remained a painful thorn in Britain's side, and Thugut refused to remove it. More and more Grenville's hopes turned on the outcome of his brother's mission at Berlin. If Britain could win Russia and Prussia to the concert, he was ready to let Vienna follow its own devious course in isolation. In such a case, British subsidy money would be divided between the Tsar and Frederick William.[58]

For the third time within a year Britain bent every effort to pry Prussia loose from her neutrality. In this she was zealously supported by the Tsar. Less than a week after the signing of the Anglo-Russian subsidy treaty, Paul instructed his minister at Berlin to urge Prussia to act openly against France. Panin set to work immediately only to discover that Haugwitz would discuss nothing until the long overdue British envoy appeared. The Prussian leader was especially anxious to learn what subsidies London would offer.[59] Almost a month passed before Thomas Grenville reached Berlin, nearly exhausted after his harrowing experience. He needed only a few days to understand conditions at the Prussian court: Haugwitz was ready to unite with Britain and Russia, but his colleagues and the King were reluctant to follow this lead. Most of the Prussian ministers feared that union with the coalition would bring down the Directory's wrath on their heads. Why take such a risk when past experience proved that Britain was always ready to come to Prussia's support in time of need? "There is some disposition here," Thomas Grenville wrote his brother, "to deny the necessity of any active concert with England under the loose

57. Eden to Grenville, December 26, 29, 1798, FO 7/53.
58. Lord Grenville to T. Grenville, January, 1799, FO 64/53.
59. Paul I to Panin, January 3, 1799, and Panin to S. Vorontzoff, January 14, 1799, *Vorontsova*, XI, 273, 59.

notion that the hour of immediate attack on Prussia will always find Great Britain interested in [a] treaty to co-operate for the defence of Prussia."[60]

Everything Grenville learned at Berlin strengthened his belief that Prussia would do nothing. Even the offer of generous subsidies had no effect on ministers who were convinced that neutrality best served their interests. The blindness of the King and his advisers to the danger of their folly filled Thomas Grenville with contempt.[61] Even France's attack on Austria in March 1799 failed to arouse Prussia from her languor, although it did bring from Haugwitz a proposal that Britain, Prussia, and Russia join to protect the north German neutral zone against French aggression. Thomas Grenville disliked the plan, even though Haugwitz pointed out that "such a concert . . . might probably at no very distant period lead to offensive measures." Should such a three-power combination be formed, Prussia would require subsidies to maintain her forces on a war footing. In a word, Britain was expected to finance a Prussian army which might never have occasion to fire a shot in anger.[62]

These reports from Berlin filled Pitt and Lord Grenville with despair. The idea of a defensive combination was disappointing to ministers who sought Frederick William as an active ally against France. In any event, Britain would not subsidize a Prussian army to help it eat the bread of idleness. The foreign secretary was clearly tiring of the game and gloomily concluded "it will still be much more advantageous to know with certainty that nothing is to be expected from Prussia than to remain in a state of doubt."[63]

The coalition had yet to be formed by the time the War of the Second Coalition broke out. France's attack in March finally cut the Gordian knot for Vienna and forced her into a war she did not

60. T. Grenville to Lord Grenville, February 28, 1799, FO 64/53.

61. "Their fear of France . . . engrosses all their attention, and furnishes to them great and constant disquietude in the present, and serious apprehension for the future. But as there is no man of leading and commanding talents enough to show them the greatness of their danger . . . there is nothing done by the Government, and they are living on from day to day . . . but destitute of energy and activity" (T. Grenville to Buckingham, April 17, 1799, *Memoirs of the Court,* II, 437).

62. T. Grenville to Lord Grenville, March 10, 1799, FO 64/53. This proposal grew into a labyrinthine scheme to supplement a public defense pact with a secret convention setting forth the conditions under which Prussia would make war on France (T. Grenville to Lord Grenville, March 18, 1799, *Manuscripts of J. B. Fortescue,* IV, 501-503). See also Confidential Notes by De Luc, March 31, 1799, *ibid.,* IV, 524-527.

63. Lord Grenville to T. Grenville, March 15, 27, 1799, FO 64/53.

really want. Logically, the next step was for Britain, Russia, and Austria to unite against the Directory. The creation of such a confederacy was to be especially difficult, since diplomatic channels were clogged with the debris of Grenville's now defunct concert plan. Austria and Russia were united in an alliance which the Tsar had already honored by sending 17,000 troops to Vienna under the command of Suvoroff. Relations between Britain and Austria were worse than ever. Ratification of the disputed loan agreement was a point of honor which Pitt could not yield. Thugut's refusal to comply with this demand cast grave doubts on his sincerity.[64] The future of Britain's recent subsidy treaty with Russia was likewise uncertain since it was conditional on Prussian adherence. Even if the Tsar waived this condition, how could 45,000 Russian troops be effectively employed? Probably they would have to be sent to support the Imperial army in central Europe. An Italian campaign, however, would do nothing to effect the liberation of Holland, which was always close to Pitt's heart. That could be accomplished only by bringing Prussia to join with Russia and Britain in a northern campaign.

In the spring of 1799 British leaders were forced to make a major policy decision. On the one hand, it could be argued that since the Prussian negotiation was clearly unprofitable, Britain ought to forge a war union with Russia and Austria. Such a decision would oblige Pitt to compromise his quarrel with the Hofburg and provide subsidies. More important, Britain would commit herself to a war in Italy and the Rhineland. On the other hand, if there was the slightest chance of securing Berlin's active cooperation, Pitt might justifiably concentrate all his energies on achieving that goal. This would mean leaving Austria to her own fate and forming an Anglo-Prussian-Russian league to drive the French from Holland. Subsidies spent to finance such an alliance would at least go to promote a vital British interest. But there was always the danger that, in the end, Prussia would again prove false and leave her allies to shift for themselves.

Britain's use of subsidies between 1797 and 1799 makes clear how basically selective her policy was. The traditional idea of Pitt using bright British guineas to tempt any and all powers to fight

---

64. For the reasons why Thugut may have been reluctant to ratify the 1797 treaty, see Helleiner, *Imperial Loans,* pp. 110-122.

his war with France certainly does not apply here. The nation's resources were far too limited to permit such prodigality. At the outset, £2,000,000 a year was set as the limit for Britain's foreign aid program—a limit which the prime minister finally had to increase to £3,500,000. Russia's decision to take arms against France, together with a growing uneasiness about Vienna's plans, forced a revision of that plan. Austria's success in winning the Tsar's sympathy compelled Pitt to modify his plan once more, this time in favor of a division of the subsidy money among the three allies. But Britain's burning wish was for an alliance with the northern powers, and when, at the beginning of 1799, it appeared that Prussia might finally rally to the cause, the prime minister abandoned all idea of aiding the Hofburg. It was almost axiomatic that Britain's generosity toward Austria waxed or waned depending upon whether reports from Berlin were bad or good. If both German powers could not be brought into the concert, Pitt did not hesitate to choose between them.

While no nation was willing to fight France without British financial help, the offer of subsidies had little effect on their decision to take arms. Prussia could easily have commanded at least £1,000,000 in British money at any time. The various negotiations which occurred at Berlin make clear that what Prussia lacked was not the means, but the will. Britain's 1796 subsidy proposal to Catherine the Great lay dormant at St. Petersburg for nearly two years until French aggression in the East sparked a response from her successor. Because Austria's position was unusually delicate, her policy was more devious and unsteady. Balanced precariously between peace and war, Thugut regarded the pledge of British money as a valuable card to play in his diplomatic game with the Directory. That game abruptly came to an end in March 1798 when the French attack on the Empire left Vienna with no choice but to fight. Of all the great powers, Britain and Russia alone were committed to war with France in order to restore the European equilibrium. Separated by an entire continent, they could do little without the cooperation of either Prussia or Austria.

VI

THE SECOND COALITION

Britain's diplomatic plans were in no way altered by the fact that Austria and France were now at war. An alliance with Prussia and Russia to free Holland remained the pole star of Pitt's policy. Before the year ended, events blasted the basis on which the prime minister had built his plans; Prussia refused to give up her neutrality, while the Tsar, infuriated by Austria's obscurantism, abandoned the contest. Britain was thus forced into tardy agreement with Austria, the one power whose support she had hitherto valued least.

Although the Hofburg had gone to war without enthusiasm, the Imperial armies fought well and scored unexpected victories over the enemy. Still more surprising was the striking power of the 17,000 Russians sent by the Tsar to support his ally. This army reached Vienna in March and was joined by 33,000 Imperial troops. Supreme command was given to the Russian general, Count Suvoroff, who at once pushed forward into Lombardy.[1] The French were stretched dangerously thin along a line running from the Rhine to Naples. Suvoroff struck at the weak midpoint of that line and drove the enemy back under a succession of sledgehammer blows. Within a few weeks Verona, Turin, and Mantua had all fallen to the allies. Suvoroff then turned on the enemy's armies fleeing northward from Naples. Once they had been crushed, he proposed to invade France. The myth of French invincibility had finally been exploded, and hopes ran high that the war would be over before the end of the year.

1. Lobanov-Rostovsky, *Russia and Europe,* pp. 31-33.

The Tsar was caught up in the enthusiasm of the moment, and in March he informed London that he was ready to implement their recent subsidy agreement, regardless of what Berlin might finally decide.[2] Paul's offer presented the Cabinet with a difficult problem. What was the best use Britain could make of 45,000 Russian troops at this moment? Should they be held in reserve until Prussia agreed to join in liberating Holland, or should they be sent to swell the ranks of Suvoroff's legions? A Prusso-Russian expedition against Holland was much to be preferred, but Thomas Grenville's latest reports made clear that Berlin was not yet ready to act.[3] In the end, the Cabinet accepted the Tsar's offer and requested that the subsidized troops be sent to drive the enemy from Switzerland. Once that had been accomplished, they could join Suvoroff's army and take part in the invasion of France.[4]

Lord Grenville hoped that the succession of defeats which France had suffered in Italy would soon prove a powerful inducement for Prussia to draw the sword. If Suvoroff's victories continued, he predicted that they might "rouse the Prussians, in order that they may come in for their share of the fruits of victory; but although this would not be a very magnanimous motive of action, I should be well content to take the war, and leave the motive to shift for itself."[5]

This prediction was not merely wishful-thinking. Late in April Count Haugwitz was so impressed by the allied successes that he initiated discussions with the British envoy regarding the future of Holland. Thomas Grenville seized this opportunity to make a strong appeal to Prussia's cupidity. Britain had all along been ready to subsidize Prussia, but that guarantee could not be held out indefinitely. The Cabinet was already financing the Tsar and it might soon be necessary to subsidize Austria, too.[6] If Prussia delayed her decision much longer, she might find the British Treasury empty. Grenville warned that Haugwitz must decide

---

2. Grenville to Whitworth, March 15, 1799, FO 65/42.

3. On March 18, 1799 Thomas Grenville informed the foreign secretary that "the immediate co-operation of the Court of Berlin in open hostilities to France is now not to be relied upon" (FO 64/53).

4. Grenville to Whitworth, March 27, 1799, FO 65/42.

5. Lord Grenville to T. Grenville, April 16, 1799, *Manuscripts of J. B. Fortescue,* V, 11-12.

6. This was probably a calculated maneuver to exploit Prussia's jealousy of Austria. The Cabinet was certainly not considering offering subsidies to Austria at this time.

quickly "whether Prussia would now avail itself of the pecuniary assistance of Great Britain for an enterprize which Prussia itself will probably be calling for six weeks hence."

Thomas Grenville's arguments were effective, and a few days later Haugwitz offered him a scheme for Anglo-Prussian cooperation to drive the enemy from Holland. Since the Directory had reduced its garrisons in that country to a minimum, Haugwitz estimated that 60,000 Prussian troops could free the country within six months. If Russia joined in the campaign, the time required might be considerably less. Britain would be expected to pay Prussia £200,000 in preparation money and additional subsidies amounting to £1,000,000 for a six month campaign. However, it must be clearly understood that Prussia was only interested in liberating Holland, after which she would return to a defensive policy.[7] Haugwitz' offer was immediately sent to London, along with a private warning from the British minister. So far, Frederick William had not approved the plan, although Haugwitz believed that he finally would. Thomas Grenville was not so sure. He admitted, however, that if the King did adopt the plan, it would doubtless achieve its purpose before the close of 1799.[8]

This latest news from Berlin sent London's hopes for victory soaring; £1,200,000 was an outrageous price to pay for six months of Prussian cooperation, but the expense would be trifling if Holland could be wrenched from the French.[9] Pitt had visions of allied armies invading France's northern and eastern frontiers before the summer turned to autumn. Such enthusiasm was bound to be infectious, and the Cabinet immediately accepted the Prussian offer.[10]

More than ever Pitt was determined that the Low Countries must be free. Joint operations undertaken by Britain, Prussia, and Russia would surely accomplish it, probably within the time limit specified by Haugwitz. In the event Prussia drew back, as Thomas Grenville warned might be the case, Pitt was prepared to

7. Thomas Grenville sent the foreign secretary a detailed report of his conversations with Haugwitz, dated April 28, 1799 (FO 64/53).
8. T. Grenville to Lord Grenville, April 30, 1799, *Manuscripts of J. B. Fortescue,* V, 33-36.
9. T. Grenville to Lord Grenville, May 9, 1799, *ibid.,* V, 45-46.
10. Lord Grenville to T. Grenville, May 7, 1799, FO 64/54.

undertake an Anglo-Russian invasion of Holland by sea. This represented no reversal of the earlier British decision to use the subsidized Russians in Switzerland. That force, commanded by General Rimsky-Korsakoff, was now on its way and would probably reach Switzerland by July.[11] The prime minister proposed to hire a second Russian corps for operations against Holland during the summer. Whitworth was therefore ordered to obtain an additional 40,000 to 45,000 Russians, to be paid for at the same rate specified in the 1798 subsidy treaty.[12] It was just as well that Pitt's plans did not depend upon Prussian support. In May Haugwitz confessed that Frederick William would run no risk of war with France. Thomas Grenville remained at Berlin throughout the summer, hoping for a change in Prussian policy. In September he finally admitted defeat and left for home in disgust.[13]

Meanwhile, Austrian and Russian policies had clashed violently in the wake of Suvoroff's Italian victories. Thugut's wish to absorb the Italian lands taken from the French was at cross-purposes with Paul's plan to restore them to their legitimate rulers. The quarrel reached dangerous proportions when the Hofburg blocked Suvoroff's attempt to re-establish the House of Savoy. Unless quickly resolved, this conflict of wills would destroy the Austro-Russian alliance. At this point, Britain intervened and proposed that Suvoroff's forces be sent to join those of Rimsky-Korsakoff in Switzerland. With the assistance of the units of the Imperial army already there, the Russians could liberate Switzerland and then invade France by use of Franche Comté.[14] Undertaken in conjunction with the proposed invasion of Holland, such a campaign would materially contribute to victory over the French.

Pitt snatched enough time during these weeks of planning strategy to arrange for the subsidy payments due Russia for Korsakoff's army. The Tsar had insisted that all payments be made into his account in London since this would benefit Russia's rate

11. Rimsky-Korsakoff's army was expected to cross the Russian frontier on May 4, at which time the first subsidy payment would fall due. See Whitworth to Lord Grenville, April 30, 1799, FO 65/42.
12. Lord Grenville to Whitworth, May 3, 7, and 23, 1799, FO 65/42.
13. T. Grenville to Lord Grenville, May 13, 1799, FO 64/54. For an account of Thomas Grenville's mission see D. C. Elliot, "The Grenville Mission to Berlin, 1799," *Huntington Library Quarterly,* 18 (1954-1955), 129-146.
14. Grenville to Whitworth, June 26, 1799, FO 65/43.

of exchange. On June 6 the Treasury remitted the first subsidy installment, amounting to £75,000, to the Tsar's London bankers, Harman, Hoare and Company. This was the same firm which had handled the Prussian subsidy of 1794.[15] Two days later the prime minister requested the Commons to vote £825,000 for the Russian subsidy during the balance of the year. By now Fox had ceased to attend Parliament and his colleague, George Tierney, led the fight against Pitt's proposal. So far as paying Russian troops was concerned, Tierney frankly admitted that "if more blood is to be shed, it should be any other than English blood." The whig spokesman directed his fire chiefly against the government's war goals. This prompted Pitt to make a spirited defense of his policy which he described as "security, just security, with a little mixture of indemnification." Debate on the war soon overshadowed the subsidy issue and the House finally granted the government's request without a division.[16]

Whitworth found the Tsar eager to support the British plan for a joint invasion of Holland, but he could not spare as many troops as Pitt desired. After some negotiation, Russia offered 17,583 soldiers for this service in return for a preparation subsidy of £88,000 and monthly payments of £44,000. Britain also agreed to furnish at least 8,000 of her own troops to cooperate with the Russians.[17] The only difficulty Whitworth encountered had to do with arrangements for the transport of the Russian force. Tsar Paul was ready to supply the ships for this purpose, but he insisted that Britain pay generously for them. After much sharp bargaining, Whitworth finally promised Russia an additional £19,642 each month for the use of the Tsar's transports.[18] Payment of all subsidies under this treaty would begin as soon as the force embarked at Revel.

Britain had done everything possible to launch two major

15. Grenville to Whitworth, no. 36, June, 1799, FO 65/43; Whitworth to Grenville, June 29, 1799, FO 65/43; King's Warrant Book, Ty. 52/85, 125, 137. All payments made to Russia under the 1798 treaty appear to have been to the Tsar's London bankers. See Harman, Hoare and Co. to Charles Long, September 18, 1800, FO 65/47.

16. *Parliamentary History,* XXXIV, 1043-1055.

17. Treaty with Russia, June 22, 1799, FO 93/81(1). A secret article (FO 93/81 [2]) expressed the hope that Sweden might be persuaded to join in the invasion. Britain applied to Sweden, but that country refused to furnish troops unless heavily paid. See Grenville to Whitworth, August 1, 1799, FO 65/44.

18. Grenville believed that valuable time would be lost if British transports had to be sent to the Baltic for this purpose. See Grenville's Minute on the Expedition to Holland, July 10, 1799, *Manuscripts of J. B. Fortescue,* V, 130-133.

campaigns which hopefully would crush the enemy before the close of 1799. At a cost of about £140,000 a month (not including preparation payments) she financed the mobilization of two Russian armies which, at least on paper, totaled more than 62,000 men. In fact Korsakoff's army in Switzerland amounted to only 27,000, rather than the 45,000 specified in the 1798 subsidy treaty. On learning this, Grenville insisted that the Tsar either bring that army up to force, or accept a proportionate reduction in the subsidy.[19]

On August 27 British troops commanded by General Sir Ralph Abercrombie made an unopposed landing in North Holland. A week later they were joined by 6,000 Russians, the first of the Tsar's contingents to arrive. Nearly a month passed before the allied army, now led by the Duke of York, moved against the French near Alkmaar. The assault was a costly failure in which more than 3,500 allied troops fell, the bulk of them Russians. From this point, the fortunes of the invaders declined and the Duke of York finally had to evacuate his force from Holland. The allied troops were withdrawn to Yarmouth, where the Russians startled the townspeople by drinking the oil from the street lamps. In time, the Tsar's soldiers were transferred to winter quarters in the remote Channel Islands.[20]

19. The foreign secretary was especially irked by the fact that subsidy payments, which had begun in June, were based on the assumption that Korsakoff's army actually numbered 45,000. At the moment he chose not to make an issue of the overpayment. Instead, he ordered Whitworth to persuade Paul to bring the army up to 45,000 (Grenville to Whitworth, August 1, 1799, FO 65/44). Paul admitted the justice of the complaint, but explained that he had no more troops to spare. Instead, he proposed to attach to Korsakoff's command a small Russian force of about 10,000 under General Rehbinder which had been sent to aid Naples. This would bring the total to about 35,000.

Grenville accepted this offer, but noted that it left two problems yet unsolved. First, the overpayment of the preparation money and the monthly subsidies begun in June. This overpayment could be deducted from the postwar debt Britain had agreed to pay. Second, Grenville demanded that all future subsidies be paid on the basis of an actual monthly muster of Korsakoff's and Rehbinder's troops (Grenville to Whitworth, November, 1799, FO 65/45). The Tsar vigorously opposed this since it would result in a steady decrease of the monthly subsidy (Whitworth to Grenville, September 24, 1799, FO 65/44). No satisfactory solution to either of these problems was ever reached. In a small way, this disagreement contributed to the deterioration of Anglo-Russian relations which marred the closing months of 1799.

20. Fortescue's account of the invasion (*British Army*, IV, 639-710) should be supplemented by A. B. Piechowiak, "The Anglo-Russian Expedition to Holland in 1799," *Slavonic and East European Review*, 41 (1962-1963), 182-195. It is impossible to disagree with the latter's conclusion that the failure of the expedition "was due to military mismanagement preceded by political misconception" (p. 190). See also John A. Lukacs, "Russian Armies in Western Europe; 1799, 1814, 1917," *American Slavic and East European Review*, 13 (1954), 319-337.

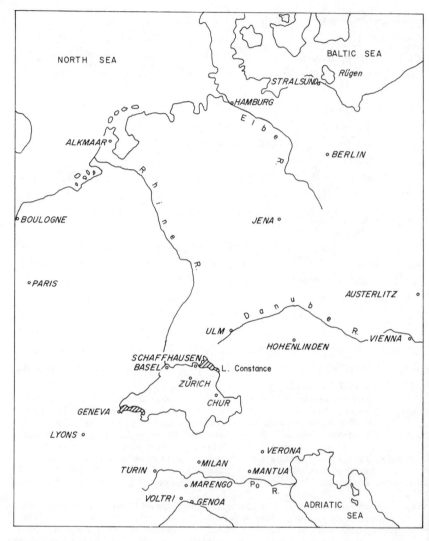

2. Campaign Area of the Second Coalition

Disaster of a different sort befell the Russian armies in central Europe. In August Rimsky-Korsakoff's corps reached Switzerland and joined the Austrians under the Archduke Charles. On the approach of Masséna's army, the Archduke withdrew, leaving his allies to defend Zurich as best they could. Masséna fell on the Russians and mercilessly drove them back to Schaffhausen. Meanwhile, Suvoroff's men were making their way northward through the Alpine passes in what was probably the most heroic undertaking of the entire war. Only on reaching Muotta did Suvoroff learn that he could expect no help from Korsakoff. The position of the Russians was now desperate. Deserted by the Austrians, who either could not or would not supply them with food and ammunition, the Tsar's army was in no condition to encounter Masséna. Suvoroff therefore decided that he must avoid the enemy by turning to the East, even though this would force his men to travel the dread Panixer pass. On October 8 what remained of the exhausted Russian force finally straggled into Chur. Burning with resentment at Austria's treatment, Suvoroff left Switzerland behind him and went into winter quarters on the north shore of Lake Constance.[21]

Grenville was undaunted by the collapse of operations in Holland and Switzerland and at once began to salvage from its remnants the materials needed to undertake a new campaign. Austria's failure to aid the Russians filled him with "rage and despair"; the Hofburg's treachery was unforgivable.[22] The next campaign must not depend on Hapsburg cooperation for success.[23] Victory could still be won if Russia was willing to pour forth her manpower. The Tsar's troops now wintering in the Channel Islands would join with British units in the spring for an invasion of Britanny. Reinforcements should be sent from Russia to swell the battered armies of Korsakoff and Suvoroff to between 70,000 and 100,000 men. If all went as planned, France would soon be forced to defend herself against invaders in both Brittany

---

21. Lobanov-Rostovsky, *Russia and Europe,* pp. 43-64. The 1799 campaign ruined Suvoroff's health. The Tsar turned against him, and he died in St. Petersburg the following May. The British minister, Whitworth, was the only dignitary to attend his funeral.
22. Grenville to Vorontzoff, September 14, 1799, *Manuscripts of J. B. Fortescue,* V, 400.
23. Grenville to Dundas, October 19, 1799, *ibid.,* V, 487.

and Franche Comté. To help Paul carry out his part in this grand design, the Cabinet proposed to give him £3,500,000 during the coming year. Illconceived and unrealistic as these plans were, Grenville ordered Whitworth to present them at St. Petersburg as a firm offer. The foreign secretary never seemed to doubt that the Tsar would be both willing and able to agree.[24]

Paul's displeasure with the failure of the Dutch invasion was trivial in comparison to his rage on learning of the Hofburg's perfidy.[25] The quarrel over Sardinia had already damaged his faith in Austria, and he now held her responsible for the debacle which had befallen him in Switzerland. Late in October he renounced his alliance with Vienna and swore that he would never again cooperate with her. Paul assured Whitworth that he would remain at war with France, but only in alliance with Great Britain.[26]

By the time London learned of this decision, the Cabinet was having serious misgivings about the value of the Anglo-Russian entente. If Paul meant that Britain must work with him to the exclusion of Austria, Grenville doubted whether the government should agree. What had happened during the last few weeks to lessen the value of that Russian cooperation for which the foreign secretary had offered £3,500,000 a year? Recently, Pitt, Grenville, and Dundas had been studying the reports on the Dutch expedition and from them they concluded that the fighting quality of the Russians had been grossly overrated.[27] At the same time, dispatches arrived from British agents which described in glowing terms the increasing effectiveness and morale of the Imperial armies. The movement of the Austrians toward the lower Rhine suggested that the Hofburg might at last be ready to fight for the freedom of the Low Countries.[28]

Grenville prepared new instructions for Whitworth on November 12, greatly modifying those sent to him two weeks before. The

---

24. Grenville to Whitworth, November 1, 1799, FO 65/45. The Cabinet had approved this war plan on October 26. See Minute of the Cabinet, October 26, 1799, Unpublished George III Letters, IX, 307-308.

25. Paul was frankly unhappy with the selection of the Duke of York to command the Dutch expedition. See F. Martens, *Recueil des Traités*, IX, 429.

26. Whitworth to Grenville, October 27, 1799, FO 65/44; Paul I to S. Vorontzoff, October 15 [o.s.], 1799, *Manuscripts of J. B. Fortescue*, VI, 35-36.

27. Pitt to Grenville, November 21, 1799, *ibid.*, VI, 35-36.

28. Wm. Wickham to Grenville, December 13, 1799, *ibid.*, VI, 72-74.

latest British war plans assumed that Austria and Russia would continue to work together in the coalition. Referring to his previous offer of a £3,500,000 subsidy for the Tsar, the foreign secretary made clear that "You are therefore to consider the whole of these Instructions as made void by any event which might arise in the meanwhile to separate that Power [Austria] from the General System which it has hitherto pursued in concert with Russia and England."[29] If the Tsar carried through his threat to break with Vienna, Austria would probably be driven to make peace with the enemy. Even if that did not happen, Britain did not want to be forced to choose between Vienna and St. Petersburg.[30]

In the best of times life for a British envoy at the Russian court was difficult enough, but the assignment given Whitworth by London made his situation unbearable. Paul's instability grew almost daily, and it was usually unsafe for anyone to discuss the war with him. In such a climate, Whitworth needed all the courage he could command to bring London's latest policy statement before the Tsar. Paul's reaction was unexpectedly temperate. Since Britain attached such importance to Austrian support, he would continue his alliance with the Hofburg on two conditions: Thugut must be dismissed and Austria would have to agree to a status quo ante territorial settlement in Italy.[31]

This decision put the British Cabinet in the very position it was most anxious to avoid. Austria would never accept the Tsar's demands, and Britain would be forced to choose between cooperation with Russia or Austria. Early in February the Cabinet reached a decision: plans for extensive military cooperation with the Tsar were canceled. The subsidies due under the 1798 treaty for the service of Korsakoff's army would be paid in full, but Britain would continue the 1799 agreement only if the Tsar agreed to allow his troops now in the Channel Islands to be used in forays against the French coast. Should Paul resent Britain's decision to strengthen her ties with Austria, rather than Russia, Whitworth was to tell him that London must use its money "in the support of that Power [Austria] which alone continues to act offensively and

29. Grenville to Whitworth, November 12, 1799, FO 65/45.
30. Grenville to Whitworth, November 23, 1799, FO 65/45.
31. Whitworth to Grenville, November 28, December 5, 1799, FO 65/45; Paul I to S. Vorontzoff, December 2 [o.s.], 1799, *Manuscripts of J. B. Fortescue,* VI, 109-110.

vigorously against the irreconcilable Enemies of His Majesty & of the General tranquillity of Europe."[32]

This only rubbed salt into the Tsar's wounds, and he rejected with contempt the suggestion that his soldiers be employed in assaults on Brittany. Orders were issued for the immediate recall of Russian troops abroad. By April 1800 they were all once more in their homeland and the British alliance was at an end. Inevitably, Whitworth was the target for Paul's scorn and he was soon declared persona non grata. Relief for the harassed emissary finally came in the form of a recall from Grenville, made sweeter by announcement of his elevation to the Irish peerage as Baron Whitworth of Newport Pratt.[33]

All that now remained was for Britain to close the Russian subsidy accounts under the treaties of 1798 and 1799. Monthly payments were made until the Tsar's troops all returned to their country.[34] Still to be settled was the problem of the postwar debt, which the 1798 treaty obliged Britain to pay. Russia insisted on receiving the full amount due, but the Treasury contended that the overpayment of subsidies for Korsakoff's armies first be deducted. Disagreement on this matter was acrimonious and the issue was not finally settled until 1802 when, out of deference to the new Tsar, Alexander I, Britain offered £263,000.[35] The remittance of that sum in 1802-1803 finally closed the account.*

On the same day the Foreign Office notified Whitworth that Britain's war union with Russia was at an end, dispatches were sent to Vienna with an offer of £1,600,000 during 1800. Thanks to the Tsar's conduct, London and Vienna were obliged to end the quarrel which had kept them apart for nearly three years. The

32. Grenville to Whitworth, February 8, 1800, FO 65/46.

33. Whitworth's recall ended eleven years of service at the Russian capital. During the brief period of peace which followed the Treaty of Amiens he served as British minister to France. He was finally given an English peerage and enjoyed it until his death in 1825.

34. Charles Long to George Hammond [?], July 29, 1800, FO 65/47.

35. Lord Hawkesbury to Lord St. Helens, June 5, 1802, FO 65/50.

*Between June 1799 and June 1800 the Treasury paid £1,934,459 in subsidies to Russia to cover Britain's obligations under the treaties of 1798 and 1799. This does not include £263,000 paid as a postwar debt in 1802-1803. However, it does include the cost of the Russian transports arranged for in the 1799 agreement. It also includes commissions to the banking firms which handled the subsidy, as well as miscellaneous charges. Excluding these extra charges, where they can be determined, subsidy payments under both treaties were as follows:

future of the coalition now depended on whether they would be able to create a partnership of trust to carry on the war.

Austria's refusal to ratify the 1797 loan treaty was as reprehensible as Pitt's insistence that there could not otherwise be any cooperation between the two governments.[36] Thugut's inexplicable perversity greatly annoyed Grenville, especially when compounded by the Austrian's quarrel with Russia in the summer of 1799. "The thing that perplexes me most," the foreign secretary wrote his brother, "in this and in every other part of my business is the conduct of Thugut. If he were paid to thwart all our measures, and to favour those of France, he could not do it more effectually."[37] For some time the Foreign Office had been less than satisfied with Sir Morton Eden's conduct of the Vienna mission. Eden was not by nature a forceful person and he had fallen under Thugut's influence. In June 1799 he was allowed to retire from the service and Lord Minto was named to take his place.[38] The foreign secretary reminded the new envoy that a

---

Treaty of 1798 (paid by Harman and Hoare)	£ 796,938
Treaty of 1799 (paid by Thornton and Smalley)	1,126,258
	£1,923,196

The payments made each year by both banks were as follows:

1799	£1,386,070
1800	537,126
1801	none
1802	200,000
1803	63,000

The data on which these calculations are based is as follows: C. Long to George Hammond, September 20, 1800, FO 65/47; Harman and Hoare to C. Long, September 18, 1800, FO 65/47; An Account of subsidies paid by Thornton and Smalley, August 23, 1800, FO 65/47. Treasury remittances to both banks are recorded in the King's Warrant Books as follows: Ty. 52/85, 125, 137. Payment of the postwar debt in 1802-1803 is recorded in the following volumes of the King's Warrant Books: Ty. 52/87, 364; Ty. 52/88, 22.

36. Eden doubted whether Austria would ever ratify the treaty; Eden to Grenville, April 10, 1799, FO 7/54.

37. Lord Grenville to T. Grenville, July 16, 1799, *Manuscripts of J. B. Fortescue*, V, 147.

38. Eden's retirement was not without honor and profit. He received an Irish peerage as Lord Henley, as well as an annual pension of £2,000.

Sir Gilbert Elliot (1751-1814) was a Scot who had served as British viceroy in Corsica between 1794 and 1796. There he had clashed with Sir John Moore, who found him difficult and unreliable (Oman, *Moore*, p. 85 and *passim*). In 1798 Elliot was created Earl Minto. His Viennese mission was his only diplomatic experience, and he is better remembered for his service as governor-general of India between 1807 and 1813.

restoration of good relations between the two governments hinged upon Austria's ratification of the disputed treaty. Privately, he warned Minto to beware the blandishments of the Hapsburg court and insisted that he be "very stout" with Thugut.[39]

Minto's first dispatches from Vienna held out no hope for any significant change in Hapsburg policy. Thugut was always willing to discuss the 1797 treaty, but he showed no inclination to ratify it. When pressed for an explanation, the Austrian statesman declared that the terms of the 1797 loan had been grossly unfair. Dutifully, Minto reported this to London but added his own belief that "Baron Thugut appears not to have acquir'd the first elements of the science of finance." The Austrian minister's chief interest was in swallowing Italian land, and Minto correctly guessed that this was "the pivot, on which their whole system would hereafter turn." Should Britain and Russia thwart this ambition, it might throw the Hofburg into the arms of France.[40] Here was the real source of trouble between London and Vienna, rather than the wretched 1797 loan treaty. Pitt and Thugut looked in opposite directions; the one toward the liberation of the Low Countries, the other toward gains in northern Italy.

The breakup of the Austro-Russian alliance and the imminent withdrawal of the Tsar's armies from central Europe made it impossible for the Hofburg to keep Britain at arm's length much longer. In November 1799 Thugut announced that a mercenary force must be recruited in Germany to replace the Russian troops who were soon to withdraw. Since Austria lacked the means to recruit such a corps, she must look to Britain for the money. Minto seized this opportunity to reopen the question of the 1797 treaty, a maneuver which led Thugut to end the conference. A few days later, however, the British envoy was told that the Emperor had at last decided to ratify the loan treaty of 1797. Almost at once, Thugut explained to Minto the aid which Austria would require of Britain in the coming year. To begin with, London must hire 30,000 German mercenaries to serve with the Imperial forces.

39. Grenville to Minto, June, 1799, FO 7/56; Grenville to T. Grenville, September 29, 1799, *Manuscripts of J. B. Fortescue,* V, 431. Grenville himself was ready to be "very stout" with Austria. During the summer of 1799 Starhemberg had the temerity to request a subsidy for Austria. The foreign secretary cut him very short. See Grenville's account of the incident in his letter to Lord Mulgrave of August 3, 1799, *ibid.,* V, 234.
40. Minto to Grenville August 11 and 17, 1799, FO 7/56.

She must also continue the payments on the loans of 1795 and 1797 and make fresh advances toward a third, which Austria would undertake at the close of the war. The size of the advances would depend on whether Britain was willing to allow Austria to mobilize and pay the 30,000 mercenaries, the arrangement which Thugut preferred. In that case, Vienna would require a total of £2,400,000 for the year. Should Britain prefer to deal with the mercenaries herself, then Vienna would need only £1,600,000. In either case, all remittances must be made to Austria on the Continent in specie.[41]

The bitter winter weather delayed the arrival of Thugut's proposal in London until early February 1800. It could scarely have been more welcome. One month before, Pitt had spurned a peace proposal offered by the new French government under Bonaparte as First Consul. At the same time, there were serious doubts whether Britain's alliance with the Tsar could last much longer. Since the future of the war clearly depended on cooperation between London and Vienna, the Cabinet promptly accepted the Austrian plan. Grenville informed Minto that Britain would undertake the formation of the mercenary corps and advance £1,600,000 to Austria during 1800. Although the foreign secretary was delighted with Thugut's decision to ratify the 1797 treaty, his suspicions had not been entirely removed. Minto must insist on two conditions in return for Britain's promise of support: "The first that no negotiation shall be entered into nor overture entertained except in common—and the second that the Archduke [commanding the Imperial forces] shall not be restrained by any Secret Instructions from His Court from following up to the utmost any Successes which He may obtain."[42] Later that month Grenville and Starhemberg formally exchanged ratifications of the 1797 loan convention, thereby bringing that tiresome issue to an end. Informing Minto of this, Grenville expressed an opinion doubtless shared by all parties concerned: "It is no small satisfaction to me to reflect that I shall have no more to write, nor

41. Minto to Grenville, November 12, December 1, 10, 13, 1799, FO 7/57. Minto believed that the money hitherto used to help Russia would be better spent in employing mercenaries. See Minto to Wm. Wickham, December 4, 1799, *The Correspondence of the Right Honourable William Wickham from the Year 1794*. edited by his grandson, William Wickham (London, 1870), II, 341.
42. Grenville to Minto, February 8, 1800, FO 7/58.

you to read, on the subject of the eternal dispute about the ratification. We are now to begin a new score with our Austrian friends and we must hope the best."[43]

Since London had accepted Austria's terms, a treaty of alliance and subsidy should have been concluded at once. It was not. Thugut's fondness for intrigue drew him along a different course, which confirmed all Grenville's deep-seated fears. In March, when Minto informed the Austrian leader that London had accepted his proposal, the chancellor received this news with what seemed to Minto "the greatest possible coldness in language and manner." Instead of £1,600,000 in advances, Thugut announced, Austria would require £2,000,000. Certain that Austria was secretly negotiating with France, Minto now charged Thugut with double-dealing. The Austrian admitted that France had offered him virtually a free hand in Italy.[44] The heated exchange which followed ended all hope of alliance between the two governments for the moment. Grenville was not surprised when he learned of this, for he had already predicted that "it will all end in a separate Austrian peace, whenever Bonaparte feels himself sufficiently pressed to think it worth his while to give the conditions, whatever they are, which Thugut means to require."[45]

In spite of this setback, Britain went ahead with the mobilization of the German mercenaries. The handling of the many complex problems involved required the service of an agent of unusual capacity. Grenville knew the one man the government could count on to undertake the mission with perfect confidence: the onetime British envoy to the Swiss cantons, William Wickham. Between 1795 and 1797, Wickham had served his country well in Switzerland, both in his official capacity and secretly as chief British espionage agent. His conduct won Grenville's respect for his ability and integrity. It also won him the hatred of the Directory, which finally forced the Swiss to expel him. Wickham returned to Switzerland in the summer of 1799, and the following

43. Grenville to Minto, February 13, 1800, *Manuscripts of J. B. Fortescue,* VI, 124. On February 17 Pitt informed the House of Commons that £2,500,000 would be needed to carry out plans for cooperation with Austria during 1800. Only nineteen members voted against giving the money. See *Parliamentary History*, XXXIV, 1438-1458.

44. Minto to Grenville, April 10, 1800, FO 7/58. As early as February 23, 1800, Minto warned Grenville that secret discussions were taking place between Vienna and Paris. See *Manuscripts of J. B. Fortescue,* VI, 139-140.

45. Grenville to Minto, March 28, 1800, *ibid.,* VI, 186.

February he was instructed to recruit the 30,000 troops needed by Austria. One million pounds were set aside for his use in hiring the mercenaries.[46]

Wickham first applied to the Elector of Bavaria for 12,000 troops, and after much intrigue and haggling the Elector finally agreed. By the treaty of March 16 Britain promised to pay the Elector the traditional preparation money and to maintain the troops while in her service. The Bavarian treaty was the prototype for all other engagements Wickham made with the German states. In one important respect it differed from the treaties for the employment of mercenaries Britain had concluded during the First Coalition: the Elector received no subsidy other than the specified preparation money.[47] Early in April the Circle of Swabia undertook to provide between 6,500 and 8,000 infantry on the same terms. Agreements signed that same month with Württemberg and Mayence added another 8,000 men to the growing corps. By the time the summer ended, Wickham had sent more than 30,000 auxiliaries to serve with the Imperial army at British expense.[48]

Austria's victory over Masséna at Voltri in April 1800 placed Thugut in a truly enviable position. On one side, Britain was ready to pay £1,600,000 to obtain an Austrian alliance. On the other, France offered Vienna extensive lands in northern Italy. London would have to pay dearly for her alliance with Austria, and early in May Thugut announced that the price would be increased. Britain must advance £2,000,000 to Austria during the present year and agree to support Vienna's plans for annexation of Italian land.[49]

Under the circumstances, Grenville had to submit to this blackmail. He informed Minto that Britain would agree to almost any Austrian demands, provided only that she were really in earnest about the war. "But while we remain in total uncertainty

46. Grenville's instructions to Wickham, February 11, 1800, are to be found in FO 74/29. William Wickham is one of the most interesting figures of this period, and he has at last begun to attract the attention he deserves. See Harvey Mitchell, *The Underground War Against Revolutionary France: The Missions of William Wickham, 1794-1800* (Oxford, 1965), and W. R. Fryer, *Republic or Restoration in France, 1794-1797* (Manchester, Eng., 1965).

47. Wickham to Grenville, March 5, 1800, FO 74/29; Treaty with Bavaria, March 16, 1800, FO 74/29.

48. Wickham to Grenville, April 5, 1800, FO 74/30; Wickham to Grenville, July 14, 1800, FO 74/31; Wickham to George Rose, August 4, 1800, FO 74/31.

49. Minto to Grenville, May 2, 8, 1800, FO 7/58.

as to the Main Question of Peace and War and see the Austrian Minister at the same moment professing a desire of intimate union and concert with this Government and on the other hand carrying on Negotiations with the common Enemy which he refuses to communicate to you, all our Measures and Resolutions are necessarily at a stand." Even so, Minto was given no blank check; he was to sign no treaty without London's prior approval. As proof of Britain's goodwill, £150,000 would be remitted to the Austrian treasury to replace military stores lost by the Imperial forces in the spring.[50]

Austria's response to the British offer was decided on the battlefield. In May Bonaparte led 40,000 troops across the Alps and within a month they had taken Milan. Thugut kept Minto at a distance while awaiting the results of a counteroffensive launched by the Imperial army. On June 14 the Austrians fell upon the enemy with such force that at the end of the day a message was sent to Vienna announcing a major victory. Although the French were badly beaten, Bonaparte refused to yield the field of Marengo. He returned to the attack and so badly mauled his opponent that the Hapsburg commander was forced to sue for an armistice.

Marengo put an end to Thugut's pirouette. On June 23 he and Minto hastily concluded an alliance agreeable to the terms endorsed by Grenville one month before. In line with Minto's latest instructions it was understood that the pact would not be binding until the Cabinet had approved it.[51] The first of the three

50. Grenville to Minto, May 13, 17, 21, 1800, FO 7/58.
51. The treaty was composed of three separate agreements. The public treaty (FO 94/14) contained the important terms. The second instrument (FO 94/15) was a joint declaration by the allies that they would take from France none of the lands which she had held prior to the Revolution. The third (FO 94/16) was a secret article setting forth in great detail the Italian territory Britain was ready to allow Austria to absorb. At Thugut's insistence, the agreement omitted the fact that Austria bound herself to maintain the Imperial army at 200,000 men. See Minto to Grenville, September 7, 1800, FO 7/60.

The dating of the alliance presents a curious problem. The text of the treaty indicates that it was signed on June 20, 1800, two days before the results of Marengo were known at Vienna. From this it has been concluded that the outcome of the battle had no effect on the conclusion of the treaty (*Camb. Hist. Brit. For. Pol.,* I, 296-297). However, on June 24 Minto explained to Grenville that while the treaty was *dated* June 20, it had actually been *signed* on June 23, the day after Vienna learned of Marengo (Chatham Papers, vol. 339). There is a gap in Minto's official correspondence in the Foreign Office papers. None of Minto's letters between May and September 1800 (including the dispatch just cited) are to be found in the Austrian volumes of the Foreign Office papers. The missing dispatches were discovered in vol. 339 of the Chatham Papers.

advances, amounting to £666,666:13:4, would be paid to Austria only when Downing Street had authorized it. For the moment, the Hofburg had no obligation to its ally and was free to do as it wished. The Italian campaign was over, but a second Austrian army was locked in combat with the enemy in southern Germany. A Hapsburg victory there would cancel out the defeat she had suffered at Marengo. Under the circumstances, Vienna might be well advised to enter into peace discussions with France. A few days after the Anglo-Austrian pact had been signed, Thugut informed Minto that an emissary had been sent to Paris for this purpose, although nothing was said about the instructions given him. When the British minister expressed concern over Austria's action, Thugut assured him that the real purpose of the mission was to gain time. Minto was not convinced.[52]

Although the Cabinet shared Minto's anxiety, it promptly approved the convention with Austria. On July 17 Grenville instructed Minto to pay the first installment of £666,666 due the Hofburg. Whether the two remaining advances (due in September and December) would be forthcoming depended upon Austria's future conduct. In the event Austria and France undertook a peace negotiation, the foreign secretary hoped that Britain would be invited to participate. Uncertain as to what Thugut would finally do, Pitt had no alternative but to assume that the recent alliance would hold fast. Minto's treaty was presented to Parliament on July 18 and the Commons voted £1,500,000 to help finance the government's policy.[53]

The Treasury encountered serious difficulty in remitting money to the Continent during the summer of 1800. For seven years England's great volume of trade with Germany helped her meet her war costs, but in 1799 the German money market collapsed and British exports sagged dangerously. Heavy subsidy payments to Russia in 1799-1800 reduced the volume of British credits in Germany. By the spring of 1800 bills of exchange issued by British agents on the Continent were being heavily discounted. Wickham, for example, complained that the commercial paper he used to pay for the mercenaries was being discounted at 10 percent and more. Unless the government sent specie to Hamburg to cover

52. Minto to Grenville, July 1, 1800, Chatham Papers, vol. 339.
53. Grenville to Minto, July 17, 1800, FO 7/59; Minto to Grenville, August 7, 1800, Chatham Papers, vol. 339; *Parliamentary History,* XXXV, 433-454.

these bills, the discount rate would go even higher.[54] Pitt came to the same conclusion. Over the stiff opposition of the Bank of England, the prime minister ordered specie sent to Hamburg for Wickham and Minto to use. Although Spanish silver made up the larger part of these shipments, the government was obliged to ship guineas as well.[55] For the first time, the legend of Pitt's guineas had some basis in fact. Fortunately, a rapid increase in Britain's export trade with the Continent soon ended the exchange problem—at least for the moment.[56]

The collapse of Austria's campaign in Germany settled the fate of her alliance with Britain. By the end of June, Munich had fallen to the enemy and the war was over. The best that Britain could now hope was that she might join her ally in arranging a general peace with France. Since the future was so uncertain, Minto was told to delay paying the second advance to Austria until orders were sent from London.[57] Thugut had been driven from power in the wake of Austria's debacle, and his position was now held by Count Louis Cobenzl, formerly Austria's minister to Russia. Early in November 1800 Cobenzl wrote directly to Grenville, explaining that so far he had resisted Bonaparte's demand that the Emperor conclude a separate peace. However, he warned that the war could begin whenever the French chose to renounce the armistice.[58] Within less than a month this prediction was borne out.

Cobenzl's good faith made a deep impression on the Cabinet. Since France clearly did not want peace, Britain must stand firm by her ally. In this spirit, Minto was directed to pay the second advance to Austria immediately upon the renewal of hostilities.[59] These instructions were dated December 2. That same day, General Moreau completed his preparation for the French attack on the Imperial army at Hohenlinden, scheduled to begin at dawn

54. Wickham to Grenville, March 26, 1800, FO 74/29.
55. On May 9, 1800 Pitt sent a sharply worded letter to the governor of the Bank reminding him that "The Expediency of making any remittance and the Amount to which it should be made are Points which I conceive to rest solely with the Direction of the Government, and the Legislature, and no part of the Responsibility which I consider thrown upon the Court [of the Bank]" (Chatham Papers, vol. 195). The export of specie was handled by Thornton's bank. The government's payments are recorded in the King's Warrant Book, Ty. 52/85, 7; Ty. 52/86, 4, 109-110. See also Samuel Thornton to Charles Long, September 24, 1800, FO 7/60.
56. Gayer, Rostow, and Schwartz, *British Economy*, I, 34-35.
57. Grenville to Minto, October 31, 1800, FO 7/61.
58. Cobenzl to Grenville, November 8, 1800, FO 7/61.
59. Grenville to Minto, December 2, 1800, FO 7/61.

the next day. In that battle, the Austrians, together with Wickham's mercenaries, were badly beaten. The total collapse of the Hapsburg war effort on all fronts forced Cobenzl to yield to the inevitable. In February 1801 a spearate treaty of peace between France and Austria was signed at Lunéville.

The circumstances leading to Austria's surrender made it impossible for the Cabinet to blame her for the decision to negotiate separately. Even before the Lunéville treaty was concluded, Grenville advised Minto that the ministers considered Austria guiltless: "The necessity under which the Emperor has acted, being unquestionably such as fairly to come within the description of those circumstances which release a Power from any engagements of this Nature however direct or positive."[60] On the other hand, the foreign secretary considered the payment of the second advance due Austria a waste of money, and he explained the simple logic of the matter to Minto: "It surely cannot be contended that it would be the same thing either in principle or in effect if, now that Austria is about to conclude an immediate peace, and when this aid is consequently no longer wanted for exertions in War, nor can be so applied, Great Britain left alone in the contest were obliged to distract and divide Her efforts, and to diminish her own defence by furnishing in any shape pecuniary relief to the finances of Her Ally no longer engaged in the War." If Minto's judgment on this matter was muddied by generous impulses, let him remember that Britain was still at war.[61]

Britain's brief and unsuccessful reunion with Austria cost her just over £2,000,000. Nearly two thirds of this went to pay for the mercenary corps created by William Wickham. Aside from Britain's gift of £150,000 to replace Austria's loss of war materials, the Hofburg received only £666,666:13:4. This was the first and only advance which Britain made under the short-lived alliance of June 1800. Since Vienna was never asked for repayment, it may be regarded as a direct subsidy.[62]

---

60. Grenville to Minto, January 13, 1801, FO 7/62.
61. Grenville to Minto, January 30, 1801, FO 7/62.
62. A total of £2,083,333:6:8 was remitted by the Treasury to Thornton's bank during 1800-1801 (King's Warrant Book, Ty. 52/85, 7; Ty. 52/86, 4, 109-110). This covered payments to Austria and the expenses of Wickham's mercenaries.

	Austria	*German princes and army expenses*
1800	£816,666	£1,066,667
1801		200,000

In addition to subsidizing Prussia, Russia, and Austria during the first two coalitions, Britain also had to assist her Portuguese ally. While this program was never more than a matter of secondary importance, its examination is worthwhile. In several important respects it foreshadows the vastly more ambitious policy Britain was to follow in the Peninsula after 1807.

In 1793 Portugal and Spain joined forces to make war on the French Republic, but the allies soon had their fill of fighting and two years later Spain made peace with the enemy. Given a free choice, the Portuguese Regent, D. João, would happily have done the same. However, the Directory was unwilling to allow Portugal to withdraw quietly into a state of neutrality; she must be subjugated and her alliance with England dissolved. France drew Spain into her plans in 1796, and shortly thereafter the two powers agreed to partition Portugal. Driven to distraction by visions of the enemy's hordes massed along Portugal's frontiers, the Regent appealed to Britain to save him from destruction.

Both treaty obligation and self-interest prompted London to answer this appeal. The alliance of 1793 had renewed all of Britain's obligations toward Portugal. Moreover, she simply could not afford to allow her ally to fall into enemy hands. The forced withdrawal of the British navy from the Mediterranean in 1796 underlined Portugal's strategic value as a base for future British military operations in that area. It was also vital for Britain to retain access to Portugal's harbors, which the French were so anxious to close. England's growing textile industry depended on the purchase of Brazilian cotton at Lisbon. The rapid increase of trade with Portugal in recent years was another compelling reason for keeping those ports open.[63]

In July 1796 the Portuguese minister in London asked for arms and war supplies to outfit 16,000 troops. Since gunpowder and saltpeter were virtually nonexistent at Lisbon, Britain was urged to give as much of both as she could spare. The Regent also hoped that 12,000 British troops could be sent to help the Portuguese army defend the kingdom. Inspired perhaps by the Austrian loan

---

63. Alan K. Manchester, *British Preëminence in Brazil: Its Rise and Decline* (Chapel Hill, N. C., 1933), pp. 52-53.

Table 1. Military supplies to Portugal and credit to her agents, 1796-1801[a]

Year	Muskets	Carbines	Pistols	Swords	Powder (Barrels)	Saltpeter (Tons)	Cannon	Credit
1796	12,000	3,300	1,300	3,300	–	200	–	–
1797	–	7,000	2,000	6,000	4,000	200	20	£ 10,009
1798	500	–	–	–	4,228	–	–	103,004
1799	16,000	1,000	–	5,000	1,772	–	–	87,675
1800	3,000	–	–	–	–	–	–	10,000
1801	–	–	–	–	–	100	–	–
Total	31,500	11,300	3,300	14,300	10,000 (900,000 lbs.)	500	20	£210,688

[a] Compiled on the basis of data contained in two reports from the Ordnance Office to the Foreign Office: that for 1800, dated December 27, 1800, is found in FO 63/34; that compiled in the following year is found in FO 63/38. The only aid in money paid directly to Portugal was the £200,000 subsidy in 1801. The King's Warrant Book (Ty. 52/84, 199-202) shows that in March 1798, £459,205 was paid by the Treasury to the Ordnance Office, the Paymaster General to the Army, and the Navy Treasury for the use of British forces in Portugal. The credit given to Portuguese agents was to enable them to purchase materials for direct shipment to Lisbon.

of the previous year, Portugal announced that she too wished to borrow money in London.[64]

Lord Grenville complied with Portugal's demand for war materials immediately. Within a few weeks the first consignment of arms, drawn from Britain's own arsenals, was on its way to Lisbon. By the end of the year Britain had sent its ally 12,000 muskets, 3,300 carbines, 1,300 pistols, 3,300 swords, and 200 tons of saltpeter. Additional shipments were made in the next year to insure that the Portuguese would want for nothing. (See Table 1.)

The dispatch of a British army to Portugal proved more difficult and it was not until November that Grenville announced that 6,000 men would soon leave for the Tagus. One third of this force would be drawn from garrisons at Gibraltar and Corsica, while the remainder would be made up of what the foreign secretary described (with great license) as "the choicest Foreign Regiments

64. R. Walpole to Grenville, July 13, 1796, FO 63/22; Almeida to Grenville, July 27, 1796, FO 63/22; Grenville to Walpole, August 24, 1796, FO 63/23.

in His Majesty's Service"—that is, units of French émigrés. Command of the army was assigned to General Charles Stuart, who was ordered to place himself at the disposal of the Portuguese commander-in-chief.[65] The first troops reached Lisbon in February 1797, but it was June before the force was complete.[66]

Raising a Portuguese loan in London presented serious problems which were never solved. Money was scarce in the City and Portugal's reputation so poor that even such a speculator as Walter Boyd refused to manage the Regent's loan. Quite possibly, Pitt privately discouraged Portugal's efforts in view of the effect which such a loan might have on England's troubled money market.[67] The Bank Crisis of 1797 put a halt to the project, but in July Pitt persuaded the Commons to vote £500,000 for Portugal's service. This would cover the cost of supplies already sent to Lisbon and enable the government to provide such future help as might seem desirable.[68]

The Cabinet's policy was to defend Portugal, rather than launch an offensive campaign against France and Spain. Within limits, that policy was successful for five years. The role of the British commander in Portugal was especially difficult. The French émigré regiments under his command gave Stuart nothing but trouble, and he bluntly declared, "I never in the course of my service saw two regiments more disgraceful to the British name." Orders sent from the Horse Guards were usually confusing and sometimes contradictory. Something of Stuart's feeling is reflected in a letter he sent to Dundas stating, "I am determined to be guided by your instructions so long as they are within the reach of my comprehension." More important than these vexations was the uncertainty of the British commander's position relative to the Portuguese army. Although Portugal was a small country, its army enjoyed the luxury of three commanding officers, no one of whom was accepted by his colleagues as the supreme commander. Stuart's unhappy experience would lead Britain, during the

65. Grenville to Walpole, November 25, 1796, FO 63/23.
66. Walpole to Grenville, February 1, 1797, FO 63/24; Fortescue, *British Army*, IV, 601-602.
67. Walter Boyd to Almeida, September 6, 1796, FO 63/23. As early as January 4, 1796, Pitt wrote Boyd urging him to discourage Portugal's efforts to borrow money (Chatham Papers, vol. 102).
68. *Journal of the House of Commons*, LII, 715-716.

Peninsular War, to insist that a British officer be named as the Portuguese generalissimo.[69]

In spite of Britain's generous help, relations between London and Lisbon were often troubled. The Regent came to see himself as a pawn in the struggle between England and the Directory. He was naturally anxious to free himself from the tangle. The Anglo-French peace negotiation at Lille in 1797 encouraged João to undertake discussions of his own with the enemy. The result was a secret peace treaty signed at Paris in August, in which Portugal agreed to close her ports to Britain. When Grenville learned of this he ordered his agent at Lisbon to persuade the Regent to withhold ratification of the pact.[70] João reluctantly disavowed the Paris agreement to the great annoyance of France. Now Portugal was more than ever bound to Britain's cause.

The meagre contribution Portugal made to her own defense irritated Grenville even more than the unceasing demands of her envoy for British arms and troops.[71] Convinced that the Regent's lassitude had now gone beyond all reasonable limits, the foreign secretary halted the flow of war materials to Portugal early in 1798. He explained his decision in straightforward terms: "But as our own pressure increases, and while on the other hand all exertions of the Portugueze Government continue so languid as to indicate a fixed persuasion & certain expectation of Peace, the drain upon this Country must cease."[72] At once the Regent gave assurances of greater energy in the future. This pledge apparently satisfied London, for the following July shipments of arms were resumed. Between July 1798 and February 1800 when British aid ended, Portugal was sent 19,000 muskets, 1,000 carbines, 5,000 swords and quantities of gunpowder which brought to 900,000 pounds the total sent since 1796.

The successful opening of the War of the Second Coalition strengthened the belief that Portugal was safe for the future, and Grenville ordered a reduction of the British garrison there.[73] However, the picture changed completely by the close of 1800.

69. Fortescue, *British Army*, IV, 602-604.
70. Grenville to Walpole, August 18, 1797, FO 63/25.
71. Cornwallis to Grenville, March 19, 1798, FO 63/27.
72. Grenville to Walpole, April 17, 1798, FO 63/27.
73. Grenville to Walpole, June 18, 1799, FO 63/30.

Now that France had triumphed over Austria, the Regent feared that Bonaparte's forces would certainly strike at Portugal. Grenville minimized the possible danger of a Franco-Spanish invasion. So far as Madrid was concerned, he declared, "The means which the Spanish Government possesses for carrying on such a War, are not of a nature to create any very serious alarm to any Government which was possessed of more energy than that of Portugal."[74] In October 1800 the Cabinet had to decide whether to use its available manpower in the Mediterranean to defend Portugal or drive the French from Egypt. A month later, the Egyptian expedition was decided on and all British troops were withdrawn from Portugal except the émigré regiments.[75]

This decision sealed Portugal's fate, and the following February a Franco-Spanish army poured across her borders. Renewed appeals for help fell on deaf ears in London. Given the vast quantity of arms sent to Lisbon since 1796, the Portuguese ought to be able to do something to defend themselves. In effect, the government had abandoned Portugal in order to drive the enemy from Egypt. Early in 1801 the new foreign secretary, Lord Hawkesbury, explained the government's policy to his envoy at Lisbon. The Regent should make peace with France on the best terms he could obtain. If Portugal continued the struggle, however, Britain would give her a £300,000 subsidy and support the Regent's efforts to borrow another £500,000 in London.[76] Hawkesbury was as good as his word. In May the House of Commons voted £300,000 for Portugal, of which £200,000 was remitted before the Regent's defense collapsed. No arms were sent, but one hundred tons of saltpeter was delivered at Lisbon in the spring of 1801.[77]

Without British troops to help him, the Regent had to make peace with his enemies; the Treaty of Badajoz (June 6, 1801) ended the war and compelled Portugal to shut her ports to Britain. Bonaparte's refusal to ratify this agreement prompted Lisbon to beg Britain for troops. Hawkesbury had nothing to offer beyond the suggestion that the Regent transfer his government and navy,

74. Grenville to John H. Frere, October 1800, FO 63/34.
75. Grenville to Frere, December 15, 1800, FO 63/34.
76. Hawkesbury to Frere, February 27, 1801, FO 63/36.
77. *Parliamentary History*, XXXV, 1420-1427; King's Warrant Book, Ty. 52/86, 380.

under British protection, to Brazil and carry on the war from there.[78] France's decision to ratify the Badajoz treaty saved João from having to take action. Hawkesbury continued to regard removal of the Portuguese government to Brazil as eminently desirable, and he returned to the idea in 1803 when Portugal was again threatened by France.[79] Four years were to pass before circumstances forced the Regent to accept this recommendation and abandon Lisbon for Rio de Janeiro.

Several features of considerable importance mark the history of this early British aid program for Portugal. The shipment of arms is the first instance of such British aid to her allies. During the last years of the Napoleonic war, the allied powers were to regard the arms given by Britain as important as her financial assistance. General Stuart's difficulties in establishing effective liaison with the Portuguese commanders foreshadows in small the problem which Sir John Moore and Wellesley encountered in the Peninsula ten years later. Finally, it is worth noting that as early as 1801 Hawkesbury saw the wisdom of moving the Regent's government to Brazil. Experience proved that without a major British army in Portugal the country could not be successfully defended against the French and Spanish. Since Britain could not assume a large military commitment in Portugal, she must think in terms of getting the Regent to Rio. In 1807 George Canning and Lord Strangford saw the question in exactly the same light as it had appeared to Hawkesbury.

The experience of the Second Coalition drove home the fact that Britain must be ready to finance the war programs of all her allies. Pitt's attempts to give shape and direction to that league by granting or denying subsidies was a complete failure. No offer of money was attractive enough to break the paralysis which had gripped Berlin since the Peace of Basel. Only Russia responded to Britain's call for a concert with anything like the determination required to gain victory. But even the Tsar could do nothing without the £2,000,000 given him by Britain between 1799 and 1800. Distrust and a diversity of interests, symbolized by the

78. Hawkesbury to Frere, July 14, 1801, FO 63/37.
79. Writing to Lord R. S. Fitzgerald in October 1803, Hawkesbury recommended that the Regent leave for Brazil. "This Proposition," he explained, "would have the double Effect not only of securing the Portugueze Settlements but under possible circumstances, the Portugueze Navy against the designs of France" (FO 63/42).

unratified loan convention of 1797, held Britain and Austria apart until they alone were left to carry on the war. Even then the British offer of alliance and subsidy went begging at Vienna for nearly six months while Thugut used it as a counter in his secret parleys with France. Only Austria's defeat at Marengo finally brought him to accept the British proposal. By then the game was up. The ineptitude of Austria's commanders gave the victory to France in the last days of the war. The mercenary corps, with which Britain had strengthened the Austrian army, was wasted as completely as the £1,200,000 its service cost the Treasury.

Circumstances alone saved Britain from the necessity of paying more than one of her allies at a time between 1797 and 1801. By now, the pattern was well established, however. With their own treasuries empty, the European powers expected to be helped by Britain. Should there ever be a third coalition, no allied army would take the field without British money.

The Portuguese aid program represented Britain's first attempt to meet an ally's deficiencies in war materials. In the end, Portugal was left to her fate because no British troops could be spared to protect her. The years of unsuccessful war which lay ahead would exhaust both the coffers and the arsenals of the major powers, leaving them dependent on Britain for muskets as well as money.

Although the Second Coalition was a failure, Britain at least emerged from it with new glory for her arms. Abercrombie's Egyptian campaign restored to the army some of the luster it had lost in the Low Countries. The navy made good its claim to supremacy in the Battle of the Nile and went on to confirm it by its victory at Copenhagen. Due in part to these successes, Britain was in a favorable position to seek peace through negotiation by 1801. But Pitt was to have no share in it. His health gave way in the autumn of 1800 under the strain of unsuccessful war and the vexing problems of Irish union. The tangled question of Catholic emancipation placed him in an impossible position with George III, and early in 1801 he announced his decision to resign.

VII

THE THIRD COALITION

If it was true, as Lord Rosebery said, that Henry Addington "carried into politics the indefinable air of a village apothecary inspecting the tongue of the State," it could be argued that in 1801 Britain sorely needed the services of a skilful physician.[1] Eight years of unremitting war had left the patient in a state of exhaustion. The new prime minister was confident of recovery once the source of the trouble had been removed. Peace talks were begun and finally led to a preliminary agreement in October 1801. Britain was to restore most of her overseas conquests and hand back the island of Malta to the Knights of St. John. In return, the First Consul would recall his forces from Naples and Egypt and promise to respect the neutrality of Portugal and the Ottoman Empire.

These terms were not universally approved in England. Some thought Addington had given up too much in return for too little. Lord Grenville was one of these, but Pitt observed that "if once the question of peace or war is looked at only as a question of terms, I am far from thinking that those now agreed to can, upon the whole, be denied to be honourable and reasonably advantageous."[2] The nation's crying need for peace outweighed concern for the details, and in March 1802 the definitive Treaty of Amiens was signed.

During the months which followed, Addington was appalled by the ruthless measures Bonaparte took to consolidate his position

1. Lord Rosebery, *Pitt* (London, 1915), p. 230.
2. Pitt to Grenville, October 5, 1801, *Manuscripts of J. B. Fortescue*, VII, 49. Pitt's opinion had changed by the time the definitive peace was concluded. See *Malmesbury*, IV, 78-79.

of supremacy in Europe. The prime minister decided to sound out Russia's reaction to this new expansion of French power. In October the foreign secretary prepared instructions for the British minister at St. Petersburg, Sir John B. Warren.[3] "The system of Ambition and Aggrandizement which has been manifested by the French Government since the conclusion of the General peace . . .," Hawkesbury explained, "render it indispensable that the Independent Powers of Europe should concur in some plan for opposing a barrier against such Encroachments." If Russia showed any interest, Warren was to propose a defensive alliance which Austria should be invited to join.[4]

The climate at St. Petersburg in 1802 was unfavorable to this call for joint action. Good relations between the two governments had recently been restored, but the new tsar, Alexander, was in no position to take any decisive action. After the experience of the Second Coalition, Russian leaders wanted as little to do with western Europe as possible. The chancellor, Count Alexander Vorontzoff, was vaguely sympathetic with Warren's proposal, but confessed that Russia and Austria were powerless to oppose France.[5]

A few months later, the tension between London and Paris reached new heights when it became clear that Bonaparte was planning some move in the East. Addington therefore decided to retain Malta and proposed that Britain and Russia jointly guarantee Turkey against French aggression. For the second time, Russia declined to cooperate with Britain.[6] Disappointed though he was by the Tsar's reaction, Addington was convinced that Britain could afford no further delay. On May 18 he obtained from Parliament a declaration of war against France. For the better part of another year, during which Britain fought alone, Addington served as war leader. This lack of allies was not the prime minister's fault; until 1804 there were simply no materials out of which he could create a coalition against France.

3. Sir John Borlase Warren (1753-1822) was a naval officer with a good war record. He was sent to St. Petersburg in 1802, but found the service uncongenial. Shortly after the outbreak of war he requested permission to return to sea.
4. Hawkesbury to Warren, October 27, 1802, FO 65/51.
5. Warren to Hawkesbury, November 17, 27, 1802, FO 65/51.
6. Hawkesbury to Warren, February 1, 1803, and Warren to Hawkesbury, March 25, 1803, FO 65/52.

Even the most perceptive observer of the European scene would have found little evidence of any spirit of continental resistance. In the Peninsula there was no hint of that national fury which would some day flame forth against Bonaparte. Austria had been plunged into a kind of stupor by the military disasters of the Second Coalition, and she now stood helpless and confused as Bonaparte turned Switzerland and the Italian republics into vassal states. When French troops seized Hanover, the British envoy at Vienna angrily reported that "not even a remonstrance has been made by the Court of Vienna to the French Government."[7] Prussia was as firmly attached to the policy of neutrality as ever, especially since Bonaparte was now in a position to dangle Hanover before her eyes as a bribe. For several more years Prussia was to remain in an uneasy state of equipoise while her leaders pondered the riddle of Hanover.

Regardless of the bleak prospects for success, Addington had to promote a coalition against France. In the summer of 1803 he made a third overture to St. Petersburg. If Russia would join with Britain and at least one of the major German states, London would provide her with subsidies at the same rate as during the Second Coalition.[8] At the same time a firm proposal was sent to Berlin: £250,000 would be given her as soon as she went to war with the promise of a second payment of the same amount once Bonaparte had been forced out of Hanover and across the Rhine.[9]

Both British bids fell on fallow ground. The Russian chancellor exactly caught the mood of his government when he observed with brutal frankness: "It is not for us alone to leap into the flames to save Hanover."[10] At Berlin, the British minister saw so little chance for success that he did not even present Hawkesbury's proposal.[11] The hard fact was that no major power would even consider alliance with Britain. The only subsidy paid by Adding-

7. Arthur Paget to Hawkesbury, June 23, 1803, *Paget Papers,* II, 91-93.
8. Hawkesbury to Warren, July 12, 1803, FO 65/53.
9. Hawkesbury to F. J. Jackson, June 28, 1803, FO 64/63.
10. F. Martens, *Recueil des Traités,* XI, 71.
11. Jackson to Hawkesbury, July 16, 1803, FO 64/63. Francis James Jackson (1770-1814) was a career diplomat who went to Berlin in 1802. He remained there for four years and was then sent as Britain's representative to the United States. Francis' brother, George Jackson, was with him at Berlin. For a vivid description of Frederick William III, see George Jackson's Diary for May 4, 1803, *The Diaries and Letters of Sir George Jackson, K. C. H., from the Peace of Amiens to the Battle of Talavera,* ed. Lady Jackson (London, 1872), I, 138.

ton was a small one to Naples to help strengthen her defenses against the oncoming tide of French power.[12]

Prospects for a new coalition remained dim until evidence of French ambition in the Balkans effected a change in Russia's attitude. The activities of French agents in Corfu and the Morea finally aroused Russia's fears, and in the autumn of 1803 a quarrel broke out between the two powers over the status of the Ionian Islands.[13] Symbolic of this reawakening of Russia's interest in the world outside was the entrance of Prince Adam Czartoryski into the Tsar's councils. Within a year the fiery young Pole succeeded Count Alexander Vorontzoff as foreign minister. Convinced that France seriously threatened Russia's eastern interests, Czartoryski argued warmly in favor of cooperation with Britain. In November 1803 Russia invited Britain to join her in diplomatic action against France.[14]

Downing Street showed less interest in the Russian offer than might have been expected. By now the Addington government was suffering from those internal ills which soon would end its life. Perhaps the Cabinet felt it was in no position to do more than listen to what the Tsar had to propose. In discussing the matter with Vorontzoff, the foreign secretary made quite clear that while the cause of European unity was dear to Britain, the Tsar must take responsibility for bringing the powers together. London was ready to subsidize the allies on two conditions: first, that any coalition include both Austria and Prussia; and, second, that all members accept a status quo ante territorial settlement as their common objective. Hawkesbury would be ready to discuss the question of subsidies for the allies in detail once the Tsar had won agreement from the German powers on these points.[15]

If the foreign secretary counted on mounting tension between Paris and St. Petersburg to spur Russia on to greater efforts, his judgment was sound. By the spring of 1804 Czartoryski was rapidly winning the Tsar to the cause of European union.[16] The

12. On November 11, 1803 Hawkesbury authorized the British envoy at Naples, Hugh Elliot, to draw up to £170,000 from the military chest at Malta for the service of Naples (FO 70/21).
13. Vernon J. Puryear, *Napoleon and the Dardenelles* (Berkeley and Los Angeles, 1951), p. 21.
14. A. Vorontzoff to S. Vorontzoff, November 20 [o.s.], 1803, FO 65/54.
15. Hawkesbury to S. Vorontzoff, February 26, 1804, FO 65/54; Czartoryski to S. Vorontzoff, April 30, 1804, FO 65/54.
16. Czartoryski to S. Vorontzoff, March 20, 1804, *Vorontsova*, XV, 168-171.

major obstacles in the way of success were the conditions set by Hawkesbury. To insist that a new coalition include both Prussia and Austria was unrealistic in the extreme. Prussia could not be counted on at all, and, so far as Austria was concerned, she would require a very generous British subsidy. Russia herself could not possibly accept Hawkesbury's demand that the allies agree on a status quo ante territorial settlement.[17]

At the end of April Czartoryski drafted new instructions for Vorontzoff in which he reviewed the difficulties involved in forming a concert. The conditions Britain had imposed simply could not be met. Would the foreign secretary reconsider the matter?[18] By the time Czartoryski's letter reached London, the Addington government had fallen. It was, therefore, with Pitt that Vorontzoff reopened the question of a new European concert against what had just become the Napoleonic Empire.

The problem of forming a new government in the spring of 1804 left Pitt with hardly any time for other business. His attempt to bring Fox into the Cabinet was vetoed by the King and, as a direct result, the Grenvilles went into opposition.[19] As finally constructed, the Cabinet was a poor one even by the standards of the day. The selection of Lord Harrowby as foreign secretary was especially unfortunate. Plagued by ill-health and melancholia, he had no capacity for managing that important department. Grenville may have been a difficult colleague at times, but Pitt soon had reason to regret his absence from Downing Street. An even worse appointment was that of Dundas (now Lord Melville) to head the Admiralty; within a year, charges of financial irregularity drove the genial pluralist from office.[20] Except for the young Viscount Castlereagh at the Board of Control, the ministers were a

17. Czartoryski himself considered the status quo ante condition distasteful. His own goals could not be achieved simply by setting the clock back. See Marian Kukiel, *Czartoryski and European Unity, 1770-1861* (Princeton, N. J., 1955), pp. 41-60.

18. Czartoryski to S. Vorontzoff, April 30, 1804, FO 65/54. Writing privately to Vorontzoff the same day, Czartoryski especially stressed the fact that "If war breaks out again, [Britain] should intervene by the payment of subsidies to those powers who by their strength and position, are alone capable of checking on land the torrent of the First Consul's ambition" (*Vorontsova*, XV, 180).

19. During Addington's ministry, Grenville and Fox had joined in an alliance which Pitt hoped to respect by bringing both men into the government. The King's opposition to Fox obliged Grenville to remain in opposition with his ally.

20. Pitt's appointment of Charles Middleton (Lord Barham) to replace Melville at the Admiralty was a fortunate one.

lackluster group with little to contribute. As a result, the prime minister was obliged to handle more of the details of administration than should have been the case.

A heavy concentration of French troops at Boulogne conjured up the spectre of invasion which hung over England in the spring of 1804. To meet this threat the new government hastily threw together a scheme to expand the army. The plan was presented to the Commons in June, and although the general purpose of the measure was acceptable, many of its details encountered opposition. The bill was finally passed by a vote of 265 to 233, thereby saving the new government by a narrow margin from defeat at the outset.

With the army bill successfully launched, Pitt took time to consider Czartoryski's appeal for help in building a new coalition. On June 26 the British reply was handed to Vorontzoff in the form of a letter bearing Harrowby's signature. This important policy statement (which was really Pitt's own work) made plain that the new Cabinet did not insist on the conditions put forward by Hawkesbury a few months before. Although a coalition would be the stronger for including both Prussia and Austria, "The co-operation of either, even for the limited object of preventing the further progress of French arms is of great importance in itself, and with a view to ulterior consequences." Nor did Pitt insist that the allies agree to a status quo ante settlement, desirable though it might be.

Once the concert powers had decided to wage war, Britain would provide them with £5,000,000 a year in subsidies.[21] Should the coalition include Russia and both the German powers, a fair division of that sum might be for Austria to receive £2,500,000, with £1,000,000 each going to Russia and Prussia. Troops could be hired from the smaller states with the remaining £500,000. Austria's wretched financial condition justified giving her a disproportionate share. Should Prussia remain neutral, the entire amount would be divided evenly between Vienna and St. Petersburg. Tsar Alexander was perfectly at liberty to refer to this offer in any discussions he might have with the Prussian and Austrian governments. In conclusion, the memorandum made

21. Subsidies for a defensive union were out of the question. The letter to Vorontzoff is very clear on this point.

explicit what its tone had implied throughout: Russia must take the lead in bringing the continental states into concert. For the time being, Britain would do no more than indicate the financial assistance the other powers might expect.[22]

Never before had Pitt offered £5,000,000 in subsidies to the continental powers. It was as much as the government could spare for foreign aid and the prime minister was ready to spend it all in order to finance a war coalition against France.[23] This unprecedented generosity was only made possible by the dramatic increase in the government's revenue which had occurred in recent years. Thanks to the war taxes Pitt had introduced five years before, the annual revenue now exceeded £46,000,000. Nor had this trend lost its momentum; revenue receipts would rise steadily until a peak of £67,000,000 was reached in 1810.[24] Not only were subsidies to be awarded generously, but they were to be offered to all powers prepared to make war. Gone forever was the policy of selective subsidization which Pitt had followed earlier. By 1804 no government would take arms against France without direct aid. Loans were out of the question. Britain's experience with the Austrian loans of 1795 and 1797 justified abandoning that device entirely.

Pitt's decision to leave the work of forming a new concert to Russia contrasts sharply with his eager search for allies during the Second Coalition.[25] This decision may have been inspired partly by the belief that Russia would be more effective in this work than Britain. Alexander had already gained an impressive personal ascendancy over Frederick William, which he was now ready to use in the cause of European union.[26] At Vienna Russian influence was far greater than anything the British envoy possessed.[27] If Alexander really meant to build a concert, he now knew the extent to which Britain would finance it. Quite possibly, Pitt may

22. Harrowby to S. Vorontzoff, June 26, 1804, FO 65/55.

23. Vorontzoff to Czartoryski, June 29, 1804, *Vorontsova*, XV, 231.

24. Gayer, Rostow, and Schwartz, *British Economy,* I, 44, 76, 103.

25. In July Harrowby sent instructions to the British ministers at Berlin and Vienna explaining the government's position. These instructions make clear that Russia was expected to take the lead. See Harrowby to Paget, July 24, 1804, FO 7/70; Harrowby to Jackson, July 24, 1804, FO 64/65.

26. Louis A. Thiers, *History of the Consulate and Empire of France under Napoleon,* trans. D. F. Campbell and J. Stebbing (Philadelphia, 1893-1894), III, 162-166.

27. Paget to Harrowby, April 9, 1804, FO 7/70.

have been unsure what Russia's intentions really were. St. Petersburg had ignored Addington's three invitations to joint action until French imperialism threatened her interests in the Balkans. Perhaps Russia's real goal was a *continental* union, financed by Britain, to protect her interests in the East. Pitt would not pay British money to support such a strategem. However, he was prepared to spend £5,000,000 to finance a war league against France. It was now up to the Tsar to prove his zeal for the cause by rallying the European powers.

Even though Pitt had withdrawn all conditions to alliance, the important policy statement of June 26 was not well received at St. Petersburg. Czartoryski described the offer of £5,000,000 in subsidies as "nugatory"—far below what was required.[28] With Franco-Russian relations worsening daily, Czartoryski chaffed at the difficulties he encountered in forming a European league. Russia's efforts to win Berlin's unqualified support for the concert dragged on throughout the autumn of 1804 and proved especially discouraging.[29] Czartoryski also attempted to enlist the support of Sweden whose king, Gustavus IV, was probably Europe's most violent enemy of the French. While Sweden could contribute only a few troops, Russia needed access to her Pomeranian possessions in the event of war.[30]

Agreement with the Hofburg was vital, especially since Russia could not rely on Prussia. Count Cobenzl lived in such great fear of France, however, that he hesitated to take a firm stand against her. It was out of the question for Austria even to consider going to war without a pledge of at least £6,000,000 in British subsidies. Knowing that this was more than double the aid Britain was ready to give, Czartoryski urged Cobenzl to moderate his demands. As part of a new Austro-Russian alliance, Czartoryski had to promise to do everything possible to persuade Britian to pay the Hofburg's price.[31] Russia at last had obtained an ally. Significantly, the

28. Warren to Harrowby, July 24, 1804, FO 65/55.
29. The question of British subsidies appears to have played no part in Russia's negotiation with Prussia. See F. Martens, *Recueil des Traités,* VI, 308 and *passim.*
30. Czartoryski hoped that Britain would provide Gustavus with a subsidy. See Warren to Harrowby, August 14, 1804, FO 65/55.
31. Czartoryski to A. Vorontzoff, November, 1804, *Mémoires du Prince Adam Czartoryski et Correspondance avec l'Empereur Alexandre Ier* (Paris, 1887), II, 57; Czartoryski to S. Vorontzoff, October 28, 1804, FO 65/56. Article IX of the Russo-Austrian alliance of November 6, 1804, obliged the Tsar "to use his good offices to

British minister at Vienna had never been invited to participate in the discussions leading to the treaty.[32]

It was now imperative for Russia to reach an understanding with Britain on the goals of the coalition and the subsidies to be paid the allies. For this purpose Czartoryski decided to send a special envoy to London rather than rely on the resident Russian envoy. The assignment was given to Count Nicolai Novosiltzoff, a young Russian diplomat whose Anglophilism guaranteed his favorable reception in Downing Street. While the Tsar's instructions to his envoy dealt at great length with half-mystical, half-realistic plans for the reorganization of Europe, they offered no concrete suggestions for the formation of the concert. In a word, Russia invited Pitt to bring forward a plan for organizing and financing the league.[33]

Novosiltzoff conferred with British leaders immediately on his arrival in London in mid-November. The burden of representing the British viewpoint soon fell entirely on Pitt, since Lord Harrowby suffered an accident at this time which completely unfitted him for business. Lord Mulgrave was soon named to take his place at the Foreign Office, but he was in no position to contribute much.[34] Occasionally, Vorontzoff would take part in the meetings between Pitt and Novosiltzoff. Such sessions offered a curious interplay of personalities and ideas. Vorontzoff had been in England so long that he sometimes forgot he was Russian. If Alexander's selection of Novosiltzoff for this mission hurt him, Vorontzoff was too much of an aristocrat to allow it to show. He had little to say at these meetings, in which Novosiltzoff played the role of an enthusiastic advocate of the Tsar's plans. Perhaps Novosiltzoff sensed the historic nature of his mission; perhaps it

---

obtain from the court of London . . . subsidies alike for the opening of the campaign and annually for the whole duration of the war, which shall as far as possible meet the expectations and wants of the court of Vienna" (Thiers, *Consulate and Empire*, III, 344-357 gives the text).

32. Paget to Harrowby, November 1, 1804, FO 7/72.

33. Novosiltzoff's instructions, dated September 11 [o.s.], 1804 are printed in Czartoryski, *Mémoires*, II, 27-45.

34. Henry Phipps, first Earl of Mulgrave (1755-1831) seems to have been regarded as a temporary head of the Foreign Office. However, he held the post during the remainder of Pitt's life. Mulgrave's management of that office, like that of his predecessor, was far below the standards set by Grenville.

was the energy and self-confidence of a fledgling diplomat. His reports exhibit boyish enthusiasm and optimism.[35] Although Pitt was only eleven years older than the Russian emissary, his responses were those of a worldly statesman listening with marked deference to the Tsar's ideas. Naturally, he took pains to stress how close Alexander's thinking came to Britain's own interests and aspirations. If Novosiltzoff alluded to the future of Malta or the problems of Britain's Maritime Code, Pitt would gently steer their discussion into less troubled areas.

Stripped of its generalizations, Alexander's proposal aimed at the re-establishment of a European balance and the creation of a permanent concert to guarantee it. Pitt must surely have seen the close connection between this scheme and that conceived by Grenville in 1798. Clearly, the time had come for the prime minister to prepare a specific plan for the formation of the new coalition. The result of Pitt's work was a major policy statement, dated January 19, 1805, addressed to Count Vorontzoff. Although the document was signed by the new foreign secretary, Pitt's responsibility for the text is clear.

In that masterful state paper, the prime minister examined three major propositions: first, that Europe could be saved only by rolling France's boundaries back to where they had been before the war. Second, provision should be made for creating barriers around France to insure against future aggression. Finally, some system must be developed to guarantee the future security of these arrangements. Russia and the German powers would probably be able to back up their ultimatum to France with a combined army of at least half a million men, but it was unrealistic to expect either German state to act "without the prospect of obtaining some important acquisition to compensate for its exertions." That is, Prussia and Austria would expect territorial rewards as well as British subsidies. Pitt recommended that Austria be invited to look for her gains in Italy, while Prussia might absorb the larger part of Belgium. Such territorial readjustments would not only be inducements for them to act, but would also build an effective system of barriers to hold France in check once the war had been won. The ideas contained in the January 19 paper

35. See Czartoryski, *Mémoires,* II, 47.

dealing with the resettlement of Europe constitute the most comprehensive plan Pitt ever proposed. In a very real sense, it was his legacy—a legacy which would profoundly influence Castlereagh's work ten years later.[36]

Pitt also took this occasion to bring his subsidy policy into sharper focus. Two days after the memorandum to Vorontzoff was finished, instructions were sent to the British minister at St. Petersburg to guide him in negotiating subsidy treaties with Russia and Austria. These instructions, together with the foreign policy statement of January 19, are in fact two sides of a single program which Britain would generally follow during the remainder of her war with France. If Russia and Austria found that they could impose their will on France only by making war, Britain would subsidize them at the annual rate of £1,250,000 for every 100,000 troops they put into action. Remittances would be made monthly on the basis of the actual number of effective troops each power had in the field. To help Austria overcome her financial handicap, she would receive an advance equal to four months' subsidies upon the outbreak of war. However, £5,000,000 was the most the two powers could expect since "it will not be possible to carry the relative proportion of men and money to any higher scale." Subsidy treaties with the allies ought also to incorporate details of the territorial gains they were to make at the end of the war. Pitt clearly conceived of such gains both as rewards and as the foundation of that barrier system he wished to forge around France.[37]

Britain was ready to pour £5,000,000 into the war chests of Austria and Russia in order to promote a coalition. Should Prussia throw in her lot with the allies and offer 100,000 men, Pitt would subsidize her at the same rate.[38] The desperate need to find allies forced the prime minister to anticipate an annual outlay of £6,250,000 in subsidies. Impressive as this figure is, it involved a

36. Mulgrave to Vorontzoff, January 19, 1805, FO 65/60. All but a small portion of this document is printed in Charles K. Webster, *British Diplomacy, 1813-1815* (London, 1921), pp. 389-394. Castlereagh himself claimed that he had assisted Pitt in the preparation of this paper. See Castlereagh to Lord Cathcart, April 8, 1813, *Correspondence, Despatches, and Other Papers, of Viscount Castlereagh, Second Marquess of Londonderry,* ed. by the 3rd Marquess (London, 1851-1853), VIII, 356.

37. Mulgrave to Lord Granville Leveson Gower, January 21, 1805, FO 65/57.

38. Mulgrave's instructions of January 21, 1805 to Leveson Gower (FO 65/57) make this quite clear.

rate of subsidization considerably less than that of Britain's previous aid treaties. The 1794 agreement with Prussia, the first major subsidy treaty, provided for payments at an annual rate of £29 for each soldier Prussia was to supply. The 1798-1799 conventions with Russia called for subsidies at a rate of £35 for each of the Tsar's soldiers. By comparison, the latest proposal, involving an annual rate of £12 10s., seems less generous than the total sum suggests. The difficulty is easily resolved. The earlier agreements were to secure the service of troops in *addition* to those Prussia and Russia had already put into the field. The 1805 proposal, on the other hand, offered subsidies for all the troops the allies were able to bring forward. For the first time, Britain was ready to help underwrite the total war expenses of her allies. A special concession was made to Austria's penury, but otherwise the proposal was based on the principle that financial aid should be given in direct proportion to the number of troops each power supplied. This principle continued to influence Britain's subsidy policy throughout the remainder of the war. Castlereagh respected it in negotiating the treaties of alliance and subsidy with Russia, Austria, and Prussia at Chaumont in 1814.[39]

The decisions Pitt took at the beginning of 1805 make clear how anxious he was to hasten the formation of a coalition. Although Alexander was expected to take the lead in forming such a union, the prime minister put a powerful tool in his hands. Pitt had been forced to take a more active part in coalition-building than he had intended during the previous summer. Over a year and a half had gone by since Britain declared war on France, but the enemy was as far from beaten as ever. Britain had driven her foe from the sea, but ultimate victory could only be won on land. Napoleon's position in Europe was stronger than before. Thanks to Spain's declaration of war on England at the close of 1804, he had the use of her ships and ports in his struggle with the island power. Pitt's decision to flood his allies with British money was a desperate measure, but it was the only contribution he could make to the formation of a new league.[40] With the British proposals now on

39. The Chaumont Treaty of 1814 divided £5,000,000 equally among the three major allies on the assumption that each of them would maintain at least 150,000 effective troops in the field. This represented a rate of about £11 per man. Castlereagh agreed to supplement this at the end of the war, however, by the payment of "return money."

40. See Pitt's statement to Vorontzoff, as reported by the Russian envoy in his letter of October 10, 1804 to Czartoryski (*Vorontsova*, XV, 273-274).

their way to St. Petersburg, the prime minister presented his budget for the coming year to the House of Commons. He drew members' attention to a provision calling for £5,000,000 as an "extraordinary expence," an amount intended to provide subsidies "in case they should be called for."[41]

His Majesty's envoy at the court of the Tsar, Sir John Warren, watched impatiently as the Russian autumn turned too quickly toward winter. London had finally granted his request to resume his career in the Royal Navy, but he would have to remain at St. Petersburg until his successor arrived. Warren had not been happy in the diplomatic service. It was no life for a man whose heart was at sea in pursuit of French prizes. Early in November 1804 his vigil ended with the arrival of Lord Granville Leveson Gower. Within a week, Warren brought the new emissary up-to-date, sent off his final dispatch, and left for England.[42]

The King's new representative was as delighted in the possession of the Russian embassy as Warren had been glad to see the last of it. Leveson Gower celebrated his thirty-first birthday en route to St. Petersburg. The appointment of an inexperienced youth to this very important position may have caused comment even among those who knew that he was the younger brother of the influential Marquess of Stafford.[43] But Leveson Gower had the talents required for diplomatic success and he was soon to have the experience.

In February 1805 a Foreign Office courier delivered to Leveson Gower the important instructions which Pitt had prepared one month before. These proposals were the groundwork for alliance with Russia and Austria, the details of which remained to be settled at St. Petersburg. The British minister carefully prepared for his conference with Czartoryski, who, Leveson Gower knew, had received a detailed account of the plan from Vorontzoff.

Czartoryski began the first meeting by announcing that he was distressed with some features of the British scheme. The subsidy

41. *Hansard's Parliamentary Debates,* 1st Series, III (1805), 544 (hereafter cited as *Hansard*).

42. Warren's return to sea service was fully as satisfying as he hoped it would be. By the end of the war he reached the rank of admiral and had been awarded the Order of the Bath.

43. Lord Granville Leveson Gower (1773-1846) became a career diplomat and in 1824 was named ambassador to France, a position he was to hold for nearly twenty years. In 1833 he was raised to the peerage as Lord Granville.

proposed for Austria fell far below what the Hofburg required. Britain must respond more generously to her pressing needs. The Russian minister sharply vetocd Leveson Gower's suggestion that the Tsar share his subsidy with the Hofburg. There were important parts of Pitt's plan which Russia considered even more objectionable. Certainly, Alexander would never support the offer of territorial rewards to the German powers. "It was not to be expected that His Imperial Majesty should exhaust his own resources in rendering over-powerful the only two great States whose frontiers were in contact with his own empire." Reporting this first meeting to Lord Mulgrave, Leveson Gower admitted that its general tone was discouraging. Perhaps the return of Novosiltzoff would "produce a more just estimation of the fairness and liberality of our propositions."

Leveson Gower's conversations with the Austrian envoy, Count Stadion, were equally disappointing. Stadion was willing to discuss the British proposal, but pointed out that he had no instructions from Vienna on the matter. In the event of war, Austria could mobilize 250,000 troops, but she would require a generous British subsidy. Leveson Gower sensed a trace of hesitancy in Stadion's responses, which suggested that Austria's cooperation might be harder to win than he had anticipated. There was also something a little ominous in the fact that during the following weeks Stadion heard nothing at all from Vienna.[44]

Nearly a month passed before Czartoryski again conferred with the British emissary and disclosed his other objections to Pitt's plan. The prime minister's terms for the three-power ultimatum to be presented to France were too extreme; unless materially modified, Russia could not accept them. To insist, as Pitt had, that France withdraw from Italy was unreasonable. Would it not be better to compromise this issue? Furthermore, the terms to be proposed to France would certainly be more palatable if Britain offered to cede her some small territory in India. Leveson Gower at once protested these alterations and declared that his instructions allowed him no room to modify Pitt's terms.[45]

44. Leveson Gower to Mulgrave, March 6, 1805, FO 65/57. Stadion received no word from Vienna between February and mid-May 1805. See Leveson Gower to Mulgrave, May 12, 1805, FO 65/57.
45. Leveson Gower to Mulgrave, March 22, 1805, FO 65/57.

It was abundantly clear that the three powers were dangerously at cross-purposes. Pitt aimed at winning allies in the war against France on the basis of a mutually acceptable set of war goals. Russia, however, regarded hostilities with Napoleon as a last resort, a solution to be adopted when all else failed. Infinitely preferable was a negotiated territorial settlement which would reduce France's threat to Russia's eastern interests. Russia's motives in this were not entirely selfish. Czartoryski knew how unwilling Austria was to go to war. With British and Austrian interests poles apart, he must find some common ground on which all three powers could unite to form a counterpoise to France. Even at that, war might be impossible to avoid. Vienna would never run that risk without positive assurances of far greater subsidies than Pitt had offered. Czartoryski's role was clear. While working to stiffen Austria, he must persuade Pitt to temper the demands contained in his January state paper. Furthermore, Britain must also be induced to pledge more extensive aid to the continental powers should they be forced into war by France's rejection of even a moderate demand for territorial adjustments. Leveson Gower's stubbornness presented a problem. He must be brought to accept major changes in the terms the three powers would offer Napoleon as an alternative to war—a war which two of those powers were most anxious to avoid.

For more than two weeks, Czartoryski hammered away at Leveson Gower to prove that it was impossible to form a coalition without modifying Pitt's peace terms. By now, Novosiltzoff had returned to St. Petersburg only to join with the Tsar's foreign minister in pressuring Leveson Gower. The British minister defended his government's policy bravely, despite the excruciating agony of an ulcerated tooth.[46] On April 7 the diplomat finally yielded and agreed to fundamental changes in the manifesto the allies would offer France. The most important of these was that, if Napoleon insisted, British troops would be withdrawn from Malta to be replaced by a Russian garrison.[47] Bad as this provision was, it could have been still worse. At first Czartoryski not only insisted

46. On March 31 he wrote to Lady Gower, "I can neither walk about, nor sit still" (*Lord Granville Leveson Gower (First Earl Granville), Private Correspondence 1781-1821*, ed. Castalia, Countess Granville [London, 1916], II, 70).
47. These changes are summarized in *Camb. Hist. Brit. For. Pol.*, I, 338.

that Britain give up Malta, but also agree to submit her Maritime Code to an international congress for revision. Only by accepting the Malta provision, Leveson Gower explained to the foreign secretary, had he been able to protect the Maritime Code. All concessions had been made on one condition: the British envoy would sign the treaty with Russia *sub spe rati.* No ultimatum would be sent to Paris without prior approval by the Cabinet. This understanding, Leveson Gower rather brightly observed to Mulgrave, "renders the provision itself [regarding Malta] quite null."[48]

Now the time had come to negotiate the three-power alliance which was to support the modified ultimatum. Since the Austrian minister remained uninstructed, Czartoryski and Leveson Gower agreed to conclude a treaty to which he could accede as soon as the Hofburg sent him authority. It was expected that, in the event of war, the three powers could mobilize half a million men. Alexander would provide 115,000 (a number later increased to 180,000), while Austria was expected to offer 250,000.[49] The balance would consist either of British troops or mercenaries hired from the lesser powers. Leveson Gower offered subsidies to Russia and Austria according to Pitt's formula: that is, £1,250,000 for each 100,000 men under arms. Czartoryski, however, took strong exception to the demand that subsidies be paid monthly on the basis of an actual count of each power's troops in the field. It would be humiliating to have a British officer make a monthly muster of the allied armies to determine the subsidy money due the powers. Furthermore, this would penalize the army which fought the hardest and, as a result, suffered the heaviest casualties. In the end, Leveson Gower agreed that payments would be made on the basis of the total force each power brought forward at the beginning of the campaign.[50] He also pledged his government to advance a large part of the subsidy due Russia and Austria to help them meet their mobilization costs. Austria was to receive

48. Leveson Gower to Mulgrave, April 7, 1805, FO 65/57. What can one make of the letter Leveson Gower sent Pitt a few days later (April 12, 1805) which contains the following? "Upon the Question of Malta, he [Novosiltzoff] assures me that you said to him, 'trouvez nous le moyen de la render neutre et nous serons contents,' and it was this Assurance that in some degree induced me to agree to any mention of Malta" (The papers of Lord Granville, deposited in the Public Record Office, London, vol. 384).

49. The increase was provided for in an additonal article to the Anglo-Russian alliance of May 10, 1805, FO 93/81(8).

50. Leveson Gower to Mulgrave, April 12, 1805, FO 65/57.

£1,000,000 as soon as she acceded to the convention; Russia would be entitled to about £360,000.[51] At Czartoryski's insistence, the treaty of alliance virtually ignored Pitt's wish to use territorial rewards as an added inducement to the German powers.[52]

The Anglo-Russian pact, setting forth the terms of the ultimatum to France and the subsidy agreement, was signed by Leveson Gower and Czartoryski on April 11.[53] Novosiltzoff's signature also appeared on the treaty. He would soon leave for Berlin to await a passport which would allow him to carry the allies' ultimatum to Paris. Once again, Leveson Gower reminded Mulgrave that the Cabinet was perfectly at liberty to reject the changes made in that ultimatum. Perhaps it was just as well that the British emissary did not know that the courier carrying the treaty to London also bore a letter from Czartoryski to Vorontzoff. Unless Britain accepted the Malta provision, the Tsar would not ratify the agreement.[54]

No part of the April treaty corresponded exactly to the original British proposal. However, the slight modifications Leveson Gower had made relative to subsidies were unimportant compared to his revision of Pitt's plans for a territorial settlement. The prime minister was dumbfounded when he learned from Vorontzoff that the Tsar regarded the evacuation of Malta as a sine qua non. He assured the Russian envoy that public opinion in Britain would never tolerate the surrender of Malta. Even if the new alliance died stillborn, Malta could never be given up.[55]

During the days which followed, Pitt considered the matter again. Deeply discouraged and physically spent, he made an agonizing search for some way out of the impasse. By the first week of June, he produced what might prove a workable solution. Britain would agree to the Malta provision if Alexander accepted four conditions. First, Malta must be garrisoned by Russian troops. Second, Spain must cede Minorca to Britain as a naval base

51. In this, Leveson Gower anticipated new instructions sent him by Mulgrave on March 15, 1805 (FO 65/57).

52. The Convention merely declared that Austria would be allowed to enlarge her frontiers, while Prussia might regain the lands on the left bank of the Rhine she had yielded the French in the Treaty of Basel.

53. Treaty with Russia, April 11, 1805, FO 93/81(6), (7).

54. Mulgrave to Leveson Gower, June 7, 1805, FO 65/58.

55. F. Martens, *Recueil des Traités,* XI, 109-111.

in place of Malta. Third, France must agree to an unconditional restoration of Piedmont under the House of Savoy. Finally, Napoleon would be required to accept the erection of a land barrier between France and Holland under Prussian control.[56]

After sending off this counterproposal to St. Petersburg, Pitt undertook to finance the coalition which he soon hoped to see take shape. On June 21 he asked the Commons to vote £3,500,000 for subsidies to the allies during the remainder of the year. The ambiguities which hung about the recent negotiation with Russia and Austria gave Fox an excellent chance to charge the government with fomenting troubles in Europe. The prime minister brushed aside the indictment and insisted that Britain had a moral responsibility to arouse the continental powers to their danger: "If you . . . could open the eyes of the continental nations to their true interests, if you could clearly shew them that not only their interests but their salvation depended upon their joining you in opposing an enemy whose object it was to destroy you both, then surely it was not only not unjust, but it was even meritorious, to secure their co-operation if possible."[57] The plain truth was that, as yet, Pitt had failed to convince Russia and Austria of this fact.

The character of fantasy which so often clung to coalition diplomacy was never more evident than in June 1805. Pitt had obtained, without a division, a vote of £3,500,000 to subsidize a league which would probably never be born. The conditions on which Britain was prepared to yield Malta were certain to be unacceptable to the Tsar. In June the Hofburg broke its long silence to announce its refusal to adhere to the Anglo-Russian alliance. Vienna found even the modified terms of the ultimatum to be offered France too likely to involve her in war.[58] The French Empire had nothing to fear from three governments whose tragic diversity of interest made it impossible for them to unite.

Only Napoleon's sword could cut through the twisted and snarled knot of coalition diplomacy. Throughout the spring, the Emperor hovered over Italy like an eagle in search of prey. On May 26 he seized upon an Italian crown to add to that of the

56. Mulgrave to Leveson Gower, no. 16, June 7, 1805, FO 65/58.
57. *Hansard*, V (1805), 541-542.
58. Leveson Gower to Mulgrave, June 10, 1805, FO 65/58.

French Empire. Nine days later he startled Europe even more by annexing the Genoese Republic. This rapine shocked the Tsar, and he recalled Novosiltzoff from Berlin at once. The British alliance was revived, and in July Alexander ratified it, having first struck out the offensive Malta provision.[59]

The Italian crisis also jolted Austria into acting with uncharacteristic energy: Stadion was ordered to accede to the Anglo-Russian convention.[60] Predictably, the Hofburg asked for more British money than had been specified in that pact. Stadion informed Leveson Gower that his government planned to mobilize 320,000 troops instead of the 250,000 expected. The British envoy hesitated to accept this gift (which would increase the Austrian subsidy by more than £850,000) since the extra troops were intended solely to defend the Rhine. However, the Hapsburg plan was adopted, and Britain pledged £4,000,000 a year in subsidies to Austria. Stadion had other demands which Leveson Gower found more difficult to accept. Austria must receive £3,000,000 during the remainder of the present year, of which half must be paid at once as preparation money. The British minister appealed to Czartoryski for help in moderating Austria's greed, but the response was disappointing. Until Vienna was satisfied, the Tsar could undertake no campaign. In desperation, Leveson Gower offered to advance Austria £1,666,665 as preparation money. The offer was grudgingly accepted, and on August 9 Stadion and Leveson Gower exchanged solemn assurances and declarations which summarized the terms of their agreement.[61]

The strategic position of Naples and Sweden made it essential for the new coalition to secure their cooperation. Naples was the only possible bulwark against the rising tide of French imperialism in Italy. Furthermore, the British navy needed access to her ports to enable it to maintain its vigil in the Mediterranean. Russia would be better able to check Napoleon's Balkan plans if southern

59. Leveson Gower to Mulgrave, July 31, 1805, FO 65/58.
60. Harold C. Deutsch, *The Genesis of Napoleonic Imperialism* (Cambridge, Mass., 1938), p. 284.
61. Leveson Gower summarized his discussions with Stadion in a letter to Mulgrave, dated August 14, 1805. Copies of the declaration which Leveson Gower and Stadion exchanged on August 9 are to be found in FO 94/17. Mulgrave accepted the subsidy concessions made to Austria, but indicated that the Hofburg need expect nothing more. See Mulgrave to Gower, September 10, 1805, FO 65/59.

Italy could be kept from his grasp. The contribution which Sweden could make to the coalition's success was quite different. Russia's participation in a war in Germany would be infinitely more effective if she could use the Swedish port of Stralsund or the island of Rügen as a supply depot, especially during those months of the year when the upper Baltic was choked with ice. During 1804-1805 Pitt made every effort to insure that the coalition would be properly supported on both its southern and northern flanks.

Since the Second Coalition, Britain and Russia had both made a point of helping Naples. In 1803 Addington quietly paid her £170,000, and a year later, Pitt pledged an annual subsidy of £150,000. When the shadow of French aggression once more fell across Italy, London promised to double that subsidy in the event of war.[62] In the autumn of 1805 France attacked Naples and both Britain and Russia went to her defense. Not only was the British subsidy increased, but 7,000 troops were brought from Malta under the command of General Sir James Craig to help halt the enemy. The British force was joined by a Russian army, but their efforts were in vain. Craig finally withdrew to the island of Sicily, accompanied by the Neapolitan royal family. Thanks to the British navy, Sicily was safe, and King Ferdinand soon established his government at Palermo. The Bourbons now became troublesome pensioners of the British government which, in turn, converted the island into a military and naval base.

Efforts to win Sweden as a partner in the Third Coalition were beset with complications. The most dramatic of these was the eccentricity of the king, Gustavus Adolphus, who insisted on personally conducting all negotiations with the envoys sent by Russia and Britain. The excessively high monetary value Gustavus placed on his support made it all but impossible for Britain to reach agreement with him. To make matters worse, the British minister at Stockholm was constantly plagued by his Russian colleague's reminders that the success of the Tsar's military plans depended on Swedish cooperation.

In the autumn of 1804 Pitt offered Sweden £60,000 for permission to use Swedish Pomerania as a base for military

62. Harrowby to Hugh Elliot, July 3, 1804, FO 70/22; Mulgrave to Prince Castelcicala, March 2, 1805, FO 70/24.

operations. It was also expected that British merchants in the Baltic would be allowed to establish a commerical depot at Stralsund. A treaty along these lines was concluded in December. Since Gustavus feared French reprisals, the agreement was kept secret and the subsidy paid from Secret Service funds.[63]

Gustavus was ready to fight in any coalition organized against France, but he expected to be well paid. In December 1804 he offered England the service of 25,000 of his soldiers. The subsidies which he required were astronomical: preparation money and the monthly payments would come to more than £2,000,000 a year. London refused to take this proposal seriously. Pitt was ready to subsidize Sweden, but only at the rate already established for the major allies—that is, £12 10s. a year for each soldier offered.[64]

Stung by Britain's rejection, Gustavus now played his trump card. He would allow the Tsar's soldiers access to Stralsund only if Britain signed a subsidy agreement with him. Since Alexander had now decided to make war, his envoy at Stockholm urgently pressed the British minister, Henry Pierrepont, to submit to Gustavus' terms. Russian troops were expected to sail soon from Kronstadt to Stralsund and it was vital that they be allowed to land. To move things along, the Tsar's emissary grandly announced to Gustavus that Alexander himself would pay the difference between what the King demanded and what Britain offered. Privately he told Pierrepont that, of course, the Tsar would expect Britain to reimburse him for his largesse.[65]

Pierrepont's resistance gradually collapsed, and in August 1805 he offered Gustavus £7,200 a month to maintain 8,000 troops at Stralsund.[66] A month later Sweden agreed to send 12,000 men into battle with the allies in return for an annual subsidy of £12 10s. per man. On the surface it seemed that Britain had gained a victory since the subsidy rate was that on which Pitt had always insisted. However, other provisions of the treaty, together with a secret article, make clear that Gustavus was enriching himself outrageously at Britain's expense. Although Sweden would be paid £150,000 a year for the service of 12,000 troops, she would not in

63. Treaty with Sweden, December 3, 1804, FO 93/101(2).
64. Lord Camden to Henry Pierrepont, December 7, 1804, FO 73/32; Mulgrave to Pierrepont, June 25, 1805, FO 73/33.
65. Pierrepont to Mulgrave, September 1, 1805, FO 73/34.
66. Treaty with Sweden, August 31, 1805, FO 93/101(3).

fact be expected to furnish more than 10,000. In that number she could include the 8,000 men at the Stralsund garrison, for which Britain was already paying £7,200 a month. Over and beyond this, Gustavus would be given a preparation subsidy of £62,500 and a special grant of £50,000 toward the upkeep of the already over-financed Stralsund garrison. In return for supplying 10,000 troops, Sweden would receive an annual payment of nearly a quarter million pounds sterling, the rate of subsidy being almost twice the £12 10*s.* Pitt originally offered.[67]

Necessity alone justified Pierrepont's treaties. Twenty thousand Russians were already en route from Kronstadt, and to guarantee that they might land at Stralsund, the British envoy had to yield. The Russian transports reached Stralsund just two days after the subsidy treaty of October 3 was signed. In London, Mulgrave read the text of the Swedish treaty with grave disapproval, but admitted that his envoy had really no choice in the matter.[68] Swedish Pomerania and Stralsund were now available to the allies for whatever use they might be able to make of them, together with the 10,000 Swedish auxiliaries whose service Britain had bought at a scandalous price.

The ineffectiveness of Britain's leadership in coalition diplomacy was never more apparent than during the formative period of the third alliance against France. Her call to union against Napoleon awakened no response except at St. Petersburg. Even Russia took strong exception to the proposal for European reconstruction proposed by Pitt in January 1805. A desperate need for allies finally forced Britain to yield to Russia's demands, even to the point of giving up Malta. However, only Napoleon's Italian thunderbolt finally jarred Russia and Austria into making common cause with Britain. That the three powers were at last allies could not hide the fact that each of them viewed the purpose of the war in a different light.

If Pitt was not the architect of the Third Coalition, he was certainly its paymaster. For the first time, Britain agreed to subsidize her partners in proportion to the effective fighting force each was to supply. The standard rate of £12 10*s.* for each soldier, laid down by Pitt in 1805, would cost Britain more than ever

67. Treaty with Sweden, October 3, 1805, FO 94/306.
68. Mulgrave to Pierrepont, October 23, 1805, FO 73/34.

before. Originally, Pitt hoped to limit subsidies to £5,000,000 a year, but the heavy and insistent demand of the continental powers finally forced him to raise it to nearly £7,000,000. An extra £1,000,000 would undoubtedly have to be added if Prussia finally supported the cause.

The anticipated £7,000,000 expenditure for subsidies during 1806 amounted to nearly half Britain's entire naval expense for the year which witnessed Trafalgar.[69] Never before had she undertaken such heavy responsibilities to her allies. In return, they had promised to put in motion armies which, at least on paper, would exceed half a million men. Weeks would pass before the military plans of Russia, Austria, and Sweden could be coordinated. Meanwhile, Napoleon would have to decide whether to persist in his plans for an invasion of Britain, or turn about and challenge the scattered armies of his continental enemies—armies created not by British gold, but by his own ambition.

69. The cost of the three services during 1805 was as follows: Army, £18,581,127; Navy, £15,035,630; Ordnance, £4,456,994. See Pablo Pebrer, *Taxation, Revenue, Expenditure, Power, Statistics, and Debt of the Whole British Empire* . . . (London, 1833), p. 154.

VIII

THE END OF AN EPOCH

At the end of August 1805 the Grand Army broke camp at Boulogne and began its march to the upper Rhine; plans for an invasion of England had been shelved. Napoleon summoned his distant army corps to join him and moved quickly to grapple with the Austrians. He forced his new ally, the Elector of Bavaria, to place his army at France's disposal. Treaties of alliance, yielding another 16,000 troops, were imposed on the German states of Baden, Württemberg, and Hesse-Darmstadt. Undoubtedly, the German recruits included some who had served the British as mercenaries ten years before. However, Napoleon's treaties with the German princes made no provision for subsidies.

Most of the Austrian army was in southern Bavaria, awaiting the arrival of their Russian allies. Predictably, the progress of the Tsar's army fell behind schedule. The vanguard of 50,000 men crossed into Galicia at the end of August, to be followed by 70,000 more Russians a month later.[1] War had come so swiftly that the usual delays in the remittance of British subsidy money were more aggravating than ever.[2] It was not until the battle of Ulm had been fought and lost that Mulgrave decided how the Austrian subsidy should be paid. All remittances would be made by Britain's agent at Hamburg, Edward Thornton, who had been ordered to turn over £1,000,000 at once to Austria's treasury. Additional payments of £250,000 each were scheduled for December and January. Since the size of the Austrian subsidy

---

1. Stroganoff to C. J. Fox, June 30, 1806, FO 65/66.
2. In August 1805 the British minister at Vienna responded to Cobenzl's appeals for money by giving him £200,000 in bills of exchange. See Paget to Mulgrave, August 30, 1805, FO 7/74; Jenkinson to Mulgrave, October 12, 1805, FO 7/75.

depended upon the number of men the Emperor had in the field (a figure unknown to London), these first payments were made on account.[3]

Remittance of the Russian subsidy was delayed still longer since the first installment was not due until the Tsar's forces had crossed their frontier. Even then a technicality intervened to complicate matters. When Leveson Gower concluded his agreement with Austria in August, he and Czartoryski exchanged notes formally recognizing that all three powers were now united within the framework of the April convention. Unaccountably, the Russian government neglected to ratify this note, and Mulgrave would make no payments of the Tsar's subsidy until the oversight had been corrected.[4] Russia's immediate needs were so urgent, however, that Leveson Gower took it upon himself to provide her with £300,000 in bills during the closing months of the year. Another £50,000 was paid in February when the Tsar finally ratified the agreement.[5]

With the outbreak of war, Pitt was again tempted to undertake a major campaign in north Germany. A well-aimed blow now might free Hanover and open the door to an allied invasion of Holland. At the moment there were about 30,000 Russian and Swedish troops at Stralsund which could cooperate with any force Britain might send. If only Prussia could be persuaded to join, success would be almost certain. The idea of creating a massive army in the north strong enough to destroy the Napoleonic Empire so charmed the prime minister that he decided once more to appeal to Prussia's greed. On September 10 the British envoy at Berlin was instructed to offer an annual subsidy of £1,250,000 in return for 100,000 Prussian troops.[6] As an added inducement, the

3. Mulgrave to Paget, October 25, 1805, FO 7/75. The agent sent by Britain to count the Austrian army did not reach his destination until about a week after Ulm; General John Ramsay to Mulgrave, November 9, 1805, FO 7/78.

Thanks to Napoleon's curtailment of British trade in north Germany, Thornton had great trouble in finding money at Hamburg with which to make subsidy payments. Heavy shipments of silver from England enabled him to remit £1,000,000 to Austria's bankers by the end of the year. See Thornton to Mulgrave, November 12, 1805, FO 33/30. See also Memorandum respecting the Austrian Subsidy, October, 1805, FO 120/1.

4. Mulgrave to Leveson Gower, December 21, 1805, FO 65/59.

5. Leveson Gower to Mulgrave, October 15, 1805, and February 1, 1806, FO 65/59, FO 65/62.

6. Since Prussia had been so long at peace, Pitt offered her no preparation money. However, if it was insisted on, Britain would pay her the equivalent of five months' subsidy.

Cabinet would agree to support Prussia's claim for territorial expansion in the west at the close of the war.[7]

Prussian policy was so evenly balanced between peace and war at this time that the British plan had some chance for success. On the ministerial level, Hardenberg and Haugwitz were in bitter opposition on the question. Haugwitz was by now a firm advocate of neutrality, but Hardenberg was thoughtful enough to see that Prussia might reap a generous reward from forceful intervention in the war at the strategic moment. The final decision was in the hands of the King, whose friendship with the Tsar encouraged the hope that he would decide in favor of the allies. Napoleon placed a realistic value on Prussia's support, and in August he offered her Hanover in return for a military alliance. Once again Prussia was pressed by two suitors, each of whom made attractive offers. At the moment, Frederick William was undecided. Hardenberg, however, was greatly interested in Britain's latest proposal and urged her minister to obtain more precise instructions from London.[8] Austria's defeat at Ulm left even more of the responsibility for the war on the Tsar. Late in October, Alexander went to Potsdam to confer with Frederick William, hoping to win from him a promise of military support.

Encouraged by this apparent stiffening of Prussia's policy, Pitt decided to open a second front in northern Europe. On October 16 orders were prepared for the dispatch of 11,000 British troops to the Elbe. Before the end of the year, reinforcements brought the British expeditionary force to 60,000.[9] Downing Street would now have to guarantee that this army have Prussian support.

To accomplish this, Pitt sent Lord Harrowby to Berlin with full power to conclude a treaty of alliance and subsidy. It is hard to imagine a worse choice than Harrowby. Melancholy and hypochondriac, he had no qualification for the mission other than the fact that he enjoyed the prime minister's confidence. The offer

---

7. Mulgrave to Jackson, September 10, 1805, FO 64/68.

8. Jackson to Mulgrave, September 20, 1805, and October 7, 1805, FO 64/68, FO 64/69.

9. The largest unit in this force was the 5,000 men of the King's German Legion. This group was formed in England in 1803 of Hanoverian exiles. Later, the legion fought well with Wellington in the Peninsula. It was disbanded in 1816. Its history was written by North Ludlow Beamish, *History of the King's German Legion,* 2 vols., (London, 1832-1837).

Harrowby was to make was merely a more generous version of the plan Pitt had proposed one month before. At that time, it was hoped that Prussia would mobilize 100,000 men. Now she was asked to go to war with double that number, in return for which Britain would pay her £2,500,000 a year. At the end of the war, Britain would do everything possible to see that Prussia received at least a part of Belgium, with such additional territory as would be required to connect her to her new possessions. If Prussia was unwilling to take an active part in the war, Harrowby was to offer her £1,250,000 for her armed mediation.[10]

Harrowby's instructions were almost entirely out-of-date even before he reached Berlin. At Hamburg he learned that the previous week Alexander and Frederick William had concluded an alliance. Prussia was to present France with an ultimatum embodying the terms of a territoral settlement roughly similar to those agreed to by Britain and Russia in the spring. Should Napoleon reject it, Frederick William would send 80,000 men into battle against him. To obtain this much, the Tsar had agreed that Prussia was to receive Hanover. Reporting this to Downing Street, Harrowby observed, "I do not conceive any part of the instructions which were given me under very different circumstances can apply to the present case." He would go on to Berlin, traveling slowly so that any new instructions sent would reach him before his arrival at the Prussian capital.[11]

When Pitt learned that Alexander had bartered Hanover in return for Prussian support, he could not comprehend the news. Britain had all along accepted, even advocated, territorial rewards for Prussia as an inducement for her to act. Belgium, yes; Hanover, never! With Nelson's splendid victory at Trafalgar only one month ago, why should Britain be asked to yield her King's patrimony? The bitter truth was that glorious as Trafalgar had been, it in no way affected France's dominant military position in Europe. Pitt struggled to adjust himself to this latest turn of events. At the end of November new instructions were sent to Harrowby: Britain would never give up Hanover, but she was ready to enlarge the reward in the Low Countries she had already offered Prussia. Presumably, this meant that all Belgium would go to Frederick

10. Mulgrave to Harrowby, October 27, 1805, FO 64/70.
11. Harrowby to Mulgrave, November 10, 1805, FO 64/70.

William. Otherwise, Harrowby was to consider his original instructions still applicable.[12]

Once more the fortunes of war intervened to make nonsense of Pitt's plans. On December 2 Napoleon's army, now refreshed from its exertions at Ulm, fell upon the allied armies at Austerlitz. Within a matter of hours Russia and Austria ceased to be military powers. Shocked at the disaster which had overtaken him, the Tsar agreed to an armistice binding him to withdraw the remnant of his army behind his own frontier. By the end of the year all Russian troops, excepting only those in north Germany, had been removed.[13] Meanwhile, the Austrian emperor, a fugitive from his own capital, accepted the humiliating terms of peace dictated by France at Pressburg. Austria undertook to pay her conqueror £4,000,000 in reparations. In all probability the £1,000,000 she had received in British subsidies found its way into Napoleon's war chest.

Austerlitz extinguished the tiny ember of hope that Prussia would join the allies. At Berlin, Harrowby desperately tried to resurrect that hope by showering Hardenberg with extravagant offers of money. He offered to make subsidy payments retroactive to the previous October, even though the Prussian army could not possibly complete mobilization until February at the earliest. He promised an additional four months' subsidy to be paid as a bonus at the end of the war. In ultimate despair, he may even have offered to let Prussia have Holland as well as Belgium if she would only intervene on the side of the coalition.[14] Few sights could have been more pitiful than Lord Harrowby, sick and probably demented, dangling before Hardenberg subsidies and the promise of lands Britain did not possess. The Prussian minister was almost embarrassed by Harrowby's absurd conduct and, in mid-

12. Mulgrave to Harrowby, November 23, 1805, FO 64/70.
13. Stroganoff to C. J. Fox, June 30, 1806, FO 65/66.
14. Harrowby to Mulgrave, December 7, 1805, FO 64/70. In his memoirs *(Denkwürdigkeiten des Staatskanzlers Fürsten von Hardenberg,* edited by Leopold von Ranke [Leipzig, 1877], II, 353), Hardenberg claimed that Harrowby offered Holland to Prussia. This offer, if it was really made, had not been authorized by Pitt. It is entirely possible that Harrowby did make it, only to be badly shocked later when he realized what he had done. This would at least explain the very mysterious letter he sent Pitt on December 12, 1805. It is printed in full in Rose, *Pitt and the Great War,* pp. 545-546. Harrowby was probably suffering a physical and mental breakdown at this time. See Jackson, *Diaries,* I, 377 and *passim.*

December, he curtly told him that he must see "the total impossibility in which the King finds himself of taking at this moment any positive engagement."[15] Prussia would yield to that suitor who could deliver what he promised.

During the last weeks of the year, Pitt's health broke down completely, forcing him to seek recovery at Bath. Meanwhile, his Cabinet colleagues salvaged what they could from the wrecked coalition. Thornton was ordered to pay no more subsidies—the war was over.[16] Even Nature favored the French emperor. Storms in the North Sea badly battered the British troop transports bound for the Elbe, causing a heavy loss of lives. Should Frederick William accept Napoleon's offer of Hanover and join with him in arms, British units already in the Electorate would have to defend themselves against a Prussian attack. Surveying the disaster which had fallen on every part of Britain's war plans, Lord Mulgrave could find no good news to send the ailing premier at Bath. Only Prussia's intervention could save the allies. "No bribe," the foreign secretary wrote Pitt, "seems to me too high for Prussia at this moment." It might be as well to offer her Holland as a reward.[17] Frederick William's decision to accept Hanover as a *pourboire* from Napoleon's hand put a merciful end to Harrowby's futile mission at Berlin. By mid-January he was on his way home.

The tragedy of the Third Coalition brought Pitt within the darkest shadow of despair. Everything to which he had set his hand had failed. The coalition itself was a monstrous travesty of his original plan. His decision to open a second front in north Germany had exposed the British expeditionary force there to possible disaster. His scheme to win Prussian support failed because it bore no relation to that country's real goals. What little benefit Pitt found in the waters of Bath was wiped out by news of Austerlitz. On January 9 he set out on his return to London, still unaware that his last hope for good news from Harrowby was gone. Five days later he collapsed; the end was not far off.

During the evening of January 22 an east wind, heavy with the promise of rain, enfolded the unpretentious villa on Putney Heath which Pitt and his niece had occupied for a little more than a year.

15. Hardenberg to Harrowby, December 15, 1805, FO 64/70.
16. Harrowby to Thornton, December 12, 1805, FO 64/70.
17. Mulgrave to Pitt, January 6, 1806, Chatham Papers, vol. 162.

Inside, a small group of friends ministered to the dying man, but he required little of them. In his final moments of consciousness, some thought stirred him to ask the direction of the wind. On being told that it came from the East, from the Continent, from the direction of Berlin, he quietly replied, "East; ah! that will do; that will bring him quick." In the final moments of life, Pitt clung to the hope that his country did not fight alone. But Harrowby was no longer in Berlin. Seven tragic years were to pass before Prussia and the other powers would finally unite, as he had vainly urged them to do. Just before dawn of the new day, the twenty-fifth anniversary of his entrance into the House of Commons, William Pitt's life ebbed quietly away.[18]

The ministry which Pitt led could not survive without him, and upon its collapse in February 1806 Lord Grenville was invited to form a government. Prominent in the new Cabinet were some of the late premier's opponents, including Charles James Fox, who became foreign secretary. The new regime was committed to peace with France, if it could be had without too great a sacrifice of national interests. That Grenville should lead such a government seems strange, given his earlier zeal for the war against France. Since 1804, however, he had grown hostile to foreign alliances, perhaps the result of his bitter experience as Pitt's foreign minister. This conversion to isolationism was hastened by his personal break with Pitt and thereafter he became a severe and sour critic of the government's war program in the Lords. Distrust of continental alliances strengthened his partnership with Fox, who hated the war. Under their joint leadership, the new ministry set out to win lasting peace for the war-weary country.

Even if the Cabinet had been pledged to continue Pitt's war program, it would have been hard-pressed to do so. Fox found the Foreign Office almost barren of any information about the latest events on the Continent. It was known that Prussia had reached some sort of agreement with France, but the details were a matter of guesswork. Whether Austria would accept the humiliation of Pressburg or go to war in order to erase it was unknown. No information had reached London regarding Russia's future course of action. Communication with Leveson Gower broke down

18. Stanhope, *Pitt*, IV, 378-382.

completely when that envoy decided that duty required him to accompany the Tsar into the field. By January he was back in St. Petersburg. Despite Russia's dreadful losses, Czartoryski assured him that Alexander meant to continue his alliance with Britain.[19]

Both British armies sent to the Continent by Pitt had been recalled before Grenville came to power. The dangerously exposed British force in Hanover had been withdrawn just before Pitt's death. In Italy General Craig had been obliged to abandon the defense of Naples and remove his forces to Sicily. Although the new government was pledged to peace, it decided to continue its war alliance with Sweden. Fox ordered the subsidy arrears paid up and thereafter his envoy saw to it that the monthly payments were punctually made.[20]

Within less than a month after taking office, Fox initiated discussions with Napoleon's government. The peace negotiation which followed continued until Fox's death the following September. However, the foreign secretary was too intelligent and responsible to ignore the obligation to prepare for war should peace prove beyond his reach. Replying to Leveson Gower's report that Alexander meant to stand by the allies, Fox declared, "A good understanding among the principal Powers in Europe is of the utmost importance, and will greatly contribute to add weight to their representations in time of Peace, as well as power to their Arms, if they should be driven to the necessity of War."[21]

Fox's plans were rudely shaken when he learned that France insisted on negotiating separately with Britain and Russia. This was expressly forbidden by the terms of the Anglo-Russian alliance. While Britain sincerely desired peace, the foreign secretary insisted that it must be arranged conjointly with the allies. Painful though it was, Fox now had to consider what steps should be taken to renew the war. During the past month, major changes had occurred in the European situation. Prussia had at last annexed Hanover and closed the north German ports to British commerce. London retaliated by seizing her shipping and block-

19. Leveson Gower to Mulgrave, January 26, 1806, FO 65/62. This information was not worth much. Three days later Czartoryski announced to Napoleon's agent that Russia would not be averse to a rapprochement. See Puryear, *Napoleon and the Dardenelles*, p. 69.
20. Fox to Pierrepont, March 14, 1806, FO 73/35.
21. Fox to Leveson Gower, February 25, 1806, FO 65/62.

ading her coasts. In June Britain declared war on Prussia, thus holding as an enemy not only Napoleon but also his ally and vassal, Frederick William III. Meanwhile, there were unmistakable indications of a resurgence of French intrigue in the Balkans. Rumours reached London that Napoleon's agents were urging the Porte to join in an attack on Russia.[22]

Any British attempt to storm the salients of French power which Napoleon had thrown up in Germany and Turkey required Russia's cooperation. As early as the first week of April, Fox directed Leveson Gower to invite the Tsar to join in applying pressure to Prussia. "The Emperor might decide to lend His Aid by Sea as well as by Land to blockade the Prussian Ports, and to attack the Frontier of the Enemy. In such a project the King of Sweden . . . might be particularly useful."[23]

A few weeks later, Fox completed his plans for stepping up the war with France. "It is the opinion of His Majesty," he informed Leveson Gower, "that nothing remains for the Allied Powers [Britain and Russia] but to carry on the most vigorous War." The Tsar ought to invade Prussia's Polish lands at once. If Napoleon came to Berlin's aid, the foreign secretary pledged that "The English will assist [Russia] in the manner that shall appear most desirable[?], either by such land forces as she can spare, by naval exertions, or by pecuniary aids, if the amount required be not too exorbitant; or by all, or any, of these means." Should Turkey attack Russia, the allies must "act vigorously against the Porte as well as against France, and the further Russia can push her conquests the more this Country will be satisfied."[24] Britain did not ignore Austria in these plans, although there was little likelihood that she would rejoin the coalition. Robert Adair was ordered to take Paget's place as British ambassador to Austria, but Fox hesitated to give him any special instructions. "I have none to give you," he told Adair on the eve of his departure, "Go to Vienna, and send me yours."[25]

22. Puryear, *Napoleon and the Dardenelles*, pp. 71-125.
23. Fox to Leveson Gower, April 7, 1806, FO 65/62.
24. Fox to Leveson Gower, nos. 11 and 12, April 29, 1806, FO 65/62.
25. Robert Adair, *Historical Memoir of a Mission to the Court of Vienna in 1806* (London, 1844), pp. 11-13. Adair was a good personal friend of Fox, although Fox appears to have had some doubt about the loyalty of Adair's French-born wife. According to Lord Malmesbury (*Malmesbury*, IV, 414), the foreign secretary refused to let her accompany her husband to Vienna.

Napoleon's recent conduct convinced even Fox that Britain must prepare for war. To this end, he offered the Tsar subsidies and virtually invited him to despoil those of his neighbors who were now Napoleon's henchmen. Basically, it was Pitt's old war policy, although the late prime minister might have hesitated to urge Alexander to partition the Turkish empire.[26] The Russian government had modified its policy by the time these instructions reached Leveson Gower. A recent entente with Prussia had given the Tsar stronger cards to play than any Fox could offer.[27] He therefore sent an emissary to Paris to discover what peace terms Napoleon was ready to propose. Thus, Britain's war plans were out of joint with Alexander's desire to negotiate a settlement with the enemy. Even Fox was now more optimistic since France had indicated that she would be willing to negotiate jointly with both Russia and Britain. There soon began that long and tortuous peace conference at the French capital which, dragging on into the autumn, proved such a bitter disappointment to Fox.

The foreign secretary now turned to consider Austria's claims for subsidies still due on the basis of her 1805 treaty with Britain. In January 1806 the Hofburg had put in a claim for £1,600,000. Unquestionably Britain owed something beyond the £1,000,000 already paid by Thornton, but the amount was in dispute. No acceptable data was available to Britain showing the exact number of men Austria had under arms before Ulm. The Hofburg claimed that her army then numbered 315,060—a figure which was probably too high. Furthermore, Britain had counterclaims for the value of supplies sent Austria during the First Coalition. After months of haggling, Fox offered Austria £500,000 and the matter was so arranged.[28]

Russia's claim proved more difficult to settle. The new Russian envoy, Count Stroganoff, contended that the Tsar was entitled to receive £1,176,425 on the basis of the 1805 treaty.[29] Of this sum,

---

26. Fox himself appears later to have had misgivings on this point. On June 19, 1806 he reminded Leveson Gower that this was only to apply in the event Turkey made war on Russia (FO 65/62).

27. Lobanov-Rostovsky, *Russia and Europe,* pp. 116-124.

28. Stadion to Starhemberg, January 1, 1806, FO 7/82; Charles Stuart to Mulgrave, January 6, 1806, FO 7/79; State of the Austrian Army . . . , October 1, 1805, sent to Fox by Starhemberg on February 3, 1806, FO 7/82; Declarations signed by Fox and Starhemberg, August 23, 1806, FO 7/82; Fox to Adair, August 29, 1806, FO 7/80.

29. Following Pitt's death, Vorontzoff resigned his post. Stroganoff's memorandum, dated June 30, 1806, is found in FO 65/66.

Britain appears so far to have paid only £350,000. During the course of Fox's discussions with Stroganoff, he learned that on July 20 Russia and France had signed a peace treaty at Paris. Since this was contrary to the Anglo-Russian alliance on the basis of which subsidies were now being demanded, Fox seems to have postponed a settlement of her claim.[30] Although the Tsar disavowed the peace treaty with Napoleon, relations between London and St. Petersburg remained strained. It was not until 1807 that £500,000 was given Russia to dispose of her claim against Britain.[31]

Russia's peace agreement with France placed Britain in a most difficult position. Unless Fox was ready to accept any terms France offered, the war would have to go on. Where could Britain turn for help except to Austria? At the end of July Fox instructed Adair to assure the Hofburg "that whatever measures of vigour the Emperor may be inclined to adopt, from which there can arise any reasonable probability of Advantage, this Country is ready to support Him."[32] But Vienna was not interested and Fox was forced to watch helplessly as his negotiation with Napoleon dragged wearily to an end.

In searching for peace, Fox never lost sight of the fact that in the end it might elude him. In such a case, Britain would have to renew her war union with Russia. When Alexander appeared to play his ally false by negotiating a unilateral peace treaty, Fox turned in desperation to Austria. Ironically, the only power ready to take up arms against Napoleon was Britain's latest enemy, Prussia. Fox died on September 13, the very moment when Berlin was preparing to draw the sword which had hung idle at her side for more than a decade.

Lord Grenville intensely disliked Prussia, and her unexpected belligerency frankly provoked him. Still hopeful of peace, he regarded her last-minute decision to take arms as an unwelcome complication.[33] What did Berlin hope to accomplish? Only a union

---

30. This is conjectural, but it seems likely that Fox would delay a settlement so long as the peace treaty remined an area of dispute between the two governments.

31. In January 1807, £500,000 was shipped to Russia in specie.

32. Fox to Adair, July 28, 1806, FO 7/80.

33. As late as the end of September Grenville still hoped for general peace in Europe. See Grenville to Howick, September 29, 1806, *Manuscripts of J. B. Fortescue*, VIII, 366-368.

of all the powers could defeat France. If Prussia really wished to topple Napoleon, she would have reached prior agreement with Russia and Britain. Grenville knew of no Russo-Prussian war alliance, and Frederick William had not offered to return Hanover to George III. All evidence led to a single conclusion: Prussia's policy was really more "directed to the object of extending the dominions of Prussia than to that of limiting those of France."[34] Of course, he would maintain an open mind in the unlikely event that Berlin meant to do something more. However, Grenville would certainly not shower her with promises of subsidies and land as Pitt would have done.

To obtain up-to-date information, the government sent Lord Morpeth to Germany as its special agent. On September 24, Lord Howick, who had taken Fox's place at the Foreign Office, prepared his instructions.[35] If Prussia was ready to restore Hanover, Morpeth was to conclude peace with her. He might even discuss terms of alliance, but Britain would offer no subsidies until "the necessity of it shall be proved & the prospect of advantage shall be such as to justify the Demand."[36]

Shortly before Morpeth's departure, Grenville learned that a Prussian envoy was en route to London to request a renewal of the 1794 subsidy pact. Unfortunately, Frederick William gave this assignment to his onetime minister to Britain, Baron Jacobi, for whom Grenville had little use. A letter from Jacobi preceded his arrival in England. Although this appeal for British help was touching, Grenville immediately noticed that its references to Hanover were equivocal.[37] At their first meeting the Prussian diplomat proposed that any discussion of Hanover's future be deferred until the end of the war. Grenville would have none of it. The immediate and unconditional restoration of the Electorate was a sine qua non to peace between the governments. Reporting this to Morpeth, Howick predicted, "I cannot doubt that the necessity of receiving assistance and support from Great Britain

34. Grenville to C. Stuart, September 12, 1806, *ibid.*, VIII, 325.
35. George Howard (1773-1848) was the eldest son of the Earl of Carlisle and known as Viscount Morpeth until his father's death. Lord Howick is better known by his later title of Earl Grey. He became prime minister in 1830 and sponsored the Reform Bill of 1832.
36. Howick to Morpeth, September 24, 1806, FO 64/73.
37. Jacobi to Grenville, September 23, 1806, FO 64/72; and Grenville to Jacobi, October 3, 1806, FO 64/72.

will speedily oblige her [Prussia] to comply with it. The Question of Subsidies may then, and not till then, be entertained."[38]

Debate over Hanover soon became pointless. Napoleon repeated his masterstroke of Ulm by falling on the Prussians before they could obtain help from the Tsar. The Battle of Jena-Auerstädt overturned all Prussia's plans; what remained of her army streamed eastward to join with the Russians. Lord Morpeth was at Weimar when he learned of Prussia's tragedy. Concluding that his mission was now pointless, he promptly returned to London.[39] With Napoleon's armies now occupying all Prussia's lands in the West, Jacobi accepted Britain's demand that Frederick William relinquish his claim to Hanover.[40]

Almost against his will, Grenville began to consider military reunion with Prussia and Russia, but first he would have to know the condition of the allied armies, as well as the war plans of their governments. It was useless to send the unenterprising Morpeth on such a mission. Instead, the assignment was given Lord Hutchinson, whose long military record qualified him for employment.[41] Hutchinson was not to carry any subsidy offer to Frederick William. It was understood in London that £2,000,000 in specie had been removed from the Prussian treasury before Berlin was captured. "If this be true," Howick observed, "no immediate pecuniary supply can be necessary, and time will be afforded for your Lordship to communicate with this Government upon the amount of Subsidy which may be required by Prussia for the future prosecution of the War." Hutchinson could give Prussia as much as £200,000 if he found her army in urgent need, however.[42]

A month later, Hutchinson caught up with Prussians at Königsberg and was shocked to see the shattered remnants of what had once been a first-class army. The survivors of Jena had lost all self-confidence and were poor spiritless things. Frederick William

38. Howick to Morpeth, October 11, 1806, FO 64/73. See also Howick to Charles Stuart, October 22, 1806, FO 65/64.

39. Morpeth to Howick, October 21, 1806, FO 64/73. Morpeth's mission had at least one distinction: he was the only British envoy of the period whose entire correspondence with the Foreign Office amounted to only three dispatches.

40. Howick to Morpeth, October 28, 1806, FO 64/73; Howick to Hutchinson, November 20, 1806, FO 64/74.

41. John Hely-Hutchinson (1757-1832), first Baron Hutchinson, had served in the British army since 1783. Although inclined to undue pessimism, he was well qualified for this military mission to allied headquarters.

42. Howick to Hutchinson, November 20, 1806, FO 64/74.

still hoped that Britain would renew the 1794 subsidy treaty. Estimating that this would cost the Treasury about £3,000,000 a year, Hutchinson concluded that "this would be buying the remainder of the Prussian Army at a dear rate indeed." In sending the Prussian request to London, he admitted that he had strong misgivings: "I feel myself unwilling to engage for the payment of any sum or sums of money—the Sincerity of Prussia is still in my Opinion doubtful, her resources are not only weakened and exhausted but can scarely be said to exist."[43] However, Prussia's needs were so great that Hutchinson did agree to give bills of exchange for small amounts of money during the winter months.[44]

These reports from Königsberg strengthened Grenville's belief that Prussia was a weak reed on which to lean, and, certainly, what she had to offer was not worth a subsidy. Since there was now a chance that Austria might enter the war, the government would make no financial commitment to Prussia for the moment.[45] One year before, Pitt had offered her nearly £3,000,000!

Grenville was just as cautious in his dealings with Russia, even though Alexander was reported to have 140,000 troops in the field.[46] Since this army was now in East Prussia, it could be argued that the 1805 subsidy treaty was again operative. However, Russia's needs were both greater and different from what they had been two years before. Muskets were in especially short supply and Britain was urged to send at least 60,000. Since Russia was now bearing nearly the entire burden of the war, it was vitally important for Britain to open a second front in western Europe. Finally, Russia desperately needed at least £6,000,000 to continue the campaign. The British government was invited to guarantee a Russian loan in London for this amount as she had once done for Austria. To meet the Tsar's immediate requirements, would Britain advance £1,000,000 of that loan in specie now?[47]

43. Hutchinson to Howick, December 23, 29, 1806, FO 64/74.

44. Hutchinson to Howick, January 29, 1807, FO 64/74. The remittances were handled by Robert Adair at Vienna and totalled £87,613; Adair to Howick, January 14, February 17, and March 25, 1807, FO 7/83.

45. Howick to Hutchinson, February 20, 1807, FO 64/74.

46. Charles Stuart to Howick, November 1, 1806, FO 65/64.

47. Stuart to Howick, November 4, 1806, and November 19, 1806, FO 65/64, FO 65/65; Budberg to Stuart, November 27, 1806, FO 65/65; Stuart to Howick, November 28, 31, and December 18, 1806, FO 65/65.

Grenville's response to Russia's appeals for help was disappointing. The request for arms presented no problems; 60,000 stand of arms would go to the Baltic as soon as shipping could be provided.[48] Britain's heavy military commitments outside Europe, however, made it impossible for her to send an expedition to the Continent. The proposal of a Russian loan aroused all sorts of unpleasant memories in Grenville, growing out of his experience with Austria. This request was refused. Howick explained the government's decision to Lord Douglas, the newly appointed minister to Russia.[49] Should Russia default on her obligations, the Treasury would have to pay at least £500,000 a year to meet the loan charges. "The Examples of the Austrian Loans," the foreign secretary explained, "are too recent to allow any one to doubt that a Loan thus secured must in effect be considered as a Subsidy, and would be so regarded by Parliament were such a proposition brought forward there." He went on to underline what was in fact the major objection: "It would not be wise, whatever may be our reliance on the Honour, the Good Faith, & the Steady Friendship of Russia, to implicate ourselves in an arrangement, which, if our present good understanding should at any time cease, might enable that Power in a moment of great difficulty to throw upon us the additional burthen of so large an annual taxation, as that which I have already stated." However, the Cabinet was not indifferent to Alexander's plight and would send £500,000 in silver to him at once. This would cover the balance due the Tsar under the 1805 subsidy treaty, the claim for which had never been settled. H.M.S. *Quebec* was to take the money to Göteborg in Sweden, where arrangements would be made to convey it to the Russian treasury.[50]

Coming at a time when Alexander was trying desperately to halt Napoleon's advance, the British response to his call for help appeared even more pinchbeck than it was. The Russian minister in London coldly asked Grenville "if it was no longer the intention of this Country to make common cause with Russia."[51] Bitterly

48. R. Crewe to G. Walpole, January 4, 1807, FO 65/72.
49. Leveson Gower returned to England in 1806. Alexander Hamilton (1767-1852) was the heir of the Duke of Hamilton and known as Lord Douglas. A wealthy eccentric of no capacity, his service at St. Petersburg was valueless. Upon the collapse of the Grenville government, he was recalled.
50. Howick to Douglas, January 13, 1807, FO 65/68.
51. Howick to Douglas, January 13, 1807, FO 65/68.

disappointed with the prime minister's lack of sympathy, Alexander could hardly be blamed for regarding him as a false friend. Even the king of Sweden turned treacherous. When H.M.S. *Quebec* landed her cargo of silver at Göteborg, Swedish authorities helped themselves to £80,000 of it, claiming that this sum had been owed them by Russia since 1791. Alexander did not condescend to take notice of this banditry.[52] However, he was stung to fury when the new British minister, Lord Douglas, tactlessly pressed him to renew his commercial treaty with England. The Tsar positively refused.[53] What manner of government was it that denied help to a faithful ally in her darkest hour and then asked for commercial concessions? Grenville had no opportunity to reply to that question. Early in March 1807 his government tottered and fell.

Beginning with the Prussian subsidy treaty of 1794, Britain's policy of aid to her war partners had grown steadily more generous under the pressure of events. By the time of the Third Coalition, Pitt was ready to set aside £7,000,000 a year for foreign assistance and, in the winter of 1805-1806, he tempted Prussia with impressive offers of money and land. His death brought about less of a change of policy than might have been expected. Even while seeking for peace, Fox recognized that the allies would require subsidies should the war continue. These he was ready to provide, if "the amount required be not too exorbitant." Lord Grenville was far less generous and, following Fox's death, he nearly stopped the stream of money which had flowed steadily to the allies since 1794. During the winter of 1806-1807, when Prussia and Russia called for massive help, he doled out subsidies by the spoonful.

This pinchbeck response confirmed the allies' belief that Britain's policy was utterly selfish. Early in 1807 Lord Howick laid down certain principles of subsidization which go at least part way to justify that conclusion. Writing to Robert Adair, the foreign secretary promised that Austria would be given some money should she go to war. "But even then," Howick went on, "it is to be observed, that the state of affairs will be very different from that in which subsidies have formerly been granted by this

---

52. Alexander Stratton to Howick, April 5, 1807, FO 73/39.
53. Douglas to Howick, March 7, 1807, FO 65/68.

Country. These were given to different Powers to induce them to send large armies into the field, and to maintain them for the purpose of offensive operations, at a distance from their own frontiers. Austria will now be engaged at home, in her own cause, & in support of her own independence." Continental powers must not rely too much on British money. With almost an air of unctuousness, Howick observed that, "if the great Powers now at war, or threatened by France, cannot find in themselves the means of such Exertion, it is in vain to expect that this Country, by any supplies which we could afford, would be able effectually to support them. It is now indeed more than ever necessary that we should husband our own resources."[54]

A more generous subsidy policy would probably have done nothing to check the onrushing French tide in East Prussia during the early months of 1807. However, Grenville's miserliness contributed to Alexander's growing sense of betrayal, a feeling clearly reflected in his statement to Napoleon at Tilsit, "I hate the English as much as you do."[55]

An epoch was coming to an end in the spring of 1807. Prussia and Russia would finally make peace with Napoleon and take their places on the fringe of his expanding empire. Except for a brief interlude in 1809, Britain's ties with her allies of three coalitions were severed and would remain so for another five years. During that interval, the major problem facing the nations of Europe would be to preserve what was left of their national integrity against Napoleon's steady pressure.

Prior to 1807 generous British trade credits on the Continent helped the government provide the allies with subsidies. However, the Continental System which Napoleon was creating would alter this and oblige future British leaders to rely heavily on the export of specie to implement their foreign aid program. How to provide subsidies and yet not exhaust Britain's specie supply was a constant problem after 1807.

Finally, the conduct of the war was passing to new hands. Pitt and Fox had both fallen, while Grenville withdrew to the House of Lords wearing the mantle of a prophet of doom. This cleared the stage for a new generation of actors. In the emergence of George

54. Howick to Adair, January 13, 1807, FO 7/83.
55. Albert Vandal, *Napoléon et Alexandre Ier* ... (Paris, 1891-1896), I, 58.

Canning and the steady, if less dramatic, rise of Lord Castlereagh, we find the heirs of Pitt—fresh, yet dedicated to their teacher's historic concept of Britain's role in the war with France. Disgusted with the old coalitions and their sad record of failure, they tried to forge new instruments or improve old ones. The national uprisings in the Peninsula gave Canning the chance to modify Pitt's policy of foreign aid and make it fit the needs of a new era. In so doing, he created a force against France which his teacher would have applauded. Castlereagh inherited the vision of a great continental alliance which Pitt had glimpsed in 1805, but nearly a decade would pass before he was able to graft its principles onto the final coalition which would overthrow Napoleon.

IX

A NEW DIRECTION FOR BRITISH WAR POLICY

The ministry formed by the Duke of Portland in the spring of 1807 was the most loosely knit regime to govern wartime Britain. Pitt and Grenville had been dominant figures, but Portland presided over a Cabinet he did not lead. The government's strength lay in the ability of several of its ministers whose rivalries the prime minister tried hard to moderate. Spencer Perceval, who served as chancellor of the exchequer, described the arrangement: "It is not because the Duke of Portland is at our head that the Government is a Government of Departments, but it is because the Government is and must be essentially a Government of Departments that the Duke of Portland is at our head."[1]

Two of those departments, vitally important in the conduct of the war, were headed by men whose antagonism finally brought them to the dueling field. At the Foreign Office, George Canning undertook to prove his claim to be Pitt's political heir. That claim was not without some foundation, but Canning's unquestionable ability and leadership qualities were marred by restless ambition. As Pitt's protégé, he had served briefly as undersecretary for foreign affairs to prepare himself for the larger roles he expected to play. A fondness for intrigue and lack of steadiness cost him his mentor's confidence. In his last years, Pitt relied increasingly on Lord Castlereagh. As Portland's secretary of war, Castlereagh would have to work with his rival in at least some degree of harmony. Mutual distrust prevented the two men from being genuine partners, but each contributed to the revision of Britain's war policy, which the Portland government initiated.

1. J. Steven Watson, *The Reign of George III, 1760-1815* (Oxford, 1960), p. 444.

Grenville had left behind a clutch of problems whose solution would require all the ability the new Cabinet possessed. His military expeditions to South America and the Mediterranean were proving costly failures. On the Continent, the war had been squeezed into a small arena where Prussia and Russia were vainly trying to hold back France. Thanks to Grenville's puny contribution to this work, Britain's influence and prestige had waned in the eyes of the allies now locked in mortal combat.

The Portland ministry was anxious to reverse Grenville's shortsighted policies and throw the nation's resources behind its allies, but impressive obstacles blocked the path. With so large a part of the army overseas, no more than 12,000 troops could be spared to open a new front in western Europe.[2] Sending financial help to Prussia and Russia also presented problems. The Continental System was rapidly shrinking Britain's export trade to Europe, thereby cutting into the credits she needed to pay subsidies.[3] Fortunately, the 1807 grain harvest would prove adequate, if not abundant; no heavy purchase of food overseas would be called for this year.[4] Of course, subsidies could always be paid for by the export of hard money, but the government was naturally reluctant to do so.

Far worse than Britain's military weakness or the shrinkage of her continental trade was the fact that time was fast running out for the allies. The French capture of Danzig in May signaled the opening of a campaign to decide the fate of the Russo-Prussian armies. If Britain was to intervene effectively, arrangements would have to be made at once. Castlereagh worked feverishly to prepare a British expedition to Stralsund; at the Foreign Office, Canning moved heaven and earth to send the allies the money and arms they needed.[5]

One of the most important features of Canning's policy appeared in his first dispatches to Lord Hutchinson, who was still

2. Memorandum for the Cabinet, relative to the State of the Military Force, March, 1807, *Correspondence of Castlereagh,* VIII, 46-52.

3. The value of British products sent to northern Europe fell from £10,320,000 in 1805 to £5,090,000 by the end of 1807. Even that was cut in half during the following year. See Eli Hecksher, *The Continental System; an Economic Interpretation,* ed. H. Westergaard (Oxford, 1922), p. 245.

4. W. F. Galpin, *The Grain Supply of England during the Napoleonic Period* (New York, 1925), p. 257.

5. Richard Glover, *Peninsular Preparation: The Reform of the British Army, 1795-1809* (Cambridge, 1963), pp. 246-254.

at allied headquarters. The Prussians were to be given £100,000 at once to provide for their needs until a regular subsidy agreement could be concluded. The shortage of continental credits and the disruption of normal banking services would make it difficult for Britain to remit large sums to the allies. "It is possible," Canning observed, "that these difficulties might be in some degree removed by an agreement on the part of the Continental Powers, to receive a proportion of what might be given (or lent) to them, in arms, clothing, and such other Manufactures of this Country, as may be applicable to their immediate wants."[6] No effort would be spared to send arms to the allies, but Britain wished to count their value as part of the subsidy they also expected.

Although the foreign secretary was eager to put muskets in the hands of the allied armies, it soon became clear that Britain's resources were severely limited. In April Jacobi gave the Foreign Office a list of supplies needed by Prussia, and within a month, 40 howitzers and cannon, together with 10,000 muskets, 3,000,000 ball cartridges, and 100,000 flints were on the way to the Baltic.[7] By June nearly 100,000 British muskets had been sent off and still the allies called for more.[8] Lord Chatham, Master General of the Ordnance, threw up his hands in despair. With only 2,000 pistols remaining in stock, he simply could not meet Prussia's latest request for 15,000. Russia had asked for 1,200 rifles of a type which the Ordnance could not supply. Very patiently, Chatham explained why he was unable to comply with such requests. The Ordnance Office had always relied on continental gunsmiths to supplement the home production of weapons. With the Continent now cut off, Britain was thrown on her own resources. Efforts were being made to boost arms production, but no material improvement could be expected for at least a year.[9]

The fresh point of view Canning brought to the Foreign Office is clearly seen in his negotiation of a subsidy treaty with Jacobi. That envoy, whom Grenville had so badly browbeaten, proposed

6. Canning to Hutchinson, no. 4, April 5, 1807, FO 64/74.
7. Jacobi to Canning, April 14, 1807, FO 64/77; Castlereagh to Canning, May 16, 1807, FO 64/74.
8. Seventy thousand muskets had gone to the Baltic since the first of the year, while 24,000 had been sent to Sicily. Memorandum . . . on the subject of Military and Naval Succours, May 26, 1807, *Correspondence of Castlereagh*, VIII, 66.
9. Chatham to Castlereagh, June 19, 1807, FO 64/77. See also R. Glover, *Peninsular Preparation*, pp. 61-67.

terms of such an agreement to Canning late in the spring: to maintain an army of 100,000 men, Prussia required £600,000 as a preparation subsidy together with monthly payments of £90,000. This scheme was based on the terms of the 1794 pact, which Prussia had all along wished to revive.

Canning rejected it. The time was long past for any agreement based on the outmoded principles of 1794. Then, Prussia was renting an army to Britain and Holland to do with as they pleased. The present situation was altogether different since "His Majesty is now called upon to assist the King of Prussia in the Recovery of his Dominions, and in the Defence of his Crown and Kingdom." Were it not for precedent, Canning would have had no treaty at all. During the Seven Years War, England subsidized Frederick the Great's desperate struggle for survival. Since the present state of affairs was exactly the same, the foreign secretary proposed to take the 1758 treaty as a model.[10] He then made a refreshingly simple offer: Britain would pay Prussia £1,000,000 in three installments during the year in return for her pledge to employ all her resources in the war against France.[11] This proposal threw Jacobi into some confusion, but there was little room for him to object. On June 27 the two men signed the simplest subsidy treaty of the entire war.[12] Happily, the foreign secretary also departed from the practices of his predecessors in another particular. Even before the treaty was signed, arrangements were made for the shipment of specie to cover the first installment of the Prussian subsidy. Silver was to be bought in Denmark for delivery at Kronstadt.[13]

The Tsar's demand for a British loan complicated the Cabinet's plans to aid him. Canning was as reluctant as Grenville to endorse such a transaction and he explained his ideas to Leveson Gower, who had again been named as Britain's envoy to Russia. During the balance of the year £3,000,000 was available for aid to the allies. Prussia and Sicily had already been promised help and

10. Canning was referring to the elder Pitt's treaty with Prussia of April 11, 1758. See Albert von Ruville, *William Pitt, Earl of Chatham,* trans. H. J. Chaytor (London, 1907), II, 184.

11. Canning to Jacobi, June, 1807, FO 64/77.

12. Treaty with Prussia, June 27, 1807, FO 93/78(5A).

13. Wm. Huskisson to Lord Fitzharris, May 20, 1807, FO 65/72; Memorandum of Wm. Huskisson, August 4, 1807, FO 65/73.

doubtless Sweden would require something. "What might remain unapplied . . . would be cheerfully contributed by H. M. in aid of the military expenditure of Russia."[14]

Canning selected the Earl of Pembroke as the new British minister to Austria and ordered him "to counteract an impression which is known to have been entertained at Vienna of an indifference on the part of this Country to the concerns and interests of the Continent." The Hofburg was not to be offered subsidies as a bait to enter the war, but whenever Austria was "unequivocally committed against France and embarked in the common cause . . . His Majesty will not then be backward to consider the necessities of His Ally."[15]

Since a British force was soon to sail for Stralsund, Downing Street must reach a clear understanding with Sweden. There were other reasons for maintaining the best possible relations with Stockholm. Access to Sweden's ports was more than ever important to British merchants who found themselves shut out of other harbors by Napoleon's decrees. Increasing dependence on Sweden for naval stores furnished still another reason for remaining on good terms with Gustavus Adolphus. If the Swedish king enlarged his army and joined Britain in an attack on France, it might materially affect the outcome of the East Prussian campaign. Canning was ready to be generous with Sweden. In return for adding 4,000 men to his army, Gustavus was offered an annual subsidy of £50,000 a year in addition to the payment of preparation money. A treaty incorporating these provisions was signed at Stralsund on June 23.[16] One week later, the van of the British expeditionary force, under the command of Lord Cathcart, sailed from England to that port. By that time, however, the campaign in East Prussia had already ended.[17]

---

14. Canning to Leveson Gower, May, 1807, FO 65/69. Leveson Gower was empowered to give Russia bills on England to meet her immediate requirements.

15. George Augustus Pembroke (1759-1827), eleventh Earl of Pembroke, was another military figure temporarily pressed into diplomatic service for a special mission. Canning's instructions, dated May 15 and 16, 1807, are to be found in FO 7/85.

16. Gustavus was to receive the equivalent of three months' subsidy as preparation money, with an extra month's payment due at the end of the war. See Canning to Pierrepont, May 30, 1807, FO 73/40; Treaty with Sweden, June 23, 1807, FO 93/101(6A).

17. The King's German Legion was the first unit to sail for Stralsund, just as it had been first to leave for the Elbe in 1805.

The Battle of Friedland (June 14, 1807) dashed all Canning's plans to pieces. Even the arms sent by Britain arrived too late to help the allies.[18] Leveson Gower reached Russian headquarters a few days after the battle and found Alexander bitterly resentful at Britain's failure to sponsor his loan. The envoy did his best to explain Canning's position, but admitted, with remarkable understatement, "I cannot say that the Emperor appeared perfectly satisfied." The Russian minister, Budberg, went to the heart of the matter when he grimly observed to Leveson Gower, "It is not money, it is men we want."[19] A few days later Alexander and Napoleon met on a raft in the river Niemen, and shortly thereafter France concluded peace treaties with the defeated powers. Leveson Gower grew anxious about the silver now deposited in the Imperial Bank at St. Petersburg. Since it was no longer needed to pay Prussia a subsidy, he had it carried on board H.M.S. *Astrea* at Kronstadt. By August it was safely at sea and the British minister breathed more easily. "I thought it my duty," he explained to Canning, "to take it out of the hands of this Government as soon as possible."[20]

By the end of July, Napoleon had swept all the pieces from the continental chess board except the Anglo-Swedish army at Stralsund. Britain's change of policy had come too late to halt, or even delay, the coalition's death. In line with the principle adopted by Pitt three years before, Canning had offered help to any power ready to fight Napoleon. However, he distrusted the complicated and unrealistic details of the treaties Pitt had negotiated. France could be defeated only by an inexorable will to victory on the part of the allies. There was no room for the careful numbering of soldiers as the basis for determining subsidies. Fight with all your might, he told Prussia, and we will not fail you. In this spirit, Britain offered to supply her allies with needed war materials. If British commerce and industry proved equal to the

18. This seems to be the meaning of Hutchinson's letter to Canning of July 20, 1807, FO 64/74.

19. Leveson Gower to Canning, June 17 and 18, 1807, FO 65/69.

20. Leveson Gower to Canning, August 2, 1807, FO 65/69. Master's Log for H.M.S. *Astrea,* 1807, Ad. 51/1662. Vienna learned of Friedland before the arrival of Britain's new envoy. Adair undertook a last-minute plea and told Stadion that he would guarantee "any sum that might be wanted to put their army instantly into motion." Stadion did not even bother to reply. Adair's proposal was sheer lunacy. See Adair to Canning, June 27, 1807, FO 7/84.

challenge, Canning was ready to promise unlimited support to any power animated by the will to victory. Guineas *and* gunpowder were henceforth to be the prime ingredients of Britain's subsidy program.

Napoleon used his new friendship with the Tsar to further plans to create a bloc of Baltic powers hostile to Britain. Canning was powerless to prevent Denmark from being forced into that league, but he could at least insure that her fleet would not fall to the French. Late in the summer of 1807 a British military and naval force attacked Copenhagen and returned home with the Danish ships in tow. This brilliant, if controversial, stroke was not without its cost. Russia declared war on Great Britain even earlier than she had planned. Meanwhile, a trembling Austria sought by all means to avoid the fate which had befallen Prussia as the penalty for her temerity. The French systematically plundered Frederick William's kingdom in order to keep it in a state of perpetual dependence.[21]

In order to survive, Britain would have to strengthen her ties with the few European powers still beyond Napoleon's grasp and use them as trade entrepôts to breach the Continental System. It was uncertain how long Portugal could be kept from Napoleon's clutches. Should France succeed in closing her ports, Canning would surely offset this loss by gaining admission to Portugal's colonial markets. The independence of Sweden and her alliance with Britain were also of paramount importance to London. British goods exported to Sweden had a way of being sent on to those parts of Europe behind Napoleon's blockade. Between 1807 and 1810 the value of Britain's exports to Sweden increased fourfold, thereby providing her with the means of obtaining much needed timber and naval stores from the Baltic area. Gibraltar, Sicily, and the Ionian Islands also served as entrepôts through which British goods passed on to continental consumers.[22] Both

---

21. In August 1807 Prussia requested a loan of £1,000,000 from Britain to help her pay the indemnity which Napoleon had imposed. The British government refused to help. See Garlike to Canning, August 26, 1807, FO 64/76.

22. Hecksher, *Continental System,* p. 245. For an account of Britain's use of Sweden and Heligoland as trade entrepôts, see *ibid.,* pp. 178-180. Sweden sent little timber to Britain, but her ports were entrepôts for timber quietly brought from other Baltic harbors under the Continental System. See Robert G. Albion, *Forests and Sea Power; The Timber Problem of the English Navy, 1652-1862* (Cambridge, Mass., 1926), pp. 342-343.

economic and military considerations made it essential for Britain to keep Portugal, Sweden, and Sicily free from French control.

During the summer of 1807 Napoleon put immense pressure on the Portuguese Regent to break with England and adhere to the Continental System. João only hoped that Britain would allow him to submit. From Lisbon, the British minister, Lord Strangford, sent home discouraging reports regarding the Regent's conduct. In order to make peace with Napoleon on the best possible terms, João was reported to be sending packets of diamonds to France's leaders. "I cannot help declaring my firm conviction," Strangford observed, "that any attempt on the part of England to save Portugal by any Military Succours, would be utterly unavailing."[23] Experience proved that only the dispatch of a major British army could help Portugal. Since this was out of the question, Canning fell back on the remedy prescribed by Lord Hawkesbury in 1801: the transfer of the Portuguese government and fleet to Brazil. But the Regent was reluctant to go. Caught between a Franco-Spanish army of invasion on one side and a menacing British fleet in Lisbon harbor, João finally yielded to Strangford's demands.[24] With the Portuguese court now en route to Brazil, Canning could afford to be generous; £80,000 in gold was sent to Rio for the Regent's use and he was given a £20,000 credit in London.[25]

Britain expected to enjoy the right of direct trade with Brazil, and in January 1808 the Regent responded by throwing open his New World ports to ships of friendly nations. Even though Britain would have the lion's share of that trade, Canning sought preferential treatment. Various difficulties intervened to delay the conclusion of the necessary commercial treaty for two years. However, by 1811 Britain had gained an impressive hold on Portugal's overseas markets—seventy-five British firms were doing business at Rio. In exchange for manufactured goods, England

23. Strangford to Canning, August 20, 21, 1807, FO 63/55. Percy Clinton Sydney Smythe, sixth Viscount Strangford (1780-1855) was one of the youngest British diplomats of the period. He accompanied the Regent to Rio and there won fame as Britain's spokesman in Brazil.

24. On October 22, 1807 Canning signed a treaty with Portugal's envoy calling for the removal of the Regent to Rio and the conclusion of an Anglo-Portugese trade agreement (FO 93/77 [1B]).

25. Canning to F. Hill, January 16, 1808, FO 63/63; Canning to Strangford, August 5, 1808, FO 63/59.

obtained specie, raw cotton, and other colonial raw materials, which somewhat offset the losses she suffered from the Continental System.[26]

It had been impossible to save Portugal from the enemy, but Canning hoped that something might be done to guarantee Sweden's independence. Following the Battle of Tilsit, Gustavus had been forced to abandon Stralsund. Now he found himself threatened on three sides by France's allies and henchmen: Denmark, Prussia, and Russia. In the East, the Tsar's army moved menacingly toward the Finnish frontier, while a French force in Denmark clearly intended to strike. In December 1807 Gustavus Adolphus called on London for help.

Sweden's importance to Britain guaranteed a favorable response to this appeal. No troops could be spared, but Canning promised to strengthen the British fleet in the Baltic as soon as possible. Subsidies were also offered on the basis of the type of agreement the foreign secretary always preferred. If Sweden would do everything possible to defend herself, Britain would pay her £100,000 a month during the coming year. These were the instructions handed to Edward Thornton, who would go to Stockholm as Britain's new plenipotentiary. To avoid needless delay, £100,000 in silver was sent to Göteborg for his use as the first installment of the subsidy.[27] Under the circumstances, Gustavus was not inclined to bargain, and on February 8, 1808 he accepted the British proposal.[28] A few days later, Russian troops crossed the border into Finland, and shortly thereafter, Denmark joined the war against Gustavus.

The rapid Russian advance prompted Stockholm to call on England for still more money and a supply of weapons. Canning's response was as vigorous as ever. Although additional subsidies could not be given, 35,000 muskets together with powder, cartridges, and sabres, all valued at £94,023, would be sent at

26. Manchester, *British Preëminence*, p. 69 and *passim*.
27. Canning to E. Thornton, December 30, 1807, FO 73/45. Edward Thornton (1766-1852) was one of Britain's more successful career diplomats. He was to have an important part to play in the formation of the final coalition against France.
28. Since all Britain's earlier subsidy treaties with Sweden involved the use of Stralsund, they were nullified when Gustavus abandoned Pomerania. See the treaty with Sweden, February 8, 1808, FO 93/101 (6B); and Thornton to Canning, February 9, 1808, FO 73/46.

once. As a special concession, the value of these arms would not be deducted from the monthly subsidy.[29] Sweden's extreme danger finally led the Cabinet to decide on military intervention, and in May, 10,000 British troops commanded by General Sir John Moore sailed for Göteborg. Canning was ready to aid Sweden by the same means he had offered Prussia and Russia one year before: subsidies, war materials, and finally military force.

Although it was desirable for Britain to clarify her relations with Sicily, the Foreign Office felt little urgency to do so. The exiled government of Naples was now safely ensconced at Palermo under the strong protection of the British fleet. Originally there had been some hope of using the island as a springboard for an invasion of the mainland, but that scheme had been abandoned. By the time Canning came to the Foreign Office, Sicily figured very little in Britain's war plans.

If Canning took the trouble to review the Foreign Office correspondence relating to Sicily during the past five years, he might have concluded that no amount of labor would make sense of it. Anglo-Sicilian relations involved three separate problems, each one of which was a Gordian knot. The records of the British subsidy payments to Sicily, which began in 1804, were now hopelessly confused, never to be set straight. Addington had started the payments on an informal basis in 1804. They were continued by Pitt who, without the benefit of a treaty, promised Naples £300,000 a year. After Ferdinand fled to Sicily, subsidy payments were made irregularly by the British minister, Hugh Elliot.[30] Not only were Elliot's records incomplete, but he and the Palermo government never could agree on the value of such remittances as he did bother to note. Payments were usually made by means of bills of exchange, but the shortage of hard money in the island produced severe discounting when the bills were converted into cash. Should payments be figured in terms of the

29. Canning to Thornton, March 24, April 1, 1808, FO 73/45; R. Crewe to C. Bagot, April 21, 1808, FO 73/53. A small part of the Swedish subsidy was used to create a credit for her government in London, but the bulk of it went to her in specie. Thornton's Account, in the papers of the Audit Office, deposited in the Public Record Office, London (hereafter cited as "AO"), 1/12(31) shows that between January and October 1808, £855,050 in silver was sent to Sweden.

30. Hugh Elliot (1752-1830) was a minor diplomat who began his career at Munich in 1773. Lack of interest and ability prevented him from reaching the top positions and he ended his career as a colonial governor.

face value of the bills of exchange, or of the specie they produced when negotiated? On giving up his post in November 1806, Elliot was obliged to send London an account of his payments. That account, showing a total expenditure of £424,657, was at best an estimate—at worst, a wild guess. Elliot abandoned the island with relief, leaving responsibility for future subsidies to the British commander, General Henry Fox, until the arrival of the new envoy, William Drummond.[31] Elliot, Fox, Drummond, and the Sicilian government agreed on only one point: British payments were in arrears. Drummond estimated these arrears to be £267,799, a figure which the Palermo court vociferously protested.[32] How the two parties were ever to reach agreement on this question was beyond Canning's understanding.

Quite a different problem was the Queen, Maria Carolina, who exerted a commanding influence over her husband's government. Disliking Sicily intensely, she schemed to recover Naples either by arms or diplomatic intrigue. The refusal of British officers to enter wholeheartedly into her harebrained plans inevitably won them her hatred, whch often verged on the paranoid. Maria Carolina easily achieved a remarkable record: she quarreled bitterly with every British military and civil official of first rank who came to the island. Elliot's successor dangerously underestimated his regal opponent. Not long after his arrival, Drummond decided to end her meddling and announced that he would pay no more subsidies until the Queen resigned from the Council of State. Victory came easy for the British envoy—too easy. The Queen did resign and Drummond renewed the payments. However, Maria Carolina's power was as great outside the council as it had ever been, a fact which Drummond's pride prevented him from admitting. Having thoroughly duped her antagonist, the Queen openly defied him by resuming her place on the council. There was more than a little sense in the suggestion privately made by General Sir John Moore that the Queen be shipped off to

31. William Drummond (1770?-1828) was capable of arousing strong feelings in those with whom he worked. Unquestionably, he was vain and inclined to self-deception. Conditions in Sicily were hardly of the sort to bring out his better qualities.

32. An Account of the different Payments made to the Neapolitan government up to November, 1806, FO 70/29; George Harrison to Hammond, December 9, 1807, FO 70/31; Drummond to Canning, October 29, 1807, FO 70/30. The total payments made by Elliot and Fox, prior to Drummond's arrival, seem to have amounted to £579,002.

Trieste. Thoughtful observers saw her as a symbol of the wretched relations that existed between the Bourbons and the people of Sicily. Reforms were desperately needed to check a growing tendency to revolution on the island.[33]

Finally, what ought to be the relation between Ferdinand's government, nominally sovereign, and his British protectors? During the Grenville ministry, Drummond had been instructed to demand important concessions from Sicily in return for a subsidy treaty. These included placing the Sicilian army under a British commander, a reform of the Bourbon government, and exemption from Sicilian custom duties of supplies sent the British garrison. Drummond did not press the matter and his treaty of March 23, 1807 obtained very little in return for the promise of an annual £300,000 subsidy.[34]

The Sicilian treaty remained unratified on Canning's desk for nearly six months. In December 1807 he finally approved it but insisted on a change in the text. One of the articles obliged Britain to pay all subsidy arrears within six months after ratification. Parliament had never voted any money for the Sicilian subsidy in the past; it had been taken from the Secret Service fund. Therefore, this article must be made a secret provision and thus expunged from the text to be laid before Parliament.[35] The foreign secretary took pains to underscore the fact that, henceforth, Palermo would be obliged to submit a quarterly account showing how it had spent the subsidy. "A constant and scrupulous observance of that Article" was recommended to Drummond. The House of Commons approved the agreement, but embarrassing questions were asked about unauthorized payments made in the past. Exception was also taken to the fact that no concessions had been obtained from Ferdinand's government.[36]

Like Elliot and Drummond, Canning failed to reach agreement with Palermo on the matter of subsidy arrears. His patience now sorely tried, he proposed to settle the business by increasing the

33. John Rosselli, *Lord William Bentinck and the British Occupation of Sicily, 1811-1814* (Cambridge, 1956), pp. 158-163; Oman, *Moore*, p. 389 and *passim.*

34. Howick to Drummond, October 3, 1806, FO 70/30; Drummond to Howick, March 11, 1807, FO 70/30; Treaty with Sicily, March 23, 1807, FO 93/96 (1B).

35. Canning to Drummond, December 26, 1807, FO 70/30. To carry out Canning's orders, Drummond negotiated a new treaty with Sicily on March 30, 1808. See FO 93/96(2, 3).

36. Canning to Drummond, June 25, 1808, FO 70/32; *Hansard,* XI (1808), 861-863.

annual subsidy to £400,000. To prevent further disputes, all payments would be made in London, rather than Palermo. The offer was accepted.[37] The Byzantine conduct of Ferdinard's regime soon drove Canning to fury, and only his resignation in October spared Palermo from feeling his wrath.[38] Canning's successors at the Foreign Office probably did well to forget Sicily; the strategic value of the island had greatly diminished during the past year. However, two important questions would soon force Downing Street to take action: the divided command over British and Sicilian troops on the island and the execrable conduct of the Bourbon government toward its long-suffering subjects.

During the first year of the Portland ministry, British foreign policy tried to conserve what little remained of her continental connections; it was a policy dictated as much by economic as military considerations. Unable to save Portugal, Britain obtained some equivalent for her loss in the opening of Brazil. Canning struggled to hold Sweden by sending her money, arms, and troops. If relations with Sicily were still uneasy, military and financial support for the island had at last been put on a regular basis. None of this was exciting, but it was necessary. Canning's experience with foreign aid and its attendant problems prepared him for the far more important work which came to hand with the outbreak of the national revolts in the Peninusla during the spring of 1808.

Instead of being rewarded for her part in the conquest of Portugal, Spain discovered that collaboration with Napoleon would cost her dearly. In the spring of 1808 more than 100,000 French soldiers were in Spain to back up the Emperor's decision to place his brother Joseph on the throne of the degenerate Bourbons. Fires of revolt against French oppression blazed forth in Madrid and quickly spread to every corner of the land, even leaping the border into Portugal. By June representatives from three Spanish juntas were in London in search of arms and money which, they insisted, were all they required to drive the usurper from their country. Reports of French defeats in the Peninsula

37. Canning to Drummond, August 5, 1808, FO 70/32; Canning to Lord Amherst, March 7, 1809, FO 70/36; Treaty with Sicily, May 13, 1809, FO 93/96 (4).

38. Canning to Amherst, August 16, 1809, FO 70/36; Amherst to the Marquess Wellesley, February 5, 1810, FO 70/39.

encouraged the hope that, properly supported, the uprising might indeed topple Napoleon.

Canning sensed the excitement of this historic moment, and on June 15 he explained the government's policy to an enthusiastic House of Commons. While his remarks deal with the Spanish crisis, they reflect the viewpoint which had marked his leadership of the Foreign Office for the past year. "We shall proceed upon the principle," he declared, "that any nation of Europe that starts up with a determination to oppose a power which ... is the common enemy of all nations, whatever may be the existing political relations of that nation and Great Britain, becomes instantly our essential ally."[39] His heart leaped at the prospect of victory now opening before him. With a British army in Sweden and the French on the defensive in the Peninsula, Napoleon might soon have his wings clipped. The foreign secretary instructed his agent at Stockholm to persuade Russia and Denmark to abandon their war with Sweden. Surely they must now see the folly of cooperating with the tyrant. Once free from France's orbit, they should unite with Britain in a defensive coalition, "while the Flames continue spreading in the South from Spain to Italy and thence perhaps to Austria."[40] Canning's dearest wish was to weld the nations along the edge of Napoleon's empire into a steel chain with which to strangle the tyrant.

The Cabinet's enthusiasm kept pace with the foreign secretary, and it agreed to send British troops to the Peninsula. Command over this force, which finally numbered 15,000 men, went to Sir Arthur Wellesley, with orders to secure a foothold in Portugal. A month later the government learned, to its dismay, that more troops were available for this service than it had anticipated. The expeditionary force sent to Sweden was returning to England with an account of its luckless adventure which was almost beyond belief. On reaching Göteborg, Sir John Moore had conferred with Gustavus Adolphus regarding the employment of the British troops. By this time the Swedish king was verging on insanity and so extreme were his views that Moore had to object. As a result Gustavus refused the British permission to land and threatened

39. *Hansard,* XI (1808), 890-891.
40. Canning to Thornton, June 10, 1808, FO 73/45.

Moore with arrest. Upon returning to England, the corps was sent to join the expedition already en route to Portugal. Command over the now enlarged army in the Peninsula was vested in Sir Hew Dalrymple.

In June Canning met with the representatives of the Spanish juntas, who vied with each other in pressing their claims for British help. The Asturian envoys, the first to reach London, asked for at least 5,000,000 Spanish dollars (about £1,000,000). Those from Galicia submitted a request for only $3,000,000, which they promptly raised to $5,000,000 on learning of the Asturian demand. Uniformity was achieved with the arrival of a delegation from Andalusia with a plea for $5,000,000. Canning returned the same answer to all of them: Britain would send as much specie and arms as she could spare.[41] No time was lost in making good that pledge. Early the next month, Charles Stuart sailed for Corunna with £200,000 in Spanish dollars for the junta of Galicia.[42] Before the summer ended £1,100,000 in silver had been given the five major juntas with the promise that more would be forthcoming as soon as a Supreme Junta for all of Spain was formed. Payments made to the provinces fell short of their original demands, but they were solid proof of Britain's determination to support the national revolt. Portugal did less well since her petition reached London only after the British government had undertaken commitments to the Spanish. At the end of July Canning learned that the Bishop of Oporto, leader of the resistance movement in that city, needed arms, equipment, and money to outfit 40,000 men. At the moment Britain could spare only about £60,000, which was given at once.[43]

41. The value of the Spanish dollar varied between four and five to the pound sterling (Canning to John Hunter and Charles Stuart, July 27, 1808. FO 72/57). Canning's replies to the envoys from the Asturias (June 12, 1808) and from Galicia (June 29, 1808) are found in FO 72/66.

42. Charles Stuart (1779-1845) was a son of General Sir Charles Stuart, who commanded the British troops sent to Portugal during the Second Coalition. The younger Stuart remained in the diplomatic service and in 1828 was created Baron Stuart de Rothesay.

Payments to the local juntas were all in silver as follows: Galicia, £500,000; Asturias, £200,000; Seville, £200,000; Leon, £100,000; Cadiz, £100,000. In addition, £50,000 was given to the troops of the Spanish Marquis de Romana (Memorandum of Supplies furnished by Great Britain to Spain . . ., FO 72/137).

43. Canning to John H. Frere, November 16, 1808, FO 72/60; Bishop of Oporto to de Souza, July 7, 1808, FO 63/65; Canning to de Souza, August 4, 1808, FO 63/65. In November 1808 Britain advanced £95,000 to Portugal on a loan which she planned to float in London; Canning to Strangford, November 26, 1808, FO 63/60.

Arms were sent the Spanish as quickly as they could be loaded aboard ships; more than 30,000 muskets accompanied the British troops when they sailed for the Peninsula in mid-July. Lord Chatham promised to deliver 70,000 more before the end of the year, but under the ceaseless proddings of Canning and Castlereagh, the languid Master General did even better. In November he reported that at least 160,000 muskets had already been sent, with another 30,000 to 40,000 due to follow within a month.[44] Most of these arms were consigned to Britain's military agents in Spain with orders to distribute them to the local juntas.[45] Portugal's needs were not neglected. During the last half of 1808 Britain sent her 26,766 stand of arms along with 17,000 pikes. Britain also shipped to the insurgents in the Peninsula enough clothing to outfit 100,000 men.[46]

Results on the battlefield quickly confirmed the wisdom of British support of the nationalists. In July a Spanish army soundly beat the French at Baylen and forced 18,000 of them to lay down their arms. A month later, Britain celebrated the first victory of its own army in Portugal. At Vimiero, thirty-five miles north of Lisbon, Wellesley repulsed a heavy French attack, but the fruits of victory were snatched away by his superior's unfortunate Convention of Cintra with the enemy.[47] Although the French agreed to withdraw from Portugal, several features of the Convention aroused bitter opposition in England. Dalrymple and Wellesley were called home to answer charges, leaving Sir John Moore in command of the British troops in Portugal. Across the frontier in Spain, a series of defeats compelled the French to withdraw to a defensive position along the Ebro River. This so encouraged London that it ordered Moore to enter Spain and join the nationalists in driving the enemy from the Peninsula. In mid-October, the British expeditionary force marched out of Lisbon on their way to Salamanca in Spain, commanded by a general who

44. Chatham to Canning, July 17, 1808, FO 72/68; Canning to Frere, November 16, 1808, FO 72/60.
45. Fortescue, *British Army*, VI, 257-261.
46. An account of the arms issued for the Service of the Portuguese Government from the Commencement of the War in the year 1808, March 24, 1813, FO 63/102; Memorandum of Supplies furnished ... to Spain, FO 72/137. Sir William F. P. Napier (*History of the War in the Peninsula* ... , [London, 1890], I, 87) claimed that very little of this equipment ever found its way to the Spanish soldier.
47. Michael Glover, *Wellington's Peninsular Victories* (London, 1963), pp. 14-15.

was frankly disturbed by the uncertainties which lay ahead. As yet, no Spanish commander had been given authority to co-ordinate the several armies which the Junta had in the field. Furthermore, Moore was troubled by the lack of any reliable information as to where he might find the Spanish and how many of them were actually under arms.

In London, Canning was trying to reach formal agreements with Britain's new allies before the first flush of enthusiasm passed. His efforts to persuade the separate Spanish juntas to unite finally bore fruit with the formation of the Supreme Junta at Aranjuez in September 1808. To no one's surprise, one of its first acts was to ask Britain for an annual subsidy of £2,000,000, together with arms and equipment for 300,000 troops.[48] The foreign secretary appointed John Hookham Frere as his envoy to the Junta and explained the policy he was to follow.[49] The money and arms already sent Spain would be considered as a gift, although future British aid must be on a somewhat different basis. Frere was given £650,000 in silver to help the Junta, pending the conclusion of a formal subsidy agreement. Britain's supply of hard money had been nearly exhausted by the massive shipments to the Peninsula during the last few months, and future aid would depend upon Britain obtaining access to the markets of Spain and her colonies. "An intercourse with South America," the foreign secretary declared, "is indispensably necessary for the obtaining, by this Country, the means of continuing its Aid to the Spanish cause."[50]

Canning stressed this point in his meeting with Admiral Apodaca, the Junta's envoy in London, and proposed that any alliance between the two governments incorporate both subsidy provisions and a commerical agreement. Apodaca protested that he had no authority to revise commercial relations between Spain and Britain. The foreign secretary decided not to press the point; perhaps Frere could accomplish more by dealing directly with the Junta. Consequently, the Anglo-Spanish treaty, signed in London

48. Count Florida Blanca to C. Stuart, October 5, 1808, FO 72/59.
49. John Hookham Frere (1769-1846) was an intimate friend of Canning and had enjoyed some success as a writer. However, he had no capacity for diplomacy. See Fortescue's harsh judgment on his services in Spain in *British Army,* VI, 300.
50. Canning to Frere, October 5, November 16, 1808, FO 72/60. The high Spanish tariff of 1806 caused British merchants much trouble. See John Holland Rose, "Canning and the Spanish Patriots in 1808," *American Historical Review,* 12 (1906-1907), 47.

on January 14, 1809, merely expressed the intention of the two powers to conclude a commercial convention at some future time. Under the circumstances, Canning decided to avoid any specific subsidy commitment and the alliance simply provided that "A Treaty shall forthwith be negotiated, stipulating the amount and description of Succours to be afforded by His Britannick Majesty."[51] For five years this loose pact was Britain's only diplomatic tie with Spain. The Junta was unwilling to follow Portugal's example and Frere's reports offered very little hope that she would ever throw open her markets to Britain.[52]

Britain's problems with Portugal were different from those which troubled her Spanish negotiation. To begin with, the Regent had already opened Brazil to England's merchants, althrough Canning had yet to win the preferential trade agreement he desired. By now, enemy troops had been driven from Portugal and it seemed unlikely that the country would again be the scene of military operations. London believed that Portugal could contribute most by sending all her available manpower to fight beside the British and the nationalists in Spain. This was the point Canning urged upon John Charles Villiers, whom he named as British minister to the newly created Council of Regency at Lisbon.[53] The council had already begun to mobilize a Portuguese army, even though this imposed a heavy burden on the tiny country. To help with the work, Canning offered to provide completely for the expense of 10,000 Portuguese troops who would be incorporated in the British army as auxiliaries. The council would receive additional British aid to help it maintain its own national force. In return, Canning insisted that Villiers be given a seat on the Council of Regency so that he might there represent London's views. The intrigue and bitter infighting which had taken place in the formation of that body was a poor augury for its future. Unless the Council agreed to allow Villiers a voice in its deliberations, British aid to Portugal might be reduced or cut off entirely.[54]

51. Canning to Frere, January 14, 1809, FO 72/71; Treaty with Spain, January 14, 1809, FO 93/99 (6).
52. Frere to Canning, January 21, 1809, FO 72/72.
53. John Charles Villiers (1757-1838) held the Lisbon post for only two years and did not distinguish himself. In 1824 he succeeded his brother as Earl of Clarendon.
54. Canning to Villiers, nos. 1, 2, and 3, November 22, 1808, FO 63/74.

By 1809 Canning had developed a policy of aid to the Peninsular powers based on several assumptions which still remained to be tested. It was expected that a joint effort by the British army and the Spanish nationalists would drive the enemy from the Peninsula. Portugal would help with this work by sending her men to serve with the allies in Spain. In return for British financial assistance, Canning expected to exert a considerable degree of influence on the Portuguese Council of Regency through his emissary at Lisbon.

The first of these assumptions, on which the others depended, was proved false in the opening weeks of 1809. Early in the previous November, the British army entered Spain and a month later it reached Salamanca, where Moore found a heavy budget of bad news awaiting him. At least one of the Spanish armies on whose support he was counting had been destroyed, while the location and condition of the other nationalist units were unknown. With all hope gone for the success of his campaign, Moore decided to fall back into Portugal. On learning this, the British minister to Spain, John H. Frere, protested that such a withdrawal would have a disastrous effect on the Junta's plans and the morale of the Spanish insurgents. Political considerations, he argued, were more important in this case than any others. Moore hesitated, but early in December he reached a decision: he would continue his advance and tempt the enemy to pursue him. In the end, of course, he would have to retreat, but it was just possible that he could draw the French after him and thereby save the south of Spain from conquest. At best, it was a calculated risk, but it could be justified. "I was aware," Moore explained, "that I was risking infinitely too much but something I thought was to be risked, for the honour of the Service, and to make it apparent that we stuck to the Spaniards long after they themselves had given up their cause as lost."[55]

The army moved out of Salamanca and, as Moore predicted, the French came storming after it. By the end of December 1808 the British were at Sahagun, about one hundred miles north of Salamanca. So far, Moore's timing had been perfect, but to postpone his retreat any longer might prove fatal. He therefore

55. Oman, *Moore*, p. 559.

ordered his forces to fall back toward Corunna in the west, where British transports were expected to evacuate them. Thanks to Moore's superb leadership, the withdrawal was a success and by January 11, 1809, the army reached Corunna. The French were so close on their heels that Moore had to turn about and give battle in order to buy time for the evacuation. The Battle of Corunna on January 16 gave Britain victory, but at a heavy price: in the last hours of the engagement, Moore was cut down. The 10,000 troops left behind to hold Lisbon were all that remained in the Peninsula of the largest army Britain had sent to the Continent since Marlborough's time. After Corunna, the French turned south to destroy this remnant of Britain's power, but they were so exhausted by the chase Moore had led them that it was spring before the tricolor was carried into Portugal.

Although the long-range value of Moore's campaign was enormous, at the time the evacuation of Corunna seemed a disastrous setback for hopes which had been unrealistically high.[56] Gone forever was the dream of a quick and victorious union in arms with the Spanish patriots, its place now taken by an equally uncritical condemnation of all things Spanish. During the past six months, Britain had sent money and arms to the Peninsula valued at more than £2,500,000. Never had so much been spent in such a short time only to yield a bitter return. On the same day that Moore's exhausted veterans disembarked at Portsmouth, Canning wrote scathingly to Frere: "In addition to the claims which this Country had already acquired to the confidence of Spain, we have now that of having shed some of our best blood in its cause, unassisted, (I am concerned to say) by any efforts of the Spaniards, or even by the good will & good offices of that part of the country through which our army passed!"[57]

Canning's enthusiasm for Spain now turned to a cold resentment from which he was never thereafter entirely free. The British aid program to the Junta ended abruptly in February 1809.[58] In an

---

56. Fortescue's analysis of Moore's work (*British Army,* VI, 394-413) still seems eminently fair.

57. Canning to Frere, January 23, 1809, FO 72/71.

58. Memorandum of Supplies furnished . . . to Spain, FO 72/137. About £7,000 worth of arms and ammunition was sent to the patriots in Galicia between February and June, 1809. See statement no. 47, Payments on Account of the Spanish Government, AO 3/756.

effort to mollify Britain, the Junta offered to begin discussions of a trade agreement with her, but with this went a request that Downing Street guarantee a loan of between £10,000,000 and £20,000,000 which the Junta hoped to raise in London. Canning was incredulous and responded with biting sarcasm: "The Undersigned confesses himself to have been . . . for a long time in doubt whether there must not have been some mistake in the translation of the phrase." He consigned the Junta's request to oblivion with the observation that "A loan of twenty, or ten millions could not be raised in the City of London for any Foreign Power whatever."[59] Spain's poor showing on the battlefield and the hopeless obscurantism of her government put an end to the foreign secretary's sympathies.

The Cabinet had to decide whether to retain Britain's remaining foothold in Portugal. The decision to remain came easier when the Council of Regency, terrified at the prospect of French invasion, begged that a British officer be named to command Portugal's army. At the close of February Canning instructed Villiers to hasten the mobilization of the 10,000 Portuguese auxiliaries to serve in British ranks and, if possible, obtain another 10,000 on the same terms. Nothing was now said of Villiers' admission to the council as a sine qua non. The Lisbon Regency had protested when the matter was first raised; this was not the moment to bring it up again. One of Canning's goals was attained when General William Beresford of the British army took command of all Portugal's troops, except the auxiliaries, and began the hard work of turning them into an army. That same month, Villiers reported that 9,000 Portuguese auxiliaries were now serving under the British flag, and he hoped the number would soon increase.[60]

Having decided to remain in Portugal, Britain had to give her government some promise of financial help. Equipment, supplies, and pay would be provided for the 20,000 auxiliaries Villiers had been ordered to obtain to serve the British. Money and supplies would also be given to the council to raise and maintain its own national army, now commanded by Beresford. Canning had strong reservations about entering into any concrete subsidy agreement

59. Canning to Don Pedro Cevallos, April 19, 1809, FO 72/86.
60. Canning to Villiers, February 28, 1809, FO 63/74; Villiers to Canning, March 20, 1809, FO 63/75.

with Lisbon, however. Assurances of a regular monthly payment would only encourage the council to relax its efforts. Without a treaty to bind her, Britain could use her control of the purse strings to goad the Regency into action whenever it showed a tendency to lassitude. Furthermore, as Canning frankly explained to Villiers, "There is no corresponding Engagement which the Regency could take with an assurance of being able to fulfill it."[61]

London decided to send Sir Arthur Wellesley back to Lisbon, along with 9,000 British troops to reinforce those already there. He was to command all British troops in Portugal, as well as the Portuguese auxiliaries, which now numbered 13,000.[62] The council's own army, under Beresford, was expected to cooperate with Wellesley. The instructions prepared for Wellesley reveal how the disaster of Corunna had affected Downing Street's outlook: his immediate task was to defend Portugal—a general campaign in Spain was to be undertaken only on instructions from London.[63]

Britain's decision to defend Portugal was no commitment to all-out war in the Peninsula. Relations with Spain, tangled since Corunna, were still very unsatisfactory, while Portugal was being held on a strictly limited liability basis. Canning had almost written off his early plans of crushing the French in Spain where the heavy expenditure of British blood and treasure had so far accomplished nothing. He turned with relief from the frustrations of the Peninsula to Germany where, in the spring of 1809, he believed that materials existed for the construction of a new coalition against France.

The early successes of the Peninsular revolts in 1808 did not blind the Foreign Office to the fact that it was fast losing its only friend in northern Europe. Sweden's defenses in Finland were being pounded to pieces by the Russian army and nothing could be done to save her. The increasingly irrational behavior of Gustavus Adolphus made it almost impossible for Britain to treat with him. Late in the summer of 1808 Sweden was forced to buy an armistice from the Tsar by abandoning nearly all of Finland to

61. Canning to Villiers, May 19, 1809, FO 63/74.
62. Wellesley to Castlereagh, April 27, 1809, *The Dispatches of Field Marshal the Duke of Wellington . . .*, ed. Lieut.-Col. John Gurwood (London, 1837-1838), IV, 272.
63. Fortescue, *British Army*, VII, 129.

him. The Russians could be relied on to renew hostilities as soon in the coming spring as conditions permitted.

Britain's 1808 subsidy treaty with Sweden would expire at the end of the year, and in November the British minister at Stockholm, Anthony Merry, was instructed to renew it.[64] If Gustavus wished to make peace with the Russians, however, Britain would not object.[65] Merry was not prepared for the violent reception he received on reaching Stockholm in December 1808. Gustavus demanded that the subsidy for the coming year be increased from £1,200,000 to £2,000,000. Since the King's needs for money were so pressing, Merry must pay him £300,000 at once. If that amount was not delivered within six days, Gustavus would break with Britain and forbid his subjects to trade with her. Merry had not expected to negotiate with a pistol at his head, but he was wise enough to see that such was the case. Sweden's ports were now filled with shipping ready to sail for England with much-needed timber and hemp as soon as navigation reopened in the spring. To save these precious cargoes, the British envoy knew that he must submit. Early in December he gave Gustavus' treasury £300,000 in bills of exchange. It was unquestionably blackmail, but the British minister had no choice.[66]

Canning was furious when he learned of Gustavus' profitable treachery; it was the sort of "outrage" which could be repeated on any occasion which suited the King's lunatic whims. If Britain were not so dependent on Gustavus, Canning would have been pleased to throw him to the Russians. The foreign secretary informed Merry that Britain would not yield to Sweden's demand for a subsidy increase. Britain would still make available £1,200,000 for Gustavus during 1809, but the £300,000 extorted from Merry must be considered as the first quarterly payment. Unless this offer was immediately accepted, Merry was to leave Stockholm.[67] Armed with these orders, the British minister took his revenge upon Gustavus Adolphus and demanded compliance. The King was sane enough to know when his bluff had been

64. Thornton had recently become *non grata* at Stockholm and Merry was sent to replace him.

65. Canning to Merry, November 10, 1808, FO 73/50.

66. Merry to Canning, December 6, 1808, FO 73/50; Account of Anthony Merry with the Audit Office, AO 1/12 (32).

67. Canning to Merry, December 23, 1808, FO 73/50.

called; without British money he could not continue his war with the Tsar. His submission was as ungracious as possible, but on March 1 he approved the new subsidy treaty which exactly accorded with London's demands.[68]

Twelve days later, a palace revolution swept Gustavus from his throne and plunged Sweden into a political crisis from which she emerged with a new monarch and a written constitution. The new king, Charles XIII, was well disposed toward Britain, but it was impossible for him to continue in alliance with her. Weary of a war which had already cost her Finland, Sweden was ready for peace with Russia on almost any terms. Canning could scarely object to Sweden's search for peace and the British diplomatic mission was soon withdrawn from Stockholm.[69] Peace with Russia obliged Sweden to adhere to the Continental System against British commerce, but Napoleon was never able to obtain her strict compliance. British goods continued to find their way into Sweden's markets under the protection of the Royal Navy, which retained control over the Baltic.[70] The loss of the northern timber market was more serious, but Britain soon found compensation for this by turning to new sources in British North America.[71]

Long before the collapse of the Swedish alliance, Canning had turned his attention to Austria, where there was a steadily growing demand for war with France. In recent years a war party had developed at Vienna intent on wiping out the humiliation imposed on the nation by the 1805 Treaty of Pressburg. At the head of this movement was the Hapsburg minister, Count Philip Stadion, who wished to recreate the old German empire under Austrian control.[72] France's entanglement in Spain encouraged the belief that the hour was fast approaching for Austria to strike. Secret appeals for support went to Berlin and St. Petersburg, but the responses were most discouraging. At the end of 1808 Metternich returned from Paris, where he had been serving as Austrian envoy, and threw all his influence on the side of war. Even without help

---

68. Merry to Canning, February 24, 1809, FO 73/54; Treaty with Sweden, March 1, 1809, FO 93/101 (7).
69. Canning to Brinkmann, April 3, 1809, FO 73/59.
70. See A. N. Ryan, "The Defence of British Trade with the Baltic, 1808-1813," *English Historical Review,* 74 (1959), 443-466.
71. Albion, *Forests and Sea Power,* pp. 346-349.
72. Enno E. Kraehe, *Metternich's German Policy* (Princeton, N. J., 1963), I, 80.

from Prussia and Russia, Austria could put at least as many men in the field as Napoleon. This argument clinched the Hofburg's decision to act, even through hostilities could not be undertaken until the spring.[73]

Austria might be able to do without military support from Prussia and Russia, but she could not succeed without British subsidies. As early as October 1808 a proposal was sent to Downing Street: the Hofburg would mobilize 400,000 men in the spring if Britain supplied £2,500,000 in preparation money together with the promise of an additional £5,000,000 to be paid during the year.[74] The Austrian bid remained on Canning's desk for nearly a month before he replied. British hopes were still high for a successful conclusion of the war in Spain. Moreover, the Hapsburg request for £7,500,000 in aid was breathtaking, especially in view of Britain's heavy expenditures in the Peninsula. When finally drafted, the foreign secretary's response was cautious and noncommital. Naturally, Britain would be happy to renew her old ties with Austria, but the financial help requested was "utterly beyond the power of this Country to furnish." Instead of offering a counterproposal, Canning restated his well-known position on subsidies: if Austria goes to war, she may rely on all the support Britain is able to give. No money was offered her as an inducement to take arms, however. "The British Government is . . . intimately persuaded," Canning argued, "that the only assurance of success in War, would be found in the general Conviction of its necessity, and in the Efforts which such Conviction must command."[75]

The failure of Sir John Moore's campaign in Spain led Canning to renew communication with the Hofburg, and in February 1809 he sent Benjamin Bathurst to Vienna as his secret emissary.[76] At almost the same time, two Hapsburg agents were beginning their journey to England: Ludwig von Wallmoden, a Hanoverian nobleman well known and trusted in London, and Lieutenant August Wagner. On their arrival the two envoys presented Canning

73. *Ibid.,* I, 68-70.
74. Substance of a Communication from the Austrian Government, October 11, 1808, FO 7/89.
75. Canning's reply to the Austrian government, December 24, 1808, FO 7/89.
76. Canning to Benjamin Bathurst, February 16, 1809, FO 7/88. Benjamin Bathurst (1784-1809) was a distant relative of Earl Bathurst, at this time head of the Board of Trade. Young Bathurst seems to have taken his time getting to Vienna, for he did not reach the Austrian capital until the end of April.

with an elaborate "tableau" indicating how Vienna was prepared to put 443,000 soldiers into action at a moment's notice. Since Britain had objected to the first Austrian subsidy request, it had been reduced to the bare minimum: a preparation grant of £2,000,000 to be followed by a £400,000 monthly subsidy.[77] Canning was willing to discuss the matter with the Hapsburg envoys, but he seemed reluctant to make a decision.

Part of this hesitancy was due to the fact that Vienna's demands, even as modified, were still excessively high. But there was more to it than that. At this same time, Canning had been called on by another German, Ludwig von Kleist, who claimed to be the secret agent of the central insurrectionary committee of Berlin. The Austrian resistance movement had its counterpart in Prussia but, lacking Frederick William's blessing, it was obliged to work underground. Gneisenau and other Prussian leaders were prepared to cooperate with Austria in what they hoped would be an all-German uprising against Napoleon. Kleist did not claim to represent the entire Prussian resistance movement, but such credentials as he offered seemed valid.[78] The foreign secretary questioned him closely and insisted that he answer in writing. From the memorandum prepared by Kleist on March 25 it was clear that the Prussian resistance movement wanted Britain to establish an arms depot at Heligoland. A British invasion of Hanover, timed to coincide with the Prussian uprising, was also desired. Naturally, money was needed and Kleist asked for at least £50,000 in specie for immediate expenses.[79]

Canning had to decide whether the German insurrection movement was promising enough to justify British support. In several important respects it differed from that in Spain which had burst forth the year before. So far as Canning knew the Austrian and Prussian uprisings were still in the planning stage; hostilities had yet to begin. Kleist presented a special problem since he clearly did not speak for the Prussian government, but rather for a secret movement. What assurance was there that the real object might not be the overthrow of the Prussian monarchy? The

77. Wagner to Canning, March 12, 1809, FO 7/90; Wallmoden to Canning, March 29, 1809, FO 7/90.
78. Fortescue, *British Army*, VII, 40.
79. See Kleist's memorandum to Canning, March 13, 1809, and his two letters to Canning of March 13 and April 11, 1809, FO 64/80.

Austrian proposals made Canning uneasy, but for different reasons. Aside from the fact that Britain would be hard-pressed to supply even half of what Austria asked for, Canning disliked the Hofburg's proposal with its demand for preparation money and monthly subsidies. This was precisely the sort of arrangement he had always opposed in the belief that its folly had been amply demonstrated by Pitt's subsidy treaties.

Early in April 1809 Canning announced his decision to the envoys of Austria and Prussia. Britain would send £250,000 in silver to an Austrian port in the Adriatic, while a military chest of between £750,000 and £1,000,000 would be established on the island of Malta for Vienna's use in the event of war. The foreign secretary was ready to conclude a subsidy agreement with Austria at once, provided its terms corresponded to Britain's present subsidy policy. The original Austrian proposal was unacceptable, based as it was on a concept of subsidization now outmoded.

"His Majesty will be prepared," Canning explained, "to give cheerfully whatever he can give consistently with the vast and complicated demands upon the resources of this Country: in the confidence that in a War, into which Austria enters in defence not only of Her interest and Her honour, but of Her very existence as an independent Power, She will not calculate the extent of Her efforts by any rule of imaginary proportion to the Assistance which she may expect to receive from an Ally, but will put forth bonâ fide, and without reserve, the whole Strength of Her Monarchy in a struggle, on the issue of which Her Monarchy itself depends." Any assistance given Austria beyond £1,000,000 in specie, Canning insisted, must be in some form other than hard money. Bills of exchange had obvious drawbacks, especially now that Britain's trade with the Continent had shrunk. The foreign secretary proposed a device, never before employed, to provide the Hofburg with between £3,000,000 and £4,000,000 during the coming year. British 5 percent Exchequer Bills would be offered for sale at Vienna with the proceeds to go directly to the Austrian treasury. Purchasers would be guaranteed the payment of interest twice a year at Vienna, with redemption to be undertaken at the end of the war. In this way, British credit would call out money in Germany which was clearly unavailable to the Austrian government. This arrangement obviated the need for a heavy export of

British specie to the Continent; only modest remittances would be required to meet the biannual interest payments.[80]

Canning's offer went far beyond anything Wallmoden had been authorized to accept. Since it was now known that Austria had gone to war with France, the two men agreed to conclude an alliance between their governments at once. Settlement of the terms of the subsidy agreement would be postponed until Vienna had responded to the British proposal.[81] For the moment, the £250,000 in silver, already on its way to the Adriatic, would cover the Hofburg's immediate expenses and be proof of Britain's desire to assist her.

At the same time, the foreign secretary informed Kleist how far Britain would go to assist the Prussian patriots. An arms depot would be established immediately at Heligoland for their use. Kleist must return to Prussia at once, going by way of Hamburg where he would be given a letter of credit for £20,000. He would be accompanied by a British agent who was to learn all he could about the Prussian movement and its plans, as well as to discover whether the movement was "independent of and unknown to the legitimate Government of Prussia." In such a case, no further British help could be expected, but if the movement had the blessing of the Prussian government, London would do everything possible to support it.[82]

Far from spurring on the German nationalists, Canning had been cautious and even slow in responding to their appeals for support. Events moved so swiftly that Britain could do nothing to save the Prussian and Austrian patriots from the disasters which befell them in the summer of 1809. Stirred by word of Austria's attack on France, the standard of revolt in Prussia was prematurely raised by Major Ferdinand Schill on April 29. Successful at first, Schill and his supporters were denounced by their king, whose fear of Napoleon had crushed nearly all his spirit. The insurgents fell back to the crumbling fortress of Stralsund in Swedish Pomerania,

80. Canning to Wallmoden, two letters of April 20, 1809, FO 7/90. On April 7 Canning informed Bathurst of the sending of £250,000 in silver to Malta for Austria's use.

81. Treaty with Austria, April 24, 1809, FO 93/11 (5A).

82. Canning's response to Kleist is undated, but it is to be found in FO 64/80 together with his instructions of April 24 to Lieutenant Maimburg, the British agent who accompanied Kleist on his return.

where they were finally destroyed by the troops Napoleon sent against them. The Austrian War of Liberation opened badly, but in May the battle of Aspern ended in a victory for the Imperial forces which they were too exhausted to exploit. Hostilities were suspended for seven weeks while the opposing armies prepared to seek a final decision on the battlefield.

Austria was severely handicapped by the lack of British money and devised a unique expedient to meet her needs. The Hofburg obtained cash from several continental banks by offering them bills amounting to £300,000 drawn on the British Treasury. Hopefully, Britain would honor these drafts when presented for payment. Canning took the matter up with Starhemberg shortly after the latter's return to London to resume his role as Austria's minister. The bills would be honored, the foreign secretary explained, but Vienna must never again resort to such a device. Starhemberg quietly accepted the reproof and then announced that he had been instructed to renew his government's request for a £2,000,000 preparation subsidy together with an additional £400,000 each month. The Hapsburg finance minister had declared unworkable Canning's plan to sell Exchequer Bills at Vienna.[83]

The foreign secretary refused Starhemberg's request for a massive subsidy, and for the time being British aid to Austria remained on an informal basis. In addition to the £250,000 in silver sent in April, bar silver valued at £337,500 was delivered to Austria's agents at Fiume in July.[84] The collapse of the Continental System in Germany which followed the outbreak of war in 1809 resulted in a marked upswing of British trade there.[85] Once again the British government was able to use bills of exchange, and £300,000 was given Austria in that form. On July 5, 1809 the Imperial Army was decisively defeated at Wagram, whereupon all British subsidy payments were ended. So far, £1,187,500 had been

83. Starhemberg to Canning, May 22, 1809, FO 7/90. The Austrian finance minister, Count Joseph Odonell (surely the descendant of an expatriate Irishman) explained to Lord Bathurst that the agrarian economy of Austria made the British plan impractical (Bathurst to Canning, June 6, 1809, FO 7/88).

84. Bathurst to Canning, July 16, 1809, FO 7/88.

85. The value of colonial and domestic goods sent by Britain to northern Europe in 1809 was £14,570,000, as compared with £5,430,000 during the previous year. See Hecksher, *Continental System,* p. 245.

remitted in specie and paper to help finance the Hapsburg war effort.[86]

When the war began in the spring, Austria had urged Britain to launch a diversionary attack on the north German coast where smouldering resentment against France gave promise of support. Instead, the Cabinet decided to undertake an amphibious assault on the French naval base at Antwerp, which was regarded as a serious threat to British security. At the end of July a British force occupied the island of Walcheren in the Dutch province of Zealand which was to be used as a base of operations for the advance up the Scheldt river. The invaders attempted to move forward, but by the time Austria withdrew from the war in the autumn, the Walcheren expedition had completely bogged down.

Military decisions made at Wagram, Walcheren, and Talavera in Spain determined the course of the war against Napoleon for the next three years. Wagram crippled the national spirit which had inspired the Austrian War of Liberation and led to the downfall of Count Stadion. Thereafter, the spirit of the Hofburg was that of Metternich, who now became the leading exponent of Hapsburg coexistence with Napoleon. The cost of the war and the crushing indemnity imposed by France weakened Austria's economy by a third of what it had been.[87] Vienna's tie with Britain was now broken, and the murder of the British agent, Bathurst, while making his way back to London was an appropriate finale to the short-lived Anglo-Austrian alliance.[88] Austria's fate was a dreadful object lesson to German nationalists who now despaired of even

---

86. Canning to the Lords of the Treasury, June 24, 1809, FO 7/91; Harrison to Hammond, October 14, 1809, FO 7/95; Canning to Starhemberg, July 29, 1809, FO 7/90. See also François Crouzet, "La Crise Monétaire Britannique et la Cinquième Coalition," *Bulletin de la Société d'Histoire Moderne,* 11th ser., no. 8 (Oct.-Dec. 1953), 14-19.

87. Kraehe, *Metternich's German Policy,* I, 119.

88. Metternich was wise enough to see the value of maintaining secret contact with London, even though formal diplomatic relations were suspended. For a detailed study of how this contact was established and maintained, see C. S. B. Buckland, *Metternich and the British Government from 1809 to 1813* (London, 1932), pp. 18 and *passim.*

With the ending of the war, Benjamin Bathurst had to leave Vienna. The French now held the Adriatic port by which he had entered the country, and he was therefore obliged to make his way overland through Prussia. At Berlin he obtained a Prussian passport and headed for Hamburg, but he never reached there. Probably he was slain by French agents or brigands, thus becoming the only British diplomat to lose his life during this period.

ultimate success.[89] Late in July the British army in Spain, acting with Spanish nationalists, threw back a heavy French assault at Talavera. Wellesley was finally compelled to part company with his allies and withdraw into Portugal, but Talavera came as close as anything in the summer of 1809 to qualify as a victory over France. The collapse of the war in Germany and the failure of the British thrust against Antwerp led to a single stark conclusion: if Britain meant to continue her war against Napoleon, she must fight him in the Peninsula.

During the two years he served at the Foreign Office, Canning redirected Britain's subsidy policy along lines which it would follow during the remainder of the war. By a series of forceful decisions he made clear that any nation ready to take arms against Napoleon could count on Britain for support. Canning was too late to save the Third Coalition, but his generous response to the Peninsular uprisings in 1808 materially strengthened the Spanish and Portuguese. Here was a war spirit which had no room for subsidy treaties based upon the counting of allied troops. What Canning wanted was a total commitment on the part of both Britain and her allies to wage war with all the strength they could muster. If the first fruits of the Peninsular War were disappointing, the fault did not lie in the British aid program. The particularism of the juntas and the chaotic condition of the nationalist armies were problems which would require dedication and hard work to solve.

Napoleon's Continental System seriously hampered Britain's ability to meet her allies' financial requirements. Short of specie and continental trade credits, Canning sent the arms, ammunition, and supplies which the allies needed as much as money. British industry stretched itself to produce the vast quantities of cloth and commodities needed in the Peninsula, while an increasingly efficient ordnance service guaranteed that there would be no lack of guns, powder, flints, and shot. Even so, help in the form of British money remained important, a fact made abundantly clear by Austria's pleas in 1809. To repair the damage caused by Britain's declining trade in Europe, Canning looked to the colonial

89. After Austria's collapse, several insurrections against France took place in the Tyrol and Switzerland. The effect of these movements on Metternich's policy is examined by Buckland, *Metternich*, pp. 222-260.

markets of the New World. Portugal responded generously to his appeal for free trade, but Spain's refusal to follow this example was to trouble British foreign ministers for the duration of the war.

No longer could it be argued that while Britain was ready to send money to Europe, she was unwilling to spill her blood there. The expeditions to Sweden, Portugal, and Walcheren made clear that the British government was ready to use what military strength it could command for more important purposes than "filching sugar islands." Thanks largely to Canning, Europe knew by 1809 that Britain would support any defiance of France by supplying money, arms, and military assistance. By now, the tide of the Napoleonic Empire was running stronger than ever before. If Britain hoped to turn that tide, she must pour her treasure and her manpower into the Peninsula—the only arena in Europe remaining to her.

X

BRITISH SUBSIDIES AND THE WAR
IN THE PENINSULA

After a stormy passage of one week from Portsmouth, H.M.S. *Surveillante* entered Lisbon harbor on April 22, 1809, and let go her anchor. On board was Sir Arthur Wellesley with orders to take command of the British troops defending Portugal against the French. No one in the spring of 1809 could foresee that almost exactly five years later Wellesley's legions would drive the enemy from the Peninsula and carry the war into France itself. At the moment British operations were frankly exploratory, intended to feel out the enemy and exploit such opportunities as might be found.[1] The tragedy of Corunna, three months before, had blasted all hope that Anglo-Spanish cooperation in arms would easily brush Napoleon back across the Pyrenees. Now the Peninsular War was about to enter a more active phase, but it was still essentially a war of improvisation whose outcome no man could predict.

The absence of long-range planning was evident also in the informal nature of Britain's subsidy arrangements with the Peninsular powers. No subsidy treaties were ever negotiated with Portugal or Spain, although Britain did promise to send them as much money and arms as she could spare. Portugal was expected to maintain her own army and, in addition, to send at least 20,000 troops to serve in the British ranks. Hopefully the time would come when Spanish troops could join with the Anglo-Portuguese. The attainment of even these general goals involved problems of which British leaders had no inkling in 1809. Subsidies to the Peninsular powers, in addition to the expense of Britain's own

1. Castlereagh to Wellesley, April 2, 1809, *Correspondence of Castlereagh,* VII, 47.

military operations, would oblige London to spend more liberally than at any time since the war began in 1793. To help Britain bear this burden, Downing Street urged the Junta to allow her free trade with the Spanish colonies, a boon she was still soliciting when the war ended. Military operations in the Peninsula carried on by three allied but sovereign governments proved especially difficult since success in the field required unified command. These problems were never really solved, but the necessity of prosecuting the war against France forced the allies to compromise their differences at least enough to maintain their union in arms. Regardless of what the future might hold, the Cabinet decided to carry on the war in the Peninsula, and in June 1809 the House of Commons appropriated £3,300,000 for subsidies to the allies during the year ahead.[2]

By the time Wellesley reached Lisbon, Portugal had made considerable progress in girding herself for war. For more than a month, General Beresford had been hard at work training the men drafted into military service by the Council of Regency.[3] Of the 20,000 Portuguese Canning had offered to take into British service, only 13,000 had been mobilized so far. Since these auxiliaries were still raw, they could not be formed into separate line-of-battle regiments. Instead, Wellesley decided to send the Portuguese batallions to serve as components of the larger British brigades.[4] Meanwhile, reinforcements from England brought Britain's own army in Portugal to nearly 30,000.

Portugal's war effort was hindered by the fact that she had so far received very little money from Britain, although generous quantities of arms and supplies had been sent her. In April 1809 a special department of the British Military Commissary was established at Lisbon to pay subsidy money to the council. This department, known as the British Aid Office, was supplied with money by the British Commissary General from his war chest.

2. Payments of the 1809 Austrian subsidy were to come out of this appropriation. On June 7, 1809 the bill passed its final reading in the Commons. One of its opponents, General Banastre Tarleton, sarcastically referred to recent British victories in the Peninsula as "skirmishes." Noting that Castlereagh had chosen to attend the House that day in his militia regiment uniform, Tarleton observed that people would say "that we were the animal in the lion's skin—and that the noble lord was the daw in borrowed feathers" (*Hansard,* XIV [1809], 919).
3. For Beresford's work, see Fortescue, *British Army,* VII, 428-429.
4. *Ibid.*, VII, 149.

Payments to the Portuguese government were made by the Aid Office at the direction of the British minister at Lisbon. On April 12 the first remittance of the year (amounting to £15,378) went to the Portuguese Commissary General for the use of the council's own troops.[5]

Help of a different kind was given to Portugal when, on April 21, Britain agreed to guarantee a £600,000 loan the Regent proposed to raise in London. Although the loan was intended to finance the government at Rio, one third of the yield was to go to the Lisbon Council of Regency for its use. Canning had long wished to have the British minister to Portugal named as a member of the council, and shortly before the signing of the Loan Convention he again brought this matter to the Regent's attention.[6] João took the hint and made some effort to meet his ally's wishes. He named Wellesley generalissimo of all Portugal's troops with the right to attend the council whenever it dealt with military or financial matters.[7]

Two important features of the Anglo-Portuguese alliance had taken shape by the summer of 1809. All Portugal's troops were now either directly or indirectly under British command.[8] Machinery had also been set up for supplying Portugal with British money and supplies, although as yet it operated sporadically. Such was the nature of the military union between the two powers soon to be tested on the battlefield.

By the time Wellesley led his army out of Lisbon, three French armies were in the field to challenge him. The major threat was from Soult, who held Oporto, and Wellesley moved north to strike at him. On May 12 the Anglo-Portuguese forced a crossing of the Douro river at Oporto and compelled the French not only to abandon the city, but to withdraw into Spain. This victory revived Downing Street's hope for success, and Wellesley was soon authorized to cross into Spain for combined operations with the nationalists.

5. Portuguese Subsidy Account, 1809, AO 3/746.
6. Treaty with Portugal, April 21, 1809, FO 93/77 (5); Canning to Strangford, April 5, 1809, FO 63/69.
7. Strangford to Villiers, July 10, 1809, FO 63/77; Wellesley to Stuart, January 1, 1811, *Dispatches of Wellington*, VII, 98.
8. Money for the pay and maintenance of the auxiliaries came from the British Commissary, but was handed over to the Portuguese Commissary for distribution. The Portuguese Commissary was also responsible for the upkeep of its forces under Beresford's command.

Almost at once the changed character of the war was reflected in the British aid program. On June 24 the British Aid Office resumed subsidy payments to the Lisbon Council of Regency and made them regularly during the balance of the year, by which time a total of £270,538 had been paid. In July 30,000 muskets with cartridges, flints, and accoutrements were shipped from England to Lisbon on board three merchant vessels, aptly named "Hope," "Experiment," and "Fame." The flow of supplies which followed soon became a flood; boots, uniforms, caps, blankets, and greatcoats, valued at £109,082, were shipped for the use of the Portuguese auxiliaries.[9]

The decision to send a British army into Spain once again forced London to take stock of its relations with the Junta, which had been strained since the first of the year. No money had been given the Junta since February, but plans for a renewal of military cooperation obliged London to be generous. In June 1809, £213,750 in Treasury Bills was turned over to the Junta at Seville, and in the following month supplies and field equipment for 30,000 men, together with 10,000 muskets, were sent for the use of the Spanish nationalists.[10] In an effort to improve relations with Spain, Canning recalled John Hookham Frere from Seville. That envoy's reputation had been damaged by his unfortunate role in Sir John Moore's campaign, and he had offended the Junta by the imperious manner in which he urged them to appoint Wellesley as supreme commander of Spain's armies. To replace Frere, Canning named the Marquess Wellesley (Arthur's older brother) and at the end of June presented him with his instructions. Although Britain was still unwilling to make a long-term subsidy commitment to the Junta, money, arms, and supplies would be sent as circumstances permitted. The Anglo-Spanish alliance of 1809 looked to the prompt conclusion of a formal subsidy engagement, but Lord Wellesley was warned not to discuss this matter at Seville.[11] Clearly, caution and improvisation continued to regulate the Foreign Office's thinking about future help for Spain.

9. Portuguese Subsidy Account, 1809, AO 3/746.
10. Statement no. 28, Spanish Subsidy Account, AO 3/765; Memorandum of Supplies furnished by Great Britain to Spain, FO 72/137.
11. Canning to Lord Wellesley, June 27, 1809, FO 72/75. These instructions are printed in *The Despatches and Correspondence of the Marquess Wellesley K. G. during His Lordship's Mission to Spain . . . in 1809,* ed. M. Martin (London, 1838), pp. 183-191.

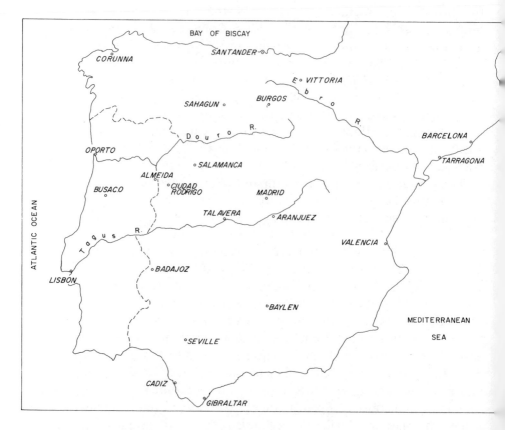

3. Campaign Area of the War in the Peninsula

In July 1809 Wellesley's army entered Spain and joined the patriots under General Cuesta. Shortly thereafter, they were attacked by the French at Talavera, but at the end of two days of battle, the bulk of which fell on the British, the enemy fell back exhausted. Wellesley was unable to take the offensive, however, since the failure of the Spanish to provide supplies had brought his troops close to starvation. He also found it utterly impossible to reach any agreement with Cuesta as to future operations. Prudence required the British to fall back to the Portuguese frontier, despite Spanish charges that this was desertion. A month later the army was once more in Portugal, and Wellesley (now Viscount Wellington of Talavera) was as bitter about the conduct of his Spanish allies as Moore had been under similar circumstances.

If the Spanish army and its commander annoyed Wellington, the Junta's latest diplomatic maneuver trenched dangerously on what little of Canning's good-will remained. With some justice, the Junta protested the informal basis on which British aid was still being given, and shortly after the Battle of Talavera, the Spanish minister in London proposed terms of a formal subsidy agreement. Britain was invited to place an army of 30,000 men at Spain's disposal for use either in Europe or South America, where rumblings of colonial revolt were already being heard. In addition, the Junta demanded arms and supplies for 500,000 men and asked Britain "to accommodate H. C. M. [Ferdinand] during the whole of the war & as long as he may want it with two millions of Dollars every month by way of loan." Canning rejected this "utterly extravagant" demand at once and refused to consider it even as a basis for further discussion. British support for Spain would remain on an informal basis for the foreseeable future. Shipment of arms and supplies were continued, but the Junta received no more British money during the remainder of 1809. With specie hard to come by, London had difficulty enough providing for the minimum needs of the Anglo-Portuguese army. The Junta must realize that future British aid depended upon the "opening to British commerce the Ports of Spanish America; and thereby enabling this Country to recruit the Stock of Specie which has been exhausted in the service of Spain."[12]

12. Treaty project offered by Apodaca, August 7, 1809, FO 72/85; Canning to Lord Wellesley, September 16, 1809, FO 72/75.

The appeal was fruitless. By the end of 1809 the Junta had done nothing beyond lowering the duty on salt fish imported from Britain and her colonies. Spain's refusal to make concessions came at a time when the Junta's need for help was as great as ever. Soult had overwhelmed the nationalist army at Ocaña in November 1809, and the French were now pushing south of the Sierra Morena to suppress the rebellion in Andalusia. Except for the guerrilla forces and a few scattered units of the Spanish army, the Junta had nothing with which to defend itself. Viewed in retrospect, the Battle of Talavera seemed less of a victory than it had five months before. Wellington's army remained in Portugal, where it seemed incapable of doing anything other than licking its wounds. As the year ended, the Cabinet once more had to decide whether to continue the war in the Peninusla. Before any intelligent decision could be made, certain military and financial factors had to be carefully considered.

The military evidence available to the Cabinet at the end of 1809 was most discouraging. Seville had fallen to the French and the Junta was now at Cadiz, which would certainly come under enemy attack. Support for Spain in 1810 would oblige Britain to spend her money, arms, men, and seapower in the defense of that city. So far as Portugal was concerned, Wellington believed that it could be held if the Anglo-Portuguese army were enlarged.[13] One conclusion was inescapable: even a defensive war in the Peninsula would require far greater military and financial exertions on Britain's part than before.

Britain had spent about £2,600,000 on the war during 1809, and the Cabinet's best estimates were that at least twice that amount would be needed for the coming year. Britain's own army would cost at least £1,700,000 and Wellington urged that the Portuguese subsidy be much enlarged.[14] Although the Lisbon Council of Regency had received £270,538 in subsidies during 1809, it was ending the year with a deficit of nearly £1,000,000. Unless Portugal were to go bankrupt, Wellington calculated that London must give her nearly £1,000,000 during 1810.[15] Aid to Spain,

13. Wellington to Liverpool, November 14, 1809, *Dispatches of Wellington,* V, 275.
14. Wellington to Liverpool, November 14, 1809, January 3, 1810, *ibid.,* V. 275, 408.
15. Portuguese Subsidy Account, 1809, AO 3/746; Wellington to Villiers, December 6, 1809, *Dispatches of Wellington,* V, 338. See also Wellington to Liverpool, November 14, 1809, *ibid.,* V, 276-278.

which in 1809 amounted to £473,919, would also have to be increased.[16]

Even if Parliament could be persuaded to vote these vast sums, there was another grim problem to consider. Would it be possible to send enough bullion to the Peninsula to cover those British expenses which could be paid in no other way? Hard money was needed to pay Wellington's soldiers, and nearly all his bills for supplies and transport must also be met in coin. Scarcity of specie had already forced the Treasury to limit cash shipments to the army in the Peninsula. About three quarters of the 1809 war costs there had been paid by using bills of exchange.[17]

The problems of remittances to cover military expenses and those needed for subsidies to the allies are so intermingled that they may be treated as one. Nearly all subsidy payments to Portugal were made from the British Military Chest under Wellington's control. Each month the British commander transferred a portion of the money in this chest to the British Aid Office for payment to the Lisbon council. Wellington varied the monthly allocation so that in any month when the Military Chest was low, the amount of money remitted as a subsidy to the council would be reduced. Occasionally specie would be sent from England for Portugal's use, but this was exceptional. In general, the size of Portugal's monthly subsidy depended on how much cash Wellington felt he could spare her from his Military Chest. Payments to the Spanish Junta were handled in a different manner: acting on instructions from Britain's envoy to Spain, the British consul at Cadiz would pay either specie or Treasury Bills to the Junta's treasurer.

The Military Chest, from which the bulk of the Portuguese subsidy came, was the responsibility of the Commissary General acting under Wellington's orders. The chest was supplied in two ways: by specie shipped from England or by hard money obtained locally in exchange for bills drawn on the Treasury. The Commissary General's agents were regularly employed in obtaining coin in exchange for Treasury Bills at Lisbon, Cadiz, Gibraltar, and

16. Spanish Subsidy Account, AO 3/765.
17. During 1809, £465,667 was sent to the Peninsula in specie, while £2,174,097 was paid out in commercial paper. See Account of Money sent to Spain and Portugal, FO 63/120.

other commercial centers in the area. The balance of payments between Britain and the Peninsula was so unfavorable, however, that Treasury Bills found few buyers and such as did appear insisted on massive discounts. As specie became difficult to procure in the Peninsula, the Commissary General called increasingly on London for shipments of coin. But the Treasury found it difficult to meet his demands. Consequently, the Military Chest shrank, the army went into debt, and the British Aid Office at Lisbon had nothing to pay the Portuguese government.[18]

The Treasury could not be blamed for the fact that very little hard money was available in Britain. During the early days of the Spanish uprising in 1808, London had flooded the Peninsula with more than £2,500,000 in silver.[19] Having spent their majority like gentlemen, the ministers were now hard-pressed to lay hands on more. Commerical difficulties during 1809 made it impossible for them to recoup this loss of coin. Britain's rapidly expanding trade with Brazil yielded less hard money than had been expected; the bulk of British goods sent there were bought on credit or paid for in colonial raw materials. Because of the Continental System, these colonial goods accumulated in London's warehouses awaiting buyers.[20] Despite all Canning's pleas, no material opening had been made for British trade in Spanish America. On rare occasions, the Junta allowed the Treasury to purchase silver at Vera Cruz in return for bills of exchange.[21] With specie so hard to come by, the government simply could not send Wellington all that he asked for. The British commander's outspoken criticism of the Treasury for this failure finally provoked one of its officials, William Huskisson, to ask him, "How can you expect us to buy specie here with the exchange thirty percent against us, and guineas selling at twenty-four shillings?"[22]

18. Shortage of hard money forced Wellington to delay his march on Talavera for five weeks until coin was received from England. The operation of the Commissary General's Department is discussed in S. G. P. Ward, *Wellington's Headquarters* (Oxford, 1957), pp. 73-101.

19. During 1808 Britain spent £2,778,796 in the Peninsula, of which all but £185,520 was in specie. See Account of Money sent to Spain and Portugal, FO 63/120.

20. Hecksher, *Continental System*, p. 241.

21. In April 1809 the Junta agreed to allow Britain to buy $3,000,000 in silver at Vera Cruz in exchange for £593,750 in bills of exchange; Frere to Canning, April 25, 1809, FO 72/72.

22. Huskisson to Wellington, July 19, 1809, in Fortescue, *British Army*, VII, 435. During the autumn of 1809 an improvement of conditions enabled the Treasury to send

In determining whether to continue the war in the Peninsula during the coming year, the Cabinet had to consider three major problems. First, what were the prospects for military success? With Spain almost at the mercy of her oppressor, and Wellington's army immobilized in Portugal, it required a cheerful optimism, bordering on foolhardiness, to believe that the prognosis was good. Second, would Parliament be willing to approve requests for still larger amounts of money to underwrite a war program which so far had failed to produce results? Finally, would commercial conditions during the coming year enable the Treasury to make at least minimal remittances of coin to the British army and its allies in the Peninsula? Given questions such as these, it required great courage for the Cabinet to decide to persist in the contest.

A political crisis late in the summer of 1809 precipitated a major reorganization of the Cabinet which had been in the making for some time. The disastrous Walcheren expedition, the duel between Canning and Castlereagh, and the prime minister's fatal illness all played important parts in the breakup of the Portland regime. Responsibility for forming a new administration fell to the former chancellor of the exchequer, Spencer Perceval, who sought in vain for Lord Grenville's support.

Failure to reach agreement with Grenville saved the new ministers from having to soften their war policy, but it left their parliamentary strength weaker than that of any government since the outbreak of the war. Castlereagh and Canning had both withdrawn from office, leaving the new Cabinet to get along as best they could without their skills. Perceval himself was an effective debater and floor-manager, but not even his friends saw him as a dynamic war leader. Castlereagh's place at the War Office was now held by Lord Liverpool, who had once served as Addington's foreign secretary. Uninspired and plodding though he was, Liverpool was a steadfast supporter of the war in the Peninsula. The Foreign Office went to the Marquess Wellesley, although the year was nearly over before he returned to London

---

more specie to the Peninsula, but this condition proved only temporary. See Wellington to Huskisson, August 30, 1809, *Dispatches of Wellington,* V, 98; Wellington to Liverpool, December 13, 1809, *ibid.,* V, 369; and Wellington to Liverpool, May 16, 1810, *ibid.,* VI, 121.

from his diplomatic post at Seville. For nearly two years Wellesley presided over the Foreign Office, where his indolence appeared even worse than it was in contrast to the force and energy of his predecessor. Lacking oratorical ability, he was a poor spokesman for the government in the Lords, where he had to face Grenville's tireless attacks on the conduct of the war.[23]

Short on talent and glamour, the new Cabinet derived vigor from its determination to wage war against France with all the strength it could command. Whether this agreement would have been quite so firm had the ministers foreseen the years of disappointment and mounting expense which lay ahead is another question.[24] Although the war in the Peninsula was to be supported to the hilt, the Cabinet recognized that circumstances might force them to reverse that decision and even withdraw their armies. Perceval's caution struck Wellington as a sign of weakness and indecision, but the charge seems unfair given the many hazards threatening the new government.

Early in 1810 Liverpool informed Wellington that 5,000 British troops would be sent to reinforce him. The government had also decided to assist with the defense of Cadiz, the only important city in southern Spain not in enemy hands. British troops, together with some of Wellington's Portuguese, would be sent to strengthen the Cadiz garrison. For nearly two years the city defended itself successfully and, in so doing, tied down a French army which might have been more effectively employed elsewhere.

The Cabinet was also ready to increase its aid to Portugal, a step which Wellington regarded as absolutely essential. During 1810 the Lisbon Regency could depend on receiving £980,000 in return for which the Portuguese auxiliaries should be increased from 20,000 to 30,000.[25] Parliamentary approval for this step was difficult to obtain, and in the Lords, Grenville attacked ministers for their prodigality in supporting Portugal at a time when there was not "the least ground of rational expectation of success." On an amendment offered by Grenville, which Liverpool declared to

23. Charles K. Webster, *The Foreign Policy of Castlereagh* (London, 1947-1950), I, 44; *The Wellesley Papers* (London, 1914), II, 7-8.
24. Spencer Perceval to Wellington, July 5, 1810, in Spencer Walpole, *The Life of the Rt. Hon. Spencer Perceval* (London, 1874), II, 131.
25. Lord Bathurst to Villiers, January 5, 1810, FO 63/74.

be nothing other than a no-confidence proposal, their Lordships approved the government's policy by a fairly close vote.[26] Although the Commons finally voted the £980,000 required for Portugal, Opposition speakers made an unusually vigorous effort to bring down the government.[27] Perceval succeeded in weathering a serious legislative crisis, but his position was still far from secure.

With the future of the war in Spain so uncertain, the government hesitated to make any commitment to its ally beyond assistance in the defense of Cadiz. Arms and supplies would be shipped to local Spanish resistance centers, but improvisation remained the keynote of the British aid program. Henry Wellesley was named to replace his brother as British minister to Spain, an assignment which the youngest member of the Wellesley family was probably happy to have. The new envoy was to make a special effort to obtain the right of free trade with the Spanish colonies, a concession considered essential to a continuation of British aid to the Junta.[28]

In 1810 the Junta delegated its authority to a Council of Regency set up at Cadiz. The fact that Cadiz was a major center for the South American trade partly explains the Regency's reluctance to surrender its commercial monopoly in the New World. Almost at once the council impressed on the new British emissary its desperate need for funds, a condition which Henry Wellesley tried to turn to his advantage. Confident of the support of his brother, the foreign secretary, he advanced money to the Regency for repayment as circumstances might permit. By July 1810 these advances amounted to about £400,000.[29] This generosity left the Regency in no position to refuse Wellesley's invitation

---

26. For Grenville's amendment see *Hansard*, XV, (1810), 511-525.

27. *Ibid.*, XVI (1810), 15**-11****. Writing to Wellington on September 10, 1810, Liverpool admitted that in the Commons "the Portuguese subsidy was carried by a small and unwilling majority" (Charles Duke Yonge, *The Life and Administration of Robert Banks, Second Earl of Liverpool* [London, 1868], I, 335).

28. Lord Wellesley to Henry Wellesley, January 4, 1810, FO 72/93. Henry Wellesley (1773-1847) was a neophyte in diplomacy. In March 1809 he suffered a severe blow when his wife abandoned him and their two children to elope with Lord Paget. Wellesley may have welcomed the Spanish mission as a means of helping him overcome his grief. He remained in Spain until 1822, and six years later he was created Baron Cowley.

29. Henry Wellesley to Lord Wellesley, July 11, 1810, FO 72/96. Perceval was a little annoyed that H. Wellesley's advances made it difficult for Wellington to obtain hard money in Spain. See Perceval to Lord Wellesley, July 14, and 23, 1810, in Walpole, *Perceval*, II, 124-128.

to discuss terms of a commercial agreement. Wisely, the British envoy asked for only modest concessions, but even these elicited a Spanish demand for massive financial aid. At first, the Regency spoke of a loan of £2,000,000 from Britain, but within a month they asked for £10,000,000.[30] Discussions went on fitfully for a while but came to nothing in the end. The hard fact was that the Regency gambled that Britain's involvement in the Peninsula would force her to tolerate Spain's refusal to abandon her trade monopoly.[31]

As a matter of fact, British commerce with Spanish America was more extensive than Canning and Lord Wellesley ever admitted. A considerable amount of illegal trading had been going on for some time, and in 1809 the Junta reluctantly acquiesced in the decision taken at Havana to open that port to foreign traders.[32] The outbreak of revolt in Venezuela also brought improvement, for in 1810 the Caracas junta declared its harbors open to all shipping. If the South American uprisings benefited Britain's trade, they caused her some embarrassment as well. However, Lord Wellesley deftly threaded his way between the demands of the colonists and the Spanish authorities without committing his government to any policy which would hopelessly antagonize either.[33]

The flow of British war supplies to Spain in 1810 went chiefly to Cadiz, where British soldiers and the Royal Navy took part in the defense of that port city. Other centers of Spanish resistance also depended on Britain for arms. In the spring, 12,000 muskets with accoutrements and equipment were given to patriot forces in Galicia and the Asturias, while shipments also reached the insurgents in Catalonia, Guadalajara, and the Eastern Provinces. Ordnance supplies sent to Spain during 1810 were valued at £291,991, while money given the Regency and its agents was somewhat in excess of £445,000.[34]

30. Henry Wellesley to Lord Wellesley, June 29 and July 15, 1810, FO 72/95, FO 72/96. See also C. W. Crawley, "French and English Influences in the Cortes of Cadiz, 1810-1814," *Cambridge Historical Journal*, 6 (1938), 176-206.
31. William W. Kaufmann, *British Policy and the Independence of Latin America, 1804-1828* (New Haven, Conn., 1951), p. 48.
32. Dorothy B. Goebel, "British Trade to the Spanish Colonies, 1796-1823," *American Historical Review*, 43 (1937-1938), 298.
33. Kaufmann, *British Policy*, p. 54.
34. Memorandum of Supplies . . . , FO 72/137; An Account of the value of . . . Ordnance . . . supplied . . . for the Service of Spain and Portugal, March 27, 1811, FO 63/120. The Spanish Subsidy Account shows that during 1810 £445,155 was paid to the Spanish government (AO 3/765).

The Spanish subsidy was intended to help the nationalists hold out against the French, but more significant results were expected from the recently expanded aid program to Portugal. The British Aid Office in Lisbon was able to make regular payments to the Council of Regency since Wellington was now giving the Aid Office half of all the money received in his Military Chest.[35] Management of the subsidy payments entailed heavier responsibilities for the British envoy at Lisbon than before. In 1810 Villiers returned to England and was succeeded by Charles Stuart, an able and forthright agent who had been in the Peninsula for two years. Under Stuart's direction, the Aid Office paid more than £1,000,000 to the council during 1810, but even this amount fell short of meeting the expenses of the Portuguese auxiliary troops. It was expected that the council, on receiving money from the Aid Office, would turn it over to the Portuguese Commissary General, which was responsible for feeding and paying the auxiliaries. Often, the Portuguese Commissary had neither food nor pay to issue the auxiliaries, in which case Wellington was compelled to supply their deficiencies from his own commissary. Stuart would sometimes purchase food in Portugal or abroad for delivery to the Portuguese Commissary, the value of the purchase being considered a part of the subsidy.[36] Much of the difficulty arose from the fact that during 1810 food prices in Portugal increased at a fantastic rate; Stuart estimated that they had doubled during the first half of the year.[37] Bad harvests and the diversion of such a large part of the nation's manpower into military service accounts for this state of affairs. By the close of 1810 the total of all payments in money and provisions to Portugal exceeded £1,800,000—twice what Wellington had estimated Portugal would require.[38]

Although the Portuguese auxiliaries might go without food and pay, they never lacked arms and ammunition. By August 1810, the year's shipment of ordnance stores for Portugal had been completed. These included 51,200 muskets and nearly 7,500,000 cartridges, along with smaller quantities of other weapons. Shipments of clothing and supplies during that year were valued at

35. Wellington to C. Stuart, June 11, 1810, *Dispatches of Wellington,* VI, 184-185.
36. Napier, *War in the Peninsula,* III, 48.
37. Stuart to Lord Wellesley, June 16, 1810, FO 63/91.
38. Portuguese Subsidy Account, 1810, AO 3/746.

about £142,000 and consisted of 30,000 uniforms for the auxiliaries, 40,000 shirts, and two pairs of shoes for each man. Also included were 42,000 knapsacks, which Wellington thought to be of unusually poor quality.[39]

The Anglo-Portuguese army spent the spring of 1810 preparing for the expected French invasion. Wellington carefully supervised the construction of heavy fortifications around Lisbon, although the casual observer could not tell whether they were intended for a last-ditch stand against the enemy or simply as a cover for a British evacuation. Under Beresford's fierce eye (he had only one), Portugal's own army was being trained mercilessly for the part it would soon have to play.[40] Meanwhile, in Spain, Masséna put in motion the 100,000 troops under his command with which he expected to crush the Anglo-Portuguese. Wellington relied on the two border fortresses of Ciudad Rodrigo and Almeida to delay the invader. Ciudad Rodrigo was garrisoned by Spanish troops, whose zealous defense cost Masséna more than a month's siege. Almeida, on the Portuguese side of the frontier, was less fortunate. About 5,000 Portuguese troops under a British officer were determined to hold the fort for as long as possible, but the explosion of their powder magazine ended resistance. With the border now open, Wellington withdrew his army toward Lisbon. The forces he commanded were almost equally composed of British and Portuguese.[41] The latter had a chance to prove themselves when, late in September, the allied army faced about to offer battle to the pursuer at Busaco. Masséna suffered a bloody repulse when he attempted to drive his opponents from the heights which they occupied. Although the engagement only delayed the French advance, it gave tangible proof of the fighting quality of the Portuguese.[42]

39. The 1810 arms shipment to Portugal also included 2,000 rifles, 3,000 pairs of pistols, 6,000 swords, 30,000 sets of accoutrements, and 512,000 flints. See An account of Arms and Ammunition issued to Portugal . . ., March 22, 1811 [the Account is misdated "1810"], FO 63/120. Wellington sent 20,000 of these muskets for the use of the Spanish. See Wellington to Henry Wellesley, August 30, 1810, *Dispatches of Wellington,* VI, 394-395; Wellington to Liverpool, June 20, 1810, *ibid.,* VI, 217; Portuguese Subsidy Account, 1810, AO 3/746.

40. Wellington to Villiers, June 5, 1810, *Dispatches of Wellington,* VI, 170.

41. Charles Oman, *A History of the Peninsular War* (Oxford, 1902-1930), III, 547.

42. Wellington declared that at Busaco the Portuguese army had "shown itself capable of engaging and defeating the enemy" (Wellington to Liverpool, September 30, 1810, *Dispatches of Wellington,* VI, 476). British and Portuguese casualties in the battle were exactly the same: 626 killed, wounded, or missing. See Oman, *Peninsular War,* III, 551.

The summer of 1810 also witnessed the first serious outbreak of hostility toward Britain in the Lisbon Council of Regency. The storm had been brewing for some time before it broke out into an ugly quarrel between the council and Wellington. To all appearances, the British commander seemed to have no other plan than to fall back on Lisbon and leave the country to the invader. The capital was crowded with refugees who added to the rapidly rising hysteric fear that the British would evacuate Lisbon as they had Corunna in 1809. To make matters worse, the war was plunging the Portuguese government into hopeless debt. Despite the enlarged British subsidy, the council would end the year 1810 with another £1,000,000 deficit.[43] Anti-British feeling in the council found a spokesman in Jose de Souza e Coutinho, usually known as the Principal de Souza.[44] In alliance with the Bishop of Oporto, himself a member of the council, De Souza tried to recover control over Portugal's military operations before Wellington's apparent cowardice lost them the war. Secret appeals for support were sent to England, backed by the argument that Portugal could only be saved by abandoning Wellington's disastrous strategy.[45] Responsibility for resisting the De Souza faction fell to the British minister, Charles Stuart, who had just been named to the Council of Regency. Thoroughly outraged by the council's conduct, Wellington showered Stuart with complaints against De Souza and the Bishop. They were obstructing his defense plans by refusing to carry out orders to destroy everything in that part of the country through which the enemy must pass on his way to Lisbon. The council had only itself to blame if it was in debt, since it was unwilling either to impose an effective tax system or properly enforce the one now operative.[46] Left to himself, Wellington would have removed De Souza from the council by force. Fortunately, Stuart had the temperament and skill for negotiation, and he was able to hold the influence of

---

43. Stuart estimated that the council had spent £2,000,000 of its own money during 1810; Stuart to Lord Wellesley, February 2, 1811, FO 63/106.

44. Three De Souza brothers were active in Portuguese affairs at this time. In addition to Jose (the Principal), Domingos was Portugal's minister to London, and Rodrigo was with the Regent at Rio.

45. Napier, *War in the Peninsula,* III, 48-57; Fortescue, *British Army,* VII, 497; Oman, *Peninsular War,* III, 415-418.

46. Wellington to Stuart, October 6, 1810, *Dispatches of Wellington,* VI, 494-495; Wellington to Liverpool, October 27, 1810, *ibid.,* VI, 545-546.

the malcontents in check. Should the situation become unmanageable he had a powerful weapon in his hands: the suspension of the British subsidy without which the Regency could not survive more than a few days. Wisely, this weapon was reserved for a more critical period.

In mid-October, Wellington brought his army into the lines of Torres Vedras near Lisbon where he was joined by about 8,000 Spanish under the Marquis Romana.[47] During the following winter the operations at Torres Vedras developed into one of the major turning points of the war. Short of supplies and living in a country almost stripped of provisions, Masséna was condemned to conduct a siege in which the besiegers suffered the greatest deprivation.

Wellington's greatest deficiency was not food but specie, which was now in shorter supply than ever. The Commissary General's agents had to accept extremely heavy discounts in converting bills drawn on England into hard money. Although the Treasury was sending more specie to the Peninsula than before, the proportion of the war expenses it paid for fell sharply. Rocketing military expenses, together with greater aid to Portugal and Spain, frustrated the government's efforts to maintain a healthy balance between specie and Treasury Bills in paying its debts in the Peninsula.[48] Meanwhile, the army's bills piled up, and pay for the troops was again several months in arrears. "If you cannot supply us with money," Wellington angrily wrote to Liverpool, "you ought to withdraw us. We are reduced to the greatest distress."[49]

---

47. Romana's troops cost the British Commissary about £110,000 to maintain during 1810. See Oman, *Peninsular War*, III, 432; Spanish Subsidy Account, AO 3/765.

48. Wellington to Liverpool, May 16, 1810, *Dispatches of Wellington*, VI, 121. Account of Money sent to Spain and Portugal (FO 63/120) shows the relation of paper and specie sent to the Peninsula during this period:

	1809	1810
Paper	£2,174,097	£5,382,166
Specie	465,667	679,069

Hecksher (*Continental System*, pp. 354, 362) contends that the British Commissary's cumbersome methods had much to do with its difficulty in procuring specie at this time. The relative ease with which Rothschilds Bank accomplished the work in 1813 seems to him a further argument in favor of the efficiency of such transactions when handled by a private bank. One might wonder whether the improved prospects of victory in 1813 made it easier for Rothschilds to call out hard money than it had been for Wellington's Commissary in 1810.

49. Wellington to Liverpool, May 23, 1810, *Dispatches of Wellington*, VI, 147; for the government's point of view, see Liverpool to Wellington, June, 1810, in Yonge, *Liverpool*, I, 330-331.

The worsening of Britain's financial health naturally excited much speculation as to its causes. Heavy outlays for military operations and subsidies in the Peninsula was a fairly common explanation offered, but some observers were unwilling to accept this as the only answer. The poor grain harvest of 1809 had necessitated heavy purchases of food abroad, while grain importation during 1810 rose to more than 2,321,000 quarters—not far from an all-time high. Expansion of British trade might have paid for both the military expenses and food imports, but the Continental System and the American Non-Intercourse Act restricted it considerably. The new South American markets offered compensation, but a large part of Britain's exports there were bought on credit. By 1810 three closely related phenomena caused uneasiness among Britain's economic leaders: the shortage of specie, the unfavorable balance of payments between England and the rest of the world, and the dangerous degree of speculation which marked her trade with Latin America.

The shortage of hard money was most dramatic since it manifested itself in the premium which gold commanded over paper in the money market. One school of thought found the cause for this in the 1797 Restriction Act, which freed the Bank of England from the obligation of redeeming its notes in specie. Without this healthy check, the Bank had outrageously over-issued notes which, in turn, had driven hard money from the market. Such was the argument effectively set forth in a pamphlet entitled *The High Price of Bullion; a Proof of the Depreciation of Bank Notes,* which came from the pen of David Ricardo late in 1809. Ignoring war expenses, subsidies, and foreign food purchases, Ricardo fastened on the expansion of Bank notes as the basic cause for the shortage and offered an easy solution. Repeal the Bank Restriction Act and the specie shortage would end.

Ricardo's pamphlet supplied a powerful and cogently argued case for those who had never ceased to oppose the 1797 suspension of specie payments. Now the cry for "conversion" was renewed by many, including Francis Horner, who had long been in the forefront of the movement.[50] From his seat in the House of Commons Horner pressed for the creation of a committee to

50. Horner's work and that of other opponents of the 1797 Restriction Act has been examined by Silberling, "Financial and Monetary Policy," p. 397 and *passim.*

inquire into the causes of the specie shortage. Perceval was reluctant to agree, knowing well the views and remedies of Horner and his supporters. At last the demand for action proved too strong, and in February 1810 such a committee was formed with Horner as its chairman. It included George Canning and William Huskisson among its members. Four months later, the Bullion Committee presented its report and, to no one's surprise, recommended the resumption of specie payments as early as practicable, a date finally identified as 1813. The report greatly alarmed Perceval, and he confided to a friend that should Parliament adopt its recommendations it would be "tantamount to a . . . declaration that we must submit to any terms of peace rather than continue the war."[51] Whether or not this view was sound, debate on the Bullion Committee's Report inevitably turned into a debate on the war itself.[52]

One month after the appearance of the report, the bubble of commercial speculation which had been growing for a year finally broke and plunged the country into the worst panic since 1797. As if this was not enough, the Cabinet faced a new crisis in the closing weeks of 1810 when George III entered what proved to be the final stage of insanity. The threat of a Regency which had hovered over Pitt on several occasions, only to pass on, now became a reality for Perceval. Since the Prince of Wales was expected to call on Grenville and the antiwar faction to form a new government, the future looked grim for the Cabinet. The Regency Bill, however, as finally enacted, limited the Prince's power to make certain fundamental changes for one year, during which time the King might recover.

Under the circumstances, the government naturally hesitated to commit itself to another year of war in the Peninsula, but this hesitancy was swept away by Wellington's successes before the lines of Torres Vedras.[53] Certain now that the French siege must

51. Perceval to J. W. Croker, November 11, 1810, *The Croker Papers: The Correspondence and Diaries of the Late Right Honourable John Wilson Croker,* ed. Louis Jennings (New York, 1884), I, 31.

52. Compare Silberling's views ("Financial and Monetary Policy") with those of Hecksher (*Continental System,* pp. 359-362).

53. In a letter to Wellington, dated February 20, 1811, Liverpool pointed out how expensive the war had become. The 1808 campaign in the Peninsula had cost Britain £2,778,796; that of 1809, £2,639,764; that of 1810, £6,061,235. "I am under the necessity of stating it to be the unanimous opinion of every member of the Government,

fail, the Cabinet decided to continue the war, and on March 6 Liverpool informed Wellington that £2,000,000 would again be set aside for Portugal's use during 1811.[54] Twelve days later Perceval asked the Commons to support this decision by voting that amount as a subsidy for Portugal. Wellington had not only checked the enemy, but he hoped soon to resume the offensive. Furthermore, Portugal was the best theatre in which to fight the war, since it provided Britain with an opportunity "to carry on operations with most advantage to ourselves, and most inconvenience to the enemy." Opposition speakers derided this assertion, but the House finally granted the government's request for funds. In the Lords, Grenville argued zealously against the measure and urged the government to conserve its resources rather than waste them in a war which could never be won.[55]

News which justified the government's courageous decision soon reached London: Masséna had abandoned operations against Torres Vedras and was now in flight toward the Spanish frontier. For the first time since the Battle of Talavera, Wellington was ready to take the offensive, and the arrival of spring saw the Anglo-Portuguese marching eastward, determined to recover the border fortresses lost during the previous year. Possession of Ciudad Rodrigo, Almeida, and Badajoz would open the passage through which Wellington proposed to lead his army into Spain. This news inspired enthusiasm on both sides of the House of Commons, and the thanks of the House was voted to Wellington, Beresford, and the men under their command without a dissenting voice.[56]

Thanks to Wellington's victory, Perceval looked forward with greater confidence to the debate on the Bullion Committee's Report, which began on May 6. Rather than oppose the economic theories of that report, the government simply argued that a return to specie payments by 1813 would have a catastrophic effect on the war which had now begun to turn in Britain's favor.

---

and of every person acquainted with the finances and resources of the country, that it is absolutely impossible to continue our exertions upon the present scale in the Peninsula for any considerable length of time" (Yonge, *Liverpool*, I, 365).

54. Liverpool to Wellington, March 6, 1811, FO 63/120.
55. *Hansard*, XIX (1811), 393, 453.
56. *Ibid.*, XIX, 774.

Speaking to this point, Nicholas Vansittart, who would soon replace Perceval as chancellor of the exchequer, declared: "To carry on the operations of the war for the next two years, not only without the accommodation afforded by the Bank ... but under the pressure of a circulation so contracted and cramped, as it necessarily must be, is a task which no minister has yet been compelled to attempt, and which ... can be accomplished only by a pressure upon the people far greater than they have yet experienced. I suspect that it could not be effected at all, and that if we were not compelled to sue for peace, we should at last be obliged to recall our forces from abroad, and abandon the continental war, just at the moment when the concurrent opinion appears to be, that fairer prospects than we have yet known are opening."[57] On this crucial question, the government was supported by Canning, himself a member of the Bullion Committee. As the man most responsible for taking up the cause of the Peninsular powers in 1808, the former foreign secretary could hardly have taken any other position.[58]

By the time the committee's recommendations were put to a vote, the Cabinet had gained wide support. The proposal to force the Bank of England to resume specie payments by May 1813 was defeated by more than three to one. This vote of confidence in Perceval was confirmed a few weeks later by legislative approval of the new Budget. In addition to £2,000,000 in aid for Portugal, the Budget provided for a £3,200,000 vote of credit which would implement the government's aid program for Spain in the coming year.[59]

With the opening of Wellington's campaign against the border fortresses in the spring of 1811, the Peninsular War entered a new phase. Britain was now committed to the contest she had resumed with such uncertainty following the failure of Sir John Moore's campaign in 1809. Ahead lay hard fighting and disappointment, but the character of the war had undergone a major change. Never again would Portugal be invaded by the enemy. In Spain, the nationalists were still on the defensive, but all of

57. *Ibid.,* XIX, 965-966.
58. *Ibid.,* XIX, 1125-1128.
59. *Ibid.,* XIX, 1169; XX (1811), 210-211.

France's efforts to subdue Andalusia had proved barren. Now there was some reason to hope that the time would soon come when British, Portuguese, and Spanish troops could unite in a single force strong enough to drive the enemy from the Peninsula.

Subsidies had materially contributed to the change in the fortunes of war which marked 1811. For three years Britain had sent arms, money, and troops to help Spain withstand Napoleon's juggernaut, while during the same period she financed the formation of a Portuguese army nearly as large as her own force in the Peninsula. When the work was undertaken, the Cabinet had no idea of the expense it would involve. The original modest grant to Portugal had to be increased to £980,000 in 1809, while in the following year it was more than doubled.

Britain's ability to supply her Peninsular allies with vast quantities of arms and supplies is one of the most striking features of the period. In 1808 the Master General of the Ordnance had been overwhelmed by the demand for muskets to be sent to the Peninsula, but in the years which followed, it became easier to meet such demands. Accounts prepared early in 1811 revealed that the Ordnance Office had achieved a record of which it could be proud. Shipment of muskets to Spain and Portugal since the beginning of the war amounted to more than 336,000, along with 60,000,000 cartridges.[60] The Storekeeper General had done every bit as well in supplying the allies with the uniforms, cloth, shoes, and countless other items they needed.

More than 45,000 regular Portuguese troops were serving under Wellington by 1811, thus making up roughly half of that force

60. These two accounts (one for Portugal; the other for Spain) are both dated February 28, 1811, and are found in FO 63/120.

	Portugal	Spain
Artillery	6 pieces	342 pieces
Artillery Amm.	2,000 rounds	128, 040 rounds
Muskets	114,116	222,141
Carbines	600	2,600
Rifles	2,120	–
Pistols	6,916	5,640
Swords	15,024	87,229
Pikes	17,300	68,530
Accoutrements	50,000	99,000
Cartridges	16,607,200	43,358,455
Balls	60,000	8,459,142
Powder (barrels)	3,009	28,924
Flints	783,680	3,996,500

which won the respect of Masséna's veterans at Torres Vedras. The Anglo-Portuguese alliance inevitably bred disagreements, which Charles Stuart had so far been able to keep within harmless limits. It remained to be seen whether his task would be quite so easy now that Portugal was free from the danger of French invasion.

Britain fought the war in the Peninsula with money as well as muskets—the former usually proving the more difficult for her to supply. The scarcity of specie available for remittance to the Peninsula was a serious problem after 1808, and the government was convinced that a return to specie payments in England would force it to abandon the war. Happily, Wellington's victories came in time to permit the Cabinet to exorcise this threat for the duration of the war.

What ultimate goal did Britain hope to achieve in the Peninsula? The foreign secretary, Lord Wellesley, considered it a "diversion," the success of which might encourage Russia to break with Napoleon. Should the Tsar do so, he would probably be supported by Prussia, Sweden, and Denmark. Thus, victories in Spain would spark a revival of Britain's old plans for a northern coalition to end the Napoleonic menace.[61] Nothing could be accomplished in this direction until Wellington completed the work begun at Torres Vedras. To that end the Anglo-Portuguese army was now moving toward the Spanish frontier.

61. Notes on the General State of Europe by the Marquess Wellesley, May 15, 1811, *Wellesley Papers*, II, 44-45.

XI

VICTORY IN THE PENINSULA

The three keys needed to open the gate into Spain proved harder for Wellington to win than he had expected. Almeida fell to the Anglo-Portuguese in May 1811, but Ciudad Rodrigo and Badajoz remained beyond his grasp for another year. Only in the spring of 1812 was it possible for the allies to advance into the heart of Spain. Until the French were driven from the frontier, the goals of Britain's subsidy program remained modest: maintenance of the Portuguese serving with Wellington and support for the Spanish resistance movement. A massive effort to mobilize a Spanish army to cooperate with the allies would have to wait at least until Wellington had won a firm bridgehead in Spain. During the year needed to accomplish this, the British aid program encountered difficulties in the attainment of even its limited objectives.

Anglo-Portuguese relations, always uneasy, grew steadily worse during 1811. Wellington's quarrel with the Regency reached the point where heavy British pressure was required to compel the council to reform the management of its war program. Portugal's surrender bred an ill-will which blighted relations between the two governments for the remainder of the war. Experience with the Portuguese Regency led Wellington to hope that when Spanish troops were joined with his own, he might have direct and effective control over them. To accomplish this he proposed to the Cabinet that he be given the management of all British aid to Spain. "I must have the power," he wrote in January 1811, "to tell the Spanish Government, that, unless these troops co-operate strictly with me, the assistance shall be withdrawn from them."[1]

1. Wellington to Lord Wellesley, January 26, 1811, *Dispatches of Wellington*, VII, 194.

Henry Wellesley's experience with the Spanish Cortes, which convened at Cadiz in the autumn of 1810, raised serious doubts whether it would ever be possible for Wellington to have this much control. Although the Cortes was now completely dependent on British support, it stubbornly refused to make any of the concessions Wellesley sought. Refusal to invest Wellington with command over Spanish troops was as vexing as the Cortes' insistence that Britain respect its trade monopoly in South America. Under the circumstances, London had no choice but to bear patiently with Spanish pride and obstinacy.

The increasing tension between Britain and Portugal arose from two major causes: disagreement over the 1810 Commercial Treaty and the Lisbon council's management of Portugal's war program. The first of these problems did not bear directly on the war except to the extent that it was another source of irritation between the allies. For years Britain had wished to end the trade monopoly of the Oporto Wine Company. Believing that the Anglo-Portuguese trade treaty of 1810 obliged the Regent to abolish the company, London resented his unwillingness to do so. Downing Street also charged that João was lamentably lax in carrying out the provisions of the treaty calling for suppression of the Portuguese slave trade. Neither of these difficulties was resolved by the time the war ended. The urgency with which Britain pressed her demands seriously damaged her prestige both at Rio and Lisbon.[2]

Far more important was Wellington's persistent charge that the Lisbon Council of Regency was mismanaging the war and wasting the British subsidy. Each year Portugal received £2,000,000 in British help to meet all the costs of its auxiliaries serving with Wellington and to support its own army under Beresford. The council was responsible for supplying all Portuguese troops with pay and provisions through its own commissary, the Junta de Viveres. Wellington had long complained of the inefficiency of the Junta de Viveres, but the frequency of these complaints, as well as their sharpness, increased dramatically during 1811. Failure of the Junta to get pay and food to their troops in the field was positively criminal, hunger, sickness, and desertions were reducing the Portuguese regiments faster than French bullets.[3] The Council

2. Manchester, *British Preëminence,* p. 99 and *passim.*
3. "Although there are, I understand, provisions in Lisbon in sufficient quantities to last the inhabitants and army for a year, about 12,000 or 14,000 Portuguese troops,

of Regency had also failed miserably to provide the army with transport at times when it was desperately needed. Wellington did not conceal the fact that, in his opinion, Britain should have assumed direct control of all branches of the Portuguese government at the outset of the war.[4]

Serious as such charges were, the council was not entirely without defense. It could hardly be blamed for the shortage of food in Portugal, which was the cause of much of the trouble. Furthermore, in its search for provisions the Junta de Viveres had to compete with Wellington's own commissary agents, whose superior credit gave them a marked advantage.[5] It was almost impossible for a poor country of two and a half million people to bear the heavy burden imposed by the war. With nearly 100,000 men either in the army or in the militia, Portugal's revenue was unequal to the expense, especially since British financial help was proving such a weak reed.[6] Throughout 1810 a large part of the Portuguese subsidy had been paid in the form of food and commodities shipped from Britain—only about half the £2,000,000 due the council had been given in money.[7] If London complained of a shortage of cash, how much more Lisbon had to suffer! Arguments such as these made no impression on Wellington, who was convinced that Portugal's troubles were the result of the council's mismanagement. Undoubtedly the council was lax in requiring the wealthy classes to pay their fair share of taxes. Until the tax system was reformed and then stringently enforced, Wellington was sure that the Portuguese treasury would always be short.[8]

The running battle between Wellington and the Council of Regency was only one side of a problem which grew increasingly serious throughout 1811. The British envoy, Charles Stuart, was finding it more difficult to maintain his good humor in dealing with De Souza and the Bishop of Oporto. One of the most controversial questions which produced heated disagreement was

which I have on the right of the Tagus, are literally starving" (Wellington to Lord Wellesley, January 26, 1811, *Dispatches of Wellington,* VII, 192). See also Wellington to Liverpool, May 1, 1811, *ibid.,* VII, 517.

4. Wellington to Lord Wellesley, January 26, 1811, *ibid.,* VII, 193.
5. Memorandum on British Aids to Portugal, March, 1813, FO 63/162.
6. Oman, *Peninsular War,* V, 147-149.
7. Portuguese Subsidy Account, 1810, AO 3/746.
8. Wellington to Stuart, January 28, 1811, *Dispatches of Wellington,* VII, 201-202.

the exact state of the British subsidy account with Portugal. While there was no doubt as to the precise amount of aid Britain had agreed to provide each year, difficulties quickly arose when efforts were made to determine what had actually been paid. Aside from the usual question as to which party would bear the loss resulting from discounts on bills of exchange, there were perplexing details peculiar to the Portuguese subsidy. Stuart often purchased grain for delivery to the Portuguese auxiliary troops. Should such foodstuffs be counted as part of the year's subsidy? If so, what value should be placed on them?[9] Disagreement on points such as these accounts for the wide discrepancy between the Council's subsidy accounts and those kept by the British emissary. Stuart's claim that the subsidy was in fact overpaid was challenged by the Portuguese, who produced figures showing that the reverse was true. Efforts to disentangle these accounts were still being made fifteen years after the guns fell silent at Waterloo.[10]

During the summer of 1811 Stuart grappled with another problem which raised Portuguese tempers even more. Payments made by the British Aid Office went directly into the Portuguese treasury for the use of the Junta de Viveres. With British subsidy money thus intermingled with Portugal's own funds, a suspicion arose that the treasury was using the subsidy for other than military purposes. Stuart was reluctant to charge peculation, although the present arrangement clearly encouraged carelessness. Wellington was less cautious; he frankly declared that Portuguese officials were embezzling the subsidy.[11]

The hot summer months of 1811, which witnessed Wellington's unsuccessful assaults against Badajoz and Rodrigo, also saw a stormy battle fought out around the council board at Lisbon. A British appeal to the Regent at Rio for help yielded the curious suggestion that he would remove De Souza from the council if London recalled Stuart.[12] From the battlefield, Wellington sent his prescription for Portugal's ills: replace the Junta de Viveres with a

9. The British Treasury took the position that food purchases were to be counted as part of the subsidy; Wm. Hamilton to Stuart, July 17, 1811, FO 63/105.

10. At least as late as 1830 the Audit Office was working over the Portuguese subsidy accounts.

11. Wellington to Stuart, April 15, 1811, *Dispatches of Wellington*, VII, 472.

12. Napier, *War in the Peninsula*, III, 295; Wellington to Stuart, May 6, 1811, *Dispatches of Wellington*, VII, 519.

The Duke of Wellington, by Thomas Heaphy

William Carr Beresford, by Thomas Heaphy

Spencer Perceval, by George Joseph

The Marquess Wellesley, by J. Davis

new commissary under British control and overhaul the national tax system.[13] To save his Portuguese regiments from starvation, he would continue to supply them as best he could from his own commissary, but the value of such supplies must be credited to the British subsidy.[14]

Wellington may have been right in contending that Britain ought never to have undertaken to work with the council as an equal, but it was now too late to correct that error. Far better that Stuart should employ his patience and tact in urging reforms on the council. Encouraging progress was made when the Rio government at last ordered a reform of the Junta de Viveres and the Portuguese tax machinery. Results were sufficiently hopeful to bring from Wellington a promise that he would work with the Council of Regency in a new spirit of good-will and cooperation.[15] This came to an abrupt end a few months later when Stuart proposed that the council create a separate Military Chest into which the subsidy would be paid, rather than into the general treasury. Incensed at the implications of this suggestion, the council refused. Since both Stuart and Wellington now agreed that the step was essential, the British minister felt justified in employing coercion. On August 17, 1811 he announced that the subsidy would be suspended until the council adopted his recommendation. Within a week, the council yielded; clearly Stuart had the means needed to enforce his will.[16]

A few months later, a chastened council was obliged to submit to still another British demand: that they accept a substantial part of the subsidy in commodities other than military supplies, to be sent from England for Portugal's use.[17] In view of London's difficulties in finding hard money, it was obviously desirable to remit as large a part of the subsidy in supplies as possible. Unwittingly, Wellington made his government's problem worse by announcing that the value of arms and clothing given Portugal

13. See Wellington's memorandum of June 25, 1811, *Dispatches of Wellington*, VIII, 48-50.

14. Wellington to Liverpool, May 30, 1811, and Wellington to Col. Gordon, June 12, 1811, *Dispatches of Wellington*, VII, 625; VIII, 7.

15. Wellington to Liverpool, June 25, 1811; Wellington to Gordon, August 21, 1811; Wellington to Stuart, October 21, 1811; *ibid.*, VIII, 52, 212, 351-352.

16. Stuart to Lord Wellesley, no. 161, August 17, 1811, and no. 164, August 24, 1811, FO 63/112.

17. Stuart to Lord Wellesley, no. 199, October 12, 1811, FO 63/113.

would not be counted as part of the subsidy. Given the delicate state of Anglo-Portuguese relations, the Cabinet decided to accept this obligation.[18]

The Treasury quickly took advantage of the concession Stuart had won, and in January 1812 it contracted with Matthew Boulton's firm to produce a quantity of copper blanks for shipment to Lisbon where they would be stamped and used as part of the national coinage. The value of these blanks was £2,800, which was applied to the Portuguese subsidy account for the year.[19] Shipments were made of other goods Lisbon had indicated it could use—timber, coal, medicines, tools, canvas, nails, iron, paper, and a host of other items. The proportion of the British subsidy sent Portugal in this form was never unduly large. At its greatest, in 1813, it amounted to only a little more than 10 percent of the total £2,000,000 due for the year.[20]

Benefits anticipated from the council's reform of its commissary and tax system failed to materialize. In the last analysis, the nation simply could not support the great military effort. Consequently, Wellington's commissary increasingly had to provide pay and

18. Wellington to Stuart, August 18, 1811, *Dispatches of Wellington,* VIII, 208. The final account of the British subsidy to Portugal (AO 3/746) omits the value of arms and clothing sent after 1811.

19. The great industrialist died in 1809, but his business continued. It had a reputation for the production of machinery to stamp and mint coins. See an unsigned letter from the Foreign Office to George Harrison, January 28, 1812, FO 63/140.

20. The Portuguese Subsidy Account for 1812 (AO 3/746) indicates that during that year twenty-four vessels sailed from England to Lisbon with cargoes of goods for the Council of Regency. The cargoes of two of these vessels, given below, are typical:

St. Andrew	*Plough*
2,822 Dozen files with handles	3,840 lbs. of Nails
4,400 Melting Pots	3,840 lbs. ditto-smaller
5,000 lbs. of pewter	3,840 lbs. ditto-2½ inch
3,000 lbs. of steel	3,840 lbs. ditto- 1½ inch
1,200 lbs. of ditto-fine	700 chests of tin
5,000 lbs. of ditto-do.	50,000 rivets 3½ inch
2,559 ½ yds. of sacking	5,000 lbs. of lead
2,800 hoes	1,471 bullock hides
1,800 axes	
Total value - £2,985:19:4	Total value £4,084:17:1

The value of these goods, in relation to the total subsidy, can be determined from the Portuguese Subsidy Account (AO 3/746).

	Goods	Total Subsidy
1812	£160,039	£2,276,833
1813	276,756	2,486,012
1814	61,561	1,345,082

supplies for the Portuguese troops. The arrangement was not without advantage, since it gave the British commander some of the control over those troops which he had all along insisted must be his. With the bulk of the Anglo-Portuguese forces now supplied from the British Commissary, there was also less occasion for British and Portuguese agents to bid against each other in obtaining such provisions as were available in the country.

By 1812 the British subsidy to Portugal was fast becoming a military aid administered by Wellington's Commissary General. Nearly all payments of the subsidy fell under one of three headings: (1) provisions, supplies, and pay furnished the Portuguese troops either directly from Wellington's commissary or indirectly through their own; (2) goods shipped from England to Lisbon; and (3) money payments to the Council of Regency by the British Aid Office. About one half the 1812 subsidy passed through the hands of the British commissary for the service of Portugal's army. During the following year, these payments rose to 70 percent of the total subsidy, while in 1814 they amounted to more than 80 percent. This change worked to the disadvantage of the council, which received a correspondingly smaller share of the annual subsidy in money. In 1812 and 1813 cash payments to the council amounted to only about one quarter of the year's subsidy, while in 1814, the last year of the war, they dropped to a mere 7 percent. Since Britain was now responsible for maintaining the Portuguese auxiliaries from her own commissary resources, there was no need for heavy remittances of money to the Lisbon council.[21]

At the outset of the war Britain had undertaken to subsidize Portugal to help her maintain a force under Wellington's command. By 1812 this arrangement broke down. Portugal's financial weakness and administrative inefficiency obliged Wellington to dip into his own resources to maintain her units in the field. The

---

21. The relation of these three forms of aid to the total subsidy was as follows:

	Money to council	British Commissary		Goods	Total Subsidy
		[Paid in Field]	[To Port Com.]		
1812	£595,079	£699,593	£511,348	£160,039	£2,276,833
1813	637,159	918,061	634,791	276,756	2,486,012
1814	98,472	522,969	649,146	61,561	1,345,082
1815	50,908	3,057	950	–	54,915

These figures are taken from the Portuguese Subsidy Accounts, AO 3/746.

resulting advantages of this arrangement to the British commander were numerous. In the end, the British subsidy became almost entirely a direct military aid program administered by Wellington's commissary. While the council was free from all obligation to the auxiliaries, it still had to provide for the upkeep of its own army commanded by Beresford. Direct payments of British money to the council shrank rapidly after 1811, and before the war ended Portugal's leaders openly wondered whether they had been Britain's allies or her victims. London never seemed to understand that, regardless of the subsidy, Portugal had nearly bankrupted herself to supply Wellington with troops.

The early months of 1811 were probably the most discouraging period in the Spanish war of liberation. Although Cadiz still held out against the enemy, elsewhere the war went badly. France's plan to reduce Catalonia took a long step forward on the first day of the New Year, when the city of Tortosa surrendered. This enabled the French to deal separately with the resistance forces in Catalonia and Valencia. The capture of Tarragona in the late spring brought them even closer to their goal. For practical purposes, the Spanish government at Cadiz was hardly effective beyond the walls of the besieged city. Efforts by the Cortes to draft a consitution for the kingdom ended in violent disagreement among its members, while South American troubles added still another burden which the government could well have done without. This civil strife, now virtually a colonial rebellion, seriously interfered with the shipment of specie to Cadiz, thereby making the Cortes more reliant on British money than ever.

Britain's Spanish policy remained what it had been since 1808: support in money and military supplies for the Spanish resistance movement. The effectiveness of the local guerrilla units justified the high priority which Britain assigned to seeing that they were well supplied. Wellington was able to help with this since the heavy arms shipments to Portugal during 1810 left him with a surplus. In January 1811 he forwarded 16,000 muskets to the British minister at Cadiz for distribution to the patriots in eastern Spain.[22] The British government never faltered in its support of

22. Wellington to Liverpool, January 12, 1811, *Dispatches of Wellington,* VII, 135. Late in the summer of 1811 Wellington offered another 4,000 muskets to the Spanish. See Wellington to Henry Wellesley, September 4, 1811, *ibid.,* VIII, 259.

the guerrillas, and for those in hard-pressed Catalonia it made a special effort. During 1811-1812 they received money and arms valued at more than £88,000.[23] The Cortes had invited several British officers to take command of some of the units of the regular Spanish army and London promoted this by undertaking to provide money and equipment to maintain these troops.[24]

Spain's financial condition grew so perilous that in January 1811 her government proposed to resume negotiations for a commercial treaty with Britain. Only desperation could bring the Regency to this step, and Henry Wellesley informed London that "without pecuniary assistance no very considerable efforts toward the prosecution of the War are to be expected from this Government."[25] Wellesley took this opportunity to recommend to the Regency that his brother be given command of its armies. The fact that Spain's generals were held in low esteem added weight to his argument. "There is not a General in the service of Spain," he confided to the foreign secretary, "whose character has not, in some way or other, suffered in the opinion of his Countrymen by the events of the Revolution."[26] Recalling how Frere had offended the Spanish by urging Wellington's appointment as generalissimo, Wellesley proceeded with caution. In March he suggested that the Regency invest his brother with command over those Spanish troops operating in areas contiguous to Portugal. The Regency at once rejected the suggestion and Wellesley fared no better when he carried the matter to the Cortes.[27]

Irritating though Spain's obstinacy was, Wellesley could not allow her to fall for lack of money. In April 1811 he directed the British consul at Cadiz to give her treasury about £16,000 in specie. London had not authorized the payment, but Wellesley felt sure it would be approved. "The Treasury is entirely empty," he

23. Statement no. 48, Spanish Subsidy Account, AO 3/765.
24. The British officers who accepted these commands were Samuel Ford Whittingham and Sir Philip Keating Roche. The former had a distinguished career in Spain which won Wellington's praise. Whittingham's devotion to his troops was especially strong, and he took sharp exception to certain passages in Napier's *History of the War in the Peninsula.* A duel between these veterans was narrowly averted.
25. Henry Wellesley to Lord Wellesley, January 12, 1811, FO 72/109.
26. Henry Wellesley to Lord Wellesley, March 25, 1811, FO 72/110.
27. Henry Wellesley to Lord Wellesley, March 30, 1811, FO 72/110. Wellington's experience as supreme commander of the Portuguese forces led him to doubt the value of Henry's efforts. Unless real authority went with the title, it would prove almost useless. See Wellington to Liverpool, February 2, 1811, *Dispatches of Wellington,* VII, 224.

explained to the foreign secretary; "the Government have not credit sufficient to raise a Dollar in the Town, nor is there any prospect of their soon receiving a supply from the Colonies."[28] The Regency's needs continued to be so pressing that during the next two months Wellesley turned over an additional £79,179.[29] He also lent $500,000 (about £132,000) in return for which Britain was to receive an equivalent value of silver in Peru.[30]

Even after Wellington's victories over Masséna in Portugal, the Foreign Office followed a cautious policy toward Spain. Lord Wellesley approved Henry's occasional payments to the Cortes, but warned him against allowing this to become a regular practice. He specifically instructed his brother to conceal the fact "that you have received such authority; but you will state to them that you are induced, by their urgent Representations of Their Pecuniary Distresses, to make advances for their Relief, upon the Principles which you know to be those which actuate this Government in assisting Spain in her present exertions." During 1811 arms and supplies for 30,000 men would be sent to Spain, in return for which Lord Wellesley hoped that the Cortes would name Wellington as commander of all the troops which he was likely to encounter during the campaign.[31]

Britain did everything possible to help Spain defend herself against the common enemy, but nothing could be done to enable her to undertake a serious offensive campaign so long as Wellington's progress was checked by the enemy at the frontier. Cadiz considered this policy halfhearted and Henry Wellesley reported that many Spanish leaders were openly asserting that Britain would do nothing more than defend Portugal. Spanish resentment was aggravated by London's refusal to provide the Cortes with more money, a policy which Henry considered

28. The exact sum was £15,937; Henry Wellesley to Lord Wellesley, April 15, 1811, FO 72/110.

29. Statement no. 30, Spanish Subsidy Account, AO 3/765.

30. Henry Wellesley to Lord Wellesley, April 18, 1811, FO 72/110. In July Henry advanced another $350,000 to Spain on the same terms; Henry Wellesley to Lord Wellesley, July 17, 1811, FO 72/112. The practice was continued during the next year. A letter from Lord Bathurst to Henry Wellesley of September 27, 1814 (FO 72/158) suggests that the arrangement did not work well.

31. Lord Wellesley to Henry Wellesley, May 3, 1811, FO 72/108. Doubtless, Lord Wellesley had already received Wellington's views on this matter. The foreign secretary pressed Henry to demand a clear understanding with the Cortes that "all civil & military officers in those Provinces and Districts, shall be subjected to his [Wellington's] Authority."

shortsighted.[32] Several times during 1811 the Cortes renewed its petition for a British loan, but Downing Street refused to consider the matter. Clearly, everything must wait until Wellington's army was in Spain.

Early in January 1812 the Anglo-Portuguese army began their attack on Ciudad Rodrigo. Once before Wellington had tried in vain to capture it and now he was determined to succeed. On the night of January 19 an assault was carried out by the light of a frosty moon which ended with the attackers in possession of the citadel. Now only Badajoz obstructed their advance into Spain. Even before learning of the fall of Rodrigo, London had decided to increase its aid to Spain. Trusting that the New Year would see a union of the British and Spanish forces, Lord Wellesley sent new instructions to his brother at Cadiz. During 1812 Spain would receive supplies and arms sufficient for 100,000 troops, and Henry Wellesley was authorized to pay her £600,000 as a subsidy. Only one issue clouded the future of relations between the two governments. Recently the Cortes had sent troops to quell the South American insurrections armed with weapons originally given by Britain for Spain's own war for independence. The foreign secretary insisted that "the Spanish Government must be distinctly informed that this Govt. will not permit any part of the Succours so liberally afforded to Spain to be perverted to the injurious purpose of prosecuting Hostilities against the Spanish Colonies." Forceful on this point, Lord Wellesley was conciliatory on others. Nothing should be done to prejudice the success of the Anglo-Spanish union in arms which was in the offing. To that end Henry was not to press for Wellington's appointment as supreme commander of the Spanish armies.[33]

Preparation of these instructions was one of Lord Wellesley's last acts as foreign secretary; the day before signing them, he had announced his intention to resign.[34] This was only one of several

---

32. Henry Wellesley to Lord Wellesley, July 26, 1811, FO 72/112.

33. Lord Wellesley to Henry Wellesley, January 17, 1812, FO 72/127; Oman, *Peninsular War*, V, 337.

34. Wellesley's motives in resigning remain somewhat of a mystery. His public explanation (*Hansard*, XXIII [1812], 367-372) lacks conviction. It may be that he found it impossible to work easily with his colleagues. Certainly, most of them were happy to see him go. Lord Liverpool doubted whether he had bothered to appear at more than half the Cabinet meetings (Liverpool to Wellington, February, 1812, in

elements in the complex political upheaval which troubled Britain in the spring of 1812. The restrictions in the Regency Bill having lapsed, the Prince Regent, later George IV, was free to make overtures to Grenville and Grey, but in the end he decided to stand by Perceval. In March the prime minister selected Lord Castlereagh to take Wellesley's place at the Foreign Office, but scarcely had the matter been settled when Perceval's assassination reopened the whole question of the government's future. Despite strenuous efforts by Canning and Lord Wellesley to succeed the fallen premier, the final settlement of the question found Lord Liverpool in that position. The reorganization of the Cabinet left Castlereagh and Vansittart, the chancellor of the exchequer, as the only important ministers with seats in the Commons. Thus Castlereagh served not only as foreign secretary but chief government spokesman in the lower house.

Despite signs of an impending rupture between Napoleon and the northern powers, Castlereagh believed that Britain must give highest priority to the war in the Peninsula. With Wellington now hammering at the last border citadel held by the enemy, the time had come to enlarge British aid to Spain even beyond the limit recently set by Lord Wellesley. Within less than a month after taking office, Castlereagh won the Cabinet to this view, and on March 30 he instructed Henry Wellesley to increase the Spanish subsidy from £600,000 to £1,000,000. The wisdom of this policy was confirmed a few weeks later when London learned that Wellington had at last taken Badajoz. Parliament willingly endorsed the subsidy appropriation for Portugal and Spain.[35]

By June 1812 Wellington had fought off attempts by the French to regain control of the border, and he was now ready to move against Madrid. Several units of the Spanish army had recently joined forces with the Anglo-Portuguese and Wellington could expect to encounter others on his march into Spain. Predictably, the Spanish relied on the severely strained British commissary to

Yonge, *Liverpool,* I, 378). For an example of Wellesley's personal peevishness, see Walpole, *Perceval,* II, 238. While one might question Webster's verdict that Wellesley "proved a gigantic failure in the Foreign Office" (*Foreign Policy of Castlereagh,* I, 17), there is no doubt that his resignation made way for a better man.

35. Castlereagh to Edward Thornton, March 13, 1812, FO 73/71; Castlereagh to Henry Wellesley, no. 11, March 30, 1812, FO 72/127; *Hansard,* XXIII (1812), 559-584.

supply them with provisions and equipment.[36] Wellington quickly discovered that his power to grant or refuse such requests gave him more real control over the Spanish than formal appointment as their general.[37]

This fact took on greater significance when the British commander learned that his government had undertaken to pay Spain £1,000,000 during the year. Sure that the Cortes would take the money and rely on him to provide for its troops, Wellington decided to intervene. He wrote Lord Liverpool in May urging that "all the supplies sent to this country for the Spanish Government should be at the disposal of the Commissary in Chief of the King's troops." Britain's unhappy experience with the Portuguese subsidy must not be repeated with the Spanish. If London granted his request, Wellington would guarantee that every shilling given by Britain would be spent to support the Spanish military program. Furthermore, it would give him a powerful weapon to make the Spanish forces do his bidding.[38] None of this implied any criticism of Henry Wellesley, but it was a condemnation of the Cortes with which Henry had to work as British minister. The corruption and waste which characterized the Cortes' expenditure of British money was reason enough to bypass that body in the future. Writing to Henry Wellesley in May 1812, the British commander frankly declared: "I admit, that it is not very easy for the King's Ambassador to give the King's aid in any other manner than through the Spanish Government . . . but the difficulty he would experience in giving the pecuniary aid direct to those who are to enjoy the benefit of it, is the principal reason why I think that the whole ought to be at the disposal of the Commander in Chief."[39]

Wellington's proposal was logical, but it involved certain practical difficulties which he did not appreciate. At least a part of the subsidy must be given to the Cortes, which now depended on Britain for its financial survival. Some money would also have to

---

36. Wellington had already been joined by Don Carlos de España's division. Before leaving for Madrid, he detached a part of Hill's command to join with other Spanish troops in guarding the important Tagus River crossing at Almaraz. See Fortescue, *British Army*, VIII, 446.

37. See Wellington's letter to España of April 29, 1812, *Dispatches of Wellington*, IX, 96-99.

38. Wellington to Liverpool, May 6, 1812, *ibid.*, IX, 124-126.

39. Wellington to Henry Wellesley, May 14, 1812, *ibid.*, IX, 146-147.

be set aside for the use of the local guerrilla units operating at a considerable distance from the main theatre of the war. As Castlereagh studied Wellington's plan, the obvious solution to its difficulties occurred to him: the £1,000,000 subsidy should be divided between Wellington and Henry Wellesley. For the moment, the British commander would have to be satisfied with this compromise.[40]

Management of the £1,000,000 subsidy expanded Henry Wellesley's normal diplomatic duties to include those of paymaster and accountant. The number who looked to him for help was legion. In addition to paying the Cortes and sending money to Wellington, he had to supply the Spanish guerrilla leaders and the British officers in command of Spanish units. All his remittances were either in Treasury Bills drawn on London, or in specie. Occasionally, he followed the example of his Lisbon colleague and purchased food for delivery to Spain's troops. By the end of the year, Wellesley had almost exhausted the £1,000,000 grant, of which about 8 percent had gone for Wellington's use.[41]

Hopes for victory, so low at the beginning of 1812, went soaring in midsummer. Wellington's triumph at Salamanca in July threw open the road to Madrid, and within a month the allies occupied the Spanish capital.[42] The position of the French was now dangerous, and they abandoned their useless siege of Cadiz. Anxious to attack before the scattered enemy armies united, Wellington decided to strike at Clausel's force in the north. Leaving a part of the allied army at Madrid, the British commander moved against his opponent at Burgos. If Clausel could be beaten, the rest of Napoleon's legions might be in flight toward the Pyrenees by the time the year ended.

Wellington's operations during 1812 involved problems of military administration bearing directly on the British aid pro-

40. Castlereagh to Henry Wellesley, June 2, 1812, FO 72/127.

41. Wellesley's account of his 1812 expenditures (Account of Money advanced to the Spanish Government ... under the authority of the Right Honble. Sir Henry Wellesley ... between the 31st of December, 1811 and the 31st of December, 1812) enclosed in Henry Wellesley to Castlereagh, February 16, 1813, FO 72/143, itemizes his payments. Exclusive of the money lent to the Cortes to be repaid in specie, these remittances totaled $3,503,118. At the prevailing rate of exchange, this amounted to about £945,000.

42. Fortescue (*British Army,* VIII, 631) states that at Salamanca the allied army consisted of 30,562 British troops, 18,017 Portuguese, and 3,360 Spaniards.

gram. His commissary had to provide for the British forces, as well as issue pay, provisions, and equipment to the larger part of the Portuguese and Spanish units serving with them. Difficulties in finding an adequate food supply in the war-torn Peninsula made the commissary's job even harder, and he turned for help to his superior, the commissary-in-chief, who directed operations in London. John Charles Herries had been named commissary-in-chief in October 1811, and he held that position for the remainder of the war. Working closely with Wellington and his commissary general, Sir Robert Kennedy, Herries often found himself the target of their complaints, but he was, fortunately, thick-skinned and their grumblings hurt him little.

The commissary-in-chief was responsible for the collection and shipment of the arms and supplies Britain had undertaken to send her allies in the Peninsula. Early in 1812 the Cabinet had promised Spain equipment for 100,000 troops and, thanks to Herries' industry, the bulk of these supplies were on their way within ten weeks.[43] One of Herries' most aggravating problems was caused by the defaulting of British manufacturers on their contracts to provide him supplies. Almost as vexing was the fact that uniform patterns sent by the Spanish and Portuguese were often so carelessly done that when the finished product was delivered by literal-minded British tailors, the jackets were much too small and the trousers would fit only giants. The commissary-in-chief struggled cheerfully with these difficulties, but he was distressed that the Spanish were so unappreciative of his accomplishments.[44]

Providing an adequate food supply for Wellington's army was Herries' constant nightmare. Conditions improved a little in 1813 when he began to buy food and forage in Britain for shipment to the Peninsula, thereby relieving Wellington from the necessity of using his scanty supply of specie to obtain them locally. Winter storms and privateers made such shipments of foodstuffs un-

43. *Memoir of the Public Life of the Right Hon. John Charles Herries* ..., ed. Edward Herries (London, 1880), I, 60; Bunbury to Hamilton, March 10, 1812, FO 72/138.
44. Herries, *Memoir,* I, 34. On July 1, 1812 Herries wrote the British Storekeeper-General at Cadiz: "In truth we have supplied their [Spanish] wants so liberally and so readily that we have misled them into exaggerated notions of our powers, and they receive our loans rather as the proofs of inexhaustible means than of generous efforts in the common cause. Instead of being surprised at our furnishing the equipment for 100,000 men in a few months, they wonder why we do not produce them in a few days" (*ibid.,* I, 61-62).

dependable, however.[45] Wellington regularly complained of Herries' shortcomings, but the commissary-in-chief never lost his government's confidence. During the closing years of the war, he was given the added responsibility of handling nearly all subsidy payments to the allies. Herries' services as commissary-in-chief between 1811 and 1816 surely justify his title as "the unsung Carnot of Whitehall."[46]

The scarcity of hard money, which had troubled Wellington from the beginning of the war, grew steadily worse throughout 1812. The troops who stormed Badajoz and drove the French before them at Salamanca had not been paid for several months, while the army's bills multiplied so fast that Britain's creditors despaired of repayment.[47] Without the rapid increase of British trade with the Peninsula, conditions would have been still worse.[48] Even so, Britain's expenditures for military operations in the Peninsula rose at a fantastic rate. The 1809 campaign had cost about £3,000,000, while double that amount was spent by the government on the Peninsular War in the next year. In 1811 the war cost had jumped to nearly £11,000,000, of which three quarters had been paid for in bills drawn on England. Discount on this paper was not far from 25 percent, while the exchange rate dropped so low that one pound sterling would buy only 3.5 Spanish dollars, rather than 5.[49] Wellington devised numerous plans for obtaining hard money in Spain, but the Treasury found none of them workable.[50] When the allies entered Madrid in the summer of 1812 the specie shortage was critical, and Wellington sternly warned the new secretary of war, Lord Bathurst, "The want of money in the army is become a most serious evil; and we may trace to this want many of the acts of plunder and indiscipline by which we are disgraced every day. We must be

45. Ward, *Wellington's Headquarters*, p. 94.
46. Denis Gray, *Spencer Perceval: The Evangelical Prime Minister, 1762-1812* (Manchester, 1963), p. 330. Herries' work deserves more attention than it has received. His papers are deposited in the British Museum, but as late as the autumn of 1965 they were not available to students.
47. Inevitably this led to wild speculation in British paper, about which there was so much complaint during the last years of the war.
48. François Crouzet, *L'Economie Britannique et le Blocus Continental, 1806-1813* (Paris, 1958), II, 688.
49. Castlereagh to the Duke Del' Infantado, March 25, 1812, FO 72/134.
50. Fortescue, *British Army*, IX, 92-94.

regularly supplied, or we cannot go on." London would have to send him at least £100,000 in coin each month.[51]

In recent years, the British Treasury had resorted to nearly every known means to obtain specie, but the results never came up to expectations.[52] To meet Wellington's latest demand, the Cabinet would have to strip the country of its specie and even send guineas to him—an act prohibited by law. It would, however, be criminal to withhold the help the British commander called for at a time when the war was nearing its climax. Over the strenuous opposition of the Bank of England, the ministers resolved that, come what may, Wellington would have his money. By means of an Order in Council £100,000 in guineas was obtained at the Bank for shipment to Spain. During the last half of 1812 a total of £775,213 in gold was sent to Spain by a government which had now staked everything on victory.[53]

Wellington did not provide that victory. His campaign in northern Spain bogged down completely when Clausel defied his best efforts to take Burgos. French armies commanded by Soult and Joseph Bonaparte had at last united and were moving against the allies. The hunter was now the hunted. Wellington abandoned operations against Burgos in October and withdrew to the Portuguese frontier. His army now included about 12,000 Spanish troops.[54]

The British retreat was a crushing blow, but the situation was not nearly as bad as it appeared. All of Spain south of the Tagus was now free, and the French position in the north was seriously threatened by guerrilla action along its perimeter.[55] In desperation, the Spanish Cortes offered Wellington command of all its armies. If Henry Wellesley is to be believed, the offer was made without pressure or persuasion on his part.[56] Perhaps the appointment strengthened Wellington's position with the 46,000 soldiers

---

51. Wellington to Bathurst, August 18, 1812, *Dispatches of Wellington,* IX, 369.

52. Some of these methods are discussed in Gray, *Perceval,* pp. 323-352.

53. Herries, *Memoir,* I, 78-79; Fortescue, *British Army,* IX, 12-13. The gold sent Wellington in 1812 included French, Portuguese, and Spanish coin, as well as bar gold. See Memorandum of Consignments of Specie to Portugal since August 10, 1812, Historical Manuscripts Commission, *Report on the Manuscripts of Earl Bathurst Preserved at Cirencester Park* (London, 1923), p. 219.

54. M. Glover, *Wellington's Victories,* p. 94.

55. *Ibid.,* pp. 96-97.

56. Henry Wellesley to Castlereagh, September 20, 1812, FO 72/132.

making up the Spanish army, but it was not clear gain. The Spanish general, Ballasteros, commanding in Granada, resented the appointment and refused to obey Wellington's orders. Although Ballasteros' attempt at a coup d'état ended in failure, it revealed how deeply the pride of some Spaniards had been hurt.[57] Less dramatic, but in the long run more important, events bore out Wellington's original prediction: now that he commanded the Spanish, the Cortes expected his commissary to feed and pay them.[58]

Since coming to the Foreign Office, Castlereagh had grown increasingly annoyed at the Spanish habit of offering too little and asking too much. Scarcely had he assumed that post, when the Spanish minister reminded him that three years had gone by without any subsidy treaty between Britain and Spain. A specific proposal for such an agreement was now offered: Britain should provide her ally with arms and equipment for 100,000 men and lend her £10,000,000. In return the Cortes would allow Britain to share in the South American trade for three years. Castlereagh very patiently explained why this offer could not be accepted. So far as arms were concerned, Britain planned to send the requested quantity to Spain during the coming year, in addition to which she would give the Cortes £1,000,000. For the time being the government preferred to give Spain all the help it could rather than to undertake a specific obligation which it might find impossible to meet. Spain's request for a £10,000,000 loan was excessive. As Castlereagh explained, "The mere statement of such a proposition is sufficient to demonstrate its impossibility." The puny trade concessions offered by Spain as an inducement for a treaty were too insignificant to be seriously considered.[59]

Although Castlereagh's support of the Peninsular War never wavered, the events of 1812 made it impossible for him to give it his undivided attention. The long-awaited break between Napoleon and the northern powers had come at last, and by midsummer, the Grand Army had crossed the Niemen river on its

57. Oman (*Peninsular War,* VI, 753) gives the strength of the Spanish army at the end of the summer of 1812 as 46,292. For Ballasteros' activities see *ibid.,* VI, 59-62.

58. Wellington to Don Estevan Mexia, December 11, 1812, *Dispatches of Wellington,* IX, 623-624.

59. Del Infantado to Castlereagh, March 2, 1812, FO 72/134; Castlereagh to Del Infantado, March 25, 1812, FO 72/134.

way to Moscow. Before the year ended a new coalition was in the making, one which Britain would have to support with money and arms. This might strain the nation's resources to the bursting point, but Castlereagh did not propose to finance such a coalition at the expense of his commitments in the Peninsula.

In February 1813 the foreign secretary explained to Henry Wellesley the government's Spanish policy for the coming year. Spain would again be given £1,000,000, in addition to which there would probably be a supplementary subsidy of between £300,000 and £400,000. Clothing, arms, and supplies would also be furnished in sufficient quantity to meet all reasonable expectations which the Spanish government might have. Since Britain also was expected to arm the northern enemies of France, he hoped that Spain could make do with only 50,000 muskets. If Wellington believed that more than that number was needed, however, the government would see that they were sent.

Britain had undertaken obligations to Portugal and Spain which might require her to lay out £3,400,000 during 1813, in addition to paying for her own military operations in the Peninsula. Over and above this, she would also have to provide equally massive subsidies for her new allies in northern Europe. In view of this unprecedented degree of aid to Spain, the foreign secretary urged Henry Wellesley once more to request the Cortes to open its colonial markets. With commendable restraint he reminded his envoy that "Spain ought to do something to conciliate the feelings of this Nation: continued Sacrifices, & no return, may shake the popularity of the War."[60]

Since the aid program for Portugal and Spain was almost entirely military in character, the British government had always been willing to take into account the opinions of its commander. By 1813 Wellington's reputation stood so high that the Cabinet was ready to leave the management of that program in his hands. Accumulating experience strengthened his belief that, so far as

60. Castlereagh to Henry Wellesley, February 15, 1813, FO 72/142. In the end Britain supplied clothing for 100,000 Spanish (Hamilton to Bunbury, October 8, 1813, FO 72/155). So far as arms were concerned, Wellington believed that 60,000 muskets would be sufficient for the year. Fernan Nuñez to Castlereagh, August 22, 1813, FO 72/149. For the development of Castlereagh's thoughts on the Spanish subsidy, see his letters to Henry Wellesley of January 26, March 4, and April 14, 1813, FO 72/142.

possible, the subsidy should be used exclusively to meet the needs of the Spanish and Portuguese forces in the field, and this was the goal he now set out to attain. Before the war ended, nearly all British money given the Peninsular powers passed through the commissary general's department to provide pay, provisions, and equipment for the allied troops.

With his army safely settled into winter quarters on the Portuguese frontier, Wellington left for a brief visit to Cadiz in December 1812. He wanted to reach a clear understanding with the Spanish government regarding his authority before he accepted its recent offer of supreme command. Even this would be meaningless unless Cadiz undertook the major reforms in its military supply system that he was anxious to propose. Wellington also wished to confer with Henry Wellesley. During the past year, Henry had given him only a small part of the British subsidy to spend and he must persuade his brother to enlarge his share during 1813.

Wellington's meeting with Spanish officials at Cadiz ended in agreement over the nature of his authority as supreme commander of their armies. Although it fell short of what the British general desired, he was satisfied that it would serve if only the Spanish honored it.[61] His discussions with Henry Wellesley were still more satisfying. Wellington may have pointed out that with a large part of Spain now liberated, the Cortes would find it easier to raise its own revenue. There was therefore no reason why most of the British subsidy should not go to the support of the Spanish troops he was to command.

The result of these discussions was an agreement between the two brothers that Wellington would control the spending of most of the subsidy for 1813. No record of this understanding appears to have survived, but its details are not difficult to infer. Wellington was to have as much of the 1813 subsidy as he wished for his own commissary to use in maintaining the Spanish units under his command. What remained would be spent by Henry upon Wellington's recommendation. Finally, the brothers seem to have understood that the value of arms and war materials sent from England was not to be counted as a part of the total Spanish

61. Fortescue, *British Army*, IX, 74-75; Wellington to Bathurst, January 27, 1813, *Dispatches of Wellington*, X, 51-55.

subsidy. When Wellington later learned that London proposed to spend £1,400,000 on Spain during 1813, he was doubtless pleased to know that nearly all of it would go to the support of the Spanish soldiers.[62] That this was in fact the case is clear from Henry Wellesley's account of his own payments during 1813, which amounted to only about £545,000, the bulk of which went to help Spanish forces operating apart from Wellington's army. The chief loser by this arrangement was, of course, the Cortes, which received only about £65,000 in British money during 1813.[63]

When the allies began their advance into Spain in the spring of 1813, Wellington's prediction was quickly fulfilled. The Spanish troops attached to his command depended almost entirely on the British commissary for their supplies and pay. Provincial authorities refused to make provisions available, and such food and pay as the Cortes had collected remained at remote magazines for lack of transport. On the eve of the battle of Vittoria, Wellington informed the Spanish war minister that the 24,000 Spanish troops in the north had so far received nothing from their own government. "If it were not for the sums which are given to these troops from the military chest of the British army . . . ," he observed icily, "these troops would not have a shilling to pay. Their provisions are forced from the country by a description of plunder."[64] The British commissary general did his best to provide the Spanish with what they needed, but his resources were limited. Lacking sustenance and transport, Wellington found it impossible to unite the scattered Spanish units with his own army, and at the Battle of Vittoria on June 21, only about 7,000 Spanish troops shared the honor of that victory with their allies.[65]

---

62. The description of this agreement is based on evidence which, although circumstantial, seems valid. On January 8, 1813 Wellington wrote Generals Whittingham and Roche that Henry Wellesley "has been so kind as to leave to me, in a great measure, the decision on the application of the pecuniary funds applied by Great Britain for the support of the cause of Spain." *Dispatches of Wellington*, X, 24. See also Henry Wellesley's letter to Castlereagh of January 20, 1813, *Supplementary Despatches and Memoranda of Field Marshal Arthur, Duke of Wellington, K. G. . . .* , ed. 2d Duke of Wellington (London, 1858-1872), VII, 529-530.

63. See Henry Wellesley's account of his payments during 1813, enclosed in his letter to Castlereagh, March 4, 1814, FO 72/159.

64. Wellington to Don Juan O'Donuju, June 14, 1813, *Dispatches of Wellington*, X, 441.

65. Jac Weller, *Wellington in the Peninsula, 1808-1814* (London, 1962), p. 268.

Vittoria virtually destroyed Napoleon's power in the Peninsula, and the Spanish Cortes was less inclined than ever to make the exertions in the cause which Wellington urged. The Spanish regiments marching with their allies toward the Pyrenees depended almost completely on the British commissary. By the close of the year that department had issued nearly £400,000 in pay, provisions, and field equipment to Wellington's Spanish units.[66]

The British commander's resentment toward the Cortes grew with each passing week. Not only had they neglected to provide for their soldiers, but they had reneged on the agreement which he had made with them at Cadiz in January. Wellington's recommendations were either ignored or treated with haughty indifference by a government no longer fighting for survival. On entering France, the Spanish troops supplemented with plunder the meagre allotment of provisions issued them by the British commissary. Convinced that such troops were more of an embarrassment than a help, Wellington decided to be rid of them before going into winter quarters. In November 1813 he ordered 20,000 of them back into their own country, keeping with him only Morillo's division of 4,500 men.[67]

Wintering the Spanish troops south of the Pyrenees solved an immediate problem, but Wellington knew well that success in the spring campaign might depend on those very troops. No reinforcements could be expected from England, and for reasons still to be examined, his Portuguese regiments were rapidly dwindling. To defeat Soult and push on to the Garonne, he must rely on the Spanish, which meant, in effect, that he would have to devise some means of supporting them. On November 24, 1813 he wrote Henry Wellesley explaining the only plan which could accomplish this. The 1813 subsidy had been divided almost equally between the maintenance of the Spanish units serving with the allies and those engaged against the enemy in the eastern part of the country. During the coming year, he recommended that the entire subsidy go to upkeep of the Spanish forces serving under his immediate command in the south of France. If the Cortes wanted to continue operations against the remaining pockets of enemy

66. Statements nos. 14 and 19, Spanish Subsidy Account, AO 3/765.
67. Oman, *Peninsular War,* VII, 216-218. For Wellington's difficulties with the Cortes, see *ibid.,* VII, 142-143.

resistance in Spain, it ought to pay the cost itself. All the British subsidy for 1814 should be used by the British commissary to support the Spanish army which Wellington intended to collect north of the Pyrenees. In this way the money would not only be spent exclusively for military purposes, but it would finance the campaign which, above all others, must prove decisive.[68]

Making provision for a large Spanish army was all the more important now that Britain's military alliance with Portugal was fast falling apart. The farther the war moved from Lisbon, the greater grew Wellington's difficulties with the Council of Regency. He bitterly complained that while the Portuguese commissary at Lisbon was well supplied with provisions, very little was sent to Portugal's troops in Spain. Like the Spanish, the Portuguese forces depended on the resources of Wellington's commissary. Charging that the Lisbon council was using subsidy money to pay off past debts rather than maintain its soldiers, he again proposed his old remedy: replace the Portuguese commissary with a new supply system under direct British control.[69] The Council of Regency violently objected and added fuel to the fire by charging that Wellington intentionally played down the achievements of its troops in his battle reports. Once again, as in 1811, letters flew between Lisbon and headquarters with increasingly shrill charges and countercharges.

The approaching end of the war created new difficulties for the Lisbon council, leading it to follow the Cortes' example and relax its military efforts. Lisbon's wartime prosperity abruptly ended in the summer of 1813 when the British supply base was transferred from there to the northern Spanish port of Santander in order to serve Wellington better. This deprived the Council of Regency of the revenue from customs duties on which it had long relied. Furthermore, Portugal again feared the likelihood of Spanish aggression, and in an effort to conserve the national resources for use in the future, the council allowed the Conscription Laws to lapse. As a result, no replacements were sent to make good Wellington's losses from death and desertion. At Vittoria, the

---

68. Wellington to Henry Wellesley, November 24, 1813, and March 11, 1814, *Dispatches of Wellington,* XI, 315-316, 570.

69. See Wellington's letter to the Portuguese Regent of April 12, 1813, *ibid.,* X, 283-287.

allied army included 30,000 Portuguese, but six months later, their effective strength had fallen to about 18,000.[70]

Funneling the British subsidy through Wellington's commissary made one long-standing problem still worse: how could the Military Chest be supplied with the greater quantity of hard money now required? With ever larger numbers of Portuguese and Spanish to feed and pay, the British commander needed every bit of specie the Treasury could send. Now that the allies were in France, he argued that it was essential that provisions bought from the French be paid for in coin. In 1812 the Cabinet had promised to send Wellington at least £100,000 a month in specie. They had done even better than that; £400,000 in coin had been sent from England during the one month of January 1814.[71] Wellington now asked ministers to do still more.

The crumbling of the Continental System made it easier for Britain to remit money to her allies in northern Europe, but it did not materially help conditions in the Peninsula. Fortunately, a considerable amount of gold coin in India became available in 1813, which, when brought to England, was converted into the last issue of guineas ever to be struck. Since most of these coins were sent to Wellington, they were usually referred to as "military guineas."[72] The upswing in the fortunes of war made it easier for the commissary's agents to exchange Treasury Bills for specie at Cadiz and elsewhere in the Peninsula, but now shortage of transport often delayed the delivery of this coin to Wellington's headquarters in the north.[73] More than £2,500,000 passed through Wellington's Military Chest during 1813, but his insatiable demand for still more led the Cabinet to solicit the assistance of Rothschilds bank in London.[74] By the end of 1813 Nathan Rothschild and the commissary-in-chief were cooperating to obtain gold coin on the Continent for Wellington's use. Gold pieces (many of them French in origin) were bought in Holland

70. Oman, *Peninsular War*, VII, 145-146; Weller, *Wellington*, 266-268; Fortescue, *British Army*, X, 425. So far as desertion was concerned, Wellington had this to say about the Portuguese: "The Portuguese (to their honor be it recollected) do not desert to the enemy. When they go, it is to return to their own country" (Wellington to Bathurst, November 9, 1813, *Dispatches of Wellington*, XI, 273).
71. Oman, *Peninsular War*, VII, 288.
72. *Ibid.*, VII, 147, 288.
73. Wellington to Bathurst, December 22, 1813, *Dispatches of Wellington*, XI, 389.
74. Wellington to Bathurst, January 8, 1813, *ibid.*, XI, 426-427.

and Germany for shipment to Spain from the port of Helvoetsluys in the Low Countries. In time Rothschild was able to buy gold in France itself for direct overland shipment to the allied army in the southern part of the country.[75]

When the campaign resumed in February 1814, control of the subsidy enabled Wellington to recall the Spanish troops which had wintered south of the Pyrenees. The withering away of the enclaves of French resistance in eastern Spain justified his decision to order all of the Cortes' forces to join him in France. With a military chest overflowing with guineas, Commissary General Kennedy was able to provide for the Portuguese and Spanish units which made up the larger part of the allied army. By the time Toulouse fell in April, Wellington had 40,000 Spanish under his command in France, although the Portuguese levies had shrunk to only 13,000.[76]

Military considerations account for the British decision, taken during the last years of the war, to divert most of the subsidy from the governments of Spain and Portugal to the service of their armies with Wellington. Ever since 1812 the British commander had pressed for this diversion. How completely he attained that goal is clear from the accounts of his commissary general.[77] About 70 percent of the £3,900,000 paid as a subsidy to Portugal in 1813-1814 was disbursed by Wellington either directly to Portuguese troops in the field, or indirectly through Portugal's own commissary and paymaster departments. The case of the Spanish subsidy was even more striking. Of the £1,820,932 given Spain during the final year of the war, about 80 percent passed through the hands of the British commissary. Because of London's unlimited confidence in him, Wellington was given almost complete control over the spending of the subsidy to the Peninsular powers. But the Cabinet's support of their general went far beyond acquiescence. By providing him with a steadily increasing flow of hard money and vast quantities of arms and supplies, the

75. Herries, *Memoir*, I, 85-86; Hecksher, *Continental System*, pp. 354-362.

76. Oman (*Peninsular War*, VII, 556-557, 563) states that only about 10,000 Spanish troops were with Wellington at the capture of Toulouse. The remaining 30,000 were either at Bayonne or elsewhere in southern France.

77. The Portuguese Subsidy Accounts for 1813 and 1814 (AO 3/746) and statements 15 and 20 of the Spanish Subsidy Account (AO 3/765) provide the data on which the following is based.

ministers guaranteed the success of his operations. Final victory in the Peninsula was won with the help of the Portuguese and Spanish soldiers who, before the war ended, were almost entirely clothed, fed, paid, and armed by Great Britain.

Consideration of the Sicilian subsidy in connection with the Peninsular War is more appropriate than might appear. The only military advantage Britain gained from that subsidy was the participation of Sicilian troops in the Spanish campaign after 1812. In one respect, the subsidization of Spain and Sicily are much alike: in both cases, British money came to be used almost exclusively for the upkeep of their armies. Sicily was remote from the center of military operations, however, and British authorities were able to deal more forcefully with its government than was possible in the case of the Spanish Cortes.

When the Bourbons and their British protectors were forced to flee to the island of Sicily in 1806, it was hoped the exile would be brief. Events soon demonstrated that Naples was not to be recovered easily, and for the time being the British subsidy became merely a pension for the Bourbon court at Palermo. Dissatisfaction with this state of affairs led Canning to place the subsidy on a more satisfactory footing in 1809, and he insisted it be used solely to support the Sicilian army which should be placed under the direction of the British commander on the island. The Bourbons vigorously opposed these demands, and a crisis was only averted by Canning's resignation as foreign secretary. His successor was content to continue the subsidy without asking much in return, but the arrangement was not really satisfactory. Should the French invade the island, lack of unified command over British and Sicilian troops might prove disastrous. Furthermore, Queen Maria Carolina's intrigues to recover Naples, even at the cost of an accommodation with France, cast serious doubts on the value of the Anglo-Sicilian alliance.

Sicily's problems were forcefully brought to London's attention in the autumn of 1810 when the French attacked the island. British troops threw back the invaders with the assistance of Sicilian peasants. The inactivity of the Sicilian army during the crisis, together with the ambiguous conduct of the Palermo government, convinced the British envoy, Lord Amherst, that the court was in league with the enemy. A new complication appeared during the following winter when Bourbon disregard for the rights of the island's parliament called forth a vigorous protest from some members of the Sicilian nobility.[78]

Downing Street could no longer close its eyes to these difficulties, and in the spring of 1811 Lord Wellesley took the first step toward their resolution: the amiable but ineffective Lord Amherst was relieved of his duties as British minister at Palermo. As his replacement the government selected Lord William Bentinck and gave him supreme command of all British troops on the island.[79] Even before taking up his post, Bentinck had reached certain conclusions regarding Sicily which went far beyond what Canning had vainly tried to achieve two years before. Britain must control the Sicilian army and demand a major reform of the Palermo government. Wellesley was unwilling to go so far without more information, however, and the instructions given Bentinck were more limited than the new minister desired.[80]

On reaching Sicily in July 1811, Bentinck learned that Maria Carolina had exiled five members of the island nobility who had protested against her tyranny. Two months spent on the island convinced the British envoy that his original recommendations had been correct, and he returned to London to urge them on the foreign secretary. Bentinck added force to his argument by pointing out that Italy was fast moving toward a national uprising against the French similar to that which had taken place in Spain. If Britain created a strong army under her control in Sicily and promoted a reform of the island's government, it would materially promote the cause of Italian liberation.[81]

78. Rosselli, *Bentinck,* pp. 12-15.
79. Lord William Cavendish Bentinck (1774-1839) was the second son of the Duke of Portland. An early military career was climaxed by his appointment as governor of Madras in 1803. His experience in India had already made him a controversial figure by the time he was given the Palermo post. Bentinck's rule in Sicily has usually been viewed in a critical light. Sir Charles Webster characterized him as "a brilliant and unbalanced egoist, all the more dangerous because he was also imbued with a species of idealism" (*Foreign Policy of Castlereagh,* I, 75).
80. Wellesley to Bentinck, May 30, 1811, and June 12, 1811, FO 70/44. Wellesley still expected to keep the Sicilians well supplied with arms. During the summer of 1811 arms, ammunition, and supplies to the value of £40,058 were sent them. See W. Griffin to Robert Peel, August 16, 1811, FO 70/49.
81. Rosselli, *Bentinck,* pp. 24-25.

Lord Wellesley was now prepared to impose this program on Palermo, and on October 7 he suspended payment of the Sicilian subsidy until King Ferdinand agreed to adopt a program of reform. For the future, Bentinck was empowered to halt subsidy payments whenever he found it necessary to do so. If indisputable evidence came to hand showing that the Bourbons were in league with the French, he could use the full authority of his dual position as envoy and military commander to correct the situation in whatever manner might seem appropriate.[82]

Bentinck now had all the authority required to bend the Bourbons to his will when he returned to the island in December. The contest between the all-powerful, if erratic, British viceroy and the malevolent Maria Carolina reached its climax a month later. Bentinck was on the verge of seizing control of the island's government when he learned of the Queen's surrender. Within a short time, he was able to inform Wellesley that his victory had been complete. Changes were being made in the government and the exiled barons were free to return. More important, Bentinck had been named Captain General of the Sicilian army. In view of Palermo's unconditional surrender, he resumed the subsidy and sent the Bourbon treasury £66,666 to cover the two months during which payments had been suspended.[83]

The experiences of an earlier British envoy under similar circumstances should have warned Bentinck that Maria Carolina's capitulation was more apparent than real. She was no more prepared to withdraw from the government to please Bentinck than she had been to comply with William Drummond's ultimatum in 1807. In some respects, the present situation was more complicated. King Ferdinand had finally been persuaded to name his son, the Hereditary Prince, as Vicar. Despite the King's nominal retirement, he continued to play a significant if devious role. Since he had not formally abdicated, Ferdinand might reappear on the scene at any moment and resume his full authority. For the time being the Hereditary Prince was left to carry on the government and to mediate the quarrel between his mother and the British minister. This well-meaning but weak

82. Wellesley to Bentinck, nos. 12 and 13, October 7, 1811, FO 70/44.
83. Bentinck to Wellesley, January 29, 1812, FO 70/51.

young man ran the risk of being crushed between these towering antagonists for his trouble. So far as Bentinck was concerned the road was now open to attain the major reforms on which he had set his heart: a revision of the Sicilian constitution and a thoroughgoing reorganization of the island army which he now nominally commanded.

On both these points the British proconsul met with resistance from the Hereditary Prince, and his dispatches to London were filled with detailed complaints. When Castlereagh came to the Foreign Office in March 1812 he immediately promised Bentinck to support him to the hilt. If Maria Carolina was in communication with the French, as Bentinck claimed, then the treaty with Sicily would be abrogated and war declared. Bentinck's control of the subsidy was confirmed, and Castlereagh made clear that he could use that control in any manner required to gain his point.[84] As yet, the £400,000 paid Sicily each year had accomplished nothing. The war in the Peninsula had reached a point where good use could be made of the Anglo-Sicilian army in Spain. From his position on the Portuguese frontier, Wellington could do nothing to help the Spanish check enemy operations in Catalonia. Since Sicily was in no danger, the foreign secretary proposed that at least a part of the Anglo-Sicilian army be sent to help the Spanish nationalists in Catalonia.

Bentinck now had carte blanche at a time when strong measures were most needed. The Hereditary Prince delayed the calling of the Sicilian parliament, which was to prepare a new constitution, while Ferdinand worked from behind the scenes to frustrate the constitutionalists. Worst of all, Bentinck had not yet persuaded the Prince to authorize a reorganization of the Sicilian forces. Almost every mail reaching Sicily brought Bentinck letters from London and from Wellington calling on him to send at least a part of the Sicilian army to Spain. The time had come to prod Palermo into action. As a foretaste of what the Hereditary Prince might expect if he continued to be stubborn, Bentinck did not pay the subsidy for the month of June.[85] The hint was too gentle. Early in July he formally announced that the subsidy would be suspended

---

84. Castlereagh to Bentinck, March 6, 1812 and May 19, 1812, FO 70/50.

85. Whether Bentinck's failure to pay the June subsidy was intentional is not positive, but it seems likely that it was no accident. Bentinck to Castlereagh, March 10, 1813 (FO 70/57) shows Bentinck's payments for 1812.

until the Sicilian army had been remodeled along the lines set forth by Britain.[86] For the second time within the year, Bentinck and the Bourbons were at war. With the purse-strings in the hands of the British viceroy, the outcome was not long in doubt.

When the Hereditary Prince finally made his peace with Bentinck in September, the British minister seized the opportunity to revise the entire character of the Anglo-Sicilian alliance. The treaty of alliance, concluded in 1807, was to be replaced by one of Bentinck's invention. One division of the Sicilian army, amounting to about 7,000 men, would be placed under the absolute control of the British commander. All their expenses would be met by Britain, but the money would be deducted from Sicily's £400,000 annual subsidy. Another deduction would be made to provide the Sicilian forces with the arms, artillery, and equipment it desperately needed. A third and final deduction would be made to reimburse Britain for her expense in maintaining the Sicilian flotilla. What remained of the subsidy would be given the Palermo government to use as it wished. By a conservative estimate, this would leave the Hereditary Prince with only about £150,000 a year. The Prince had no choice but to agree, and on September 12 a new Anglo-Sicilian alliance was signed incorporating these provisions. In effect, Britain had acquired the service of 7,000 mercenaries.[87]

Bentinck was now able to present London with a well-armed and trained force of 7,000 Sicilians for use in the Peninsula. In June 1812 he had sent a part of the British garrison on the island to Spain, but London continued to call for more. Although still enchanted by the dream of leading a force to liberate Italy, Bentinck finally agreed to send a part of his Sicilian troops to Catalonia. During the last half of 1812, 9,000 men were sent from Sicily to Spain, of whom a large number seem to have been drawn from the Sicilian division.[88]

86. Bentinck to the Hereditary Prince, July 4, 1812, FO 70/52.

87. The Treaty with Sicily of September 12, 1812 (FO 93/96 [5]) refers to the division as numbering 7,314 men. The monthly deductions are itemized, but they are expressed in ounzes, the Sicilian monetary unit. On April 12, 1813 Castlereagh told the Commons that nearly two thirds of the annual subsidy to Sicily was spent on the upkeep of the Sicilian division; *Hansard,* XXV (1813), 790.

88. The 6,638 troops sent from Sicily to Spain in June 1812 all seem to have been British, except for 353 Calabrians. See Fortescue, *British Army,* VIII, 555-556.

Bentinck's army in Sicily consisted of three kinds of troops: British, Sicilians, and Neapolitans. Although Castlereagh claimed that by the end of 1812 there were 6,000

By the spring of 1813 Bentinck at last felt free to go to Spain to take command of his Anglo-Sicilians. The new Sicilian Constitution of 1812 was well launched and its chances for success had been immeasurably improved by Maria Carolina's announcement that she would soon leave the island forever. The British proconsul sailed for Spain in May, but he could not shake himself of the notion that Italy was on the verge of revolution against the French.[89]

The Anglo-Sicilians won no glory on the battlefields of Spain; bad luck and poor management haunted them throughout the remainder of the war. An outbreak of political turmoil at Palermo forced Bentinck to cut short his military career and return to the island in the autumn of 1813. No notice need be taken here of his violent quarrel with the Palermo government, since it did not involve Britain's subsidy policy. When, at long last, circumstances permitted Bentinck to lead an expedition to the Italian mainland, conditions there had completely changed. In March 1814 he landed at Leghorn with 14,000 British and Italian troops to join with the Austrians and Murat in breaking France's hold. His conduct, increasingly eccentric and unsure, embarrassed Castlereagh's Italian policy and ultimately led to his recall to England.[90]

The Anglo-Sicilian alliance of 1812 left Palermo in an extremely tight financial position and Bentinck had occasionally to lend it money in order to meet daily expenses.[91] Although the Sicilians regarded the word "loan" as a euphemism for a gift, the British minister fully expected repayment. Before leaving the island for

---

Sicilians in Spain, it seems likely that he included the Neapolitans in his count, as well as the Sicilians (*Hansard*, XXV [1813], 790). Fortescue, (*British Army*, IX, 27) makes clear that the two expeditions Bentinck sent to Spain in November and December 1812 consisted of British troops, Sicilians, Neapolitans, and the "Italian Regiments."

89. Fortescue, *British Army*, IX, 31.

90. Fortescue (*ibid.*, X, 61) believes that by the time Bentinck went to Italy he had "lost his mental balance." Even Rosselli (*Bentinck*, p. 169) concedes that his conduct showed signs of "muddle-headedness."

91. These "loans" began at least as early as 1812. See Bentinck to Castlereagh, March 10, 1813, FO 70/57. The money was needed by Sicily for various purposes. Bentinck was probably happy to grant Sicily's request for funds to pay Maria Carolina's debts in preparation for her departure from the island. Money was also advanced to ransom Sicilians from the Barbary pirates. In 1812 the Palermo government conducted a lottery to raise money, but the prizes were drawn in such a way that the government ended by owing the winners more money than it had collected. Bentinck advanced the additional money required to relieve Palermo of its embarrassment. See Bentinck to Belmonte, May 5, 1812, FO 70/51.

the last time in the summer of 1814, Bentinck suspended the subsidy to remind Palermo of its obligation, but his successor, William A'Court, seems to have resumed the payments. When the war ended London instructed A'Court to continue the monthly payments at a half-rate through February of 1815, when the subsidy would end.[92] "Loans" were made at least until November 1814, by which time they totaled about £280,000. So far as repayment was concerned, A'Court came close to the truth of the matter when he observed to Castlereagh, "Our only chance of payment rests upon the liberality and justice of the Parliament of Sicily, and a worse security could not be offered."[93] In the end, nothing seems to have been accomplished toward recovering the money.

92. Rosselli, *Bentinck,* pp. 210-211; Bathurst to A'Court, September 7, 1814, FO 70/65.
93. A'Court to Castlereagh, August 14, 1815, FO 70/70; British Commissary General in Sicily to A'Court, November 14, 1814, FO 70/65.

XII

BRITAIN AND THE RISING OF THE NATIONS

Lord Wellesley often annoyed his Cabinet colleagues by demanding that they throw even more money and men into the Peninsular War. He did not claim that the French empire could be destroyed on the battlefields of Spain, but British victories there would certainly inspire the northern powers to turn on Napoleon. Britain must, therefore, wage total war in the Peninsula and, at the same time, encourage any spirit of resistance which might appear elsewhere in Europe. The latter was especially difficult to accomplish since the collapse of normal diplomatic channels of communication in 1809 left London woefully ignorant of continental affairs. Reports from Hanoverian envoys at Berlin and Vienna and from British agents elsewhere in Europe were of limited value. Incomplete and unreliable as such intelligence was, it was preferable to silence.

Efforts made by the Foreign Office to obtain accurate and up-to-date information were seldom entirely satisfactory and, on occasion, they proved embarrassing. In 1810 Wellesley sent John Harcourt King to Vienna to gather news and promote the re-establishment of diplomatic relations between London and the Hofburg. King remained at Vienna for nearly two years but his fondness for intrigue finally led Metternich to expel him.[1] A premium was placed on news from St. Petersburg, and in the autumn of 1811 a Portuguese army officer passed through London on his way to the Russian capital and agreed to send Wellesley reports written in sympathetic ink. The secret agent was as good as

---

1. Buckland, *Metternich*, pp. 261 and *passim*.

his word, but a few months later, the Foreign Office had to inform him that, thanks to some defect in the ink, the invisible writing in his dispatches was clearly visible.[2]

What little information reached London made clear that when the time came for a rising of the nations against France, Britain would be expected to support it with both arms and money. When Napoleon occupied Vienna following the Battle of Austerlitz in 1805, he removed 100,000 muskets from the Hapsburg arsenals. Russia had suffered a great loss of equipment in her last war with France, while Prussia was especially short of powder and artillery.[3]

During the winter of 1810-1811, Wellesley learned from the London banker, Samuel Thornton, that the Russian government wished to receive 500 tons of gunpowder from England. Thornton explained that the request had been sent him by Henry Cayley, his financial correspondent at St. Petersburg. The foreign secretary appears to have done nothing until Thornton relayed another such appeal the following spring. This time Russia proposed to exchange naval stores for British powder and lead. Wellesley submitted the proposal to the prime minister and Perceval approved it.[4] In July 1811 four merchant ships carrying 500 tons of gunpowder and 1,000 tons of lead sailed for the Baltic under the protection of H.M.S. *Grasshopper,* an eighteen-gun ship commanded by Captain Henry Fanshawe. The cargo, valued at about £90,000, was consigned to Henry Cayley with instructions to exchange it for 2,500 tons of Russian hemp. The whole business was so fantastic that probably no one was surprised when Russian authorities refused the flotilla permission to land.[5]

Of more substance were the appeals reaching London at this time from the secret Prussian resistance movement. Four years before, Canning had responded to a similar request. The call for help which now lay before Wellesley bore the endorsement of Gneisenau, the great Prussian leader.[6] The foreign secretary quickly made his decision, and orders flew from the pen of his secretary directing the Ordnance Office, the Transport Office, and

---

2. C. C. Smith to Capt. Antonio Guedes, January 10, 1812, FO 65/77.
3. William O. Shanahan, *Prussian Military Reforms, 1786-1813* (New York, 1945), pp. 179-180.
4. Perceval Memorandum, June 15, 1811, FO 65/76.
5. Documents relating to this operation are to be found in FO 65/76.
6. Gneisenau to General Decken, September 10, 1811, FO 64/84.

the Treasury to make the necessary arrangements. At least 60,000 stand of arms with powder and accoutrements, as well as cannon, were sent to the Prussian coast between September and November 1811.[7] On returning from the Baltic, H.M.S. *Grasshopper* was ordered to take her convoy to Prussia and there deliver the powder and lead originally intended for Russia. How much of these war materials were landed is uncertain, but probably a large portion found their way into Prussian army arsenals.[8]

In the autumn of 1811 Wellesley undertook a secret overture to Sweden, with whom Britain had been nominally at war for the last year. By this time, Bernadotte had appeared in the curious role of Prince Royal of his adopted country. His desire to annex Norway as compensation for Sweden's loss of Finland puzzled Wellesley, if it did not discourage him. Nevertheless, in October 1811 he sent Edward Thornton to Stockholm to promote peace between Britain and Sweden. Although Thornton was to hold out a general assurance of British financial aid, he had no specific offer to make. He conferred with the Swedish ministers, but it soon became clear that the Prince Royal would take no step which might antagonize France.[9]

For a foreign secretary best remembered as indolent and careless of detail, Wellesley had been energetic in paving the way for a continental uprising. His hopes and plans ran far beyond the available opportunities, however; conditions for a real resistance movement did not yet exist. Premature as these efforts were, at least they made clear to the northern powers that Britain would support them when they were ready to act.

A decisive break between the Baltic powers and Napoleon was in the making by the time Castlereagh came to the Foreign Office in March 1812. To turn it to Britain's advantage would call for all the skill and patience which Pitt had taught him were essential in coalition diplomacy. Although the rift between Napoleon and Alexander was widening, Britain was in no position to influence

7. Stores ordered for Prussia, November 1, 1811, FO 64/84.

8. C. C. Smith to Croker, October, 1811, FO 64/84. Some of these arms were probably deposited on the island of Heligoland, which Britain later used as a major arms depot. FO 64/84 contains many documents relative to this enterprise.

9. Wellesley to Thornton, October 9, 1811, FO 73/70; *Camb. Hist. Brit. For. Pol.,* I, 382.

Russian policy in any material way.[10] Sweden was a different case.
Napoleon's seizure of Swedish Pomerania in January 1812
produced an immediate change in Bernadotte's policy. A Swedish
envoy was sent to St. Petersburg to obtain an alliance with the
Tsar, while the Prince Royal informed London that he was now
ready to make common cause with her in return for money, arms,
and British support for his territorial ambitions.[11]

Bernadotte's message was the first strong bid sent Britain by any
of the northern powers, and Castlereagh now had to respond to it.
For the second time within a year Thornton was ordered to
Sweden. The foreign secretary explained that any proposal of a
subsidy for Sweden was premature at this time, especially in view
of Britain's very heavy commitments to Portugal and Spain.
Nonetheless, Thornton was to assure the Prince Royal that Britain
would send him arms and supplies in the event he found himself at
war with France. Sweden's territorial aspirations presented a
problem. London was willing to part with a West Indian island, as
Bernadotte seemed to wish; under certain circumstances, the two
powers might even agree on a plan to transfer Norway from
Denmark to Sweden. At the moment, however, it was far too early
for Britain to undertake anything on this question.[12]

Thornton's reception at Stockholm justified the cautious line
Castlereagh had adopted. The Swedish ministers happily accepted
Britain's pledge of war materials, but they were disappointed that
Thornton could offer them no money. For Sweden to make peace
with Britain would inevitably involve her in war with Napoleon
and she must, therefore, insist on a prior guarantee of £1,200,000
a year in subsidies.[13] Sweden had recently won an alliance with
Russia which bound the Tsar to work for her annexation of
Norway. Before breaking with Napoleon, Bernadotte must have
the same promise from London, together with a pledge of
generous subsidies.

10. Russian agents were in England during the spring of 1812 to buy muskets and
saltpeter. As an inducement to Britain to second their efforts, they proposed to include
in such shipments to Russia British trade goods of equal value. See S. Cock to
Castlereagh, April 21, 1812, FO 65/81.
11. Franklin D. Scott, *Bernadotte and the Fall of Napoleon* (Cambridge, Mass., 1935),
p. 13.
12. Castlereagh to Thornton, March 13, 1812, FO 73/71.
13. Thornton to Castlereagh, April 9, 16, 1812, FO 73/72.

For the time being, Castlereagh could only allow events to take their course. Even if the Prince Royal could be trusted, and there was serious doubt about that, he was obviously more interested in annexing Norway than going to war with France. Russia's conduct was so ambiguous that it was impossible for Britain to approach her with any specific proposal. While at Stockholm, Thornton conferred with some of the Tsar's agents and learned that Alexander was ready to make peace with Britain as the first step toward diplomatic reunion. One of the agents, Baron Nicolai, suggested to Thornton that Britain could promote this development by assuming responsibility for the repayment of Russia's indebtedness to certain Dutch banks. Acknowledging receipt of this news, Castlereagh pointed out that these overtures were hardly strong enough to justify any British reply. After all, the Tsar was still carrying on discussions with Napoleon.[14]

As had happened so often, French military action cleared the air and provided a new framework for continental diplomacy. Napoleon's invasion of Russia cut the ground out from under attempts by Alexander and Bernadotte to make Britain pay for peace treaties with them, and in July 1812 Thornton concluded formal agreements with both powers without having to concede any of the demands they had originally made. The formation of a three-power concert for joint action against France would prove more troublesome in view of Castlereagh's reluctance to lavish subsidies on Russia and Sweden. Bernadotte attempted to reduce the difficulty by lowering his demand for British money from £1,200,000 to £1,000,000, but he now brought forward a new condition which was bound to heighten Castlereagh's suspicion: that he be allowed to occupy Norway before undertaking military operations against Napoleon. The foreign secretary rejected Sweden's demand and told Thornton, "till Sweden has arrived at that Point in Her exertions, which is to bring Her Army in contact with the Enemy, She cannot expect to enter into Competition, in Her claim for Pecuniary Aid, with Powers at this moment actually opposed in the Field to France."[15]

14. Thornton to Castlereagh, April 29, 1812, FO 73/72; F. Martens, *Recueil des Traités*, XI, 157-161; Castlereagh to Thornton, May 7, 8, 1812, FO 73/71.
15. Thornton to Castlereagh, June 25, 1812, FO 73/73; Castlereagh to Thornton, July 18, 1812, FO 73/71.

Although Castlereagh was not yet ready to pay Sweden, he regarded Napoleon's attack on Russia as justification for Britain to arm Bernadotte. Even before learning of Thornton's peace treaty with Stockholm, the Cabinet allocated £500,000 to cover the cost of war goods for the Prince Royal. On July 25 the Ordnance Office was ordered to send 20,000 muskets and 23 pieces of artillery to Sweden, while Bernadotte's agents in London were given credit with which to purchase gunpowder.[16]

The time had come for the re-establishment of direct relations with Russia, and Castlereagh appointed Lord Cathcart as the new British minister to St. Petersburg. Lacking any accurate information regarding conditions in Russia, the foreign secretary's instructions to Cathcart were necessarily general. Although the new envoy might ultimately receive authority to offer a subsidy, Castlereagh had nothing to say on the subject at the moment. However, Cathcart was positively to discourage any hope that Britain would assume Alexander's debts with the Dutch banks. Estimating this indebtedness at about £4,500,000, Castlereagh flatly declared that Parliament would never assume such a burden. Should Cathcart find either Sweden or Russia in need of immediate help, he was authorized to spend £500,000. The new envoy was to proceed to Russia by way of Sweden in order to confer with Thornton and any of the Tsar's envoys who might be in Stockholm.[17]

Lord Cathcart was not the only agent the Foreign Office sent to Russia during the critical summer of 1812. A second mission was launched which, while not diplomatic in character, was to have a significant effect on Britain's subsidy policy. With Russia now fighting for her life, it was obvious that the wretched condition of the Tsar's finances would hamper his ability to survive. Residing in London was a financial expert of some reputation who had already offered to reform the Russian fiscal system and place it on

16. Castlereagh to Thornton, July 18, 1812, FO 73/71; Castlereagh to the Master General of the Ordnance, July 25, 1812, FO 73/77.

17. William Schaw, first Baron Cathcart (1755-1843) was a professional military officer who had seen service in the American Revolution. He had commanded the expedition against Copenhagen in 1807 and for his service, his Scottish peerage had been exchanged for an English one. Cathcart's selection for the Russian mission in 1812 was a poor one. Although a career officer, he had no skill in diplomacy. See Castlereagh to Cathcart, nos. 1 and 2, July 24, 1812, FO 65/78.

4. Campaign Area of the Final Phase

a sound footing. Sir Francis d'Ivernois, a native of Switzerland, had won the confidence of the British government, and it now proposed to send him to St. Petersburg.[18] These envoys, one a soldier-diplomat, the other a monetary expert, were both to play major parts in the formation of Britain's alliance with Russia.

At Stockholm, meanwhile, Edward Thornton had convinced himself that only the lack of British money prevented the Prince Royal from going to war with France.[19] On his own initiative he decided to return to London in order to press Bernadotte's claims on the foreign secretary. On August 8 Thornton's vessel was beating its way out of the Baltic when it encountered another ship with Cathcart aboard. The two envoys conferred at sea, thus giving Cathcart a chance to bring his colleague up-to-date. In this way Thornton learned that London had decided to appropriate £500,000 to aid Sweden: £300,000 would be used to furnish arms to Bernadotte while Thornton was to pay him the remainder in cash as it was needed.[20] Encouraged by this latest news, Thornton returned to Sweden with Cathcart, and thereafter made small advances to the Swedish treasury which totaled £200,000 by the end of the year.[21] The first shipment of arms sent by Castlereagh arrived in Sweden in September 1812, to be followed during the winter by clothing and gunpowder.[22] The major question of an Anglo-Swedish alliance continued to drag, however. The season was now too far advanced for a Swedish army to take the field. More important, Castlereagh was not yet ready to pay the price which the Prince Royal had attached to his cooperation against Napoleon.

Lord Cathcart's search for the Tsar ended in late August at Åbo in Finland where Alexander had gone to meet Bernadotte.[23] For a ruler whose land was overrun by an invading army bent on destruction, Alexander seemed almost unconcerned about his own peril. Instead of asking help for himself, the Tsar explained to

---

18. Vansittart to D'Ivernois, July 14, 1812. Otto Karmin, "Les Finances Russes en 1812 et la Mission de Sir Francis D'Ivernois à St. Pétersbourg," *Revue Historique de la Révolution Française et de l'Empire,* 8 (1915), 180.

19. Thornton to Castlereagh, June 25, 1812, FO 73/73.

20. Castlereagh to Cathcart, no. 1, July 24, 1812, FO 65/78.

21. Thornton to Castlereagh, September 12 and November 20, 1812, FO 73/74.

22. Castlereagh to Baron de Rehausen, December 11, 1812, FO 73/76.

23. While at Åbo, Alexander and Bernadotte concluded a more refined version of their original alliance, which had been signed in the prevous April.

Cathcart why Britain ought to allow Bernadotte to annex Norway before intervening in north Germany on behalf of Russia. Alexander's own danger was serious, but Britain could help him most by sending a supply of arms.[24] Unknown to the Tsar, Castlereagh had already ordered 50,000 muskets sent to the Baltic for the use of the Russians along with a half ton of "Peruvian bark" for their medical service. When the foreign secretary learned of the French capture of Moscow, he ordered off another 50,000 stand of arms with the offer of still another shipment of the same size. Unfortunately, the second consignment of 50,000 muskets could not be delivered before winter shut fast Russia's Baltic ports.[25]

Alexander's indifference to British money, which had impressed Cathcart at Åbo, continued to amaze him in the months which followed. During the historic winter which witnessed Napoleon's retreat, the British envoy had no occasion to draw on any part of the £500,000 given him at the beginning of his mission. This seemed so remarkable that Cathcart made a special point of it in writing to Castlereagh: "No mention has been made to me by the Emperor or His Government of Subsidy, on the contrary, in times of the greatest difficulty . . . the Emperor said that a supply of arms in the North and in the Black Sea would be more valuable to him than any possible supply of Guineas."[26]

Cathcart completely misunderstood the Tsar's refusal to mention subsidies in their discussions. Had the British envoy not taken such a marked dislike to Sir Francis d'Ivernois, whom he met at St. Petersburg, possibly the Swiss financier would have been willing to enlighten him on this matter.[27] D'Ivernois was warmly welcomed by the Tsar on his arrival at the Russian capital in September 1812. Alexander created a special committee to solve

24. Alexander was particularly anxious to obtain some of the new shrapnel shot from Britain. See Cathcart to Castlereagh, August 30 and September 22, 1812, FO 65/79.

25. Castlereagh to Cathcart, October 20, 1812, FO 65/78. On their return from the frozen Baltic, the vessels carrying the muskets were ordered to sail for Russia's Black Sea coast (E. Cooke to Croker, December 23, 1812, FO 65/82). The Turks denied the vessels passage through the Dardenelles and, once more, the guns were returned to England. They were finally delivered to the Russians at Riga in the summer of 1813 (Castlereagh to Lieven, July 31, 1813, FO 65/89). See also Castlereagh to Cathcart, August 30, 1812, FO 65/78; E. Cooke to S. Billingsley, August 31, 1812, FO 65/81.

26. Cathcart to Castlereagh, December 6, 1812, FO 65/80.

27. D'Ivernois to Vansittart, November 7, 1812. Karmin, "Les Finances Russes," p. 10.

Viscount Castlereagh, by Sir Thomas Lawrence

Lord Liverpool, by Sir Thomas Lawrence

Francis I, by Sir Thomas Lawrence

Frederick William III, by Sir Thomas Lawrence

the nation's financial problems and included in its membership five Russians, D'Ivernois, and the Prussian Baron vom Stein who was then in St. Petersburg.[28] At one of the early meetings, the Russian members pointed out that, without massive financial help from Great Britain, their country must soon abandon the war. Some of the Tsar's advisors were using this as an argument to persuade him to give up the contest as soon as the French had been driven from Russia. D'Ivernois reported all this to Vansittart, the chancellor of the exchequer, and added that his Russian colleagues seemed oblivious to the fact that Britain herself was staggering under a tremendous financial burden.[29] During the final months of the year, D'Ivernois and Stein tried to devise some method by which Britain could aid Russia without bankrupting herself.

Alexander much preferred to deal directly with London on the matter of subsidies, rather than with Cathcart who had no proposal to make. The instructions given to Count Lieven, whom he appointed to represent him in England, especially stressed Russia's need for money. Lieven arrived in London in December 1812 and soon discussed the matter with Castlereagh. Out of special consideration for Britain, the Tsar would not insist on resurrecting the terms of the 1805 Anglo-Russian subsidy pact. Instead, he asked only that Britain give him £4,000,000 a year, which was the bare minimum required to finance Russia's war. Castlereagh declared this sum excessive. Clearly it would not be easy to bridge the gap between what Russia asked and what Britain could pay.[30]

Although the continental situation had improved by the close of 1812, it was difficult to see in it the making of a grand alliance. Napoleon's invasion of Russia had turned into a disorganized rout, which might end in the destruction of the Grand Army if the Tsar could only be kept steady.[31] Bernadotte seemed ready to draw the sword as soon as Britain paid his price. Reluctantly, Castlereagh

28. Otto Karmin, *Sir Francis D'Ivernois 1757-1842* (Geneva, 1920), pp. 493-494.
29. D'Ivernois to Vansittart, January 10, 1813. "Les Finances Russes," pp. 54-55.
30. F. Martens, *Recueil des Traités,* XI, 167-168; Alexander to Lieven, January 20, 1813, FO 65/89.
31. As late as the spring of 1813 Lieven reported that the Cabinet was haunted by the fear that Russia might make a separate peace with France (F. Martens, *Recueil des Traités,* XI, 168).

was now ready to meet most of the Prince Royal's demands in order to involve him as an active belligerent against France.

On the other side of the ledger, the picture was far less bright. Wellington's retreat to the Portuguese frontier after his failure at Burgos blasted hopes for victory in the Peninsula this year. The failure of the German powers to respond to the turning of the tide against Napoleon was also most discouraging. Even at this historic moment, Prussian policy was marked by languor and inactivity. Powerless to overcome this inertia, Britain was forced to grab at straws. In January 1813 Castlereagh studied a plan sent him by Gneisenau to win over the Kolberg garrison and arouse Pomerania against the French. Britain agreed to furnish the Prussian leader with 20,000 muskets and supplies to help him raise a partisan army to cooperate with the Russians in northern Germany.[32]

Prussia's conduct appeared weak and cowardly, but that of the Hofburg was maddeningly devious. The British agent, John Harcourt King, tried in vain to speed Austria along the road to resistance by his intrigues with the Archduke John and the patriot leaders in the Tyrol. The Tsar begged Cathcart to do something to pry Austria loose from her obstinate neutrality. In the autumn of 1812 Cathcart sent his own personal agent to Metternich with an offer of £500,000 if it would help Austria take the field, but Metternich had no intention of giving up his alliance with France and Cathcart's envoy accomplished nothing.[33] Almost the last hope for Austria's intervention was extinguished by a message Metternich sent to London at the close of 1812: if Austria intervened at all it would be to persuade the belligerents to negotiate a general peace in Europe.

By the opening of 1813 British war diplomacy had identified three major goals. First, the Peninsular War must be given all the support needed to guarantee Wellington's success. Second, a major army must be created in north Germany to aid the Russians. Swedish intervention would go a long way toward attaining this goal. Pressure on the French would be still greater if British troops or Gneisenau's partisans could be united with the Swedes. Finally,

32. Gneisenau's memorandum of January 17, 1813, FO 64/94; E. Cooke to Gneisenau, January 25, 1813, FO 64/94.
33. Webster, *Foreign Policy of Castlereagh,* I, 112-113; Buckland, *Metternich,* pp. 412-423.

some firm agreement would have to be reached with the Tsar in order to guarantee his continued participation in the war.

Attainment of each of these goals would require a heavy expenditure of British money. Subsidies to Portugal and Spain during the coming year would cost at least £3,000,000. Bernadotte's cooperation could not be had for anything less than £1,000,000, while the formation of a north German corps to join with the Prince Royal would cost about the same.[34] It was impossible to guess how much Russia would finally be willing to settle for in British subsidies. If the war was to be carried on during 1813 according to London's plans and expectations, she might have to lay out more than £7,000,000 in subsidies.

Castlereagh never closed his eyes to the difficulties involved in building a coalition against France, or to the strain it would put on Britain to finance it. The calm and steady policy he would follow during the all-important year which lay ahead is clearly foreshadowed in a letter he sent to Cathcart in January 1813. "The crisis is of that magnitude," he declared, "that *we must not starve the cause* by suffering any great object to fail, which can by an effort be brought within our grasp."[35]

Castlereagh had no way of knowing that, within a few weeks after the arrival of the New Year, the character of the war against Napoleon would be dramatically altered by Prussia's decision to throw her weight into the balance. Until then his plans were based on the expectation that Russia and Sweden would carry the burden of the war in northern Europe. High priority in Britain's plans was assigned to the conclusion of a firm military pact with Bernadotte, who had followed such a slippery policy during the past year.

Mutual need brought Sweden and Britain so close to agreement that the foreign secretary was ready to bridge the narrow gap which remained. Denmark's stubborn refusal to cut her ties with Napoleon made it easier for Castlereagh to agree that the Prince Royal should have Norway, although he was unwilling to

34. Castlereagh to General Alexander Hope, January 17, 1813, FO 73/79.
35. Castlereagh to Cathcart, January 22, 1813, *Correspondence of Castlereagh*, VIII, 313.

guarantee him in the possession of his loot.[36] Britain was likewise ready to cede to Sweden her right of possession to the island of Guadaloupe; the sacrifice of that war prize taken from France would not be painful.[37] British subsidies were more than ever needed to insure the effectiveness of Bernadotte's military intervention, for real distress had fallen on Sweden as a result of the near failure of the 1812 grain harvest. Furthermore, Bernadotte had already spent nearly £1,000,000 on military preparations during the past year.[38] Since the Prince was now acting as if he really meant to break with France, Castlereagh was willing to go a long way to satisfy him.

Because Thornton was so easily swayed by Bernadotte, Castlereagh decided to entrust the negotiation of the Swedish alliance to a special envoy. Union with Sweden must be accompanied by agreement as to the role she would play in the spring campaign. Therefore the services of a British military officer at Stockholm were especially desirable, and the mission was entrusted to General Sir Alexander Hope.[39] Castlereagh's instructions to Hope make clear that the principal goal of the alliance was to obtain Swedish military assistance for Russia in Germany, for which Hope was to offer £1,000,000 in subsidies for the current year. Bernadotte was also to be told that Britain was ready to spend another £1,000,000 on the formation of a German volunteer corps to cooperate with the Swedes.[40] Hope reached Stockholm in February 1813, and he spent nearly a month haggling with Bernadotte before a treaty was finally concluded. Sweden's decision to accept the British offer probably was hastened by Prussia's entrance into the war.

The treaty of March 3, 1813 obliged Britain to pay her ally £1,000,000 by October, when a new agreement would be arranged

36. Castlereagh was never happy about the Norwegian cession. In a letter of April 28, 1813 to Cathcart he admitted, "We never have disguised from ourselves the embarrassments of the Norwegian point; but it was an engagement made in the day of adversity, for the preservation of Russia" (*ibid.,* VIII, 383).
37. In the final peace settlement France regained Guadaloupe and Britain met her obligation to Bernadotte by a grant of money.
38. Hope to Castlereagh, February 24, 1813, FO 73/79.
39. General Sir Alexander Hope (1769-1837) was a career army officer who was serving as governor of the Royal Military College at Sandhurst at the time of his diplomatic appointment.
40. Castlereagh to Hope, January 17, 1813, FO 73/79.

if the war had not ended. Bernadotte was to put 30,000 men into the spring campaign against Napoleon in accordance with operational plans to be worked out with General Hope. The treaty also included some important trade privileges for Britain which would benefit her commerce in the Baltic.[41] Bernadotte proved a hard bargainer, especially when it came to the money he was to receive. Not only did he insist on receiving £1,000,000 during the coming eight months, but also that a sizable part of the subsidy be remitted immediately to cover his mobilization costs. Hope and Thornton both agreed that there was some justice to this last demand, and even before the formal signing of the treaty, they turned over £215,000 in bills of exchange to the Swedish treasury. This was to be regarded as the preparation advance provided for in the treaty.[42] Considering that Bernadotte was only bound to put 30,000 men into the campaign, the British subsidy was certainly generous, even lavish. It involved a payment of about £33 per soldier for eight months' service, a rate far in excess of Britain's grants to other powers in 1813. Such liberality was justified by the necessity of bringing Bernadotte into overt opposition to France. Only time would tell whether the benefits to be derived from Swedish intervention would repay Britain's efforts to secure the alliance.[43]

41. Britain obtained the right of entrepôt at three Swedish ports while Sweden agreed to keep her tariffs on British colonial products to a specified minimum.

42. The Treaty with Sweden, March 3, 1813, FO 93/101 (9), (10); Thornton to Castlereagh, February 24, 1813, FO 73/81; Castlereagh to Thornton, March 26, 1813, FO 73/80; An Account of the Bills of Exchange . . . issued for the Service of the Swedish Government . . . , FO 73/87. An extra financial benefit for Sweden, not provided in the treaty, arose from Britain's desire to promote peace between Bernadotte and the legitimate government of Spain. The conclusion of such a pact had long been a British goal, since it would involve a formal break between the Prince Royal and Napoleon. In November 1812 a treaty of peace between Sweden and Spain had been signed but never ratified. The troubled course of Sweden's relations with Spain particularly annoyed Castlereagh. Part of the difficulty arose from Bernadotte's demand that the agreement be loaded with conditional clauses and that Spain give him a small subsidy. In February 1813 the foreign secretary proposed that if Sweden would only sign a simple peace treaty, Britain would agree to pay the sum Bernadotte demanded of the Cortes. The arrangement seemed reasonable since the Spanish government had almost no money except what it received from Britain. On this basis agreement was reached, and in March 1813 a treaty was concluded between Sweden and Spain. Spain's obligation to Bernadotte was finally fixed at $500,000 (about £137,300), which sum Britain assigned to Sweden's credit in London for the purchase of war supplies. See Scott, *Bernadotte*, 31; Castlereagh to Thornton, February 16, 1813, FO 73/80; Foreign Office memorandum to the Treasury, July 7, 1813, FO 73/77; Castlereagh to Rehausen, July 31, 1813, FO 73/86.

43. Scott, *Bernadotte*, p. 34.

Prussia's abrupt entry into the war was soon followed by her conclusion of an alliance with Russia at Kalisch in February 1813. This enlargement of the coalition improved the chances of victory, but it presented Castlereagh with a new set of problems. Some could be solved quickly and easily, while others would prove more difficult. Prussia naturally expected British subsidies. For Britain to furnish them and, at the same time, satisfy the Tsar's demands would prove particularly difficult. Formal alliances had yet to be negotiated uniting the belligerents in a single war league. Most important of all, Castlereagh had to act immediately to insure that the Swedes, the Prussians, and the Russians had all the arms and ammunition they required to crush the enemy. Unless this was done, there might be no coalition for British diplomacy to create.

Britain had begun to ship arms to the northern powers during the summer of 1812. Notwithstanding the heavy demands made by the war in the Peninsula, the Ordnance Office sent 120,000 muskets to Sweden and Russia before the year ended. With the arrival of 1813 the government determined to expand this flow of arms and equipment. The first shipment of the year was made in February and included 50,000 stand of arms consigned to the Russians. Almost immediately, 54 cannon, together with arms, ammunition, and stores for 23,000 men were sent to be shared by the Prussians and the Russians.[44]

During the spring and summer of 1813 an almost steady stream of transports sailed from England for Baltic ports to guarantee that the three powers lacked nothing. The Prussians received at least 100,000 muskets with powder, accoutrements, and flints— the last being in especially short supply.[45] An identical shipment reached the Tsar's armies and included, in addition, 116 field pieces and 1,200 tons of ammunition and shells. That same summer, more than 40,000 muskets with powder and uniform cloth were delivered to Bernadotte's troops.[46] A depot was established at Stralsund to receive the war supplies brought from England. One shipment alone made to Stralsund in the summer of

44. Half the muskets sent Russia in 1812 were not delivered until the following year. See An Account of the Value of . . . Supplies . . . afforded to the Foreign Powers . . . in the North of Germany during the present year, December 24, 1813, FO 64/95.

45. Castlereagh to Stewart, September 6, 1813, FO 64/86; Shanahan, *Prussian Military Reforms*, p. 211.

46. War Department Memorandum on Supplies to Russia, Prussia, and Sweden, July 7, 1813, FO 65/91.

1813 consisted of 2,000 barrels of powder, 5,000,000 musket cartridges, carbines, pistols, flints, and 20,000 muskets.[47] Considering the pressure on the Ordnance Office to maintain this flow of war equipment, it was small wonder that Castlereagh hoped the Russians could salvage some of the muskets left behind by the French in their flight.[48] Five years before, the Ordnance Office had found it difficult to send 200,000 muskets to the Spanish and Portuguese. In November 1813 Castlereagh informed the Commons that nearly 1,000,000 muskets had been sent to Britain's allies in the Peninsula and in northern Europe during that year alone, "an exertion which . . . reflected the greatest credit on the head and all the members of that department of the public service by which it was effected."[49] No tribute was ever better earned.

In spite of Britain's original plan, it was never possible for her to send an expeditionary force to join the allies in northern Germany. Wellington could spare no men from the Peninsula, and the war with the United States made it necessary to send troops to the North American theatre. With no men of her own available, Britain resorted to hiring mercenaries. In the spring of 1813 she offered to take the Russian German Legion into her pay. This unit was made up of Germans from Napoleon's army whom the Russians had captured during the winter of 1812-1813. Castlereagh proposed to take over the legion, which numbered about 4,000 men, and increase it to 10,000 by the addition of Hanoverians. It could then join forces with Bernadotte or continue operating as a part of the Russian army. Arrangements were finally made along these lines and a formal Anglo-Russian treaty was concluded on July 6, 1813.[50]

Britain had little difficulty in supplying the allies with arms, but the creation of a four-power war alliance proved troublesome.

47. Bathurst to Rear Admiral Hope, July 5, 1813, FO 73/87.
48. Castlereagh to Cathcart, April 6, 1813, FO 65/83.
49. Castlereagh referred to 900,000 muskets having been sent abroad; *Hansard,* XXVII (1813), 134.
50. The Russian German Legion should not be confused with the older King's German Legion (Russian German Legion Treaty, July 6, 1813, FO 93/81 [13]). Britain transferred the Russian German Legion to Hanoverian service at the end of 1813. When the war ended it was transferred to Prussia. Additional troops from Hanover and the Hanse towns were taken into British pay during the summer of 1813 for service with the allies (Charles Stewart, 3d Marquess of Londonderry, *Narrative of the War in Germany and France, in 1813 and 1814* [Philadelphia, 1831], pp. 18-19, 263-264).

Near the heart of the problem was the vast financial aid which the northern powers demanded. The Swedish subsidy and the cost of the Russian German Legion together would amount to about £2,000,000, while aid to the Peninsular powers might require nearly £4,000,000. Russia and Prussia certainly expected to be generously financed. If Austria finally entered the war and solicited British money, ministers might find themselves with empty pockets.

The financing of the emerging coalition hung heavily over the heads of Castlereagh and Vansittart during the spring of 1813. Lieven had already asked for £4,000,000 for the Tsar, and he hoped that the Cabinet would appropriate an additional £500,000 for the maintenance of the Russian squadron Britain had seized at Lisbon in 1808.[51] The Prussian envoy, Jacobi, had also warned that generous British aid was "indispensably necessary" for his government to remain at war.[52] Desperate for some means by which to satisfy the allies without impoverishing Britain, Castlereagh and Vansittart seriously considered a scheme recently sent them by Sir Francis d'Ivernois. This plan, developed jointly by D'Ivernois and Stein, proposed to finance Prussia and Russia by an issue of paper currency to be redeemed by the allies at the end of the war.

Although the details of the "federative paper" proposal were complicated, its four basic principles can be simply stated:

1. An issue of paper money would be made each month to Russia and Prussia, which they would use to pay their military expenses.

2. Of each monthly issue, Russia was to have two thirds, while Prussia would receive the remaining one third.

3. Once in circulation, the paper would yield no interest during the remainder of the war, but upon the return of peace it would bear a specified interest until redeemed.

4. At the close of the war, Britain, Prussia, and Russia would jointly redeem all paper in circulation. Britain would be respon-

---

51. In 1808 Britain had occupied Lisbon and taken possession of a squadron of Russian war vessels in that harbor. In return for providing £500,000 a year for the upkeep of these ships, Lieven proposed that Britain should employ them with her own navy (F. Martens, *Recueil des Traités*, XI, 151-152; James, *Naval History*, IV, 323).

52. Hardenberg to Jacobi, March 26, 1813, FO 64/87.

sible for three sixths of the total redemption costs, Russia, two sixths, and Prussia, one sixth.[53]

The use of scrip for the payment of subsidies was not a new idea, as D'Invernois admitted. The Dutch government had made a similar proposal at the time of the Prussian subsidy treaty in 1794. In 1809 Canning had offered to pay the Austrian subsidy by using interest-bearing Exchequer bills. Neither of these plans had ever been put into operation.

Vansittart and Castlereagh carefully studied this latest proposal by which the three governments would merge their credit in order to provide aid for Prussia and Russia. The major weakness of the scheme, as Vansittart saw at once, was that any paper put in circulation would be heavily discounted. Russia and Prussia might find that the purchasing power of the scrip would be only a thin shadow of its face value.[54] The use of "federative paper" would, however, solve two problems currently troubling the British Treasury. It would enable Britain to subsidize Prussia and Russia on credit and make it unnecessary for her to send specie to those powers. Probably the most attractive feature of the D'Invernois proposal was that it would postpone the actual payment of British money until the war was over. This was the view which most appealed to the Cabinet and it endorsed the scheme, provided that certain safeguards were incorporated in the final arrangements.

In April 1813 Castlereagh made known his plans to assist Russia and Prussia during the present year. He included this information in his instructions to Cathcart and the newly appointed minister to Prussia, Sir Charles Stewart.[55] The latter, Castlereagh's half-brother, enjoyed the foreign secretary's full confidence, and undoubtedly the two men discussed the proposals at length before Stewart's departure for Germany in April. The opening of the

53. Karmin, *D'Ivernois,* pp. 510-512. The plan went through many modifications, which can be traced in the correspondence of D'Ivernois, Stein, and Vansittart, published in Otto Karmin, "Autour des Négociations Financières Anglo-Prusso-Russes de 1813," *Revue Historique de la Révolution Française et de l'Empire,* 11 (January-June 1917), 177-197; 12 (July-December 1917), 24-49, 216-252.

54. Suggestions respecting the proposed Federative Paper by . . . N. Vansittart, [June], 1813; *Correspondence of Castlereagh,* VIII, 405-406.

55. Sir Charles Stewart (1778-1854) had served in the British Army since 1794 and been involved in the Peninsular War. Aside from the fact that he was related to Castlereagh, Stewart had no particular qualification for the Prussian appointment. He and Cathcart did not work well together. On Castlereagh's death, Stewart became Marquess of Londonderry.

Baltic to British trade would make it easier for the government to make foreign remittances, but the Cabinet could give no more than £2,000,000 for both Prussia and Russia during 1813. Even this might have to be reduced unless those powers revised their tariff policies in favor of British commerce.[56] The £2,000,000 subsidy was to be divided between Prussia and Russia in proportion to the number of troops each had agreed to maintain by the terms of their alliance: that is, Russia would receive two thirds of the entire amount (£1,333,334) and Prussia the remaining one third (£666,666). Since the allies needed British weapons as well as money, Castlereagh hoped that "as large a portion of the value [of the subsidy] be taken in military effects as possible." As a special aid to the Tsar, Britain would spend £500,000 a year on the maintenance of his warships now in British ports, provided that Britain was allowed to use these vessels. All subsidies would be paid in London so that any loss from unfavorable exchange rates would be borne by those receiving the money.

Russia and Prussia, for their part, must maintain 200,000 and 100,000 effective troops respectively, not including forces on garrison duty. To guarantee this, "the three Powers are to be respectively entitled to receive satisfactory proofs that the said quotas are kept constantly complete." Finally, the allies must "engage to unite their arms and their councils" and solemnly promise not to negotiate separately with the enemy.

In addition to the £2,000,000 subsidy, Stewart and Cathcart were to offer help to Prussia and Russia by means of a separate "federative paper" convention to include the following specific provisions:

1. The total of all paper issued must not exceed £5,000,000.

2. The monthly issue of scrip was to be divided between Russia and Prussia at the rate of two thirds and one third respectively.

3. All paper issued must be used exclusively by the recipients for their military expenses.

56. In his instructions to Cathcart of April 6, 1813, Castlereagh explained that "it has been in expectation of a considerable extension of British exports being the result of the total expulsion of the enemy from the north of Europe, that His Majesty's Govt. have felt themselves justified in recommending so large & unexampled an aid to our allies in that quarter" (FO 65/83).

4. All paper in circulation at the end of the war would begin to bear interest, but no more than 5 percent. Responsibility for redemption would be shared by the three powers in the following proportion: Britain, three sixths; Russia, two sixths; and Prussia, one sixth.

5. Britain must never be asked to redeem more than three sixths of the total issue; i.e., £2,500,000.[57]

Stewart carried Castlereagh's instructions with him when he set out for his new assignment. The negotiation of the subsidy treaties with Prussia and Russia would take place on the battlefields of Germany. While awaiting the results, Castlereagh turned his attention to other phases of the war program.

The Swedish subsidy convention was something of an embarrassment to the government, especially since Bernadotte showed little zeal for grappling with the French. It was not until the end of April 1813 that his troops reached Stralsund, and even then they did remarkably little. The foreign secretary hesitated to lay the treaty before Parliament until the Swedes had accomplished something. The provisions in that agreement relating to Norway and Guadaloupe would not be well received. Furthermore, the government had no desire to admit that subsidy payments had actually begun before Parliament had voted the money. Responding to a question asked in the Commons in May, the foreign secretary confessed that this had indeed happened. This admission exposed Castlereagh to the same charge which had been made against Pitt in 1796: that of advancing money to a foreign power without parliamentary approval at a time when the legislature was in session.[58]

Bernadotte's inactivity severely vexed Downing Street and gave rise to serious doubts whether he could be trusted. At one point, Castlereagh was tempted to stop the subsidy until the Prince Royal had done something to earn it.[59] This mood passed, and less than a week later, on June 11, he presented the Swedish treaty to the House of Commons. A few days later he defended the convention and effectively dealt with an opposition charge that

57. Castlereagh to Cathcart, April 9, 1813, FO 65/83; Castlereagh to Stewart, April 9, 1813, FO 64/86.
58. *Hansard,* XXVI (1813), 406-407.
59. Castlereagh to Hope, June 6, 1813, FO 73/79.

Britain "was always eager and anxious to furnish money as long as any other country was ready to take it."[60] That same month, the chancellor of the exchequer explained to the Commons the major items in the new budget which would involve heavier expenses than in the previous year. Supplies which would have appeared incredible two decades before were asked for the army and navy. Nor was this all. An additional £6,000,000 was requested for war purposes in the form of a special Vote of Credit.[61]

British plans for 1813 grew out of the hope that France must go down to defeat before the united military strength of the three northern powers, aided by the steady progress of Wellington's army in Spain. Money, arms, and men had been sent to the Peninsula to guarantee that progress, and by the spring of 1813 results were clearly visible. Meanwhile, Britain was sending mountains of war materials to equip the Swedes, the Prussians, and the Russians who even now were pushing into the heart of Germany. As well as arming Napoleon's enemies, London was supplying them with the money they needed to complete the work. Bernadotte was to have £1,000,000, and twice that sum had been offered Russia and Prussia in subsidies. By means of the "federative paper" proposal Britain was prepared to provide those powers with an additional £5,000,000 in credit, a sum she was unable to spare from her current resources. If the war could be won by generous gifts of British arms and cash, then the Cabinet would never have to apologize for its policy. The broad lines of that policy were now established. It remained for Cathcart and Stewart to complete the formation of a grand alliance of the three great powers.

60. *Hansard*, XXVI (1813), 874-880.
61. *Ibid.*, XXVI, 577.

XIII

FORGING THE GRAND ALLIANCE

The war in Germany had reached a critical stage by the time Sir Charles Stewart arrived late in April at allied headquarters in Dresden. Napoleon had won the initiative and was about to hurl his forces against the Prussians and Russians in Saxony. His success drove the allies back in confusion, and the two British envoys were often obliged to conduct their business within the sound of guns. Stewart's discussions were chiefly with Hardenberg and Stein representing the Prussian government, while Count Nesselrode dealt with Cathcart on behalf of the Tsar.[1]

Several important features of Castlereagh's subsidy proposal were bitterly protested by the Russian and Prussian ministers. They particularly objected to the British demand that all payments be made in London. With hard money almost unavailable in Germany, Prussia and Russia insisted that Britain send them specie. The quotas of troops specified by Castlereagh were unacceptable to Nesselrode. Prussia had about 100,000 men in the field, but Russia would be hard-pressed to maintain more than 150,000. Notwithstanding, the Tsar expected to receive twice as large a subsidy as Prussia.[2]

The "federative paper" scheme proved especially troublesome and much time was wasted wrangling over its details. In May Sir Francis d'Ivernois arrived at Dresden and offered his services to the diplomats, but it is doubtful whether this was much help. At least Stewart was honest enough to admit that the whole business

1. Webster, *Foreign Policy of Castlereagh*, I, 130-132.
2. Stewart to Castlereagh, May 17 and 24, 1813, FO 64/87; Stewart to Castlereagh, May 20, 1813, *Correspondence of Castlereagh*, IX, 14-16.

of paper money was far beyond his understanding; if Castlereagh wanted to get the matter settled he should send a financial expert from London.[3] More was at issue, however, than the technical details of the plan. From the start of the negotiation, Prussia and Russia asked to be relieved of responsibility for the redemption of any part of the federative paper. There was more to their request than mere self-interest. The wretched financial condition of the two governments would unquestionably prejudice the acceptance of the federative paper if it was known that they were to meet half the redemption costs. This difficulty would disappear if Britain undertook to redeem the entire issue. Such was the arrangement which Russia and Prussia favored.[4] There was another possible solution: that the paper issue be reduced to £2,500,000 (half the original amount projected), with Britain bound to redeem the entire amount.[5] Discussion of the plan finally broke down completely, and all parties wearily agreed to refer the business to London for final settlement.

By June the representatives of the three powers had reached general agreement on all other important points at issue relative to subsidies. Russia and Prussia were ready to pledge themselves to maintain armies of at least 160,000 and 80,000 troops respectively, with the £2,000,000 British subsidy to be divided between them in the same proportion. Russia would therefore receive £1,333,334 and Prussia £666,666 during the remainder of 1813. This division was unfair to Prussia since her army in Germany was nearly as large as the Tsar's, and Prussia's resentment over this discrimination caused Castlereagh considerable difficulty during the months which followed. Stewart and Cathcart refused the allies' demand that all subsidy payments be made on the Continent in hard money. Russia and Prussia finally agreed to accept payments in London, but they subsequently put great pressure on Castlereagh to modify this. Remittance of the

---

3. Stewart to Castlereagh, May 17, 1813, *ibid.,* VIII, 390-392.

4. Stewart to Castlereagh, May 17, 1813, FO 64/87; Stewart and Cathcart to Castlereagh, May 24, 1813, FO 64/87. See also D'Ivernois' memorandum of May 6, 1813 in Karmin, "Autour des Négociation Financières," *Revue Historique de la Révolution,* XI, 188-191.

5. Castlereagh was willing to accept this. See his letter to Stewart of June 22, 1813, FO 64/86.

£2,000,000 subsidy was to be completed by the end of the year; if the war continued into 1814, Britain would make a new financial arrangement with her allies. Since a separate "federative paper" convention was to be negotiated in London, only a passing reference was made to the matter in the treaties now being prepared for signature at Reichenbach. That with Prussia was signed by Stewart on June 14, while the Russian treaty was concluded by Cathcart on the following day.[6] Since Hardenberg claimed that Prussia's need for money was desperate, Stewart gave him £100,000 in bills upon the conclusion of the treaty. Informing Castlereagh of this the British envoy explained, "The fact is, Prussia cannot go on just now without a lift; the machine is really at a stand for want of oil."[7]

The Reichenbach alliances proved troublesome from the very beginning. Instead of a single pact, the three powers were now joined in separate, but interlocking, engagements. Still worse, the future of the alliances was at once cast in doubt; a few days before the formal signing, Prussia and Russia agreed to a six-week armistice with the enemy. They had done this without any reference to the envoys of that power with whom they were now officially united. The Pläswitz armistice had been the work of Metternich, who hoped that it might lead to a general pacification among the continental belligerents. Stewart and Cathcart had no part in arranging the armistice, nor were they invited to participate in the discussions which followed. Troublesome as this latest development was, Cathcart was confident that it was a necessary preliminary to Austria's adherence to the allied cause. His colleague, Sir Charles Stewart, took a different view and regarded the armistice as proof of Metternich's treachery.[8]

If the two British agents on the spot disagreed as to the meaning of the armistice, how much more difficult it was for Castlereagh to evaluate it. This turn of events caused great uneasiness in London, but Castlereagh believed that all would finally be well. Certainly the suspension of hostilities ought not to impair the flow of

6. Treaty with Prussia, June 14, 1813, FO 94/184; Treaty with Russia, June 15, 1813, FO 93/81 (11). The Russian treaty obliged Britain to pay an additional £500,000 a year for the upkeep of the Tsar's ships in her ports.

7. Stewart to Castlereagh, June 16, 1813, in Archibald Alison, *Lives of Lord Castlereagh and Sir Charles Stewart* . . . (Edinburgh and London, 1861), I, 669.

8. Webster, *Foreign Policy of Castlereagh*, I, 137-139.

Alexander I, by Sir Thomas Lawrence

Prince Metternich, by Sir Thomas
Lawrence

Prince Von Hardenberg, by Sir Thomas
Lawrence

Count Nesselrode, by Sir Thomas
Lawrence

British arms to the allies.[9] Furthermore, at the end of June the foreign secretary announced that at least a part of the subsidy due Russia and Prussia under the Reichenbach agreements would be sent to them in coin as they wished. Both Jacobi and Lieven had strongly impressed on Castlereagh how important it was for their governments to receive specie.[10] Recently the Treasury had obtained £100,000 in coin and bar silver, which the foreign secretary dispatched to the Prussian port of Kolberg on board H.M.S. *Amphion,* a thirty-two gun frigate. This specie was to be divided between Prussia and Russia. Since Britain's Baltic trade was expanding, Stewart and Cathcart were empowered to give bills of exchange in partial payment of the subsidy money due the allies, but they were not to draw for more than £200,000 a month. The remainder of the subsidy debt would be paid in London, as provided for in the treaties.[11]

For the moment, the conclusion of the Pläswitz armistice suspended the operation of the subsidy provisions of the Reichenbach alliances. Considering the nature of the discussions the allies were carrying on with the enemy, the British envoys decided to make no further payments beyond the £100,000 in bills given to Prussia at the signing of the alliance. Thus the money brought by H.M.S.. *Amphion* was allowed to lie idle for the time; nor did Stewart and Cathcart draw any bills on England. Castlereagh approved their decision and informed Cathcart that "it has been found necessary . . . to make a Reserve as to the continuance of the Instalments in the Event of a prolongation of the armistice."[12] As the foreign secretary feared, the armistice was finally extended to August 10.

No phase of coalition diplomacy was more disturbing to the Cabinet than Austria's conduct. Metternich's proposal that Austria intervene to arrange for a general peace had been coldly received in London at the end of 1812. In the spring of 1813, Baron de Wessenberg arrived in England as the Hofburg's unofficial spokesman and announced that Metternich was prepared to take a slightly stronger line involving "armed mediation.".Would Britain

9. Bathurst to Rear Admiral Hope, July 5, 1813, FO 73/87.
10. F. Martens, *Recueil des Traités,* XI, 177.
11. Castlereagh to Stewart and Cathcart, June 25 and 29, 1813, FO 65/83.
12. Castlereagh to Cathcart, July 13, 1813, FO 65/83.

provide subsidies to support this strengthening of Hapsburg policy? Castlereagh vetoed the suggestion; if Britain was to dip into her shrinking war chest to help Vienna, it would have to be for better reasons than those Wessenberg proposed.[13]

The motives which inspired Austria's policy continued to give Castlereagh great concern throughout the summer. Wessenberg was useless as a source of information since Metternich neglected even to write him. Late in June, when the continental picture was especially confused, the foreign secretary decided to undertake a direct overture to the Austrian leader. On June 30 he sent Cathcart a letter to be forwarded to Metternich inviting the latter to make known "the views and intentions of the Austrian Cabinet." Cathcart was reminded that, on leaving England the year before, he had been authorized to draw on London for as much as £500,000 for "extraordinary purposes." So far, he had used none of that money. Now he was instructed to turn the entire sum over to Austria "in the event of the Austrian army being actually engaged in hostilities against the enemy; as an aid to assist their first efforts."[14]

Even before receiving these instructions, Stewart and Cathcart had sent Metternich assurances of British aid if and when Austria joined forces with the allies in war. It is possible that they went so far as to pledge money and arms to the value of £1,000,000.[15] Metternich refused either to see Cathcart or to accept Castlereagh's letter, but he maintained indirect communication with the British envoy during the armistice through the agency of the Hapsburg minister, Count Stadion. Late in July Cathcart received a visit from General Nugent at Reichenbach. Lavall Nugent was a shadowy figure who had already served as Metternich's intermediary with London.[16] Now he asked Cathcart for money to help

13. Webster, *Foreign Policy of Castlereagh*, I, 122-124; Buckland, *Metternich*, p. 496.
14. Castlereagh to Cathcart, June 30, 1813, with a letter for Metternich enclosed, FO 65/83.
15. In May 1813 Cathcart requested Nesselrode to assure Metternich of British help in the event of war. See Cathcart to Castlereagh, June 1, 1813, in Webster, *British Diplomacy*, p. 4. Nesselrode met Metternich at Czaslau on June 2, 1813. See *Memoirs of Prince Metternich 1773-1835*, ed. Prince Richard Metternich and trans. Mrs. Alexander Napier (New York, 1881), I, 108. According to Alison (*Castlereagh*, I, 668-670), Stewart and Cathcart agreed on June 16 to pledge Metternich £1,000,000.
16. Lavall Nugent (1777-1862) was a native of Ireland who entered Austrian service in 1793. He fought with the Austrians in the first two coalitions, whereupon he appears to have entered British service for a time. He was well known in London and respected by Wellington. He lived long enough to serve as a volunteer in the Battle of Solferino.

arm the Austrian Tyrol, and after discussing the matter with Stadion the British envoy gave Nugent £30,000 in bills.[17]

The great question of peace or war which was at the heart of the allies' conferences with France during the summer of 1813 almost overshadows the problem of British subsidies. Except for the £100,000 given Prussia in June, the British agents made no payments under the Reichenbach treaties, pending the outcome of the armistice. To what extent was Austria's decision to join the allies influenced by the offer of British money made by Stewart and Cathcart? Probably very little. Metternich knew that he could rely on Britain for help, but only after Austria had gone to war. To regard this offer as a bribe seems to overstate the case.[18] Castlereagh would do as much for Austria as he had already done for Sweden, Russia, and Prussia, but only after she had "actually engaged in hostilities against the enemy." The Austrian leader knew, at least as early as June, that such help would be forthcoming, and the knowledge was doubtless valuable to him. Two other developments, however, were probably of greater significance: Wellington's victory over the French at Vittoria (June 21), and Napoleon's stubborn refusal to accept any reasonable settlement of the issues at stake between himself and the three great continental powers. Had Wellington been defeated at Vittoria and Napoleon inclined to show the same disposition to compromise which he had exhibited earlier in his career, the emerging coalition against France might not have survived the summer. Instead, when hostilities resumed in August 1813, Austria was now counted as one of the allies.

Once the scene of action had shifted from the conference table to the battlefield, Stewart and Cathcart were ready to pay Russia and Prussia the Reichenbach subsidies. On August 12 Hardenberg and Nesselrode proposed that the £100,000 brought by H.M.S. *Amphion* be equally divided between them—a suggestion Cathcart happily accepted.[19] During the next few months, an additional £200,000 in specie was received from England and was also evenly

17. Cathcart to Castlereagh, July 26, 1813, FO 65/86; Webster, *Foreign Policy of Castlereagh*, I, 150.
18. Buckland (*Metternich*, p. 522) states: "warned by the armistice, England resolved to bribe in time."
19. Cathcart to Castlereagh, August 12, 1813, FO 65/86.

shared by the two powers.[20] The allies were given an additional £300,000 in bills of exchange by the British agents, while the balance of the year's subsidy was paid them in London. Britain's debt to Prussia was almost entirely cleared off by the end of the year, but the balance due Russia was not remitted until the spring of 1814.[21]

In addition to these subsidies, the allied powers expected to receive at least £2,500,000 by means of the "federative paper" plan. Following the renewal of the war in August, the British government undertook to arrange the details of this with Jacobi and Lieven. To assist in the work, Vansittart invited D'Ivernois to come to London. Although the Swiss financier did appear in order to advise the Treasury, he was by now thoroughly disenchanted with the scheme he had originated.[22]

The "federative paper" treaty, signed in London on September 30, 1813, differed materially from the plan originally proposed earlier that year. To begin with, the issue would be limited to £2,500,000, the whole amount to be redeemed by Britain when the war ended. Russia and Prussia were to receive bills of credit in

20. Castlereagh to Cathcart and Stewart, September 3, 1813, FO 65/83. Three shipments of specie were made for the use of Prussia and Russia, the last being in Hanoverian coins in April 1814. See the Account of Lord Cathcart, AO 1/11 (20). The value placed on the specie produced disagreement. Lieven insisted that Russia had received a total of £150,000 in specie (Lieven to Wm. Hamilton, January 21, 1814, FO 65/95), while the Treasury valued it at £156,229 (C. Arbuthnot to Wm. Hamilton, December 31, 1814, FO 65/97). In the end the Treasury accepted Russia's figure.

21. The preferential treatment Britain showed Prussia in making these payments may have been in an effort to appease her justifiable resentment with the unfair division of the £2,000,000 subsidy between her and Russia. Payment of the Reichenbach subsidy to Prussia was made as follows (Treasury Minute, January 21, 1814, Ty. 29/127, 350-351):

Paid in specie on the Continent by Stewart (1813-1814)	£150,000
Paid in bills of exchange on the Continent by Stewart	283,373
Paid in London (1813)	216,666
Paid in London to close the account (1814)	16,627
	£666,666

Payment of the Reichenbach subsidy to Russia was made as follows (C. Arbuthnot to Wm. Hamilton, December 31, 1814, FO 65/97):

Paid in specie on the Continent by Cathcart (1813-1814)	£150,000
Paid in bills of exchange on the Continent by Cathcart	7,500
Paid in London (1813-1814)	1,175,834
	£1,333,334

22. D'Ivernois had turned sour on the federative paper plan and on August 19, 1813 he correctly predicted to Vansittart that, in the end, Britain "would be called on . . . to fulfill the engagement of others" (Karmin, "Les Finances Russes," *Revue Historique de la Révolution,* IX, 70).

fifteen monthly installments to be counted from the signing of the Reichenbach treaties in June 1813. Of each monthly issue, Russia and Prussia were to receive two thirds and one third respectively. In this way Russia would get £1,666,666 and Prussia £833,333 in all. A special commission representing the three governments would be created to handle the monthly issue of bills.

The treaty made special provision to prevent the discount on bills in circulation from reaching extravagant heights. It was assumed that the allies would convert the monthly bills into cash by offering them to continental banks. To make acceptance easier, the convention provided an option for those to whom the bills were offered: they could either hold them or immediately exchange them in London for interest-bearing British bonds especially issued for this purpose. These bonds would be redeemed as quickly as possible after the end of the war. Only then would the Treasury begin to redeem the bills of credit still in circulation, which were to bear one-half percent interest per month from the end of the war to the date of their redemption. In effect, those accepting "federative paper" were invited to gamble whether the returns would be greater by converting them at once into short-term bonds, or holding on to the paper in order to benefit from extended interest payments. The device was not only complicated but may also have been unsound. In any event it was never actually put into operation.

Since the "federative paper" issue was to be counted from the conclusion of the Reichenbach agreements, the allies were entitled to receive slightly more than one third of the entire £2,500,000 issue by the close of 1813. But no paper could be issued until Parliament had approved the plan and the necessary administrative machinery been established. To provide immediate relief, a secret article bound Britain to offer the allies promissory notes equivalent to the value of six fifteenths of the entire issue. Stewart and Cathcart were instructed to issue such notes on demand, and in order to secure them the government deposited £900,000 in Exchequer Bills with the Bank of England.[23] Thus the promissory notes were offered as an interim substitute for "federative paper," which itself was a substitute for British subsidy money!

23. Identical Treaties were concluded on September 30, 1813 with Prussia (FO 93/78[6],[7]) and Russia (FO 93/81[14],[15]); and Castlereagh to Stewart and Cathcart, October 18, 1813, FO 65/83.

Before 1813 ended, the "federative paper" arrangement began to fall apart. Although Stewart and Cathcart were sent the promissory notes, the allied powers seem not to have requested their issue.[24] Conversion of these notes into cash on the Continent would probably cost the allies a large part of their face value in discount. Early in 1814 Prussia asked the British Treasury to substitute a cash payment to her of £225,000 for the "federative paper" and promissory notes to which, by then, she was entitled.[25]

The discount problem proved fatal to the "federative paper" treaty, which finally evolved into an outright subsidy. Early in 1814 Amsterdam was selected as the place where the three-power commission, provided for by the treaty, would be established. The French had already withdrawn from Holland, and Dutch financial facilities were now available to the allies. In January 1814 Sir George Burgmann arrived in Amsterdam as the British representative of the "federative paper" commission. While waiting for the Prussian and Russian members to appear, Burgmann made enquiries of the Dutch banks to which the allies were likely to offer the bills of credit. Nearly all of the banks made clear that they would prefer to have nothing to do with federative paper. A few were willing to accept it, but would insist on at least a 25 percent discount. Responses which Burgmann received from German banking houses were much the same.[26]

By the time the Prussian and Russian commissioners reached Amsterdam in March, Burgmann had concluded that issuance of the bills of credit would be unwise. Since the prevailing rate of discount on bills of exchange drawn on England was considerably less than that which would be applied to the bills of credit, he recommended that all payments to the allies be made in bills of exchange.[27] The war with France was drawing to a close and the British Treasury would soon have to redeem such federative paper as might be issued. It was, therefore, more economical and practical simply to give bills of exchange to the allies rather than "federative paper."

The Treasury had reached the same conclusion, and in February 1814 it granted Prussia's plea for £225,000 in place of "federative

24. Treasury Minute, February 11, 1814, Ty. 29/127, 725.
25. Treasury Minute, February 22, 1814, Ty. 29/127, 848.
26. Burgmann to the Lords of the Treasury, February 18, 1814 and March 7, 1814; Ty. 1/1376, Ty. 1/1381.
27. Burgmann to the Lords of the Treasury, March 8, 1814, Ty. 1/1381.

paper." Burgmann's suggestion was adopted and the Treasury empowered him to issue bills of exchange to the allies for the amounts due them under the "federative paper" treaty.[28] Over-all management of the remittances to Prussia and Russia was assigned to the commissary-in-chief, who, with the ending of the war, was able to obtain cash on the Continent with which to supplement bills drawn on England. By the autumn of 1815 Prussia and Russia had received the entire amounts due them by the terms of the 1813 treaty.[*] None of the bills of credit provided for by that convention appear ever to have been issued.[29]

28. Treasury Minute, March 8, 1814, Ty. 29/128, 141-143; Burgmann to the Lords of the Treasury, March 11, 1814, Ty. 1/1381.

*Payments to Prussia and Russia under the "Federative Paper" Treaty are recorded in the final subsidy account of the commisary-in-chief, AO 3/1088. This account reveals that all remittances were either in cash or bills of exchange. Since payments were not completed until after the fifteeen-month period provided for in the treaty, the Treasury was liable for interest on its debt to the allies. Herries' account shows how the sums were paid and reveals the wide range of banking facilities which he and Nathan Rothschild used to handle the transaction. The account is expressed in thalers (Prussian) rather than sterling. The total issue of £2,500,000 was the equivalent of 15,000,000 thalers. Thus, the thaler was equal to about .1666 of the pound sterling.

Russia

Amount owed under the 1813 Treaty	10,000,000 thalers
Interest due for delayed payment	31,666
Total debt	10,031,666 thalers
	(£1,671,922)
Paid by Commissary (1814) in Warsaw	1,000,000 thalers
Hamburg	1,750,000
Dresden	750,000
Amsterdam	1,198,333
Paid by Treasury in London (1815)	5,333,333
	10,031,666 thalers

Prussia

Amount owed under the 1813 Treaty	5,000,000 thalers
Interest due for delayed payment	227,500
Total debt	5,227,500
	(£871,099)
Paid by Commissary in Amsterdam	
(1814)	339,167 thalers
Berlin (1814)	2,070,000
Berlin (1815)	2,818,333
	5,227,500 thalers

29. By the end of 1814 the House of Commons had voted a total of £2,650,000 to discharge Britain's obligations under the federative paper treaty; *Journal of the House of Commons*, LXIX, 345; LXX, 497.

Within a few days after Austria declared war on France, Lord Cathcart met with Metternich at Prague. The British envoy had already given £30,000 to General Nugent for Austria's use, and he now turned over £470,000 in bills of exchange as an advance on the British subsidy Metternich expected.[30] Nearly a month before, Castlereagh had decided to send a special agent to Metternich, and on August 6 he handed his instructions to Lord Aberdeen.[31] It was assumed that when Austria went to war, Cathcart would give her the £500,000 in his keeping. Therefore, Aberdeen was to offer another £500,000 if, on reaching Germany, he found that Austria had in fact joined the allies. At the moment, £1,000,000 was as much as Britain could spare for the Hofburg, but more would be provided if the war lasted into the coming year. Concern for British commercial interests prompted the foreign secretary to give his envoy special instructions. In view of the large subsidy Britain was ready to provide, it was hoped that Austria would "admit . . . British Colonial Produce and Manufactures upon the footing of the most favored nations."[32]

Aberdeen reached Teplitz early in September and discussed the terms of an Anglo-Austrian alliance with Metternich. The crucial question was whether the two governments could agree on the specific goals they were to fight for. By comparison, negotiation of the British subsidy was a secondary matter. Metternich was disappointed to learn that London could add only £500,000 to the money already given by Cathcart, but he gracefully accepted the terms Aberdeen had no authority to alter. Austria desperately needed arms and military stores. When Metternich proposed that the value of such goods sent by Britain be considered as over and beyond the subsidy Austria was to have, Aberdeen was obliged to object. Castlereagh had always insisted that war materials sent the allies be regarded as a part of their subsidy, and Austria must accept this principle which had already been applied to Russia and Prussia. This difference of opinion ended in a heated two-hour argument at the close of which Metternich conceded the point at

---

30. Cathcart to Castlereagh, nos. 85 and 86, September 1, 1813, FO 65/86.
31. George Hamilton Gordon, fourth Earl of Aberdeen, was only twenty-nine at this time. His youth and inexperience were a great handicap to him in his negotiations with Metternich.
32. Castlereagh to Aberdeen, August 6, 1813, FO 7/101.

issue, but insisted on giving Aberdeen a strong note to send to London.[33] The Austrian leader was on stronger ground in rejecting the British request for commercial preference and he informed Aberdeen that "it was wholly out of his power to enter into discussions on this subject; that it was one on which the Emperor himself had very strong opinions, and he saw no prospect of their being changed."[34]

The Austrian alliance signed by Aberdeen at Teplitz on October 3 conformed to the subsidy proposal Castlereagh made two months before. Austria was to maintain 150,000 effective troops in the field in return for a British subsidy of £1,000,000. The £500,000 still owed the Hofburg (beyond what Cathcart had already paid) would be remitted at the rate of £100,000 a month. New arrangements would be made when the final installment was paid in April 1814, if the war had not ended by then.[35]

Even before Aberdeen reached Teplitz, Stewart and Cathcart had sent home Austria's urgent appeal for arms. As always, Castlereagh's response was generous and prompt; in September he announced that muskets, accoutrements, and ammunition for 60,000 men would be sent for Austria's use. Various delays occurred, however, and it was not until November that five transports carrying these supplies sailed for Fiume.[36] By then, London had received a second Austrian request for arms as well as a large quantity of uniform cloth and 10,000 hides for use in making shoes. This list of requirements was sent to the Ordnance Office and the Storekeeper General, which arranged for the dispatch of the goods during the coming winter.[37] The foreign secretary also approved Aberdeen's recommendation that, as a good will gesture, nothing be deducted from the 1813 subsidy to

33. In sending Metternich's note, Aberdeen urged that Castlereagh be as generous as possible with his new ally. He recommended that the value of all arms and stores sent Austria be deducted from the 1814 subsidy, rather than from the £1,000,000 promised for 1813 (Aberdeen to Castlereagh, October 9, 1813, in Lady Frances Balfour, *The Life of George, Fourth Earl of Aberdeen K. G.* [London, 1922], I, 113).

34. Aberdeen to Castlereagh, September 13, October 9, 1813, FO 7/102.

35. Treaty with Austria, October 3, 1813, FO 93/11 (6),(7).

36. Castlereagh to Aberdeen, September 21, October 6, and November 5, 1813, FO 7/101.

37. Aberdeen to Castlereagh, October 10, 1813, FO 7/102. The uniform cloth and hides were shipped early in 1814, but the second shipment of arms (including 50,000 muskets) did not arrive until after the war had ended (Bathurst to Merveldt, September 21, 1814, FO 7/113).

Austria, but the value of all supplies sent her (about £590,000) be counted as a part of the 1814 subsidy.[38]

The course of the war in Germany during the late summer was disappointing, but no part of it gave Castlereagh greater pain than the ambiguous role played by Bernadotte. The Prince Royal commanded a mixed force of Swedish, Russian, and German troops and his handling of that army was open to serious criticism. Although it was true that in September he had thrown back a French army which had been sent to take Berlin, the fact that Bernadotte managed the campaign so that his Swedish units were not exposed to danger aroused suspicion both at the allied headquarters and in London. The Anglo-Swedish subsidy treaty was due to expire in the autumn of 1813, and the foreign secretary was reluctant to renew it until the last possible moment. For some time the Swedish minister in London had been pressing for an increase in the subsidy, pointing out that the Prince's military expenses in Germany amounted to £150,000 a month. Late in September Castlereagh authorized Thornton to offer Bernadotte £1,000,000 for the coming twelve months. This represented a reduction of the 1813 subsidy which had amounted to £1,000,000 for a period of only eight months. Thornton could increase the offer to £1,200,000 if it was *"indispensable"* to a renewal of the alliance.[39]

By the time Thornton received these instructions, the allies had scored a major victory at Leipzig. Bernadotte and his army had

---

38. Castlereagh to Aberdeen, November 5, 1813, FO 7/101. The first shipment of arms was valued at £186,851; the second (which arrived after the war ended) was valued at £142,120. See the Ordnance account, dated August 17, 1814, in FO 7/115. The value of all cloth and hides sent was £262,234 (Storekeeper General to Wm. Hamilton, August 11, 1814, FO 7/115).

Aberdeen paid the £500,000 owed to Austria in two issues of bills of exchange: December 1813 (£200,000) and March 1814 (£300,000). See Aberdeen to Castlereagh, December 21, 1813, and March 10, 1814; FO 7/103, FO 7/107.

39. Castlereagh to Thornton, September 24, 1813, FO 73/80. Payment of the £1,000,000 subsidy for 1813 was made as follows:

Payments in bills by Thornton	£214,992
Payments made to Swedish minister in London	735,008
Payment made in October 1813 to close account	50,000
	£1,000,000

See Copy of a Treasury Minute of October 1, 1813, sent to the Foreign Office, FO 73/88.

been involved in the engagement and the Prince was full of importance with the part he had played. He was, therefore, shocked and dismayed at the British offer of only £1,000,000 for the coming year. In the excitement of his discussion with Thornton, Bernadotte may have doused himself liberally with cologne water and waved his handkerchief with unusual vigor.[40] He finally accepted the offer of £1,200,000 which Thornton held out as the final proposal, but he was far from being satisfied. The shabby manner in which Britain had treated him justified his withdrawal from the war altogether. Instead, he would give the world proof of the nobility of his motives by zealously supporting the great military drive through Germany with which the allies planned to follow their success at Leipzig. When the Anglo-Swedish treaty was finally signed, Thornton probably breathed a sigh of relief. Thoroughly aroused, this Gascon prince of Sweden was likely to prove difficult for a mere British diplomat to deal with.[41]

The opening of Parliament on November 4, 1813 was an historic occasion, for on that day victory seemed closer than at any time in the past twenty years. Napoleon's power in the Peninsula had vanished in the gunsmoke of Vittoria, and Wellington was even now pushing his way into the Pyrenees. News of the Battle of Leipzig reached London only a few days before Parliament met, and it filled the nation's cup of rejoicing to the brim. The Prince Regent's speech at the opening of the session held out the brightest prospects for the future, marred only by the continuation of war with the United States. While acclaiming Wellington's latest victory, the Regent paid his allies a graceful compliment by the manner in which he referred to their triumph at Leipzig. "The annals of Europe," he declared, "afford no example of victories more splendid and decisive than those which have been recently achieved in Saxony." So infectious was this spirit of optimism that, in the Upper House, it brought from Grenville a statement of congratulation and support for the government such as their lordships had not heard from him in nearly a decade.[42]

40. Stewart noted that Bernadotte usually appeared at conferences armed with a handkerchief and a cologne bottle "inundating lavishly every thing around him with the perfume" (Londonderry, *War in Germany*, pp. 72-73).
41. Renewal of the Anglo-Swedish alliance took the form of an article signed on October 22, 1813, which was appended to the March 1813 treaty (FO 93/101 [9]).
42. *Hansard*, XXVII (1813), 3, 11-20.

Two weeks later Castlereagh explained to the Commons how the government planned to promote the formation of what all hoped would be the final coalition against France. He briefly described the subsidy treaties already negotiated with Prussia, Russia, Austria, and Sweden and called on members to vote the money needed to bring the war to a successful conclusion.[43] Canning spoke in favor of granting the £3,000,000 which the foreign secretary had asked and summed up the feeling of the House when he declared, "Is it nothing, to look back upon the fallen, the crouching attitude of enslaved Europe, at a period not long distant and compare it with the upright, free undaunted posture in which she now stands?—Living memory can recal no period when she was entitled to hold her head so high, and to bid such bold defiance to her enemy."[44] A few voices protested the government's prodigality, but the Commons would have none of such grumbling. Clearly, the Cabinet could count on Parliament's support if it could bring France to her knees by sending arms, supplies, and money to the allies.

Between March and November 1813, the British government had undertaken subsidy obligations which would involve the payment of more than £11,000,000. A good share of this had already been paid with the balance due during the coming year:

Sweden (March Treaty),	£1,000,000
Sweden (October Treaty),	1,200,000
Sicily,	400,000
Spain,	1,000,000
Portugal,	2,000,000
Prussia,	666,666
Russia,	1,333,334
Federative Paper,	2,500,000
Austria,	1,000,000
	£11,100,000

The tremendous expansion of the British subsidy program is one of the most dramatic features of the final phase of the war with Napoleon. The £11,000,000 pledged to the allies in 1813 nearly equals the sum of all subsidies and loans paid by Britain during the first two coalitions, 1793-1801. Nor was the end in sight. Within a

43. *Ibid.,* XXVII, 132-143.
44. *Ibid.,* XXVII, 146.

few months, Hanover, Holland, and Denmark joined the growing list of subsidized powers. There was some truth to the remark that God was the only ally Britain did not have to pay.[45]

Britain's help to the allies must be measured in other units than the pound sterling. Huge stores of ammunition and arms were sent to outfit the Swedes, the Prussians, the Russians, the Austrians, the Spanish, the Portuguese, and Britains's own army in the European theatre. Arms sent to the allied powers in 1813 cost the government nearly £2,000,000.[46] The Ordnance service groaned under the demands made of it by the War Office and the Foreign Office, but happily, the worst was over by the close of 1813. Requests for guns and supplies dropped sharply during the final months of the war although they did not altogether cease.[47]

Castlereagh's subsidy policy closely resembles that which Pitt followed during the formation of the Third Coalition. Like his great teacher, he was ready to help all France's enemies, but the piecemeal manner in which the 1813 coalition was formed made it impossible for him to adhere to Pitt's principle of a standard rate of aid to the allies. The overwhelming importance of involving Sweden in the campaign forced him to be prodigal with Bernadotte. Even the subsidy arrangements with Prussia and Russia had to be adjusted to meet the Tsar's demand for preferential treatment. Least generous of all was the British subsidy to Austria: the Hofburg received the same subsidy as Sweden in return for maintaining an army three times as large. This was not a matter of policy. By the time Austria entered the war, Britain's resources for the year were nearly exhausted; £1,000,000 was all she could afford to give. Castlereagh knew that the distribution of subsidy money among the allies in 1813 had resulted in flagrant inequities. In making financial arrangements with the allies for the coming year, he intended to employ Pitt's principle of dividing the available money in proportion to the size of their armies.

45. Sydney Buxton, *Finance and Politics: An Historical Study 1783-1885* (London, 1888), I, 6.

46. An Account of the Value of all Arms . . . supplied by the Ordnance Department to any Foreign Power . . . between 31 December, 1812 and 31 December, 1813 . . ., dated March 21, 1814, gives the total value as £1,963,581. See the papers of Nicholas Vansittart, deposited in the British Museum, Add. Mss. 31231.

47. Eighty thousand muskets with ammunition were issued to the allies during 1814 (Crewe to Bunbury, January 27, 1815, WO 1/795).

In 1807 Canning had proposed to make good the deficiencies of the allied powers by sending them British arms as well as money. From that time on a steady stream of muskets and ammunition went to the Continent, chiefly to help the Spanish and the Portuguese. The 1812 rising of the nations found Castlereagh ready to increase that flow of arms to benefit the northern powers as well. By the winter of 1813-1814, British muskets made up a large part of that ring of steel which was being drawn around France.

Britain's outlay of money and arms materially contributed to the success of the final coalition. Even when awarded with a free hand, subsidies did almost nothing to effect any change in the commercial, military, and diplomatic policies of the allied powers. Only the marked upswing in British exports to Europe which followed the collapse of the Continental System enabled her to remit the massive subsidies which Castlereagh had promised.[48] British efforts to improve conditions still more by persuading the continental powers to liberalize their tariff policies were generally disappointing. Economic interdependence accounts for the trade privileges which Sweden granted Britain in their 1813 alliance. This was exceptional. Spain steadily denied Britain unrestricted access to her home and colonial markets even though the Cortes' life depended on British military aid and subsidies. London's efforts to pry open the Austrian market were a total failure. Metternich accepted £1,000,000 in British subsidies, but refused even to discuss the commercial question with Aberdeen. Of the major allies, only Prussia was willing to make some concessions to British goods entering her ports.[49]

Russia's system of trade protection was especially irritating in view of the Tsar's lofty demand for British money. In 1810 a ukase had virtually prohibited the importation of certain goods and imposed heavy duties on others. Especially hard hit were refined sugar, textiles, and decorated china—all important British trade items. Since the ukase operated on all imports regardless of national origin, the "most favored nation" clause contained in the Anglo-Russian peace treaty of 1812 did not alter this situation.[50]

48. Crouzet, *L'Economie Britannique,* II, 845-846. Trade statistics dealing with British commerce for 1813 were destroyed by fire, but it seems likely that the upswing which marked 1812 continued during 1813 (*ibid.,* II, 883).
49. Londonderry, *War in Germany,* pp. 259-261.
50. Crouzet, *L'Economie Britannique,* II, 660.

Now that the two nations were partners-in-arms, Castlereagh hoped that the offending decree would be either modified or abolished. During the summer of 1813 he repeatedly urged Cathcart to demand significant trade concessions in return for the liberal financial aid given the Tsar.[51] Cathcart made no headway at all, the most Russia would offer was a temporary suspension of the ukase. By the time the war ended, the foreign secretary was still trying to persuade Alexander to abolish the decree.[52]

Britain's relations with Sweden during the closing months of 1813 make plain that subsidies bought London no real influence over her allies' military plans. Following the renewal of the alliance in October, Bernadotte joined the other allies in a drive toward the Rhine. The Prince Royal was to spearhead the advance into the Low Countries, and he adhered to that plan up to the time his troops occupied Hanover. Instead of moving on to the Rhine as planned, Bernadotte swung north and attacked the Danes. By this means, he hoped to force Denmark to cede Norway to him. Castlereagh was furious when he learned this, especially since a few weeks before he had lavishly praised the Prince Royal in the House of Commons for his willingness to subordinate Swedish interest to the greater good of the allied cause.[53] On Christmas Eve, 1813, the foreign secretary bitterly complained to Thornton that the Swedish diversion had probably ended all chance of driving the enemy from the Low Countries during the winter. The Swede was not being subsidized to take Norway! Unless Bernadotte immediately resumed his march to the Low Countries, Thornton was to declare that "the Issues of Subsidy will be suspended." By the time these instructions were handed to Thornton, the Prince Royal had compelled Denmark to make peace with him. The British envoy therefore withheld Castlereagh's ultimatum and Bernadotte led his army toward the Low Countries without knowing that Britain had meant to cut off his funds.[54]

---

51. On April 6, 1813 Castlereagh warned Cathcart that "If the allied courts do not assist us in improving the exchange, they will sacrifice a serious proportion of the Credit placed in London at their disposal" (FO 65/83).

52. Castlereagh to Cathcart, September 18, 1813, FO 65/83; Cathcart to Castlereagh, July 18, 1814, FO 65/93.

53. *Hansard*, XXVII (1813), 135.

54. Castlereagh to Thornton, December 24, 1813, FO 73/80; Scott, *Bernadotte*, pp. 141-142, 146-147.

Castlereagh fumed and grumbled at the economic obscurantism of his allies and their stubborn refusal to welcome British trade. Bernadotte's aberrations both vexed and embarrassed him. Although he occasionally threatened to force compliance from the allies by withholding their subsidies, he hesitated to do so. In the last analysis the major goal was to win the war against France and it could not be jeopardized by quarrels between Britain and her partners over what were, after all, secondary issues.

Far more dangerous was the tendency of the continental allies to overlook the interests of their British ally in the diplomatic discussions they carried on with Napoleon. In part this was due to the absence of any agreement among them as to the specific objectives they hoped to obtain. In order to supply this deficiency, Castlereagh sent his agents in Germany a plan of union based on a clearly defined set of war goals. Cathcart found the Russian ministers cool to the idea and insistent that the existing collection of treaties was entirely satisfactory for the purposes of the coalition.[55] When Aberdeen explained the British proposal to Metternich, the Austrian statesman listened with marked attention and courtesy. But even then he was opening a new channel of communication with France which he hoped would result in a renewal of peace discussions.

Castlereagh was driven to despair by the cavalier manner with which the great powers treated Britain's proposals and ignored her interests. Clearly, Cathcart, Stewart, and Aberdeen were powerless to check this trend, which threatened the future of the alliance. On December 20, 1813 the Cabinet decided that Castlereagh himself must go to allied headquarters to bring the belligerents to agreement.

Difficult as the foreign secretary's mission was to prove, he had one card to play which might prove useful. The 1813 subsidy treaties with the allies were now expiring and they had already begun to inquire what they might be able to count on in 1814. Castlereagh was ready to exploit this "power of the purse" to gain his objective. He had already told Lieven as much, and before the end of 1813 he was able to measure the effect of his words.[56] In the closing weeks of the year, Pozzo di Borgo arrived in London as

55. F. Martens, *Recueil des Traités,* XI, 197.
56. Webster, *Foreign Policy of Castlereagh,* I, 162-163.

a special envoy of the Tsar to join with Lieven in demanding a prompt decision on the question of subsidies for the coming year. Castlereagh was pleased to learn from Pozzo that Alexander was at last ready to support the formation of a single alliance among the four great powers if Britain really insisted upon it.[57]

The instructions Castlereagh carried with him on his mission had been prepared by himself, endorsed by the Cabinet, and signed by the Prince Regent. They set forth the limits within which he was to work to bring the four powers into a union strong enough to attain its goal either by diplomacy or arms. Subsidies to be paid by Britain during the coming year were specifically mentioned, but the subject was given little space. Achievement of an effective union against Napoleon was the prime object and to finance such a union the foreign secretary was authorized to divide £5,000,000 among the three great powers.[58]

57. F. Martens, *Recueil des Traités,* XI, 197-198.
58. Castlereagh's Instructions, dated December 26, 1813, are to be found in FO 139/1. The document is printed in Webster, *British Diplomacy,* pp. 123-126.

XIV

THE FINAL COALITION

H.M.S.*Erebus* waited at Harwich to convey the foreign secretary to Holland, but a dense fog smothered the coast and the New Year had arrived before the frigate at last stood out to sea. Castlereagh probably attached no significance to the fact that the vessel carrying him was named for that cheerless zone through which the Greeks believed all souls passed on their way to Hades. His destination was allied headquarters, not Hades, but he could only guess what fate awaited him there. One month before, Napoleon had accepted an invitation sent by Metternich in the name of the great powers to renew peace talks with them, but the Frankfort proposals, which offered peace to France on the basis of her natural frontiers, were now considered too generous by some of the allies. Some sort of negotiation would probably take place and the Cabinet was anxious that Castlereagh take part in order to protect Britain's interest and obligations. Should the discussions prove fruitless, the allied powers would have to press on with the war in hope either of toppling Napoleon or forcing him to accept such terms as they might decide to impose.

So long as the issue of peace or war was still in doubt, Britain must overlook no opportunity to strengthen the striking power of the allied war machine. Before leaving London, Castlereagh concluded an agreement with Hanover binding the Electorate to send 15,000 men into the field in return for an annual subsidy of £600,000.[1] Britain was also anxious to support the Dutch war of

---

1. The Treaty with Hanover, December 5, 1813 (FO 93/40 [1]), enabled Britain to transfer the Russian German Legion to the Hanoverian service. This corps, now numbering about 6,000 men, would be counted as part of the 15,000 troops the Electorate had undertaken to supply.

liberation which had broken out in November 1813. An expeditionary force, under Sir Thomas Graham, was sent to Holland with a generous supply of arms for the Dutch. The Prince of Orange was given £200,000 on leaving for his homeland at the close of the year to head the liberation movement.[2] On reaching The Hague early in January, Castlereagh assured the Prince of continued British support in money and arms during the months ahead.[3] By this time, Bernadotte had forced the Danes to surrender Norway to him and he was now reported to be on his way to help drive the enemy from the Low Countries. Castlereagh was a little annoyed to learn that the Prince Royal's army included 10,000 of his former enemies, whose service Thornton had obtained, without authority, by granting a £400,000 a year subsidy to Denmark.[4]

After a few days at The Hague, Castlereagh pushed on to Basel where he arrived on January 18 to find the division in the council of the allies even greater than he had feared. At the moment, the major question was whether to enter into peace discussions with Napoleon. Russia and Prussia now scorned the Frankfort proposals and argued that their recent military successes had nullified that offer. Metternich lived in fear that Alexander would try to substitute Bernadotte for Bonaparte as ruler of the French. If the Tsar persisted in this madness, Austria would withdraw from the war. Castlereagh's immediate task was to mediate this quarrel so that the allies could at least present a common front to the enemy. After a few days of discussion with Metternich and Hardenberg at Basel, he set out for the Tsar's headquarters at Langres where he finally achieved an agreement which at least temporarily closed the rift within the coalition. Peace talks would be undertaken with

2. By the end of 1813 the Dutch had received arms and equipment for 20,000 men valued at £219,996. See An Account of the several payments made in the year ended 5th January, 1814 . . . , FO 83/25. See also G. J. Renier, *Great Britain and the Establishment of the Kingdom of the Netherlands, 1813-1815* (London, 1930), pp. 144-145.

3. On learning that Britain expected to be repaid for the money and supplies given the Dutch, the Prince of Orange declined to accept further assistance. See Renier, *Great Britain and the Netherlands*, p. 145.

4. Thornton signed a treaty of peace and subsidy with Denmark on January 14, 1814 (FO 93/29[2]). The day before, Castlereagh had written from Mühlheim warning Thornton to undertake "no pecuniary arrangement" with the Danes "without express authority for so doing" (*Correspondence of Castlereagh*, IX, 161). The Cabinet disliked the treaty, but grudgingly approved it (Bathurst to Thornton, April 14, 1814, FO 73/89). For Liverpool's objections to the treaty, see his letter to Castlereagh of February 4, 1814, in Webster, *Foreign Policy of Castlereagh*, I, 519.

France, but hostilities would not be suspended. As a basis for these discussions, the four powers proposed to offer France her pre-war frontiers rather than the natural boundaries contained in the Frankfort proposals. Because of numerous delays, the conference at Châtillon did not begin until February 7. Since the allied foreign ministers were not themselves to participate, Britain was represented in the negotiation by Cathcart, Stewart, and Aberdeen.

Castlereagh, meanwhile, turned to a consideration of the new subsidy agreements with the allies which would be called for in the event the Châtillon meetings came to nothing. He had already discussed the matter in general terms with Nesselrode, but it was not until February 9 that he put on paper a proposal to create a single alliance among the four powers, financed by British subsidies.[5] A copy of this plan was sent the Russian foreign minister, but none went either to Metternich or Hardenberg.

There was good reason for Castlereagh's decision to open the matter with Nesselrode in advance of the other ministers. In the Reichenbach treaty of 1813, the Tsar had received the larger share of British subsidy money greatly to the annoyance of Prussia. It was now Castlereagh's intention to provide for an equal distribution of the 1814 subsidy among the three major powers. This could be justified on several grounds. It would correspond with the spirit of the Teplitz Treaty (September 9, 1813), which bound each of the three continental allies to maintain at least 150,000 troops in the field against France.[6] It would also provide some redress for Prussia who had received less than her due in the distribution of the Reichenbach subsidy.[7] No matter how valid such considerations might appear, Castlereagh would have to make a special effort to persuade Russia to yield the preferred position she had enjoyed in the division of the 1813 subsidy.

The sketch of an alliance which the foreign secretary sent Nesselrode on February 9 included most of the features finally

5. Castlereagh to Nesselrode, February 9, 1814 (Châtillon), FO 92/2.
6. F. Martens, *Recueil des Traités,* VII, 105-112.
7. Accurate figures on the size of the allied armies are difficult to obtain. The following figures show their size at the time of the invasion of France and represent the total number of soldiers, including reserves and those outside the major battle area: Russia, 278,000; Austria, 230,000; Prussia, 162,000. See Archibald Alison, *History of Europe from the Commencement of the French Revolution to the Restoration of the Bourbons in MDCCCXV* (Edinburgh and London, 1849-1850), XII, 639.

incorporated in the Chaumont treaty. The four powers were to join in a single league, binding themselves to act together in military operations or in peace discussions with the enemy. Rather than specifying the actual number of troops each power was to supply, Castlereagh simply proposed that each undertake to exert "the utmost energies . . . in the vigorous prosecution of the present war against France." Equal division of British subsidies among the allies was specified, but the total amount Britain would provide for the year was left blank. There was also provision for mutual protection against renewed French aggression after the return of peace. Each power was to send 60,000 troops to the aid of any of her partners attacked by France. Britain would have the right to meet her obligation either by hiring troops or by making a money payment to the attacked power.[8]

Before Nesselrode could respond to this proposal, the allies were thrown into confusion by the Tsar's decision to suspend the Châtillon discussions. The course of the war was now so favorable that Alexander soon hoped to enter the enemy capital and dictate his own terms of peace. Metternich threatened to make a separate peace with France unless the Tsar gave up this folly. Once again Castlereagh worked to hold the allies together, and the Tsar was finally persuaded to take a more reasonable position. By now, however, the fortunes of war were beginning to favor France and it was Napoleon's turn to delay the negotiation. The balance on the battlefield soon tipped once more toward the allies, and by the end of February 1814 they demanded that France either accept their terms or end the Châtillon conferences.

The time had come for Castlereagh to discuss the future of the war alliance with all the foreign ministers, and on March 1 he sent each of them the proposal made a few weeks before to Nesselrode. The plan was discussed by the four ministers two days later and it was accepted in principle. On the evening of March 9 at Chaumont, they signed the treaties which made up their new alliance.

The Chaumont agreements specifically bound each of the four powers to keep at least 150,000 effective troops in the field against the enemy. Britain would divide £5,000,000 equally among

8. Castlereagh to Nesselrode, February 9, 1814 (Châtillon), FO 92/2.

her three allies during the year. Payments were to be made in London each month, retroactive to the first of the year. Should peace be concluded with France, subsidies would be due to the end of the month in which the treaty was signed. One provision appeared which had not been a part of Castlereagh's original proposal: the three allies were to be given an additional grant of money at the close of the war to help meet their demobilization costs. This "return money" would equal a two months' subsidy in the case of Prussia and Austria, while Russia would be given twice that amount out of consideration for the greater distance her armies were from their own country. A twenty year mutual defense pact was also provided binding each of the four powers to put 60,000 men under arms in the event of a French attack on a member nation. Britain was to have the option either of supplying the specified number of men (which might include mercenaries), or paying the attacked power an annual subsidy of £1,300,000.[9]

Creation of the four-power alliance was a personal triumph for Castlereagh since it achieved most of the goals which he originally desired.[10] He had not haggled over subsidy money; the £5,000,000 promised the allies was the entire amount the Cabinet had empowered him to offer. In fact, he had exceeded his instructions by promising that Britain, too, would maintain an army of 150,000 men in the coming campaign. This had been urged on him by the allies, and most especially by the Tsar. National pride compelled him to agree, even though this obligation, together with the pledge of £5,000,000 in subsidies, imposed a double burden on Great Britain.[11] The only really new feature having to do with subsidies in the Chaumont agreement was that calling for an equal division of British money among the three continental allies.[12] Austria and Prussia naturally approved this, but how had Russia been brought to agree?

9. Although dated March 1, 1814, the Chaumont treaties were actually signed on March 9. Castlereagh concluded separate but identical treaties with Russia (FO 93/81 [16], [17]); Austria (FO 93/11 [8], [9]); and Prussia (FO 93/78 [8], [9]).

10. Webster, *Foreign Policy of Castlereagh*, I, 229.

11. Castlereagh to Liverpool, March 10, 1814, FO 92/3; Castlereagh to W. Hamilton, March 10, 1814, *Correspondence of Castlereagh*, IX, 335-336.

12. Webster failed to note that the equal division of British subsidies provided for in the Chaumont treaties was different from the subsidy agreements of the previous year. He observed that the Chaumont treaties represented "only a consolidation of subsidy treaties such as were already in being" (*Foreign Policy of Castlereagh*, I, 227).

When Nesselrode first learned of the British proposal to subsidize the allies equally, he entered a strong protest. The maintenance of the Russian army in western Europe imposed an especially heavy strain on the Tsar's resources, still suffering from the devastating effects of the 1812 invasion.[13] Nesselrode's description of Russia's economic misery was supported by independent evidence which the foreign secretary could not discount. Letters reaching him from Lord Walpole, the acting British minister at St. Petersburg, painted a gloomy picture of the Tsar's finances.[14]

Russia's distress was the major topic of a conversation Castlereagh had at this time with Count Razumovsky, the Tsar's representative at the Châtillon conference. Razumovsky reminded the foreign secretary that two years before Russia had invited Britain to assume responsibility for the repayment of her debt with the Dutch banks. Then the British government declined the invitation. The matter was now brought forward once more, but in a somewhat different form. Since Russian troops were currently driving the enemy from Holland, the Dutch were under some obligation to the Tsar. What better way for the Prince of Orange to show his gratitude than by taking over Alexander's £6,000,000 debt to his own country's bankers? Should the Dutch find the burden too heavy to bear, perhaps Britain would be willing to assume some share of it herself.[15]

Castlereagh's immediate reaction to this ingenious suggestion was hostile. The obvious plea for preferential treatment was at cross-purposes with his own wish to aid the three allies equally. Prussia and Austria likewise had large debts with Dutch bankers. "And why pay Russia rather than Austria and Prussia?" he asked. Parliament would never support such a plan.[16]

In spite of Castlereagh's rebuff, Nesselrode brought the matter up again two weeks later and hinted that unless Britain assumed the Russian debt, Alexander might refuse to renew his alliance with her. The foreign secretary ignored this empty threat for he knew that Alexander's need for subsidies was so pressing that he

13. Nesselrode to Castlereagh, March, 1814, FO 139/5.
14. Some of Walpole's letters are printed in vol. IX of *Correspondence of Castlereagh.* See especially his letter to Castlereagh of March 22, 1814, pp. 374-376.
15. Castlereagh to Clancarty, February 20, 1814, *ibid.,* IX, 284.
16. Castlereagh to Clancarty, February 20, 1814, *ibid.*

would not dare make the debt assumption a sine qua non. Considerations of a different nature, however, were slowly bringing Castlereagh to take a more sympathetic view of the question. He was beginning to see how the Tsar's debts might be used to further his own plan to create an enlarged Kingdom of the Netherlands. If repayment of the £6,000,000 debt was made a joint obligation on Britain, Russia, and Holland, Alexander would have a very real interest in insuring the success of the Dutch kingdom that Castlereagh was anxious to establish. On the day before the Chaumont agreements were signed, he decided to sound out Lord Liverpool on the matter: "I am aware," he wrote the prime minister, "that this transaction differs essentially in its character from any aid which the Parliament of Great Britain has hitherto been prevailed upon to afford to a foreign State; and yet practically, in its political influence, it may be of more real importance, both upon the war itself and upon the future happy construction of the Continent, than a greater sum provided in the ordinary shape of a subsidy." Castlereagh left no doubt of his own view: "If I am enabled to give encouragement to these views on the part of Russia, I am of opinion that it may be attended with the most beneficial consequences, in bringing the contest in which we are engaged to a satisfactory issue."[17]

The conclusion of the Chaumont alliance could not wait until the problem of the Tsar's debts had been settled, however. On the eve of the signing of that alliance, Castlereagh sent Nesselrode an official note on the subject. He promised to bring the question before the Cabinet at the earliest possible moment and declared that, "Whatever may be the difficulties attending the suggestion I am confident it will be considered in that spirit of friendship & liberality which has invariably marked the auspicious alliance between our respective Courts."[18]

For the moment, Russia must be satisfied with this assurance together with the promise of twice as much "return money" as the German powers were to receive. On this basis Nesselrode accepted the equal division of subsidies provided for in the Chaumont alliance.[19]

17. Castlereagh to Liverpool, March 8, 1814, *ibid.*, IX, 327-329.
18. Castlereagh to Nesselrode, March 8, 1814, FO 139/5.
19. The Russian treaty also continued the additional £500,000 British grant for the upkeep of the Tsar's squadron in her care.

Russia was to be disappointed with the sequel. Despite Castlereagh's warm endorsement, Liverpool and Vansittart strongly opposed the Russian debt assumption plan. With Britain groaning under a massive indebtedness of her own, Parliament was in no mood to absorb the Tsar's deficit. The prime minister quietly shelved the matter in hopes that it would die. Fortunately, the ending of the war in April freed London from further Russian demands for financial aid.[20]

Subsidy arrangements with the allies for 1814 were essentially the same as in the previous year, except for the fact that the three major allies were to share equally. In this Castlereagh simply applied the principle laid down by Pitt almost ten years before. On the eve of the Third Coalition, the prime minister hoped to create an army of 400,000 to be subsidized at the standard rate of £1,250,000 for every 100,000 soldiers the three powers provided. The Chaumont treaties almost exactly followed this idea since the £5,000,000 British subsidy was to be equally divided among the allies on the assumption that each would furnish at least 150,000 troops.

Pitt would have been astounded at the extent of Britain's total subsidy commitment for 1814. In addition to the £5,000,000 pledged to the major powers, Castlereagh had undertaken to pay at least that much again to the other allies. Since 1812 Sweden, Hanover, Holland, Denmark, and Sardinia had been swept into the coalition, thereby giving each of them a claim on Britain's bounty.[21] More than £3,000,000 was spent to help the Peninsular powers during the last year of the war, the larger part of which went to pay and support their troops serving with Wellington.

With the signing of the Chaumont treaties, a renewal of the war with Napoleon was a certainty. The breakdown of the Châtillon discussions occurred ten days later, by which time the noose had been drawn still tighter around France. Bordeaux declared for the

20. Liverpool to Castlereagh, April 14, 1814, Webster, *Foreign Policy of Castlereagh,* I, 532-533. Castlereagh did not bother to seek the opinion of the Dutch on this issue. In May 1814 The Hague learned of the business for the first time. When pressed, the foreign secretary admitted to the Dutch that he had conducted discussions with Russia on the matter (Renier, *Great Britain and the Netherlands,* p. 296).

21. On February 3, 1814 Britain signed a treaty with Sardinia (FO 93/87 [1B]) by which she agreed to pay and equip a force of 3,000 Sardinians who had fallen into her hands as prisoners of war. This corps was to be sent to Italy for service against the French.

Bourbons in the middle of March, and before the month ended, Wellington's army appeared before Toulouse. Two hundred thousand allied troops, commanded by Blücher and Schwarzenberg, stormed the heights of Montmartre on March 30, and the next day the Tsar and the King of Prussia entered Paris. The conclusion of a formal treaty of peace with France took longer than Castlereagh expected, but it was finally signed on May 30. Britain was thereby spared the necessity of paying her Chaumont allies an extra month's subsidy.

Now that the war was over, Britain was anxious to stop the payments to the allies as quickly as possible. The Treaty of Paris automatically halted her debt to Russia, Prussia, and Austria although they were still entitled to the "return money" provided by the Chaumont agreement. Closing out engagements with the other powers would require more time since each had to be handled separately. The settling of all accounts involved two steps: first, the amount of money owed each ally must be exactly determined; and second, arrangements would have to be made to remit these sums. With only a few unimportant exceptions, all subsidy treaties had been extinguished by the close of 1814 and nearly all final payments had been made.

Since the Treaty of Paris had been signed in May, the Chaumont allies were entitled to five months' subsidy, together with "return money." Austria and Prussia would each receive £972,222 while, thanks to the promise of double "return money," Russia could expect to receive £1,250,000.[22] All that remained was for the Treasury to pay these sums. Even before the war formally ended, the Cabinet began to close out the smaller subsidy agreements. The first to go was the unpopular obligation to Denmark which Thornton had undertaken in January 1814. Denmark was informed that the subsidy would be ended in May, although one extra month's payment would be made as a *douceur.*[23] The Swedish subsidy was also extinguished as soon as it could be done

---

22. Herries Subsidy Account, AO 3/1088.

23. Thornton paid the Danes £35,000 in bills drawn upon Rothschilds bank in Amsterdam (Thornton to Castlereagh, May 10, 1814, FO 73/91). The balance due (£86,917) was remitted to Denmark's agents in London between May and September 1814 (Army Ledgers, PMG 2/113, 59, 60, and 76).

without unduly offending Bernadotte. Monthly payments of £100,000 would be continued through August, after which the treaty would be considered as formally at an end.[24] Britain's other obligation to Sweden proved more difficult to meet: the pledge given in 1813 to transfer the island of Guadaloupe to Bernadotte at the end of the war. Since the Bourbon government of France pressed for a return of the island, Castlereagh had to cast about for an equivalent. During the summer, Sweden made it known that a British payment of £1,000,000 would be regarded as a satisfactory substitute, and in August a treaty was concluded between the two governments providing for such a payment.[25]

The Sicilian subsidy proved harder to end and, in fact, was continued into 1815. Ever since the French drove King Ferdinand from Naples, that monarch had yearned to return. It now appeared, however, that the Kingdom of Naples, currently ruled by Murat, might survive the deluge which had swept away the other Napoleonic vassal states. The allies themselves were not of one mind whether Ferdinand should be restored. Final settlement of this question would have to wait until the Congress had assembled at Vienna, and, consequently, the Cabinet decided to retain its military force in Sicily. Although the subsidy would be considered formally ended in August 1814, something would have to be done to placate the Palermo regime; additional monthly payments of half the usual amount would be made until the future of Naples had been settled.[26]

Closing out the Portuguese and Spanish subsidies involved especially difficult problems which were never satisfactorily solved. The Portuguese and Spanish troops serving with Wellington were sent back to their own countries following the surrender of France, but London was ready to continue the subsidies for at least a few more months. In August 1814 Castlereagh informed the Lisbon Council of Regency that October would mark the termination of the British aid program which had begun six years

24. Bathurst to the Lords of the Treasury, October 3, 1814, FO 73/94.
25. See William H. Robson, "New Light on Lord Castlereagh's Diplomacy," *Journal of Modern History,* 3 (1931), 198-218. The payment of the £1,000,000 was conditional on the union of Holland and Belgium and was therefore not made until 1815.
26. Bathurst to A'Court, September 7, 1814, FO 70/65.

before.[27] The accounts of the Portuguese subsidy were so confused that it was impossible to determine whether British aid had exceeded or fallen below what the council had a right to expect. Every effort would be made to clarify this, although October 1814 would be the terminal date for the subsidy.[28] Now began the "battle of the bookkeepers," which nearly led to an open break between London and Lisbon. The two governments had kept separate accounts of the British aid and there was ample room for honest disagreement about the monetary value to be assigned to shipments of supplies from England. British records were in such disorder that it was not until 1822 that London had an account of its payments which it believed reasonably correct. The Portuguese Regency had long resented its ally's highhanded methods and, in the fall of 1814, it refused outright to accept a consignment of grain sent by Britain as part payment of the aid due for that year.[29] Anglo-Portuguese relations had steadily deteriorated during the final years of the war and they were now to grow still worse.

The Spanish subsidy proved troublesome to settle since Madrid wished to use Britain's desire for a commercial treaty as a lever to obtain still more money. In February 1814 the Spanish government announced that it was now ready to negotiate such a pact with its ally. During the discussions which followed, Henry Wellesley was frequently reminded of Madrid's desperate need for money. Perhaps Britain could continue the subsidy during the remainder of the year even though the war had ended? Spain would also be grateful if Downing Street supported her efforts to borrow £10,000,000 in London.[30] As proof of her good faith, she was ready to conclude an immediate alliance and commercial agreement which would go at least part way toward meeting Britain's wishes. The treaty, signed by Wellesley on July 5, did indeed create an alliance between the two powers and extended a few commercial privileges to Britain. Provision was made for the

27. Writing to Thomas Sydenham at Lisbon on August 8, 1814, Castlereagh expressed the hope that the Portuguese forces would be kept "in a state of competent organization" (FO 63/174).

28. Britain continued to make small remittances throughout 1814-1815.

29. R. Lushington to W. Hamilton, Oct. 4, 1814, FO 63/180.

30. H. Wellesley to Castlereagh, February 26, 1814 and June 17, 1814; FO 72/159, FO 72/160.

re-establishment of commercial relations between them on the same basis which had existed in 1796. No significant concessions were made to Britain's desire for free trade with the Spanish colonies, however. Presumably this would be arranged in a supplementary convention at some future time.[31]

Castlereagh was tolerably satisfied with the Spanish treaty, but he made clear to Henry Wellesley that Britain would never guarantee a £10,000,000 loan for Madrid. "Your Excellency well knows," he wrote, "that since the period of the Austrian loan, all such Transactions are viewed in this Country in no other Light than as a Subsidy granted under a less generous Name." Originally, the Cabinet planned to halt all payments at the end of July, but if Spain undertook to abolish the slave trade within five years, Britain would pay her £800,000 during the remainder of 1814. A modest loan might also be arranged if the slave trade was stopped immediately.[32] This offer appeared so puny to Madrid that it brought forth a counterproposal: the slave trade would be abolished within five years in return for both the £800,000 subsidy balance and the promise of a loan. The Cabinet regarded this proposition as outrageous and adhered to its original decision to end the Spanish subsidy.[33] Castlereagh's future negotiation with Spain over the slave trade was therefore separated from the problem of war subsidies.

Although the end of the war freed Britain from monetary obligations to the allies, she still suffered from a serious drain on her manpower. The American war continued to drag on, and in the summer of 1814 a large part of Wellington's army was transferred to North America. During that same summer, however, the four great powers each agreed to maintain 75,000 men under arms on the Continent while the Congress of Vienna was in session.[34] In this way, Britain acquired an obligation which it would be difficult for her to meet. Parliament was naturally anxious to demobilize as quickly as possible, and by the end of

31. Spain did agree that in the event her colonial markets ever were opened Britain would enjoy a most-favored-nation status in them (Treaty with Spain, July 5, 1814, FO 93/99 [7B]).
32. Castlereagh to H. Wellesley, July 30, 1814, FO 72/158.
33. Bathurst to H. Wellesley, September 9, 1814, FO 72/158.
34. The treaties of June 29, 1814, between Britain and Russia, FO 93/81 (19); Prussia, FO 93/78 (10); and Austria, FO 93/11 (10).

1814, 47,000 men had been eliminated from the army establishment.[35] There were still British garrisons in Belgium, Sicily, and Genoa but their total fell considerably below the 75,000 men she had promised to keep under arms. It was therefore decided to retain the 15,000 subsidized Hanoverians who had served Britain in the Low Countries.[36] This decision was dictated by economy, for the expense of the Hanoverian mercenaries was appreciably less than the cost of maintaining a British force of the same size. Even with the Hanoverians, Britain still required 22,000 more troops to meet her quota. To make good this deficiency, Castlereagh offered to pay Prussia to maintain as part of her own army the additional number of troops Britain was treaty-bound to supply. This was in accord with the spirit of the Chaumont alliance, and, using the formula set forth in that convention, Britain gave Prussia £355,333 for this purpose during the eight months their bargain was in effect.[37]

Settling the subsidy accounts inevitably bred disagreement and unpleasantness. When Austria learned that the value of British arms sent her during 1813-1814 was to be deducted from the subsidy due her by the Chaumont agreement, she heatedly protested. After all, the subsidies being paid to Prussia and Russia were not being similarly adjusted. Furthermore, a part of the war supplies sent her were not received until the war had ended. Since the amount at issue was small (less than £400,000) Castlereagh yielded to the Hofburg's demands as a matter of policy.[38] The Russians made themselves most unpopular with British Treasury agents, and their imperious demands for immediate payment of the subsidies drove the commissary-in-chief nearly to despair.[39] Difficulties also developed with Prussia, who was being paid to

35. Fortescue, *British Army*, X, 228.
36. The British forces in Belgium during the summer of 1814 consisted of the subsidized Hanoverians, the King's German Legion, and the British expeditionary force sent to Holland under Graham during the past winter. For reasons of expediency, supreme command of this force was vested in the Prince of Orange. This provided London with the opportunity to propose that half the cost of the Hanoverians be borne by Holland, a suggestion the Dutch dutifully accepted (J. P. Moirer to G. Harrison, September, 1814, FO 37/75).
37. See Castlereagh's letter to the Prussian chargé d'affaires, Gruehm, of June 6, 1815, FO 64/101.
38. Merveldt to Bathurst, September 13, 1814, FO 7/113; Castlereagh to Metternich, October 8, 1814, FO 7/113.
39. Herries, *Memoir*, I, 90.

carry on her own military establishment a part of the 75,000 man police force for which Britain was responsible. Prussia insisted that those payments be increased on the grounds that British troops garrisoned in the Mediterranean could not honestly be included in the 75,000 quota Britain was bound to maintain "on the Continent." This was too much for the foreign secretary, and he rejected the Prussian demand even though the resulting ill-will badly strained relations between London and Berlin.[40]

The British Treasury was obliged to provide £10,000,000 to meet all the subsidy debts to the allies for 1814.[41] Of this sum about £3,000,000 represented aid to Portugal and Spain, almost all of which was paid by the end of the summer. The £7,000,000 due the other allies had still to be remitted by the time the war ended in May. It had originally been intended to pay all subsidies in London and this method had been specified in the Chaumont treaties with the great powers. The Treasury soon had misgivings about making payments in this manner. Once subsidies had been paid in London, the allied governments would probably transfer the money to their own accounts on the Continent. Such massive conveyances might adversely affect the rate of exchange between Britain and Europe. To prevent this, it was decided to make payments both in London and on the Continent where credits were now available to Britain. Since the war was over, a British subsidy office was established in Paris from which payments to the allies could be made as a supplement to those in London.[42]

Responsibility for managing the subsidy remittances fell to John C. Herries, the commissary-in-chief, who left for Paris in April 1814 to supervise financial operations there. Payments made in London and in Paris would have to be delicately balanced to avoid unnecessary damage to Britain's rate of exchange. Issuance of bills of exchange required careful handling to prevent speculators amassing them to the disadvantage of the Treasury. Precautions would also have to be taken to discourage counterfeiters who were

40. Hardenberg to Gruehm, May 13, 1815, FO 64/101; Castlereagh to Gruehm, June 6, 1815, FO 64/101.
41. This includes "federative paper" payments.
42. Vansittart to Castlereagh, April 28, 1814, *Correspondence of Castlereagh*, IX, 520-522.

already busy issuing spurious bills.[43] The partnership formed between Herries and Nathan Rothschild in 1811 took on special significance now that Rothschild's international banking connections were available for the use of the commissary-in-chief.

In remitting money from Paris between 1814 and 1816, Herries drew on credits available to him at nine financial centers in Europe. So efficiently did he work that, by the close of 1814, nearly all the subsidies due the allies had been paid.[44] If anything, Herries moved too quickly to suit Lord Castlereagh, who was encountering difficulties with some of the powers at the Vienna Congress. In January 1815 the foreign secretary urged Lord Bathurst to have Herries slacken the pace of his remittances: "I beg you will not give any money at present to any of the Continental Powers. The poorer they are kept, the better, to

---

43. Jean Baptiste Capefigue, *Histoire des Grandes Opérations Financières; Banques, Bourses, Emprunts* . . . (Paris, 1855-60), III, 2. Herries' management of subsidy payments between 1811 and 1816 has still to receive the attention it deserves. Some hint of the complexity of his task is revealed in his letter to George Harrison of February 28, 1822, which accompanied his final statement of subsidy payments (AO 3/1088): "It was entrusted to me by their Lordships to effect the application of this very large Sum in the discharge of foreign subsidies . . . by an arrangement entirely new which consisted principally in providing the Specie required for these Services thro' a single and confidential agency, by means of which it was collected with greater certainty and more economy; and much of the difficulty and embarrassment which had arisen in this branch of the Public Service was removed. The details of this arrangment embraced every mode by which foreign currencies could be obtained for British money or Credit; such as the purchase of Specie in all the markets of the world; the conversion of Bullion into coin at our own and at foreign mints; the coining of foreign money in England & the purchase of bills of remittance in such manner as to conceal they were for a Public Account; the negotiation of British Paper on the Continent at long date to avoid pressure upon the Exchange, etc., etc."

44. Of the £42,500,000 paid out by Herries between 1811 and 1816, Rothschilds bank handled at least half of it. See Count Egon Caesar Corti, *The Rise of the House of Rothschild*, trans. B. and B. Lunn (New York, 1928), p. 169. Herries' account (AO 3/1088) shows the following remittances during 1814 which paid off the subsidy debts of 1813, as well as those of 1814:

Austria	£ 939,523
Russia	1,925,834
Prussia	1,037,268
Hanover	525,000
Sweden	800,000
Denmark	121,917
Sicily	316,666
	£5,666,208

Payments to Spain and Portugal do not appear in this account.

prevent them from quarrelling. Time enough to settle accounts, when we know who deserves it."[45]

At Vienna Castlereagh again tried to use British money as a tool to persuade Spain and Portugal to end the slave trade. In the case of Portugal, he discovered that her agreement could be bought. In January 1815 Portugal promised to abolish the trade north of the equator in return for an outright gift of £300,000 and Britain's promise to repay the £600,000 borrowed by the Regent in London in 1809. Agreement with Spain was harder to win, and it was not until 1817 that a bargain was struck with her which also involved the payment of British money.[46]

The old problem of Russia's debt came to the surface once more on the eve of the Vienna Congress. Castlereagh was prepared to assume at least a part of the £6,000,000 debt if the Tsar would agree to the union of Belgium and Holland, but he was unable to overcome the Cabinet's determined opposition. Alexander now let it be known that he might have to make the assumption of his debts a sine qua non to the union of the Low Countries. Since this was one of the cardinal features of Castlereagh's plan for the reconstruction of Europe, the foreign secretary knew that he must come to terms with the Tsar. The great difficulty was the Cabinet's reluctance to endorse the plan. To make the assumption acceptable to ministers, Castlereagh undertook to win an additional concession from Russia. For nearly two years he had vainly urged the Tsar to liberalize his tariff policy to benefit British commerce. In July 1814 he hinted to Nesselrode that Parliamentary approval of the debt assumption would come easier if "the commercial System of Russia towards Great Britain should be previously placed upon a different and more friendly footing than has latterly prevailed." Although Russia did not respond, Castlereagh was not discouraged. Even before the assembling of the Vienna Congress, Britain had begun to press Holland to join with her in underwriting repayment of half the Russian debt.[47]

Alexander's plan for the reconstruction of Poland created a serious crisis at Vienna and pushed the Russian debt issue into the

45. Castlereagh to Bathurst, January 30, 1815, *Correspondence of Castlereagh,* X, 248.
46. There were two treaties with Portugal, signed on January 21 and 22, 1815; FO 93/77 (10), (11). Also see Webster, *Foreign Policy of Castlereagh,* II, 459.
47. Castlereagh to Nesselrode, July 11, 1814, FO 65/95; Robson, "New Light on Lord Castlereagh's Diplomacy," pp. 213-214.

background. Until the Tsar proved reasonable Castlereagh would not give him a shilling. Liverpool was as hostile as ever to the debt assumption and even Castlereagh conceded that it would be folly to strengthen "the credit of a Calmuck Prince to overturn Europe."[48] The foreign secretary still hoped that Alexander would finally back down. In this spirit, he wrote to Vansittart, warning the chancellor of the exchequer, "If his Imperial Majesty shall change his tone, and make a reasonable arrangement of frontier on the side of Poland, if he shall allow the other European arrangements to be equitably settled, including those of Holland, and alter his tariff besides, then, my dear Vansittart, I must come upon you for my pound of flesh."[49]

The Polish crisis soon passed, and the Tsar proved as ready to compromise on the other points as Castlereagh wished. By mid-February 1815 an agreement had been reached between Britain, Russia, and Holland regarding the Tsar's debts. Britain and Holland each undertook to repay one quarter of the Tsar's debt, which portion, with accumulated interest, amounted to £2,272,727. The remaining half of the loan would continue to be a charge on Russia. A dissolution of the Kingdom of the Netherlands would free Britain and Holland from their debt obligations, a proviso Castlereagh described to Liverpool as "a most valuable guarantee on the part of Russia of those possessions to the House of Orange." He was also able to inform the prime minister that Alexander would soon carry through a major revision in his tariff policy to the benefit of Britain's merchants.[50]

The foreign secretary postponed the conversion of this agreement into a treaty until May 1815, when agents of the three powers signed the Russian-Dutch Loan Convention. Although the Cabinet disliked the whole business, it finally approved the treaty at Castlereagh's insistence.[51] The financial obligation im-

48. As late as November 2, 1814 Liverpool warned Castlereagh to steer clear of the Russian debt problem and declared that for Britain to absorb a part of that debt "would be in principle one of the most difficult questions to defend that ever was brought forward in Parliament" (Yonge, *Liverpool*, II, 51; Castlereagh to Vansittart, November 11, 1814, *Correspondence of Castlereagh*, X, 200).

49. Castlereagh to Vansittart, November 11, 1814,*Correspondence of Castlereagh*, X, 200.

50. Castlereagh to Liverpool, no. 69, February 13, 1815, FO 92/12; Nesselrode to Castlereagh, February 14, 1815, FO 92/12.

51. The Russian-Dutch Loan Convention, May 19, 1815, FO 93/81(22),(23). Castlereagh's delay was unfortunate. Napoleon had returned to power by the spring of 1815, and Russia accordingly demanded an important modification in the terms of the

posed on Britain by the treaty was relatively light: repayment of her share of the principal with interest computed at 5 percent per year. Long-term amortization was provided by means of a 1 percent annual sinking fund, on the basis of which the total annual charge to Britain amounted to £136,363.[52]

Parliament's reception of the Russian-Dutch Loan Convention bore out Liverpool's gloomy prophecy. When the text of the agreement was presented to the Commons in June 1815, opposition leaders attacked it vociferously. Samuel Whitbread charged that a large part of the debt had been incurred by Catherine the Great to help finance her wars with Turkey. The British government of the day had vainly tried to protect the Turks and, as a consequence, had suffered the humiliation of Oczakoff. Now Pitt's disciples were asking the nation to pay for the mortification which their leader had suffered at the Tsarina's hands. Ministers winced at the charge, especially since they were unable to deny it.[53] Thanks to the fact that Napoleon was again loose in Europe and that Britain and Russia were allies, Castlereagh won parliamentary approval of the treaty. Opposition leaders rang the changes of Oczakoff, but they mustered only nineteen votes in Commons against the agreement.[54]

In February 1815 Castlereagh prepared to leave Vienna where, for the past five months, he had wrestled with the problems of European resettlement. All the major issues had now been settled, and he could no longer ignore the Cabinet's demand that he return to London. What little business remained could be entrusted to the Duke of Wellington, who had recently arrived to join the British delegation. The Coalition of 1814 was by now almost

---

original agreement. If Belgium (or any part of it) were taken from the House of Orange, Britain and Holland would continue to be liable for repayment of the debt, but the extent of their obligation would be reduced in proportion to the loss of population to the Netherlands which would result from the separation of Belgium.

The Cabinet may have found it easier to approve the agreement because in 1814 the Dutch bank of Hope and Co., which held the Russian loan, came under the control of the English banking house of Baring (Jenks, *Migration of British Capital,* p. 33).

52. *British and Foreign State Papers,* ed. by the Librarian of the Foreign Office (London, 1838-1841), II, 385.

53. See Liverpool's evasive answer to this question in the Lords on June 12, 1815, *Hansard,* XXXI (1815), 718.

54. *Ibid.,* XXXI, 756.

entirely dismantled. Nearly all subsidy treaties had been closed out and payments to the allies were about completed. Britain had at last ended her war with the United States and the arrival of the New Year brought a promise of the first real peace which the nation had known in a decade. In this spirit of optimism, Parliament lost no time in cutting back the military establishment and repealing the lucrative but unpopular Property Tax. Before the arrival of spring, however, clouds of war once more darkened the skies. On the first day of March, Napoleon landed on the south coast of France, and within three weeks he re-established his regime at Paris.

Word of Napoleon's escape from Elba had reached Vienna on March 7, and the reports which followed during the next few days confirmed Metternich's prediction that he would make straight for Paris. On March 12 mobilization orders were sent from Vienna to the Russian, Prussian, and Austrian armies.[55] Instinctively, the foreign ministers turned to Wellington for advice and for a promise of British money to help finance the contest which had already begun. The British general insisted that the first step was to determine how many men the allies could put into the field. Two hundred thousand Russians were in winter quarters on the Niemen river, and Alexander offered to create a second army of the same size to hurl against Napoleon. Metternich had 300,000 Austrian soldiers ready to serve in Italy and along the Rhine. One hundred and fifty thousand Prussians together with 60,000 assorted British, Dutch, and Hanoverian troops were already under arms. Thus, at least 700,000 allied troops were available to oppose the military machine Napoleon was constructing.[56]

Impressive as this force appeared on paper, its effectiveness depended upon generous grants of British money. Wellington was beset with demands for subsidies on a more lavish scale than in 1814. Lacking instructions, the Duke could make no promises, although he felt reasonably certain what the Cabinet's decision would be. The three great powers could probably expect Britain to provide them with the same aid specified in the Chaumont treaties one year before; that is, £5,000,000. Predictably Nesselrode

55. Wellington to Castlereagh, March 12, 1815, *Dispatches of Wellington*, XII, 266-268.
56. Protocol of the allied Military Conference, March 17, 1815, FO 139/11.

pressed for special consideration since Russia's needs were far greater than those of the other powers. Would Britain grant an extra subsidy if the Tsar mobilized a force in excess of the 200,000 men now on the Niemen? Wellington rejected the idea at once knowing that Castlereagh had always aimed at an equal division of subsidies among the three powers. Reporting this to London, the Duke observed, "I conceived it would be quite impossible for His Majesty's Government to grant what was required; and that it was best the subject should not now be brought forward." Nevertheless, Wellington sympathized with the allies and urged the Cabinet to go as far as possible in meeting their demands for money.[57]

The union of the four great powers against Napoleon was accomplished in their alliance of March 25, binding each of them to put at least 150,000 effective troops into motion at once. No mention was made of British subsidies since Wellington had still not heard from London. Doubtless, instructions would soon arrive on the basis of which a supplementary agreement could be concluded. The foreign ministers at Vienna were ready to rely on Britain's good faith, but they formally expressed the hope that she would provide them with more than £5,000,000.[58]

Conclusion of the four-power alliance released Wellington from his diplomatic duties and he was soon en route to Belgium in order to assume command of Britain's forces. During the three weeks following Napoleon's return, he had acquitted the responsibility thrust upon him by that event. The Chaumont alliance was now revived, and while Wellington had given the allies a general guarantee of British aid he had made no promise which might embarrass his government.

In London Castlereagh was moving swiftly to resurrect the old coalition which had been so carefully taken apart during the last year. Wellington was to assure the allies that Britain would not fail them in this crisis. *"We* can often *do more* than *we can say,"* he explained to the Duke, "and I see no reason to fear, that the Parliament or the Nation will shrink from supporting the

57. Wellington to Castlereagh, March 18 (no. 14) and March 28, 1815, FO 92/14; Wellington to Castlereagh, March 18, 1815, *Dispatches of Wellington,* XII, 271-273.
58. Treaties of alliance with Russia, FO 93/81 (20); Prussia, FO 93/78 (11); and Austria, FO 93/11 (13); and Protocol of March 25 signed by the Russian, Prussian, and Austrian foreign ministers, FO 92/14.

Continental Powers in whatever System of vigorous Policy they may be prepared to adopt against Buonaparte."[59] A few days later, he sent dispatches to Vienna containing the Cabinet's decision regarding subsidies: £5,000,000 to be equally shared by Russia, Austria, and Prussia during the year.[60] Wellington's prediction was thus fulfilled; the subsidy provisions of the Chaumont alliance would be applied to the present war. It was unreasonable of the allies to expect Britain to pay more. In addition to giving the major powers £5,000,000 she would also have to hire troops to complete her own 150,000 man quota. All this the foreign secretary explained to Wellington's successor at Vienna, Lord Clancarty, and sourly concluded, "We shall not fail them [the allies] in our due scale of Exertion, but the Powers of Europe must not expect us to subsidize all the World, or to go beyond certain limits in point of expence."[61]

Acting on these instructions, Clancarty concluded a subsidy convention with the three great powers which supplemented their alliance of March 25. Its terms exactly conformed to those of the 1814 Chaumont agreement: £5,000,000 divided equally among Russia, Prussia, and Austria and paid in monthly installments during the year. Payments would be made through the month in which a definitive treaty of peace was signed with France. At the end of the war, the German powers were to receive an extra two months' subsidy as "return money," while Russia would be entitled to twice as much.[62]

Britain's refusal to give more than £5,000,000 greatly disappointed the allies and they entered a plea for a supplementary grant which, they argued, was essential to the success of their operations. Castlereagh rejected this demand at once. Parliament was soon to vote £9,000,000 for foreign aid which, together with Britain's own war expenses, would require the reintroduction of the hated Property Tax. Surely, the continental powers did not

---

59. Castlereagh to Wellington, March 14, 1815, FO 139/7. Compare this language with that Castlereagh used in a letter to Thornton on November 29, 1812: "We can do much in support of foreign states . . . , but we must do it our own way" (Webster, *Foreign Policy of Castlereagh*, I, 101).

60. Castlereagh to Wellington, March 24, 1815, FO 92/13.

61. Castlereagh to Clancarty, April 12, 1815, FO 92/16.

62. Treaties of April 30, 1815 with Russia, FO 93/81 (21); Prussia, FO 93/78 (12); and Austria, FO 93/11 (14).

think Britain was made of gold![63] "After the unexampled Efforts of Great Britain in the two last years of the War," the foreign secretary explained to Wellington, "it is not surprizing that all Europe should hope to derive aid from her resources, but the extent to which those exertions were pushed is only an additional reason why they can now only be called forth within certain limits."[64]

But was it true economy for Britain to withold from her allies the additional funds they insisted they must have to deal with the enemy? An extra million pounds spent now might be insurance against having to spend ten times more the next year. Castlereagh himself had warned Wellington against half-measures: "If we are to undertake the job, we must leave nothing to chance. It must be done upon the largest scale."[65] Under the pressure of this idea, the foreign secretary gradually increased the original £5,000,000 subsidy limit for the great powers. Austria had an especially strong claim on Britain for extra assistance. Her troops were already in Italy to crush Murat and thus pave the way for a restoration of the Neapolitan Bourbons. Since the success of this enterprise was important to Britain, Castlereagh could not logically turn a deaf ear to Vienna's pleas. He therefore agreed to remit an additional £280,000 to the Hofburg.[66] The Tsar was ready to mobilize a second army against France, if Britain would only supply the means. When this offer was first made, Castlereagh had rejected it. Now his anxieties led him to reconsider. Several months must pass before a new Russian army could reach France, but its appearance on the scene even then might make the difference between victory and defeat. He therefore decided to give the Tsar an additional £1,000,000 a year to add between 150,000 and 200,000 to his forces.[67]

---

63. Castlereagh to Clancarty, April 24, 1815, FO 92/16. In May the Commons voted £5,000,000 for subsidies to the three major powers and a month later an additional £4,000,000 was provided in the budget for foreign aid (*Hansard*, XXXI (1815), 798.

64. Castlereagh to Wellington, April 13, 1815, FO 92/13.

65. Castlereagh to Wellington, March 26, 1815, *Correspondence of Castlereagh*, X, 285.

66. Castlereagh to Clancarty, April 24, 1815, FO 92/16. The foreign secretary managed the extra grant to Austria without recourse to Parliament. See Castlereagh to Wellington, March 12, 1815, *Supplementary Despatches of Wellington*, IX, 593.

67. Castlereagh to Liverpool, October 5, 1815, FO 92/28.

British efforts to resurrect the old war coalition encountered difficulties only with some of the lesser powers. Bernadotte refused to take part in the 1815 campaign. Professing ardent support for the good cause, the Swedish Prince Royal explained that he could not possibly put his army in motion before the end of the summer.[68] Still more disappointing was Portugal's refusal to answer the call to arms. In April Wellington had urged the Cabinet to send his old Portuguese units to Flanders. The suggestion was immediately approved by London and Castlereagh invited Portugal to supply between 12,000 and 14,000 troops for which Britain would pay £11 a year per man.[69] Considering Lisbon's grudge against Britain it is not surprising that the offer was declined. The official reply explained that threat of a Spanish invasion made it impossible for the Council of Regency to send any Portuguese troops abroad. Dispatches from George Canning, currently serving as British minister to Portugal, revealed that more than this was involved. The Regency so bitterly resented the treatment it had received at Britain's hands that it would do nothing to help her.[70] Spurned by Portugal, Castlereagh turned to Spain and offered to hire 20,000 troops to cooperate with loyalists in the south of France. Madrid promptly accepted the bid, but by then the Hundred Days was over.[71]

Within three months of Napoleon's return from Elba, the war coalition of 1814 had been rebuilt almost in its entirety. Sweden and Portugal chose to remain aloof, but in all other important respects the alliance which now faced Napoleon was the same which had overturned him one year before. At least £6,000,000 in British subsidies had been pledged to Russia, Prussia, and Austria, while Britain would have to spend nearly half that amount to bring her continental army to the 150,000 mark established by her alliance with the major powers. Since only about 50,000 British and Hanoverian troops were currently in Flanders, an additional 100,000 would have to be recruited. To mobilize and maintain a

---

68. Thornton to Castlereagh, April 6, 1815, FO 73/95.
69. Wellington to Bathurst, April 12, 1815, *Dispatches of Wellington*, XII, 301-302; and Castlereagh to Canning, April 17, 1815, FO 63/184.
70. Canning to Castlereagh, April 10 and 28, 1815, FO 63/186.
71. Castlereagh to H. Wellesley, June 22, 1815, FO 72/172; H. Wellesley to Castlereagh, July 14, 1815, FO 72/175.

British soldier in Europe for one year would cost the government between £60 and £70.[72] As a matter of pure economy the Cabinet decided to fill its quota by renting troops from other states. Russia and Prussia had already offered to supply them in exchange for subsidies, but Castlereagh disliked the idea and recommended instead that Britain apply to the states of Germany for assistance. Subsidizing the German princes would at least help them "to fight for what they are hereafter to defend."[73] The Cabinet agreed and authorized Wellington to arrange with the German rulers for the addition of 100,000 soldiers to his command. A fixed subsidy was set for this purpose amounting to £11 2s. a year for each soldier supplied.[74]

Even without this new responsibility, Wellington's hands were full with the business of converting the polyglot force under his command into an army. Of the 47,000 men on the British muster rolls, nearly half were Hanoverians or members of the King's German Legion. As commander of the Prince of Orange's army, Wellington also had 22,000 Dutch and Belgian troops at his disposal.[75] Soldiers from the German states, now marching toward Flanders, could be relied on to bring his total force to nearly 200,000 men.

In May Wellington turned to the negotiation of subsidy agreements with the German emissaries who crowded in on him in Brussels. The work was difficult since he had neither the time nor patience to deal with the demands of individual princes for preferential treatment. By the time the Waterloo campaign opened, however, five German states had agreed to supply a total of 100,854 men in return for British financial aid.[76]

Britain had pledged her credit to the extent of £9,000,000 to finance an allied army of nearly 1,000,000 men. Nothing had been neglected which would contribute to the ultimate victory of the

---

72. This was Castlereagh's estimate. See *Hansard,* XXXI (1815), 459.
73. Castlereagh to Wellington, no. 2, April 8, 1815, FO 92/13.
74. Castlereagh to Wellington, April 13, 1815, FO 92/13.
75. Fortescue, *British Army,* X, 430.
76. Wellington was especially troubled by the Bavarian envoy, Colonel J. Washington, who was probably a remote relative of the American president, George Washington. See Wellington's letter to J. Washington, May 20, 1815, *Dispatches of Wellington,* XII, 411.
The five subsidy treaties were as follows: Baden, 16,000 troops; Bavaria, 60,000 troops; Nassau, 3,050 troops; Württemberg, 20,000 troops; Saxe Coburg, 1,804 troops. Fortescue (*British Army,* X, 430) indicates that more than 7,000 Nassau troops were in the field at Waterloo. It seems clear that Wellington was subsidizing only a part of each German prince's army.

coalition over Napoleon. The original strategy, developed by the allies in the spring of 1815, called for the creation of an almost unbroken line of troops stretching from Flanders along the Rhine, and ending in northern Italy. The extreme right of this line was to be held by Wellington, and by Blücher's 113,000 Prussians. Russia's army was to take position along the lower Rhine and connect with the Austrians who were to hold the southern sector. The Russians and Austrians moved so slowly that Wellington despaired of seeing them on the Rhine until mid-June.[77]

When Napoleon led his army into Belgium at first light on the morning of June 15, only Wellington and Blücher occupied the positions assigned them in the allies' plan. So it was that the full fury of Waterloo fell on the Prussians and the conglomerate force of British, Dutch, Belgian, and German units under Wellington's command. Of the total allied manpower, only about one fifth was directly involved in the victory gained at Waterloo on June 18. The Napoleonic menace crumbled so rapidly in the wake of that engagement that the larger part of the allied armies never encountered the enemy in serious action. For Austria's forces, the high point of the war came a month before with their capture of Naples. The Tsar's 200,000 troops did not cross the Rhine until after Waterloo had been fought, and their march on Paris was hardly more than a mopping-up operation.[78]

The ease with which the resurrected Napoleonic Empire had been blasted to pieces contrasted sharply with the huge expense imposed on Britain to accomplish it. Nor did the expense end when Napoleon was at last conveyed to the security of St. Helena. Britain's treaties bound her to continue monthly subsidy payments to the allies until the conclusion of a peace treaty with France. Castlereagh reached Paris early in June, but the negotiation proved so difficult that a formal convention was not signed until the following November. The allies were thus entitled to subsidies for each of the five months which followed the Battle of Waterloo. Britain's subsidy debt was therefore much larger than it had been in 1814. As finally settled, it amounted to nearly £7,000,000 for a war which had lasted one hundred days.[79]

77. Wellington to H. Wellesley, June 2, 1815, *Dispatches of Wellington*, XII, 438.
78. Lobanov-Rostovsky, *Russia and Europe*, pp. 352-353.
79. Subsidies due the allies for 1815 were as follows: Austria, £1,668,889; Russia, £2,083,334; Prussia, £1,338,889; Minor Powers, £1,723,727. See Herries Subsidy Account, AO 3/1088.

Liverpool and Vansittart watched with horror as the subsidy bill steadily mounted throughout the summer and autumn of 1815. Obviously nothing could be done about those subsidies which would end only with the conclusion of a French peace treaty, but certain other economies might be made. The 20,000 Spanish soldiers hired by Henry Wellesley in July could certainly be eliminated.[80] Nor was there any need for the second Russian army Castlereagh had hired; their march to the west should be halted at once. Vansittart urged such steps on the foreign secretary early in July adding the hope that the latter was "sufficiently aware of the necessity of all practicable economy, and of reducing our expenses within the narrowest limits which can be consistent with vigorous and successful exertion."[81] Caught in the tangle of peace negotiations at Paris, Castlereagh was annoyed by the chancellor's lecture on economy. Of course he would spare the Treasury useless expense! The progress of the second Russian army had already been halted and he had agreed to pay the Tsar £417,666 as a final settlement for their services.[82] So far as the Spanish subsidy was concerned, Vansittart must surely know that nothing was due Madrid since the war had ended before these troops reached the French frontier.[83]

For reasons of policy Castlereagh strongly objected to the Cabinet's desire to escape its obligation to the German princes with whom Wellington had concluded subsidy treaties. Five such treaties had been signed prior to Waterloo, but many other German states had their armies on the road to Flanders before that battle had been fought and won. Were they not entitled to British help, even though no formal treaties had been concluded with them by that time? Wellington believed that they could not be turned away empty-handed. To deny to some what others had obtained only because they had arranged pacts with Britain before June 18 would generate a vast amount of ill will. Furthermore, it was not until some weeks after the battle that it became clear that

80. Vansittart to Castlereagh, August 17, 1815, *Correspondence of Castlereagh,* X, 482.
81. Vansittart to Castlereagh, July 7, 1815, *ibid.,* X, 418.
82. Provision for this was made in Castlereagh's treaty with Russia, October 4, 1815, FO 93/81 (25). See also Castlereagh's letter to Liverpool, October 5, 1815, FO 92/28.
83. Castlereagh to Vansittart, August 10, 1815, *Correspondence of Castlereagh,* X, 473-475.

the war was in fact over. Relying on the support which the Cabinet had always given him, the British field marshal continued signing treaties with the German states during the weeks which followed Waterloo. When pressed for an explanation of his conduct, he replied by pointing out that as all the princes "have performed the Stipulations of the Treaty of Accession to the General Alliance, I conclude it is not the Intention of the Government to deprive them of what others have got, and what they have had reason to expect."[84] The form of all these treaties was virtually the same: in return for a specified number of troops, Britain would pay an annual subsidy (to begin with April 1815) amounting to £11 2s for each man. Payments would be made monthly with one extra month's subsidy given as "return money" following the conclusion of peace with France.[85]

The Cabinet vigorously opposed this idea that Britain should maintain an indiscriminate system of outdoor relief for the benefit of German princes. Castlereagh immediately came to Wellington's defense, however. At Paris many of the German rulers were already claiming bits and pieces of France as prizes of war. Castlereagh would find it easier to divert them from such looting if he could promise them subsidy money. For Britain to snap shut her purse in the face of hungry German princelings might prove bad policy. But there was a still more pressing reason why London should indulge them in their passion for money, as the foreign secretary explained to Liverpool: "If we were to cancel these Arrangements, through the Effect of which alone we can establish our own pretensions of being considered as a Power serving with one hundred and fifty thousand men, we might possibly prejudice our own Claims to serve as a great Power but, at all events, should produce a great Clamour against us in Germany, which, altho' in the first instance confined to the smaller Powers, would soon drive the greater to an intervention." The Cabinet might find it easier to be generous since France had agreed to pay reparations to the major allies. Castlereagh had all along insisted on Britain's right to share in such reparations, a demand which "has been acceded to in consideration of our Subsidiary Efforts, and the effect will be that

84. Wellington to Castlereagh, August 17, 1815, FO 92/15.
85. The texts of twenty-five of these treaties concluded by Wellington are printed in *British Foreign and State Papers*, II, 484-516.

we shall take one fifth of whatever France pays."[86] There were times when considerations of economy must yield to those of policy. The foreign secretary gently chided Vansittart on this point: "As I have no doubt . . . that you have not more money than you know what to do with, you may rely upon my saving as much for you as I possibly can, consistent with the military attitude which the Confederacy must still assume, in order to secure and consolidate the peace they have so successfully conquered."[87] These arguments finally prevailed, and Wellington was allowed to continue signing subsidy agreements with the German states which had put their armies into motion prior to Waterloo. The last of such treaties, that with Holstein, was signed on September 5, 1815. Britain's generosity involved her in only a modest expense. All these treaties expired in November 1815 with the conclusion of the French peace treaty. The Treasury wasted no time in settling accounts with the German states; by February 1816 they had received the £1,723,727 owed them.[88]

Management of subsidy remittances and British military expenses was again entrusted to Commissary-in-Chief Herries, who returned to the Continent within a month after Waterloo. Following the practice of the previous year, he made payments to the allies both in London and on the Continent where credit was now available for his use. Meanwhile, the Treasury had arranged to finance the nation's war effort by offering for sale £30,000,000 in 3 percent bonds. The entire loan was allocated to the British banks of Baring Brothers and Smith, Payne and Smiths who, in turn, put up a large part of the issue for sale in Hamburg, Amsterdam, Vienna, Basel, Frankfort, and St. Petersburg. Herries was able to draw on the proceeds of the sale at these six continental cities for the payment of subsidies. So well did the arrangement work that only £1,000,000 had to be sent him from England to close all subsidy accounts with the allies.[89] In April 1816 Herries made the

86. Castlereagh to Liverpool, August 24, 1815, FO 92/24.
87. Castlereagh to Vansittart, August 10, 1815, *Correspondence of Castlereagh*, X, 475.
88. Statement of Sums paid on Account of Subsidies to Minor Powers, under Engagements made by the Duke of Wellington, *ibid.*, XI, 172.
89. Ralph W. Hidy, *The House of Baring in American Trade and Finance . . .* (Cambridge, Mass., 1949), p. 53; Jenks, *British Capital*, p. 33.

final remittance of subsidy money under the treaties of 1815.[90] Six years later he sent the Lords of the Treasury his official statement of all payments made to the allies, thereby marking the end of that long history of subsidization which began in 1793.

Problems continued to arise relating to subsidies even after Herries' account had been sent the Treasury. In 1821 Lord Liverpool's government decided to insist that Austria repay her two wartime loans. Pitt had persuaded Parliament to guarantee an Austrian loan for £4,600,000 in 1795, and two years later a similar endorsement was made to promote a new Hapsburg loan of £1,620,000. Austria abandoned all responsibility for repayment of these loans in 1797 and, thereafter, they became a charge on the British Treasury. Pitt and his successors quietly accepted the fact that they must patiently bear the expense, and the question of Austria's repayment appears never to have been raised between London and Vienna during the last ten years of the war. Matters would doubtless have remained this way had not opposition leaders forced Liverpool to act in 1821. By that time, the original Hapsburg loans of £6,220,000 had involved Britain in a debt of £23,515,890, thanks to accumulated interest. The manner in which Castlereagh, and later Canning, pressed Vienna for a settlement of the debt did them little credit. Indeed, the game was hardly worth the candle. The whole business was finally disposed of in November 1823, when Britain accepted an Austrian payment of £2,500,000 in cash as a full and final settlement of the loans. This represented a liquidation of the debt at a rate of about 10 percent.[91]

In 1831 the future of the Russian-Dutch Loan Convention, signed by Castlereagh sixteen years before, was reopened. By that treaty, Britain and Holland had promised to repay half of Russia's debt with Dutch bankers, but this obligation would be modified to Russia's disadvantage if Belgium were ever separated from Holland. When the Belgian revolt occurred in 1830, a different

---

90. Herries Account (AO 3/1088) shows a final payment to Prussia of £9,022 in 1820. Since no explanation is given, this presumably was to settle some claim arising out of the past.

91. The question has been examined by Irby C. Nichols, "Britain and the Austrian War Debt, 1821-1823," *Historian,* 20 (1958), 328-346. See also Helleiner, *Imperial Loans,* pp. 147-179.

view of British interests prevailed. Lord Palmerston argued that it was now to Britain's advantage to promote an independent and neutral Belgian state. To win Russia's approval for this, the foreign secretary proposed that Britain continue to meet her obligations under the Loan Convention, regardless of the separation of Belgium. A treaty embodying this agreement was concluded between Russia and Britain in November 1831.[92] Even the outbreak of the Crimean War in 1854 did not interrupt the annual British payments toward the reduction of her enemy's debt. Payments were made each year until 1891, by which time the balance of Britain's obligation had been reduced to £516,528. In that year, an act of Parliament made arrangements for wiping out that balance by 1906.[93] Under the advancing shadow of the World War, the British government finally closed the subsidy and loan accounts of the Napoleonic period.

92. Charles K. Webster, *The Foreign Policy of Palmerston* (London, 1951), I, 150-151.
93. 54 Vict., 26.

XV

CONCLUSION

Britain's payment of subsidies to her war partners was a time-honored practice long before the contest with Revolutionary France broke out in 1793. The hiring of German mercenaries began in the reign of Edward III and became so common that it has been characterized as "perhaps, the most long-lived feature of British foreign policy."[1] Chatham's subsidization of Frederick the Great was still remembered in 1794 when his son used it as a precedent to justify his own Prussian subsidy treaty. Between 1793 and 1815 Britain poured out her treasure in an ever increasing flow to aid her allies. By the end of the war, she had given them £65,830,228. Almost half this amount was spent during the last five years of the war, and in 1815 more than thirty European powers, great and small, shared Britain's bounty. Not until the World War, almost exactly a century later, would Europe again witness such an example of wartime aid.

The memory of Britain's massive financial contribution to victory survived long after Napoleon ceased to menace Europe. Looking back on that heroic period from the vantage point of the late nineteenth century, English writers took a certain pride in the fact that their country had financed Europe's deliverance from the Napoleonic yoke.[2] Almost inevitably, they applied to the entire war period that characteristic of feverish British spending which marked its final and most dramatic phase. Napoleon's defenders contributed to the growing legend by their frequent references to "Pitt's gold" offered as a bribe to the continental powers to join

1. *Camb. Hist. Brit. For. Pol.,* I, 3.
2. See, for example, Sydney Buxton, *Finance and Politics,* I, 6-7.

the coalitions. Even today, the myth of Pitt, the bountiful paymaster of Europe, has been uncritically accepted by students who refer to subsidy treaties which, in fact, never existed.[3] More important than these errors, the legend of "Pitt's gold" has created a false image which conceals the evolutionary nature of Britain's subsidy policy. Far from meekly accepting the role of financier to the coalitions, Pitt shunned it for as long as he was able. But the character of the war changed, forcing Britain's subsidy policy to change with it. By 1815 that policy was very different in character and scope from what it had been twenty-two years before.

Within a few weeks after the outbreak of hostilities in 1793, Britain started to hire troops from the German princes in order to enlarge her own army in the Low Countries. The practice was so well established that even Pitt's opponents raised no objection. For nearly a year after the war began, the prime minister offered no help to his country's major allies. The contest with France was not likely to last long and he was hardly inclined to be prodigal with the nation's wealth, which he had guarded so carefully as its peacetime leader. In this mood, he rejected Russia's demand for a subsidy in 1793, even though he thereby provided Catherine the Great with an excuse to remain out of the war.

Austria and Prussia had struggled with France for nearly a year before Britain joined them, and by the end of 1793 they were showing unmistakable symptoms of financial exhaustion. Prussia finally annnounced that the allies must subsidize her if they wished her to remain in the coalition. Financial distress only partly accounts for this resort to blackmail. Attracted by the possibility of new territorial gains in Poland, she wanted to be paid to continue what, so far, had been a profitless war with France. For a time Pitt tried to persuade all the major allies to join in helping Prussia, but in the end he was faced with a grim choice:

3. A case in point is the volume of the *Oxford History of England* (published in 1960) dealing with the eighteenth century (Watson, *Reign of George III*, p. 364) which has this to say of the formation of the First Coalition: "Pitt still supposed nevertheless that his rôle in Europe would be that of paymaster. In March 1793 a subsidy treaty was negotiated with Russia. By the end of August Britain had agreed to finance Austria, Prussia, Sardinia, Hesse-Cassel, Spain, and Naples, in war on France." In fact, no subsidy treaty was concluded with Russia until 1798, while only two of the other powers (Sardinia and Hesse-Cassel) received British money during the period mentioned. The same error appeared earlier in Rose, *Pitt and the Great War*, p. 123. See also the treatment of Pitt's subsidy policy in the popular textbook, W. E. Lunt, *History of England*, 4th ed. (New York, 1957), p. 601.

Britain herself must either pay Frederick William or allow him to carry out his threat. There was no alternative but to yield to his demands. The Prussian subsidy treaty of 1794 was not difficult for Pitt to defend. Thanks to Britain's advanced economy, her population (twice that of Prussia) was vastly more productive than those of her allies. The colonial campaigns, the war in Europe, and the requirements of the navy were already drawing heavily on her manpower supply. More than 200,000 of her people would serve in the navy and with the army in Europe during the coming year. Any greater diversion of her population into military service might seriously diminish the nation's ability to create wealth. Thus, as in the case of hiring mercenaries, it was economically wiser for Britain to subsidize 62,400 Prussians than to put that many of her own people under arms. The weak point in this argument was its failure to consider whether Prussia was as anxious to fight the French as Britain was to have her do so. Even when given subsidies, Prussia could not resist the lure of Polish lands and, within a year, she abandoned the coalition to give her undivided attention to the final partition of that unfortunate country. This was not the last time that British leaders discovered that subsidies, no matter how freely given, could not buy an ally's dedication to the cause.

Britain, no less than her allies, had national interests to promote in the war and they profoundly influenced her use of subsidies during the first two coalitions. Pitt had been forced into war by France's attack on the Low Countries, and for the remainder of his life the liberation of Holland was one of his most important goals. Of the German allies, only Prussia had a similar interest in the fate of the Low Countries. Geography, territorial ambition, and dynastic connection with the House of Orange account for this concern, whereas Austria had long wished to exchange Belgium for Bavaria and thereby consolidate her holdings. One of the most consistent features of Pitt's war policy was his desire to form a military combination with Prussia and Russia in order to drive the French from Holland. By 1798 Paul I of Russia was ready to support such a plan, provided Britain financed his military operations. To bring Prussia to the same point, Pitt launched five missions to Berlin between 1795 and 1805 with attractive offers of money and territorial rewards in the west.

Prussia rejected each of these offers because the chances of a successful military intervention in the Low Countries were too slim to justify her abandoning the profitable policy of neutrality she had followed since the Peace of Basel.

Pitt's failure to give the early coalitions the northern focus he so much wanted left him no choice but to fall back on his partnership with Austria as the only means of carrying on the war. By 1795, however, the Empire's finances were so shaky that Britain had either to provide support or allow her to follow Prussia's example and make peace with the enemy. Instead of subsidizing Austria, the Cabinet decided to guarantee the £4,600,000 loan she was negotiating in England. Why a loan guarantee rather than a subsidy? No positive answer can be given, but several considerations probably account for Britain's decision. For more than a year, Austria had tried to borrow money in London, but the affair languish d. A British guarantee would bring the business to a quick and successful conclusion. So far, Pitt's subsidization had been on a modest scale and he was in no position to pay his ally the several million pounds she required. If Vienna met the annual payments on the loan Britain had guaranteed, the Treasury would not have to pay anything. Even if she defaulted, as Pitt half expected, the annual charges which Britain would thereafter be obliged to meet amounted to only about £350,000. From the short-term view, and this was the view which governed Pitt's finance program during the first years of the war, the annual expenditure of £350,000 was less troublesome than the payment of £4,600,000 in subsidies at one time.

The following year, when Austria again appealed to Britain for help, the Cabinet advanced money to her which she was expected to repay from a second loan. Even with this support Austria was overwhelmed on the battlefield, and in 1797 she withdrew from the war and reneged on all her financial obligations to Britain. She not only refused to meet the annual payments on her original loan, but stubbornly withheld ratification of her 1797 loan convention with Britain. The quarrel which followed, ostensibly financial in origin, went far beyond that issue. For years, Vienna had resented London's preferential treatment of Prussia, her arch-rival. Instead of giving subsidies, such as those she had provided for Prussia in 1794, Britain never did more for Vienna than help her borrow money in London at what the Hofburg regarded as an outrageously high interest rate. The British Cabinet, for its part, was sorely distressed by Vienna's indifference to the fate of the Low Countries (a matter of prime importance to Britain) and by her regrettable habit of engaging in separate negotiations with the enemy. Austria's peace treaty with France in 1797 confirmed Pitt's darkest suspicions: in return for surrendering Belgium, Austria was to annex Venetia.

Anglo-Austrian antagonism greatly weakened the Second Coalition and led Britain to deny the Hofburg any financial aid, even though both powers were at war with France. Pitt continued to dream of a British-Prussian-Russian alliance, financed by subsidies, which would liberate Holland. The Tsar's abrupt withdrawal from the war in 1799 destroyed that dream and forced Britain to come to terms with Vienna in a last-minute effort to keep the coalition alive. Once again Pitt proposed to advance money on still another Imperial loan to be floated in London when the war ended. The collapse of the Hapsburg war effort in the summer of 1800 put an end to this plan as well as to the coalition. Henceforth, all British aid to the major allies was given as an outright subsidy and the Imperial loans of 1795 and 1797 were remembered as horrible mistakes, never to be repeated.

The year 1804 marked a major turning point in the development of Britain's subsidy policy. Before that time, Britain had used subsidies as an emergency measure to keep the coalitions alive. Pitt had made far more attractive offers to Prussia than to Austria in keeping with his wish to create a northern league which would release Holland from France's grip. By 1804 France had made good on her claim to supremacy in western Europe. If Britain hoped to defeat the enemy, and that was now the all-important goal, she must finance any nation ready to join her in the work. The time had gone by for the selective subsidization she had previously practiced.

For these reasons, Pitt followed a very different subsidy policy in the formation of the Third Coalition. The more realistic war finance program he had introduced (the British national revenue more than doubled between 1799 and 1804) now made it possible for him to offer money with a free hand to any power ready to take arms against Napoleon. Specifically, he was ready to pay

£1,250,000 a year for each 100,000 soldiers Russia, Austria, and Prussia sent into battle. This offer, the most generous Britain had ever made, did nothing to create the war league Pitt so desperately wanted. The interests of the great powers diverged wildly in 1805: Britain was anxious to step up the war, Russia preferred a negotiated settlement with France, while Austria and Prussia wanted nothing more than to be left alone. Napoleon's aggression in Italy, not the promise of British subsidies, breathed life into the Third Coalition. Pitt's desire to bring Prussia into the league inspired his final diplomatic venture: the sending of Harrowby to Berlin with a glittering promise of money and land to attract Frederick William and his ministers. Whatever basis exists in fact for the legend of Pitt the tempter is to be found in his hot pursuit of Prussia. In the end Prussia yielded her favor to France in exchange for Hanover, a territorial bribe which Napoleon (unlike Pitt) was able to deliver—and then take back.

The collapse of the Third Coalition ended all chance of another continental union for five years. Britain was too isolated to support Prussia's impulsive uprising in 1806 and that of Austria three years later. In 1808, however, the Spanish and Portuguese took arms against their oppressor and instinctively turned to Britain for money, arms, and military help. Under Canning's leadership the government responded to these appeals in a heroic manner. For the first time the French imperium was challenged not by crowned heads but by a people driven on by a national fervor as dynamic as anything seen in the early stages of the French Revolution. A great flood of British specie and war materials was let loose to support the Peninsular resistance movement. Under relentless pressure from Downing Street the Ordnance Department hastened its retooling in order to meet the insurgents' demand for arms. Muskets, carbines, pistols, cartridges, flints, accoutrements, cannon, swords, drums, and medicines, along with hundreds of other items, were sent in huge quantities to outfit the armies which Spain and Portugal were creating. Never before had British aid been given on such a scale in *both* money and muskets. This was only the beginning. In the years to come, Britian would have to send all her allies guns as well as gold since both were desperately needed.

Conclusion

The war in the Peninsula began with three allied armies in the field, each directed by its own government. Britain had promised to supply the Portuguese and Spanish forces and, at the same time, send money to their governments. Almost at once it became clear that the French could be defeated only if the three allied forces were directed by a central authority. Wellington's appointment as generalissimo of the Portuguese and Spanish accomplished nothing since the title was an empty one. By 1811 the British commander was sure that centralized control over the armies was to be obtained in only one way: the entire subsidy for Portugal and Spain must be in his hands so that he might use it to feed, supply, and pay the Iberian units under his direction. London approved this plan, and by the time the war reached its climax in 1813, almost the entire British subsidy was at Wellington's disposal. Thus, British aid to Portugal and Spain, amounting to about £3,000,000 a year, bought Wellington the service of a force larger than that sent him by his own government. In effect the subsidy became a direct military aid administered by Britain's commander in the Peninsula. For the first time since 1793, London could be sure that all her subsidy money was going for strictly military purposes.

By 1812 Napoleon's arrogant ambition was steadily forcing the great powers into a war for survival which their economies were hardly able to support. In the Peace of Tilsit (1807), the conquering Emperor of the French had stripped Prussia of nearly half her land and people, at the same time requiring that she pay the expenses of his army of occupation. The failure of Austria's ill-timed War of Liberation in 1809 placed her too at Napoleon's mercy. To gain peace, the Hofburg was forced to part with some of its most valuable possessions and submit to a crushing indemnity. Russia alone was spared the blows which had beaten Prussia and Austria to their knees, but in 1812 the French invasion brought death and devastation to the richest part of the Tsar's domain. The French imperium nearly shattered the war-making capacity of the great powers, but its terror strengthened their will to survival.

The help which Napoleon's enemies so desperately needed in 1812-1814 could only come from the resources of Britain's expanding economy. Secure in her island and blessed with a mighty navy which gave her access to the markets of the world, Great Britain found increased strength in the years which brought invasion and humiliation to the continental states. Despite occasional setbacks, such as the financial crisis of 1810, the progress of her economy was unmistakable. With the collapse of the Continental System in 1812, Britain's overseas trade leaped forward and thereby enabled Castlereagh to help his country's allies at the time they most required it. The increasing productivity of the nation's economy likewise furnished the British government with a solid base for its war finance program; between 1806 and 1816 a population of less than fourteen million people paid nearly £142,000,000 in income taxes alone.[4] Britain had never been able to give her allies the will to fight France, but by 1813 the great powers had found that essential ingredient within themselves. What they now required of Britain was what she could send them: the money and arms needed to transform that will into victory over their common enemy.

The certainty of receiving British aid encouraged the Rising of the Nations, even though it did not inspire it. Thanks to the increased efficiency of the Ordnance service, London was able to ship almost unlimited quantities of arms to the Russians, Swedes, Austrians, and Prussians during 1813-1814. So extreme were their demands for guineas and gunpowder that, with all her wealth and resources, Britain still had to strain every muscle to comply. Nearly one million muskets and £7,500,000 in subsidies went to the allies during 1813. Little wonder that Castlereagh and the harassed chancellor of the exchequer, Vansittart, hoped that "federative paper" might partly substitute for the cash Prussia and Russia insisted they must have.

Never before the summer of 1813 had Britain poured out such lavish quantities of money and weapons to support the war against France. She did so without attaching conditions to her gifts. Castlereagh deplored the fact that the northern allies ignored their benefactor's interests in their sporadic peace talks with France, but he never faltered in sending them the means to wage war.

4. Arthur Hope-Jones, *Income Tax in the Napoleonic Wars* (Cambridge, 1939), pp. 124-125.

Since the purpose of this aid was to overthrow Napoleon, Britain did well to overlook the allies' insensitivity to her wishes. The refusal of Spain, Russia, and Austria to liberalize their tariff policies irritated Downing Street, but not to the point of stopping the subsidies. Only Bernadotte's eccentric behavior drove Castlereagh past the point of endurance. Perhaps it was as well that his threat to end the Swedish Prince's subsidy was never carried out.

Massive British subsidization had become such an accepted policy that, by the time Castlereagh went to the Continent in 1814, the only question remaining was how the £5,000,000 aid for the year was to be apportioned among the allies. The foreign secretary proposed an equal division among Russia, Austria, and Prussia on the assumption that each of them would maintain at least 150,000 effective troops under arms. This formula was incorporated both in the Chaumont treaty (1814) and that negotiated with the allies following Napoleon's return from Elba in 1815. By this device, Castlereagh may have hoped to end the allies' rivalry and, at the same time, respect his own theory of the equality of the great powers, a theory fundamental to his whole idea of a concert of Europe. The hard fact was that the military strength of the great powers varied considerably. With the largest army in the field, Russia naturally opposed the principle of subsidy-equality and, in effect, argued for the strict application of Pitt's 1805 formula which apportioned subsidies in direct proportion to the size of the allied armies. Castlereagh was finally obliged to make "adjustments" so that Russia did indeed receive the largest share of British aid during the closing years of the war.

With the arrival of peace, Britain still found her money a useful means to attain diplomatic goals. Portugal and Spain were persuaded to limit the slave trade in return for British gold. Castlereagh also won trade concessions from Russia as well as her consent to the creation of the Kingdom of the Netherlands by that curious financial bargain known as the Russian-Dutch loan, a bargain which imposed a small burden on British taxpayers until 1906.

The liberalization of Britain's subsidy policy naturally resulted in a greatly increased outlay for foreign aid between 1793 and 1815. Pitt's coalitions (1793-1807) never cost the British Treasury more than £2,600,000 a year in subsidies.[5] Between the opening of the Peninsular War in 1808 and the Rising of the Nations five years later, British aid to the allies (chiefly Portugal and Spain) fluctuated between £2,600,000 and £4,400,000 a year. Even this increase was modest when compared to the final three years of the contest culminating in Waterloo when annual British subsidy payments never fell below £7,500,000. An all-time high was reached in 1814 when more than £10,000,000 was spent in subsidies to the allies. The climactic campaigns of 1814-1815, involving less than ten months of actual combat, cost Britain about £20,000,000 in subsidies alone. This equaled nearly one third of the entire amount spent on subsidies and loans between 1793 and 1816.

Impressive as these figures are, subsidies added proportionately less to Britain's total war costs than might be supposed. Maintenance of the British army, navy, and ordnance between 1793 and 1816 cost the government more than £830,000,000, yet the total of all subsidies and loans for this period amounts to only 8 percent of the figure.[6] Most important, the government's increasing revenue returns kept pace with the expansion of the subsidy program. In 1794 (the year of the Prussian subsidy) payments to the allies amounted to about 14 percent of the government's revenue for the same year. In 1814 more than £10,000,000 was paid in subsidies, but that still represented only 14 percent of the government's tax yield.

Prior to the Peninsular War, the Cabinet relied heavily on mercenaries and subsidized troops to meet its military commitments on the Continent. Therefore it is hardly surprising to discover that subsidy payments before 1808 generally exceed the expenses of Britain's national army in Europe. The sending of a British force to the Peninsula dramatically reversed this condition. Although foreign aid thereafter went soaring to new heights, it

---

5. The Austrian Loan of £4,600,000, which Britain guaranteed in 1795 brought the total of all foreign aid for that year to more than £5,000,000. Since this was a loan guarantee, rather than a subsidy, it could be argued that the amount of the loan should be excluded from the tabulation. Until 1797, that loan cost Britain nothing. The liberalization of Pitt's subsidy policy in 1804-1805 actually involved Britain in little expense. The Third Coalition did not last long enough to cost Britain much by way of subsidies.

6. Military costs determined on the basis of data in Pebrer, *Taxation*, p. 154.

regularly fell below the amount Britain spent on her own military operations. Between 1808 and 1816 it cost Britain nearly £80,000,000 (much of it in specie) to maintain Wellington's army. During this same period, all subsidy remittances amounted to only about half that sum.

Clearly, subsidies contributed less to Britain's war burden between 1793 and 1816 than their critics claimed. The British taxpayer thoroughly detested paying foreign governments, a prejudice which the antiwar party naturally exploited. How important were subsidies in worsening the balance of payments problem which troubled England during the final years of the war? Unquestionably they made a bad situation worse. More to blame than subsidies, however, was the very heavy expenditure of credit and specie required to support the all-important campaigns which Wellington carried on in the Peninsula.

By means of subsidies, Britain hoped to enable her allies to carry on a war program which was beyond their own strength. All the early coalitions, however, lacked a community of interest among the allies which kept victory out of reach. Britain's own war goals included the reduction of France's power in Europe, the liberation of Holland, and the acquisition of some of the enemy's colonies— what Pitt once called "a little mixture of indemnification." Only by defeating France on the battlefields of Europe could Britain hope to achieve the first two of these goals. As an island power with only half the population of her antagonist, she depended on coalitions to overthrow the common enemy.

But what of the interests of the continental powers on whom Britain relied—powers whose lands lay exposed to enemy attack? From the short-term view, Prussia's withdrawal from the war in 1795 was not entirely unjustified. Since taking up arms three years before, the only territorial gains she had made were in the east, and by 1795 even these were threatened by Russia and Austria. The Treaty of Basel permitted Prussia to disentangle herself from the French war and thereafter protect her interests and resources. Britain could not really expect Austria to fight to the bitter end to liberate the Low Countries when Vienna yearned for territorial rewards in Italy and eastern Europe. Austria's peace treaty with France in 1797 left the enemy in a position of great strength, but it was not entirely without honor and profit for the Hofburg. The acquisition of Venetia (which Austria very much wanted) was respectable compensation for her surrender of the Austrian Netherlands (which she did not want). So far as Russia was concerned, the mainspring of her military intervention between 1798 and 1805 was fear that French imperialism threatened her interest in eastern Europe.

France's military prowess won her such a position of strength in Europe by 1809 that Russia and Austria found it best to accept peaceful coexistence with her. Prussia had already been reduced to the condition of a French dependency in return for her challenge to Napoleon's power in 1806. Only in the Peninsula was there a real show of resistance, and Britain showered that area with money, arms, and troops in order to check the French. The money was well spent for it enabled the Spanish and Portuguese nationalists to accomplish what they burned to do: drive the invader from their land. British foreign aid never yielded a better return than that spent in the Peninsula.

Napoleon's reckless aggression toward the powers he once had cowed resulted in a major change in the international scene by 1812. Russia had now to fight for her survival, and even Bernadotte was ready to defy his former leader in the hope of winning Norway as a reward for his daring. After a brief period of indecision, Prussia declared for the new coalition and fought to wipe out the shame of Jena.

Generously supported though this union was with British money and guns, it was actually weaker than it appeared. Such unity as it had came not from British help, but from Napoleon's refusal to accept any settlement of the issues at stake between France and her enemies. The failure of the 1813 peace talks strengthened the Russo-Prussian alliance and even brought Austria into the ranks of the confederacy. As late as the winter of 1813-1814, Napoleon still might have separated the continental powers from their British paymaster. By the spring of 1814, however, it was too late. At Chaumont, Castlereagh at last created that union of the great powers which Pitt and Grenville had vainly tried to call into being. Animated by a singleness of purpose and financed by Britain's great wealth, the coalition required only a month to drive Napoleon from France. A year later, at Waterloo, it crushed all efforts to resurrect that power which too long had disturbed the peace of Europe.

356

APPENDIX

BIBLIOGRAPHY

INDEX

Appendix

TABLE OF EVENTS IN FRENCH HISTORY
1789-1815

1789	July 14	Fall of the Bastille
1791	Sept. 3	Adoption of the new French Constitution
1792	Feb. 7	Austro-Prussian alliance against France
	April 20	France declares war against Austria
	July 27	Brunswick Manifesto
	Sept. 20	Battle of Valmy
1793	Jan. 21	Louis XVI executed
	Feb. 1	France declares war against Britain and Holland
	March	Revolt breaks out in the Vendée
	April 6	Formation of the Committee of Public Safety
	June 2	Fall of the Girondins
	August	*Levée-en-masse* decreed
	Aug.-Dec.	Toulon occupied by the allies
1794	July 27	Fall of Robespierre
	Dec. 27	French armies invade Holland
1795	April 5	Treaty of Basel with Prussia
	June-July	British-émigré invasion at Quiberon
	August 22	New Constitution adopted
	Oct. 1	Belgium annexed to France
	Nov. 3	Directory installed
1796	March	Suppression of revolt in the Vendée and Brittany
	Aug. 19	France allies with Spain
	Dec. 16	French invasion fleet sails for Ireland

359

1797	Feb. 2	Mantua surrenders to Napoleon
	July 9	Cisalpine Republic formed
	Sept. 4	Coup d'état of 18 Fructidor
	Oct. 17	Treaty of Campo Formio with Austria
	Dec. 16	Opening of the Congress of Rastadt
1798	Feb. 15	Establishment of Roman Republic
	March	Formation of the Helvetic Republic
	May 19	Bonaparte sails from Toulon
	June 12	Malta surrenders to French
	Dec. 4	France declares war against Naples
1799	Nov. 9	Coup d'état of 18 Brumaire; overthrow of Directory
	Dec. 24	Constitution of the Year VIII
1800	June 14	Battle of Marengo
1801	Feb. 9	Treaty of Lunéville
	July	Concordat with the Papacy
1802	March 27	Treaty of Amiens
	Aug. 2	Bonaparte becomes First Consul for life
	Aug.	Constitution of the Year X
1803	May	Renewal of War with Britain
1804	March	French Civil Code
	March	Murder of the Duke of Enghien
	May 18	Formation of the French Empire
1805	May	Napoleon becomes King of Italy
	Oct. 21	Battle of Trafalgar
	Dec. 2	Battle of Austerlitz
	Dec. 15	Napoleon's treaty with Prussia
1806	March	Joseph Bonaparte becomes King of Naples
	June	Louis Bonaparte becomes King of Holland
	July 12	Confederation of the Rhine organized
	Aug. 6	End of the Holy Roman Empire
	Nov. 21	Napoleon's Berlin Decree
1807	July	Treaties of Tilsit with Russia and Prussia
	Nov.	French armies occupy Portugal
	Dec. 17	Napoleon's Milan Decree
1808	May	Outbreak of revolt in Peninsula; Joseph Bonaparte proclaimed King of Spain
	Oct.	Congress of Erfurt

1809	May	Napoleon's annexation of the Papal States
	Oct. 14	Treaty of Schönbrunn with Austria
1810	April	Napoleon's marriage to Marie Louise
	July 9	Holland annexed to French Empire
1812	June	Napoleon begins his invasion of Russia
	Sept. 7	Battle of Borodino
	Oct. 19	Retreat from Moscow
1813	Jan.	Concordat of Fontainebleau
	July-Aug.	Congress at Prague
	Aug. 12	Austria declares war against France
	Oct. 16-19	Battle of Leipzig
1814	Feb.-March	Congress at Châtillon
	April 11	Napoleon abdicates
	May 30	Treaty of Paris
	Sept.	Beginning of Congress of Vienna
1815	March 1	Napoleon lands at Cannes
	March 20	Napoleon enters Paris and restores the Empire
	June 18	Battle of Waterloo
	June 22	Napoleon's second abdication
	Oct.	Napoleon arrives at St. Helena
	Nov. 20	Second Treaty of Paris

SUBSIDY PAYMENTS TO THE ALLIES
1793-1816

Lists of subsidy payments for this period have already appeared in a number of books.[1] With only one exception all of them reproduce the data contained in a paper prepared by the Treasury and presented to the House of Commons on May 6, 1822, entitled "An Account of all Sums of Money paid or advanced by way of Loan, Subsidy, or otherwise, to any Foreign State, from the Year 1792, up to the present time . . . "[2] Notwithstanding the title's bold claim, the account is far from reliable. It contains errors and in a number of cases is misleading. Payments are indicated for years when Britain had no subsidy agreement with the power receiving the money. Such remittances were to settle claims rising out of past service. For example, £7,000 was paid Brunswick in 1798 to satisfy her claims against Britain on the basis of their treaty of four years before. Part of the money paid Hesse-Cassel in 1795 was the balance due her for supplying Britain with troops during the American Revolution! The government would occasionally pay subsidies without first obtaining Parliamentary approval, the money usually being drawn from the Secret Service funds. The 1822 account discreetly neglects to note such

1. For example, see the subsidy list given as Appendix A in Rosebery's *Pitt*.

2. This paper (*Accounts and Papers,* 1822, XX, Cmd. 293) was brought up to date and reprinted in 1854. The only printed subsidy list I have encountered which differs from the 1822 account is contained in Silberling, "Financial and Monetary Policy," *Quarterly Journal of Economics,* 38 (1923-1924), 227. Payments there are expressed in units of £1,000,000 and they differ more from the 1822 account than those given in this appendix.

payments. According to that paper the first Swedish subsidy began in 1808, whereas, in fact, British money had been sent to Sweden during each of the three previous years. Some omissions from the 1822 list are puzzling: in 1805 Austria received £1,000,000, of which the official statement takes no notice.

In compiling a list of subsidy payments for this appendix, reliance has been placed on data derived from the following sources:

King's Warrant Books (Ty. 52): This is particularly valuable for subsidy payments made during the early years of the war.

Declared Accounts in the Audit Office (AO 1): British officials abroad (such as ministers) who made subsidy payments were obliged to submit their accounts to the Audit Office.

Minute Books of the Lords of the Treasury (Ty. 29): These provide considerable information, especially relating to "federative paper."

Army Ledgers of the Pay Master General's Office (PMG 2): An important source of information for a number of subsidies.

Foreign Office Correspondence: Letters between the Foreign Office and bankers handling subsidy money often provide data not found elsewhere.

John C. Herries Account (AO 3/1088): This superbly compiled account is invaluable for the final years of the war. It fails, however, to include payments made to the Peninsular powers.

No claim for absolute accuracy is made for the list included in this appendix. The confused manner in which subsidy accounts were kept puts that degree of accuracy beyond the reach of even the most devoted researcher with a lifetime to give to the work. Furthermore, compiling a list of subsidy payments involves certain problems which different students would solve in different ways. For example, what year should be specified for a subsidy payment authorized by the Treasury in December and remitted in January? Payments in specie were always troublesome because the value placed on the bullion by the Treasury was seldom that given it by the recipient. Which valuation should be used? Should bankers' commissions, together with freight costs and insurance on subsidy bullion, be counted as part of the subsidy?

Payments to Portugal and Spain between 1808 and 1815 are especially difficult to deal with. British aid to those powers was given in so many forms other than money that it is almost impossible to express the total annual aid in pounds sterling. The attempt would fail altogether were it not for the Audit Office accounts dealing with those subsidies.

The Spanish subsidy ledger, compiled in 1822, is entitled "Payments on Account of the Spanish Government" (AO 3/765) and consists of forty-eight separate accounts each relating to some aspect of the aid program. The expenditures of Wellington's commissary general, Sir Robert Kennedy, are given in eleven separate accounts. Five accounts record payments made by the British consul at Cadiz on the order of Sir Henry Wellesley. Payments of British money to Generals Whittingham and Roche, commanding units of the Spanish army, are itemized in nine accounts. Many of these accounts represent payments made by individuals over an extended period of time, and they must all be coordinated year by year to determine the total annual payments to Spain. The work involved was extensive and revealed some problems which had to be solved. A few of the smaller accounts simply show the sum of payments made over a period of years, without specifying how much was paid each year. Since the amount was small, I decided to omit it. On different grounds, I also excluded Accounts No. 43 and 44 which set forth expenditures by the Admiralty and the Victualling Department for the benefit of Spain's ships between 1808 and 1822. These payments total £332,833 but had little to do with the war in the Peninsula.

The Portuguese subsidy is easier to handle, thanks to the existence of separate accounts for each year between 1808 and 1815. Unfortunately, this collection of ledgers (AO 3/746) lacks that for the year 1811. Diligent search for the missing volume by helpful staff members of the Public Record Office proved fruitless. In this one case I have been obliged to rely on the data presented in the 1822 account. I have done this with particular regret since the subsidy figures given in that account for Spain and Portugal during the Peninsular War are in almost every case simply approximations or estimates.

Subsidy figures given in the 1822 account appear below in a parallel column for purposes of comparison.

SUBSIDY PAYMENTS
1793-1816

			1822 Account
1793	Hanover	£ 452,551	£ 492,650
	Hesse-Cassel	190,622	190,622
	Sardinia	150,000	150,000
1794	Baden	20,196	25,196
	Brunswick	17,659	none
	Hanover	601,476	559,375
	Hesse-Cassel	418,132	437,105
	Hesse-Darmstadt	91,372	102,073
	Prussia	1,200,000	1,226,495
	Sardinia	200,000	200,000
1795	Austrian Loan	4,600,000	4,600,000
	Baden	6,794	1,793
	Brunswick	46,778	97,721
	Hanover	340,192	478,347
	Hesse-Cassel	317,492	317,492
	Hesse-Darmstadt	85,224	79,605
	Sardinia	150,000	150,000
1796	Brunswick	53,645	12,794
	Hanover	3,736	none
	Hesse-Darmstadt	62,651	20,075
1797	Austrian Loan	1,620,000	1,620,000
	Brunswick	15,565	7,570
	Hesse-Darmstadt	19,249	57,015
	Portugal*	10,000	none

*Paid to agents in London for purchase of supplies.

1822 Account

1798	Brunswick[†]	7,000	7,000
	Portugal[*]	103,000	120,013
1799	Hesse-Darmstadt	none	4,812
	Portugal[*]	87,675	none
	Russia	1,386,070	825,000
1800	Austria	816,666	1,066,666
	German Princes	1,066,667	500,000
	Portugal[*]	10,000	none
	Russia	537,126	545,494
1801	Austria	none	150,000
	German Princes	200,000	200,000
	Hesse-Cassel[†]	100,000	100,000
	Portugal	200,000	200,113
1802	Hesse-Cassel[†]	33,451	33,450
	Russia[†]	200,000	200,000
1803	Hanover[†]	110,155	117,628
	Russia[†]	63,000	63,000
	Portugal	none	31,647
1804	Hesse-Cassel[†]	83,303	83,303
1805	Austria	1,000,000	none
	Hanover	26,190	35,340
	Russia	300,000	none
	Sweden	132,500	none
1806	Austria[†]	500,000	500,000
	Hanover	76,865	76,865
	Hesse-Cassel[†]	18,982	18,982
	Russia[†]	50,000	none
	Sweden	311,400	none
1807	Hanover	19,899	19,899
	Hesse-Cassel	45,000	45,000
	Prussia	187,613	180,000
	Russia[1]	614,183	614,182
	Sicily[2]	1,094,002	none

1. £500,000 of this sum was due Russia from her 1805 treaty, while the balance was the value of arms sent her in 1807.
2. This is the total of all subsidies to Sicily between 1804 and 1807.
*Paid to agents in London for purchase of supplies.
†Payments for claims arising out of past service.

1822 Account

	Sweden	248,128	none
1808	Portugal	140,156	none
	Sicily	353,438	300,000
	Spain	2,325,668	1,497,873
	Sweden[3]	1,094,023	1,100,000
1809	Austria	1,187,500	850,000
	Portugal	539,369	none
	Portuguese Loan	600,000	600,000
	Sicily	313,836	300,000
	Spain	473,919	529,039
	Sweden	300,000	300,000
1810	Portugal	1,986,069	1,237,517
	Sicily	425,000	425,000
	Spain	557,952	402,875
1811	Portugal	1,832,168	1,832,168
	Sicily	275,000	275,000
	Spain	539,554	220,689
1812	Portugal	2,276,833	2,167,831
	Sicily[4]	628,532	400,000
	Spain	1,036,598	1,000,000
	Sweden[5]	500,000	278,291
1813	Austria	700,000	500,000
	Prussia	650,039	650,039
	Portugal	2,486,012	1,644,062
	Russia[6]	1,058,436	657,500
	Sicily	440,000	600,000
	Spain	877,200	1,000,000
	Sweden	1,334,992	1,320,000
1814	Austria	939,523	1,064,881
	Denmark	121,917	121,917
	Hanover	525,000	500,000
	Portugal	1,345,082	1,500,000

3. Of this amount, £94,023 is the value of arms sent that year.
4. Includes arms valued at £40,060.
5. Includes arms and credit in London, totaling £300,000.
6. Includes arms valued at £400,936.

1822 Account

	Prussia[7]	1,438,643	1,319,128
	Russia[8]	2,708,834	2,169,982
	Sicily	316,666	316,666
	Spain	1,820,932	450,000
	Sweden	800,000	800,000
1815	Austria	1,654,921	1,796,229
	Hanover	270,940	200,000
	Portugal	54,915	100,000
	Prussia[9]	2,156,513	2,294,222
	Russia[10]	2,000,033	3,241,919
	Sicily	33,333	none
	Spain	147,295	147,295
	Sweden	608,048	521,061
	Minor Powers[11]	1,723,727	1,724,001
1816	Austria	416,667	none
	Russia	972,222	1,096,355
	Sicily	117,748	117,748
	Sweden	422,766	506,098

7. Includes approximately £401,371 paid in "federative paper."
8. Includes approximately £783,000 paid in "federative paper."
9. Includes approximately £469,728 paid in "federative paper."
10. Includes approximately £888,922 paid in "federative paper."
11. These payments were completed in February 1816.

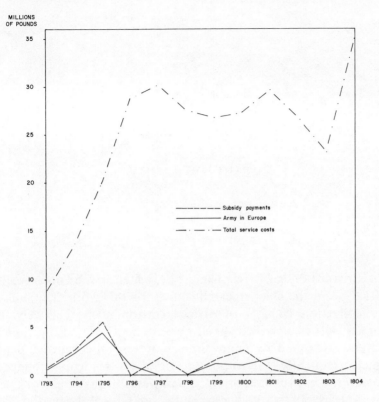

Comparison of Subsidy Payments, Cost of British Army in Europe, and Total Costs of British Army, Navy, and Ordnance, 1793-1803 and 1804-1816

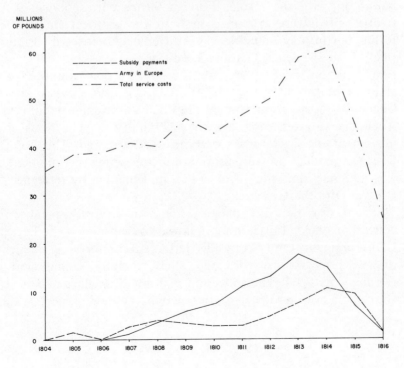

BIBLIOGRAPHY

The British Foreign Office papers, deposited in the Public Record Office, were the chief research source for this work. The bulk of the collection consists of official correspondence between the Foreign Office and British envoys. Students with little time to spare are tempted to ignore the volumes of miscellaneous papers which frequently interrupt the flow of this correspondence. However, these volumes often contain valuable material along with trivia. Nearly all treaties are in the Record Office; the protocol and ratified forms are catalogued as FO 93 and FO 94 respectively. In a few cases, the protocol forms escaped classification and are bound in with the regular Foreign Office correspondence. All treaties cited were examined in both the protocol and ratified forms, but in only one case was a difference discovered (Britain's treaty with Sweden of October 3, 1805).

Information relating to subsidy payments is found in the archives of the Treasury, the Audit Office, and the Pay Master General's Office. These sources are discussed in some detail in the Appendix. Masters' logs in the Admiralty papers reveal the movement of naval vessels carrying specie abroad. The Foreign Office dispatches provide information concerning the shipment of war materials, but they should be supplemented by reference to the War Office letters.

Except for the Pitt papers (Chatham), private manuscript collections yielded little more than was to be found in the Foreign Office archives. Lord Cornwallis' letters offer interesting sidelights on his brief service with the allies' military commission in Germany in 1794. The collection of Lord Granville's papers (the Granville Leveson Gower of this period) contain some revealing letters written during his service as British envoy at St. Petersburg.

Unfortunately, the papers of John Charles Herries, Commissary-in-Chief to the army in the last years of the war, (deposited in the British Museum) were not available for examination in 1965. When students finally are able to use them, they will doubtless yield a rich return. Herries deserves study, but for the moment we must be content with his *Memoir* edited by Edward Herries.

The correspondence of George III since 1783 is being edited for publication by Professor Arthur Aspinall. Two volumes have already appeared, bringing the work to the close of 1797. Until the project is completed, American scholars will find it convenient to use the twenty-two volumes of the King's letters in typescript deposited in the William L. Clements Library, the University of Michigan, Ann Arbor.

For the first two coalitions, the printed papers of Lord Grenville are as important as the Foreign Office archives. This ten-volume collection, published by the Historical Manuscripts Commission under the confusing title, *Report on the Manuscripts of J. B. Fortescue, Esq., Preserved at Dropmore*, is a rich storehouse for students of the period. It should be supplemented by the *Memoirs of the Court and Cabinets of George the Third*, which contain a large number of private letters written by Lord Grenville and Thomas Grenville. Fundamental for the concluding years of the war is the more familiar collection of Lord Castlereagh's correspondence in twelve volumes edited by his half-brother. Many of the printed memoirs of other British leaders of the period are disappointing, although an exception must be noted in the case of Lord Malmesbury's *Diaries and Correspondence*.

The collections of Austrian state papers edited by von Vivenot, Hüffer, and Pribram are all important. Fedor Martens, *Recueil des Traités et Conventions Conclus par la Russie . . .* , includes valuable source material taken from the Russian foreign archives. It should be used in conjunction with the papers of the Vorontzoff family published in the *Arkhiv Kniazia Vorontsova*. Prince Hardenberg's *Denkwürdigkeiten*, edited by von Ranke, has some important material relative to Lord Harrowby's unfortunate mission to Berlin in 1805.

Today's student can still make good use of the multivolume works of Alison, Sorel, von Sybel, and Thiers. Out-of-date though they are in some ways, they nevertheless provide both dramatic sweep and an encyclopedic attention to detail. As guides through the maze of diplomatic and military history of the period, nothing takes the place of the appropriate volumes of the *Cambridge Modern History* and the *Cambridge History of British Foreign Policy*.

After half a century, John Holland Rose's biography of Pitt remains the standard, and even Lord Stanhope's older work cannot be overlooked. Sir Charles Webster's two-volume study of Castlereagh's foreign policy is a fundamental work, based as it is on unassailable scholarship. Few British political leaders of the period have found suitable biographers. Lord Grenville remains unnoticed and the Earl of Liverpool still waits to be rescued from the pages of Charles Yonge's official biography. The brilliance of Canning's final years has obscured the fact that between 1807 and 1809 he served successfully as foreign secretary. Until a major study of this early period of his life appears, we must be satisfied with Temperley's work and with Dorothy Marshall's *Rise of George Canning*.

Sir John Fortescue's *History of the British Army* remains indispensable. Students of the Peninsular War will find Weller's *Wellington in the Peninsula* a handy guide through the subject which is covered extensively by Fortescue, Napier, and Oman. All but three of the twelve volumes of Wellington *Dispatches* deal with the period 1808-1815 and my debt to this work is enormous. The important changes which occurred in the ordnance supply system and the organization of the British army at this time have been skillfully examined by Richard Glover in his *Peninsular Preparation*. Detailed accounts of naval operations are found in the works of those rival historians, William James and Captain Edward Brenton.

Gayer *et al., Growth and Fluctuation of the British Economy, 1790-1850* has been faulted by some because of its conclusions. As a vade mecum through the maze of trade statistics I found it most helpful. The economics of British subsidization is treated in Norman J. Silberling's "Financial and Monetary Policy of Great Britain During the Napoleonic Wars," (*Quarterly Journal of Economics*, 38[1923-1924]), which deserves examination. Karl Helleiner's useful monograph, *Imperial Loans,* should be consulted in connection with the Austrian Loans of 1795 and 1797. Sir

Francis d'Ivernois, the author of the "federative paper" plan, has been the subject of a biography and two articles by Otto Karmin. Not to be overlooked is François Crouzet's study of the effect of the Continental System on Britain's economy—a work which largely supplants its predecessors in this field.

MANUSCRIPT COLLECTIONS AND PUBLIC RECORDS

Public Record Office, London

1. Foreign Office Papers

FO	7	Austria
FO	29	The Army in Germany
FO	33	Hamburg and the Hanse Towns
FO	37	Holland and the Netherlands
FO	63	Portugal
FO	64	Prussia
FO	65	Russia
FO	67	Sardinia
FO	70	Sicily and Naples
FO	72	Spain
FO	73	Sweden
FO	74	Switzerland, Series I
FO	83	Great Britain and General
FO	92	Continent: Treaty Papers
FO	93	Protocols of Treaties
FO	94	Ratifications of Treaties
FO	97	Supplement to General Correspondence
FO	120	Embassy and Consular Archives (Austria): Correspondence
FO	139	Continent: Correspondence

2. Treasury Papers

Ty	1	Treasury Board Papers
Ty	29	Minute Books
Ty	52	King's Warrant Books

3. War Office Papers

WO	1	In-Letters
WO	2	Out-Letters

4. Admiralty Papers
   Adm 52   Masters' Logs

5. Audit Office Papers
   AO 1   Declared Accounts
   AO 3   Accounts, Various

6. Pay Master General's Papers
   PMG 2   Ledgers

7. Collections of Private Papers
   Chatham Papers (including the papers
   of William Pitt the Younger)   (30/8)
   Cornwallis Papers   (30/11)
   Granville Papers   (30/29)

British Museum Additional Manuscripts
   Aberdeen Papers   (43073-43079)
   Grenville Papers   (41851-41859; 42058)
   Liverpool Papers   (38248-38261; 38325-38326)
   Vansittart Papers   (31230-31231; 31236)
   Wellesley Papers   (37286-37288; 37292-37294;
                        37310; 37415)

William L. Clements Library, Ann Arbor, Michigan
   Typescripts of the unpublished correspondence of George III.

PUBLISHED MEMOIRS, PAPERS, AND DOCUMENTS

Adair, Robert. *Historical Memoir of a Mission to the Court of Vienna in 1806.* London, 1844.

Arkhiv Kniazia Vorontsova. Edited by P. I. Bartenev. 40 vols. Moscow, 1870-1895.

Auckland, William Eden, first Baron. *The Journal and Correspondence of William, Lord Auckland.* 4 vols. London, 1861-1862.

Baring, Francis. *Observations on the Establishment of the Bank of England, and on the Paper Circulation of the Country . . .* 2d ed. London, 1797.

British and Foreign State Papers. The Librarian of the Foreign Office, ed. Vols. I-III. London, 1838-1841.

Calvert, Harry. *The Journals & Correspondence of Gen'l Sir Harry Calvert . . .* Harry Verney, ed. London, 1853.

Castlereagh, Viscount. See Londonderry, Robert Stewart, second Marquess of.

Cornwallis, Charles, first Marquis. *Correspondence of Charles, First Marquis Cornwallis.* Charles Ross, ed. 3 vols. London, 1859.

Bibliography

Croker, John Wilson. *The Croker Papers: The Correspondence and Diaries of the Late Right Honourable John Wilson Croker.* Louis Jennings, ed. 2 vols. New York, 1884.

Czartoryski, Prince Adam. *Mémoires du Prince Adam Czartoryski et Correspondance avec l'Empereur Alexandre 1er.* 2 vols. Paris, 1887.

George III. *The Later Correspondence of George III.* Arthur Aspinall, ed. Vols. I-II. London, 1962- (in progress).

Granville, Granville Leveson Gower, first Earl of. See Leveson Gower, Granville.

Grenville, William Wyndham, first Baron. See Historical Manuscripts Commission, *Report on the Manuscripts of J. B. Fortescue, Esq., Preserved at Dropmore.*

Hansard's Parliamentary Debates, from the Year 1803 to the Present Time, Published under the Superintendence of T. C. Hansard. First Series. 41 vols. London, 1803-1820.

Hardenberg, Karl August Fürst von. *Denkwürdigkeiten des Staatskanzlers Fürsten von Hardenberg.* Leopold von Ranke, ed. 5 vols. Leipzig, 1877.

Herries, John Charles. *Memoir of the Public Life of the Right Hon. John Charles Herries...* Edward Herries, ed. 2 vols. London, 1880.

Historical Manuscripts Commission. *Report on the Manuscripts of Earl Bathurst Preserved at Cirencester Park.* London, 1923.

—— *Report on the Manuscripts of J. B. Fortescue, Esq., Preserved at Dropmore.* 10 vols. London, 1892-1927.

Holland, Elizabeth Lady. *The Journal of Elizabeth Lady Holland 1791-1801.* Earl of Ilchester, ed. 2 vols. London, 1908.

Hüffer, Hermann. *Quellen zur Geschichte der Kriege von 1799 und 1800.* 3 vols. Leipzig, 1900-1907.

Jackson, George. *The Diaries and Letters of Sir George Jackson, K.C.H., from the Peace of Amiens to the Battle of Talavera.* Lady Jackson, ed. 2 vols. London, 1872.

Journal of the House of Commons. Vols. XLIX-LXX.

Leveson Gower, Granville, first Earl Granville. *Lord Granville Leveson Gower... Private Correspondence 1781-1821.* Castalia Countess Granville, ed. 2 vols. London, 1916.

Londonderry, Charles Stewart, third Marquess of. *Narrative of the War in Germany and France, in 1813 and 1814.* Philadelphia, 1831.

Londonderry, Robert Stewart, second Marquess of. *Correspondence, Despatches, and Other Papers, of Viscount Castlereagh, Second Marquess of Londonderry.* The 3rd Marquess of Londonderry, ed. 12 vols. London, 1851-1853.

Malmesbury, James Harris, first Earl of. *Diaries and Correspondence of James Harris, First Earl of Malmesbury...* 2d ed. The 3rd Earl of Malmesbury, ed. 4 vols. London, 1845.

—— *A Series of Letters from the First Earl of Malmesbury, His Family and Friends from 1745 to 1820.* 2 vols. London, 1870.

Manuscripts of J. B. Fortescue, Esq. See Historical Manuscripts Commission.

Martens, Fedor F. *Recueil des Traités et Conventions Conclus par la Russie avec les Puissances Etrangéres.* 15 vols. St. Petersburg, 1874-1909.

Martens, George, and Martens, Charles. *Recueil des Principaux Truités d'Alliance... Conclus par les Puissances de l'Europe...* 2d ed. 8 vols. Göttingen, 1817-1835.

Memoirs of the Court and Cabinets of George the Third. The Duke of Buckingham and Chandos, ed. 4 vols. London, 1853-1855.

Metternich-Winneburg, Clemens Fürst von. *Memoirs of Prince Metternich 1773-1835.* Prince Richard Metternich, ed. Mrs. Alexander Napier, tr. 5 vols. New York, 1881.

Minto, Gilbert Elliot, first Earl of. *Life and Letters of Sir Gilbert Elliot, First Earl of Minto, from 1751 to 1806...* The Countess of Minto, ed. 3 vols. London, 1874.

Nesselrode, Karl Robert, Comte de. *Lettres et Papiers du Chancelier Comte de Nesselrode, 1760-1850...* 11 vols. Paris, 1904-1912.

Paget, Arthur. *The Paget Papers: Diplomatic and Other Correspondence of the Right Hon. Sir Arthur Paget, G.C.B., 1794-1807.* Sir Augustus Paget, ed. 2 vols. London, 1896.

Parliamentary Debates. See *Hansard's Parliamentary Debates.*

Bibliography

Parliamentary History of England, from the Earliest Period to the Year 1803 . . . William Cobbett, ed. 36 vols. London, 1806-1820.

Pozzo di Borgo, Carlos Comte de. *Correspondance Diplomatique du Comte Pozzo di Borgo* . . . 2 vols. Paris, 1890-1897.

Pribram, Alfred F. *Oesterreichische Staatsverträge. England.* Vol. II. Vienna, 1913.

Reports from Committees of the House of Commons. Vol. XI. London, 1803.

Rose, George. *A Brief Examination into the Increase of the Revenue, Commerce, and Navigation of Great Britain during the Administration of the Rt. Hon. William Pitt.* London, 1806.

—— *Diaries and Correspondence of the Right Hon. George Rose.* L. V. Harcourt, ed. 2 vols. London, 1860.

Sidmouth, Henry Addington, first Viscount. *The Life and Correspondence of the Right Hon'ble Henry Addington, First Viscount Sidmouth.* George Pellew, ed. 3 vols. London, 1847.

Smith, Adam. *An Inquiry into the Nature and Causes of the Wealth of Nations.* Everyman edition. 2 vols. New York, 1910.

Vivenot, Alfred von. *Quellen zur Geschichte der Deutschen Kaiserpolitik Oesterreichs während der Französischen Revolutionskriege, 1790-1801.* 5 vols. Vienna, 1873-1890.

Vorontzoff, Simon. See *Arkhiv Kniazia Vorontsova.*

Webster, Charles K., ed., *British Diplomacy, 1813-1815.* London, 1921.

Wellesley, Richard, first Marquess. *The Despatches and Correspondence of the Marquess Wellesley K.G. during His Lordship's Mission to Spain . . . in 1809.* M. Martin, ed. London, 1838.

—— *The Wellesley Papers.* 2 vols. London, 1914.

Wellington, Arthur Wellesley, first Duke of. *The Dispatches of Field Marshal the Duke of Wellington* . . . Lieut.-Col. John Gurwood, ed. 12 vols. London, 1837-1838.

—— *Supplementary Despatches and Memoranda of Field Marshal Arthur, Duke of Wellington, K.G.* . . . The 2d Duke of Wellington, ed. 15 vols. London, 1858-1872.

Wickham, William. *The Correspondence of the Right Honourable William Wickham from the Year 1794.* William Wickham, ed. 2 vols. London, 1870.

Windham, William. *The Windham Papers: The Life and Correspondence of the Rt. Hon. William Windham, 1750-1810.* 2 vols. London, 1913.

Woodforde, James. *The Diary of a Country Parson: The Reverend James Woodforde.* John Beresford, ed. 5 vols. London, 1924-1931.

OTHER SOURCES

Acton, Harold. *The Bourbons of Naples 1734-1825.* London, 1956.

Adams, Ephraim D. *The Influence of Grenville on Pitt's Foreign Policy, 1787-1798.* Washington, D.C., 1904.

Albion, Robert G. "British Shipping and Latin America, 1806-1914," *Journal of Economic History,* 11 (1951), 361-374.

—— *Forests and Sea Power: The Timber Problem of the English Navy, 1652-1862.* Cambridge, Mass., 1926.

Alison, Archibald. *History of Europe from the Commencement of the French Revolution to the Restoration of the Bourbons in MDCCCXV.* 14 vols. Edinburgh and London, 1849-1850.

—— *Lives of Lord Castlereagh and Sir Charles Stewart* . . . 3 vols. Edinburgh and London, 1861.

Andersson, Ingvar. *A History of Sweden.* Carolyn Hannay, tr. New York, 1957.

Andréadès, A., *History of the Bank of England.* C. Meredith, tr. New York, 1909.

Ashton, Thomas S. *Iron and Steel in the Industrial Revolution.* Manchester, Eng., 1951.

—— Review of *The Growth and Fluctuation of the British Economy, 1790-1850,* by A. Gayer, W. W. Rostow, and A. J. Schwartz, in *Economic History Review,* 2d ser., 7 (1955), 377-381.

Bibliography

Balfour, Lady Frances. *The Life of George, Fourth Earl of Aberdeen K.G.* 2 vols. London, 1922.

Barnes, Donald G. *George III and William Pitt, 1783-1806.* Stanford, Calif., 1939.

Beamish, North Ludlow. *History of the King's German Legion.* 2 vols. London, 1832-1837.

Biro, Sydney S. *The German Policy of Revolutionary France: A Study in French Diplomacy during the War of the First Coalition, 1792-1797.* 2 vols. Cambridge, Mass., 1957.

Blease, W. L. *Suvórof.* London, 1920.

Bourgoing, François de. *Histoire Diplomatique de l'Europe pendant la Révolution Française.* 4 vols. Paris, 1865-1885.

Brenton, Edward P. *The Naval History of Great Britain . . .* 2 vols. London, 1837.

Brinton, Crane. *A Decade of Revolution, 1789-1799.* New York, 1934.

Browning, Oscar. "Hugh Elliot at Naples," *English Historical Review,* 4 (1889), 209-228.

Bryant, Arthur. *The Years of Endurance.* New York, 1942.

—— *The Years of Victory.* London, 1944.

Buckland, C. S. B. *Metternich and the British Government from 1809 to 1813.* London, 1932.

Burne, Alfred H. *The Noble Duke of York: The Military Life of Frederick Duke of York and Albany.* London, 1949.

Buxton, Sydney. *Finance and Politics: An Historical Study, 1783-1885.* 2 vols. London, 1888.

Cambridge History of British Foreign Policy, 1783-1919. A. W. Ward and G. P. Gooch, eds. Vol. I. Cambridge, 1922.

Cambridge Modern History. A. W. Ward, G. W. Prothero, and Stanley Leathes, eds. Vols. VIII and IX. Cambridge, 1934.

Capefigue, Jean Baptiste. *Histoire des Grandes Opérations Financières; Banques, Bourses, Emprunts . . .* 4 vols. Paris, 1855-1860.

Carr, R. "Gustavus IV and the British Government, 1804-1809," *English Historical Review,* 60 (1945), 36-66.

Clapham, John. *The Bank of England: A History.* 2 vols. New York, 1945.

—— "Loans and Subsidies in Time of War, 1793-1914," *Economic Journal,* 27 (1917), 495-501.

C[okayne], G. E. *Complete Peerage of England, Scotland, Ireland, Great Britain and the United Kingdom . . .* 8 vols. London, 1887-1898.

Corti, Egon Caesar Count. *The Rise of the House of Rothschild.* B. and B. Lunn, trs. New York, 1928.

Court, W. H. B. *A Concise Economic History of Britain, from 1750 to Recent Times.* Cambridge, 1954.

Crawley, C. W. "French and English Influences in the Cortes of Cadiz, 1810-1814," *Cambridge Historical Journal,* 6 (1938), 176-206.

Crouzet, François. "La Crise Monétaire Britannique et la Cinquième Coalition," *Bulletin de la Société d'Histoire Moderne.* 11th ser., no. 8 (Oct.-Dec. 1953), 14-19.

—— *L'Economie Britannique et le Blocus Continental, 1806-1813.* 2 vols. Paris, 1958.

Cunningham, Audrey. *British Credit in the Last Napoleonic War.* Cambridge, 1910.

Daly, Robert. "Operations of the Russian Navy during the Reign of Napoleon I," *Mariner's Mirror,* 34 (1948), 169-183.

D'Auvergne, Edmund. *Envoys Extraordinary: The Romantic Careers of some Remarkable British Representatives Abroad.* London, 1937.

Davies, Godfrey. *Wellington and His Army.* Oxford, 1954.

Derry, John W. *William Pitt.* London, 1962.

Deutsch, Harold. *The Genesis of Napoleonic Imperialism.* Cambridge, Mass., 1938.

Elliot, D. C. "The Grenville Mission to Berlin, 1799," *Huntington Library Quarterly,* 18 (1954-1955), 129-146.

Falk, Minna R. "Stadion, adversaire de Napoléon (1806-1809)," *Annales Historiques de la Révolution Française,* 169 (1962), 288-305.

Bibliography

Festing, Gabrielle. *John Hookham Frere and His Friends.* London, 1899.
Ford, Guy Stanton. *Hanover and Prussia, 1795-1803: A Study in Neutrality* . . . New York, 1903.
Fortescue, John W. *British Statesmen of the Great War, 1793-1814.* Oxford, 1911.
——— *A History of the British Army.* 13 vols. London, 1899-1930.
Fremantle, A. F. *England in the Nineteenth Century.* 2 vols. New York, 1929-1930.
Fryer, W. R. *Republic or Restoration in France, 1794-1797.* Manchester, Eng., 1965.
Furber, Holden. *Henry Dundas, First Viscount Melville, 1742-1811* . . . London, 1931.
Gabory, E. *L' Angleterre et la Vendée.* 2 vols. Paris, 1930-1931.
Galpin, W. F. *The Grain Supply of England during the Napoleonic Period.* New York, 1925.
Gayer, Arthur, Rostow, W. W., and Schwartz, A. J. *The Growth and Fluctuation of the British Economy, 1790-1850.* 2 vols. Oxford, 1953.
Glover, Michael. *Wellington's Peninsular Victories.* London, 1963.
Glover, Richard. "Arms and the British Diplomat in the French Revolutionary Era," *Journal of Modern History,* 29 (1957), 199-212.
——— *Peninsular Preparation: The Reform of the British Army, 1795-1809.* Cambridge, 1963.
Godechot, Jacques. *La Grande Nation: l'Expansion Révolutionnaire de la France dans le Monde de 1789 à 1799.* 2 vols. Paris, 1956.
Goebel, Dorothy B. "British Trade to the Spanish Colonies, 1796-1823," *American Historical Review,* 43 (1937-1938), 288-320.
Gray, Denis. *Spencer Perceval: The Evangelical Prime Minister, 1762-1812.* Manchester, Eng., 1963.
Grunwald, Constantin de. *Trois Siècles de Diplomatie Russe.* Paris, 1945.
Halévy, Elie. *A History of the English People in the Nineteenth Century.* E. I. Watkin and D. A. Barker, trs. Vol. I. New York, 1945.
Hansing, Karl. *Hardenberg und die Dritte Koalition.* Berlin, 1899.
Hawtrey, Ralph G. *Currency and Credit.* 4th ed. London, 1950.
Hecksher, Eli. *The Continental System: An Economic Interpretation.* H. Westergaard, ed. Oxford, 1922.
Helleiner, Karl F. *The Imperial Loans: A Study in Financial and Diplomatic History.* Oxford, 1965.
Hidy, Ralph W. *The House of Baring in American Trade and Finance* . . . Cambridge, Mass., 1949.
Hope-Jones, Arthur. *Income Tax in the Napoleonic Wars.* Cambridge, 1939.
Horn, D. B. *The British Diplomatic Service, 1689-1789.* Oxford, 1961.
Hovde, B. J. *The Scandinavian Countries, 1720-1865.* 2 vols. Boston, 1943.
Imlah, A. H. "Real Values in British Foreign Trade, 1798-1853," *Journal of Economic History,* 7 (1948), 133-152.
James, William. *The Naval History of Great Britain* . . . 5 vols. London, 1822-1824.
Jenks, Leland H. *The Migration of British Capital to 1875.* New York and London, 1927.
Karmin, Otto. "Autour des Négociations Financières Anglo-Prusso-Russes de 1813," *Revue Historique de la Révolution Française et de l'Empire,* 11 (January-June 1917), 177-197; 12 (July-December 1917), 24-29, 216-252.
——— "Les Finances Russes en 1812 et la Mission de Sir Francis D'Ivernois à St. Pétersbourg," *Revue Historique de la Révolution Française et de l'Empire,* 8 (1915), 177-191; 9 (1916), 5-71.
——— *Sir Francis D'Ivernois 1757-1842.* Geneva, 1920.
Kaufmann, William W. *British Policy and the Independence of Latin America, 1804-1828.* New Haven, Conn., 1951.
Kluchevsky, V. O. *A History of Russia.* C. J. Hogarth, tr. Vol. V. New York, 1960.
Kraehe, Enno E. *Metternich's German Policy.* Princeton, N.J., 1963.
Kukiel, Marian. *Czartoryski and European Unity, 1770-1861.* Princeton, N.J., 1955.
Lackland, H. M. "Lord William Bentinck in Sicily, 1811-1812," *English Historical*

Review, 42 (1927), 371-396.

Lascelles, Edward C. P. *The Life of Charles James Fox.* Oxford, 1936.

Lewis, Michael. *The History of the British Navy.* London, 1959.

Lukacs, John A. "Russian Armies in Western Europe; 1799, 1814, 1917," *American Slavic and East European Review,* 13 (1954), 319-337.

Lobanov-Rostovsky, Andrei A. *Russia and Europe, 1789-1825.* Durham, N.C., 1947.

Mackesy, Piers. *The War in the Mediterranean, 1803-1810.* Cambridge, Mass., 1957.

Manchester, Alan K. *British Preëminence in Brazil: Its Rise and Decline.* Chapel Hill, N.C., 1933.

Marcus, G. J. *A Naval History of England.* Vol. I. London, 1961- (in progress).

Marriott, J. A. R. *Castlereagh.* London, 1936.

Marshall, Dorothy. *The Rise of George Canning.* London, 1938.

Matheson, Cyril. *Life of Henry Dundas, First Viscount Melville, 1743-1811.* London, 1933.

Mitchell, Harvey. *The Underground War against Revolutionary France: The Missions of William Wickham, 1794-1800.* Oxford, 1965.

Moller, Herbert, ed. *Population Movements in Modern European History.* New York and London, 1964.

Napier, W. F. P. *History of the War in the Peninsula* . . . 6 vols. London, 1890.

Newmarch, William. "On the Loans Raised by Mr. Pitt during the First French War, 1793-1801; with Some Statements in Defence of the Methods of Funding Employed," *Quarterly Journal of the Statistical Society,* 18 (1855), 104-140, 242-284.

Nichols, Irby C. "Britain and the Austrian War Debt, 1821-1823," *Historian,* 20 (1958), 328-346.

Nicolle, André. "The Problem of Reparations after the Hundred Days," *Journal of Modern History,* 25 (1953), 343-354.

Oman, Carola. *Sir John Moore.* London, 1953.

Oman, Charles. *A History of the Peninsular War.* 7 vols. Oxford, 1902-1930.

Parkinson, C. N., ed. *The Trade Winds: A Study of British Overseas Trade during the French Wars, 1793-1815.* London, 1948.

Pebrer, Pablo. *Taxation, Revenue, Expenditure, Power, Statistics, and Debt of the Whole British Empire; their Origin, Progress, and Present State.* London, 1833.

Piechowiak, A. B. "The Anglo-Russian Expedition to Holland in 1799," *Slavonic and East European Review,* 41 (1962-1963), 182-195.

Pipes, Richard. *Karamzin's Memoir on Ancient and Modern Russia: A Translation and Analysis.* Cambridge, Mass., 1959.

Puryear, Vernon J. *Napoleon and the Dardenelles.* Berkeley and Los Angeles, 1951.

Renier, G. J. *Great Britain and the Establishment of the Kingdom of the Netherlands, 1813-1815.* London, 1930.

Roberts, Michael. *The Whig Party, 1807-1812.* London, 1939.

Robson, William H. "New Light on Lord Castlereagh's Diplomacy," *Journal of Modern History,* 3 (1931), 198-218.

Rose, John Holland. "Canning and the Spanish Patriots in 1808," *American Historical Review,* 12 (1906-1907), 39-52.

—— *Napoleonic Studies,* 2d ed. London, 1906.

—— *Pitt and Napoleon: Essays and Letters.* London, 1912.

—— *William Pitt and the Great War.* London, 1911.

—— *William Pitt and National Revival.* London, 1911.

Rosebery, Archibald, fifth Earl of. *Pitt.* London, 1915.

Rosselli, John. *Lord William Bentinck and the British Occupation of Sicily, 1811-1814.* Cambridge, 1956.

Rostow, W. W. *British Economy of the Nineteenth Century.* Oxford, 1948.

Russell, Lord John. *Memorials and Correspondence of Charles James Fox.* 4 vols. London, 1853-1857.

Ruville, Albert von. *William Pitt Earl of Chatham.* H. J. Chaytor, tr. 3 vols. London, 1907.

Ryan, A. N. "The Defence of British Trade with the Baltic, 1808-1813," *English Historical Review*, 74 (1959), 443-466.
Rydjord, John. "British Mediation between Spain and Her Colonies, 1811-1813," *Hispanic American Historical Review*, 21 (1941), 29-50.
Scott, Franklin D. *Bernadotte and the Fall of Napoleon.* Cambridge, Mass., 1935.
Shanahan, William O. *Prussian Military Reforms, 1786-1813.* New York, 1945.
Sherwig, John M. "Lord Grenville's Plan for a Concert of Europe, 1797-1799," *Journal of Modern History*, 34 (1962), 284-293.
Silberling, Norman J. "Financial and Monetary Policy of Great Britain during the Napoleonic Wars," *Quarterly Journal of Economics*, 38 (1923-1924), 214-233, 397-439.
Sorel, Albert. *L'Europe et la Révolution Française.* 8 vols. Paris, 1885-1904.
Spinney, J. D. "Some Vicissitudes of a 'V.I.P.,' " *Blackwood's Magazine*, 265 (1949), 301-312.
Stanhope, Philip, fifth Earl of. *Life of the Right Honourable William Pitt.* 4 vols. London, 1861-1862.
Stearns, Josephine B. *The Role of Metternich in Undermining Napoleon.* Illinois Studies in the Social Sciences, vol. XXIX, no. 4. Urbana, Ill., 1948.
Sybel, Heinrich von. *History of the French Revolution.* W. C. Perry, tr. 4 vols. London, 1867-1869.
Temperley, H. W. V. *Life of Canning.* London, 1905.
Thiers, Louis A. *History of the Consulate and Empire of France under Napoleon.* D. F. Campbell and J. Stebbing, trs. 12 vols. Philadelphia, 1893-1894.
Tilley, John, and Gaselee, Stephen. *The Foreign Office.* London, 1933.
Tooke, Thomas. *A History of Prices and of the State of Circulation from 1793 to 1837...* 6 vols. London, 1838-1857.
Treitschke, Heinrich von. *History of Germany in the Nineteenth Century.* E. and C. Paul, trs. 6 vols. New York, 1915-1919.
Turner, Eunice H. "The Russian Squadron with Admiral Duncan's North Sea Fleet, 1795-1800," *Mariner's Mirror*, 49 (1963), 212-222.
Vandal, Albert. *Napoléon et Alexandre Ier...* 3 vols. Paris, 1891-1896.
Waliszewski, K. *Paul the First of Russia, the Son of Catherine the Great.* London, 1913.
Walpole, Spencer. *The Life of the Rt. Hon. Spencer Perceval.* 2 vols. London, 1874.
Ward, S. G. P. *Wellington's Headquarters.* Oxford, 1957.
Watson, J. Steven. *The Reign of George III, 1760-1815.* Oxford, 1960.
Webster, Charles K. *The Foreign Policy of Castlereagh.* 2 vols. London, 1947-1950.
―――― *The Foreign Policy of Palmerston.* Vol. I. London, 1951.
Weil, M. H. *Un Agent Inconnu de la Coalition, le Général de Stamford.* Paris, 1923.
Weller, Jac. *Wellington in the Peninsula, 1808-1814.* London, 1962.
Wheeler-Holohan, Vincent. *The History of the King's Messengers.* New York, 1935.
Yonge, Charles Duke. *The Life and Administration of Robert Banks, Second Earl of Liverpool.* 3 vols. London, 1868.
Ziegler, Philip. *Addington: A Life of Henry Addington, First Viscount Sidmouth.* London, 1965.

Index

Abercrombie, Maj.-Gen. Sir Ralph, 121, 142
Aberdeen, George Hamilton Gordon, fourth Earl of, 305-307, 311, 313, 317
Åbo, 279, 280
A'Court, William, 271
Active, H.M.S., 46-47
Adair, Robert, 174, 176, 179n, 181, 189n
Addington, Henry: prime minister (1801), 143; negotiates peace with France, 143; renews war with France, 144; tries to organize coalition, 144-147; subsidizes Naples, 145-146, 162, 193; collapse of government (1804), 146, 147
Alexander I, Tsar of Russia: accession, 126; formation of Third Coalition, 144, 146; and Frederick William III, 149; Novosiltzoff mission, 151-152, 154; subsidy treaty with Britain (1805), 159, 160, 161; and Sweden, 163, 181; War of Third Coalition, 166, 167, 170, 173, 179, 180; offers Hanover to Prussia, 168, 169; peace negotiations with France, 175, 176; resentment of Britain, 181, 182; peace with Napoleon (1807), 182, 189; war with Sweden (1808), 205-206; quarrel with Napoleon, 274-275; relations with Bernadotte, 275, 279-280, 316; rapprochement with Britain, 276, 279-280, 282; D'Ivernois mission, 280-281; and Austria, 283; negotiations with Napoleon (1814), 316, 318; and Castlereagh, 312, 319, 320-321, 330-331; occupies Paris (1814), 323; Russian-Dutch loan convention, 277, 320-321, 330-331; Hundred Days, 333, 334, 336
Alkmaar, 121

Almeida, 230, 235, 239
Amherst, William Amherst, first Earl of, 265-266
Amiens, Treaty of (1802), 143
Amphion, H.M.S., 298, 300
Andalusia, 198, 222, 237
Antwerp, 213
Apodaca, Admiral, 200
Aranjuez, 200
Armies, allied: size in 1793, 11; in 1815, 333
Army, British: condition in 1793, 14-15; growth (1793-1797), 19, 77, 94; campaign in Low Countries (1793-1795), 17, 50, 54, 61, 77; cost of (1793-1797), 87; in Portugal (1796-1801), 137-140; expedition to Holland (1799), 121; in Egypt (1800-1801), 140, 142; in Italy and Sicily, 162, 173; expedition to north Germany (1805-1806), 168, 171, 173; expedition to Stralsund, 185, 188, 189; expedition to Walcheren, 213, 214; and the Peninsular War, 197-265 *passim;* demobilization (1814), 326-327, 333; duty on Continent (1814), 327, 328; and Hundred Days, 333, 337-338, 339
Army of Reserve Act (1804), Great Britain, 148
Aspern, Battle of (1809), 212
Astrea, H.M.S., 189
Asturias, 196, 198, 228
Auckland, William Eden, first Baron, 10
Austerlitz, Battle of (1805), 170, 171, 273
Austria
before 1793: rivalry with Prussia, 5, 6, 7, 20, 24, 27; Belgium-Bavaria Exchange, 5, 20, 23; territorial ambitions, 5; economic weakness, 11; war with

Index

Jacobi, Baron von: Grenville's dislike of, 10, 31-32, 177; Prussian subsidy treaty (1794), 30-32 *passim,* 51, 52; negotiates peace with Britain (1806), 177, 178; subsequent career, 186, 187, 289, 298, 301

Jena-Auerstädt, Battle of (1806), 178

João, Don, Prince Regent of Portugal, 136, 139-141 *passim,* 191, 218, 240, 242

John, Archduke of Austria, 283

John, Don, Prince Regent of Portugal, see João

Jourdan, Gen. Jean-Baptiste, 62

Junta de Viveres, see Commissary General, Portuguese Army

Kaiserslautern, 50

Kalisch, Treaty of (1813), 287

Kennedy, Sir Robert, 254, 264

Kinckel, Baron, 47

King, John Harcourt, 272, 283

Kingdom of the Netherlands, creation of the, 321, 330, 331, 343

King's German Legion, the, 168n, 188n, 327n, 338

Kleist, Ludwig von, 209, 211

Kloest, Baron von Jacobi, see Jacobi, Baron von

Knights of St. John, 143

Kolberg, 283, 298

Königsberg, 178, 179

Kronstadt, 72, 163, 164, 187, 189

Lehrbach, Count Ludwig, 27

Leipzig, Battle of (1813), 307-308

Leveson Gower, Granville: ministry to Russia (1804-1806), 155-159 *passim,* 161, 167, 172; second ministry to Russia (1807), 187, 188, 189

Lieven, Count Christoph, 282, 289, 298, 301, 313, 314

Lille, Anglo-French peace discussions at (1797), 94, 97, 139

Liverpool, Robert Banks Jenkinson, second Earl of: foreign secretary under Addington, 140-141, 144, 146-147, 191; as secretary of war (1809), 225, 226-227, 234n, 235; prime minister, 251, Russian-Dutch loan, 321, 322, 331-332; settlement of 1815 subsidy account, 340, 341; repayment of Austrian loans (1821), 343

Lucchesini, Jérôme, Marquis de, 27-28

Lunéville, Treaty of (1800), 135

Madrid, 196, 253

Mainz, 24, 31, 48

Malmesbury, James Harris, first Earl of, 5, 32-41 *passim,* 45-52 *passim,* 64-67

Malta, 104, 143, 144, 157-162 *passim,* 164, 210

Mantua, 90, 116

Marengo, Battle of (1800), 132, 133, 142

Maria Carolina, Queen of Naples and Sicily, 194-195, 265-268 *passim,* 270

Maritime Code, Great Britain, 152, 157-158

Masséna, General André: and the Second Coalition, 123, 131; and the Peninsular War, 230, 232, 235, 238, 249

Mayence, British subsidy treaty with (1800), 131

Mercenaries, German, in British service: (1793-1797), 18, 19, 74, 77-78; (1800-1801), 128-131 *passim,* 133, 135, 142; (1815), 338-342 *passim; see also* Baden, Hanover, Hesse-Cassel, Hesse-Darmstadt, Bavaria, Swabia, Brunswick

Mercy D'Argenteau, Count, 58, 59

Mermaid, H.M.S., 48, 49, 50

Merry, Anthony, 206-207

Metternich, Prince Klemens Wenzel von: and Austrian War of Liberation (1809), 207; and Austrian foreign policy (1809-1813), 213, 272, 283; and Pläswitz armistice (1813), 296; and Britain (1813), 298-300 *passim,* 305-306, 313, 317; negotiations with Napoleon, 313, 315; threatens to abandon coalition, 318; and Hundred Days, 333

Milan, 132

"Military guineas," 263

Minorca, 159-160

Minto, Gilbert Elliot, first Earl of, 127-135 *passim*

Möllendorf, Field Marshal Richard von, 47-51 *passim,* 53, 56, 64

Moore, Lt.-Gen. Sir John: and improvement of British Army, 14-15; opinion of Maria Carolina, 194-195; expedition to Sweden, 193, 197-198; campaign in Spain (1808-1809), 199, 200, 202-203; mentioned, 141, 208, 219, 221, 236

Moreau, Gen. Jean-Victoire, 134-135

Morillo, Maj.-Gen. Pablo, 261

Morpeth, George Howard, Viscount, 177-178

Mulgrave, Henry Phipps, first Earl of, 151, 164, 166, 171

Munich, 134

Muotta, 123

Murat, Gen. Joachim, 270, 324, 336

Naples, Kingdom of: alliance with Britain

Index

Index

Vorontzoff, Count Simon, 10, 107, 108-109, 111, 146, 147, 175n; and alliance with Britain, 21, 22; Russian subsidy treaty, 105; and Third Coalition, 148, 151-152, 159

Wagner, Lt. August, 208-209
Wagram, Battle of (1809), 212, 213
Walcheren, Island of, British expedition to (1809), 15, 213, 214, 215, 225
Wales, 86
Wallmoden, Ludwig Von, 208-209, 211
Walpole, Lord, 320
War of 1812, 288, 308, 326, 333
War of the Spanish Succession (1701-1714), 25
Warren, Sir John Borlase, 144, 155
Waterloo, Battle of (1815), 339
Watson, Brook, 47
Wellesley, Sir Arthur, see Wellington
Wellesley, Sir Henry: and trade with Spain, 227-228, 240, 258, 325-326; aid to Spain, 227, 247, 248-251 passim, 253, 258, 260; and Wellington, 240, 248, 252-253, 256, 259-260; treaty with Spain (1814), 325-326; hires Spanish troops (1815), 340
Wellesley, Richard Wellesley, the Marquess: and Spain, 219, 228, 249, 250; foreign secretary, 225-226, 238, 250-251, 272, 274; and Sicily, 266, 267; and Russia, 272, 273; and Austria, 272; and Prussia, 273-274; and Sweden, 274
Wellington, Arthur Wellesley, first Duke of Peninsular War (1808-1814), 197, 199, 205, 216; military operations, 214, 218, 230-232 passim, 234-238 passim, 239, 242, 250, 251-264 passim;

230-232 passim, 234-238 passim; and Portuguese army, 217, 218, 237-238, 244-247 passim, 254; and Portuguese subsidy, 222, 223-224, 229; specie shortage, 224, 232, 255-256, 263; and Portuguese Council of Regency, 231, 239-244 passim, 262; and Spanish subsidy, 239, 252-253, 258-262 passim; and Spanish army, 240, 247, 251-252, 256-257, 260-261
Hundred Days (1815), 332, 333-335, 338-342
Wessenberg, Baron de, 298-299
Whitbread, Samuel, 332
Whittingham, Sir Samuel Ford, 248n
Whitworth, Sir Charles, 10; and First Coalition, 20-23, 70-73, 82, 83; promotes Grenville's concert plan, 100, 103; and subsidy treaties with Russia (1798-1799), 105, 107, 110-111, 120; negotiations with Tsar (1799-1800), 124-126
Wickham, William, 130-131, 133, 135
William, Prince of Orange, 316, 320, 327n
Woodforde, The Reverend James, 1
World War I, 344, 345
Württemberg, 18, 131, 166

Yarmouth, Francis Seymour Conway, first Earl of, 18-19, 24, 27-28, 32
York, Frederick Augustus, Duke of: general, 14, 15, 54; campaign in the Low Countries (1793-1795), 31, 50, 77; and Austrian army, 59, 60, 61, 68, 69; expedition to Holland (1799), 121, 124n

Zealand, province of, 213
Zurich, 123